E L E V A T I O N S

Chicago Studies in the History of Judaism
A Series Edited by William Scott Green

ELEVATIONS

THE HEIGHT OF
THE GOOD IN
ROSENZWEIG
AND LEVINAS

RICHARD A. COHEN

The University of Chicago Press
Chicago and London

Richard A. Cohen is the Isaac Swift Distinguished Professor of Judaic Studies at the University of North Carolina, Charlotte.

The University of Chicago Press, Chicago 60637
The University of Chicago Press, Ltd., London
© 1994 by The University of Chicago
All rights reserved. Published 1994
Printed in the United States of America
03 02 01 00 99 98 97 96 95 94   1 2 3 4 5

ISBN: 0-226-11274-8 (cloth)
ISBN: 0-226-11275-6 (paper)

Library of Congress Cataloging-in-Publication Data

Cohen, Richard A., 1950–
    Elevations : the height of the good in Rosenzweig and Levinas /
Richard A. Cohen.
    p.   cm. — (Chicago studies in the history of Judaism)
    Includes bibliographical references and index.
    1. Rosenzweig, Franz, 1886–1929.   2. Levinas, Emmanuel.
3. Philosophy, Jewish.   4. Judaism—20th century.   I. Title.
II. Series.
BM755.R6C64   1994
181'.06—dc20
                                                    94-1165
                                                      CIP

To
Alasdair and Arielle
With love

Shall a man make gods to himself, and they are no gods?

Jeremiah 16:21

We now know that a man can read Goethe or Rilke in the evening, that he can play Bach and Schubert, and go to his day's work in Auschwitz in the morning.

George Steiner

Often young people ask me why I don't have it erased, and this surprises me: Why should I? There are not many of us in the world to bear this witness.

Primo Levi, The Drowned and the Saved

The pile of corpses that lie between them and me cannot be removed in the process of internalization, so it seems to me, but, on the contrary, through actualization, or, more strongly stated, by actively settling the unresolved conflict in the field of historical practice.

Jean Amery, At the Mind's Limits

It is rather for us to be here dedicated to the great task remaining before us, that from these honored dead we take increased devotion to that cause for which they gave the last full measure of devotion; that we here highly resolve that these dead shall not have died in vain.

Abraham Lincoln, "Gettysburg Address"

Preface

This volume is the result of a devotion to philosophy, and a devotion to the thought of Emmanuel Levinas especially, lasting more than two decades. I first read *Totality and Infinity* in 1970. It was not easy, and many references and allusions were beyond my reach. But what I remember distinctly to this day is the impression Levinas made on me. "This is *true*," I thought, in contrast to all the philosophers and philosophies which are *fascinating* or *provocative*. For all my reading and learning since, and for all the references and allusions that I now do understand, I am often and perhaps even more profoundly still moved in this same "naive" way.

At that time I was studying philosophy at the Pennsylvania State University, in one of the few departments in America deeply committed to the "grand tradition" of metaphysics, the tradition of great books and great thinkers, going back to ancient Greece and culminating in Kant and Hegel. Among other teachers there, I was privileged to have been a student of Alphonso Lingis, translator of Levinas's major philosophical works. He was the philosopher most responsible, for better and worse, for educating me in the paths and byways of contemporary continental thought.

Later I was privileged to have attended Levinas's classes at the Sorbonne, during the 1974–75 academic year, his penultimate of university teaching. I had the audacity, too, though trembling inside, to call upon M. Levinas at his home, where he welcomed me graciously and memorably. During the same year in Paris, on rue Soufflot, just downhill from the Pantheon, I purchased Franz Rosenzweig's *The Star of Redemption,* in the Beacon Press paperback edition, for twenty-seven francs.

Thirteen years later, coming full circle, in 1987, I gave my first public talk on Rosenzweig and Levinas (now chapter 11, "Non-in-difference," in this volume) in Paris, at the Goethe Institute.

In 1979, I completed my graduate studies in philosophy at the State University of New York at Stony Brook, writing my dissertation on "Time in the Philosophy of Emmanuel Levinas," and defending it before a committee composed of Professors Don Ihde, David Allison, Don Welton, and Alphonso Lingis. After one decade, I was still far from done with Levinas and Rosenzweig. The volume at hand is the product of a second decade of continued appreciation.

Each chapter speaks for itself. As a whole the volume expresses the vision of a new manner of thinking. The reader will see, however, that at the same time nothing is new about this thinking. It is rather a perennial thinking, or an *Altneu* thinking, that must in each generation, and in each person, be reawakened, renewed, rethought, and refined in current idiom. It is a thinking captivated by responsibilities and obligations beyond those of pure thought. It is a thinking acutely aware of its captivation, not as a fault or weakness but as its very strength and height, its dignity. It is truth beholden to goodness, as truth *should* be. Hence it is a writing at once careful and inspired, and thus, so I hope, inspiring.

There is an ancient philosophical tradition of such new thinking. The peak moments of several of Plato's dialogues point to a "good beyond being." Aristotle, at the height of his vision, would not detach or lower the virtue of genuine friendship from the excellence of active intellect. Descartes, centuries later in France, probed methodically for the unshakable foundation of a truly scientific certitude, and found himself "dazzled" by the priority of G-d. "It seems to me right to pause for awhile," he wrote, "in order to contemplate God Himself, to ponder at leisure His marvelous attributes, to consider, and admire, and adore, the beauty of this light so resplendent, at least as far as the strength of my mind, which is in some measure dazzled by the sight, will allow me to do so." His younger contemporary, Blaise Pascal, had neither hesitation nor qualm praising the heart's reasons, inaccessible to reason. Immanuel Kant, a century and a half later in Königsberg, at the highest summit of rational thought, having scrupulously and meticulously analyzed the capabilities and limits of objective knowledge, affirms that only beyond the purview of objective judgment can one find the sole "good without qualification" in all the universe. This is, of course, the *good will,* which even when partially stymied, or completely hamstrung, "sparkles" undiminished "like a jewel." These moments represent but a handful of the most striking philosophical testimonies to an elevation higher than that of knowledge and intellect alone, testifying to the moral heights of life lived fully, not without knowledge, certainly, but raising knowledge up to judiciousness and wisdom. These are the same heights towards which the writings of Levinas and Rosenzweig point.

Morality would perhaps be a far simpler matter if it were open to and limited by the same evidential standards as objective knowledge, if one could prove or disprove moral claims in the same fashion as scientific hypotheses are tested. But this is not so, and never can be so. And to make matters worse, scientific thought is driven by a hubristic telos towards a universality that can only with the greatest difficulty be brought to recognize the legitimacy of claims that are alternatives to its own. The writings of this volume will insist on imposing this "difficulty" on knowing and knowledge. "It has never been more difficult to think," comments Levinas.

In straining to establish and maintain the rights of its universality, knowledge insists on its autonomy as well, building for itself the protective hegemony of a paradigm or ideology. It resolutely remains within itself by transforming every other into "the same," from one end of its universe to the other. Such is the empire of the empirical. But the strain of establishing and maintaining its internal security and equilibrium shows. It inevitably excommunicates (as "subjective," "primitive," "infantile," "stupid," or "mad") the claims and orientations it can never comfortably make its own. Outside of science we are but fools and madmen.

When philosophy claims the title of science, its highest thought is to think itself or, second best, to think about thought thinking itself. Philosophy dreams of returning to itself and itself alone, eternally. The history of European philosophical systems, each one claiming to be more "scientific" than the next, provides ample evidence of thought's self-infatuation, whether in the guise of a solitary bravado or speaking with the megaphonic ventriloquy of "world historical spirit." But beyond and better than these second highest thoughts of first highest thoughts, and certainly better than the venom of their only partially repressed frustrations, come other claims, irreducible to empirical science or philosophical totality but more sincere and more elevated—moral claims. Better than science are the demands of morality, of goodness, and above morality itself, absolute but constituting the very sting and prod of morality, are the even higher demands of holiness, the unsurpassable "you shall be holy because I am Holy."

My own philosophical interests and training led me to ponder many years over the subtle but global significance of the "x" which crosses out *Sein* in Heidegger's later writings, and the elusive but no less consequential significance of the "a" in Derrida's famous *differance,* that postmodern resurrection of Heidegger's cross. For *better* reasons, and with no claim to originality, in these pages I make what for philosophers is an even more disturbing gesture, which I note by putting a "-" in the name "G-d." Though it may gall philosophers (or thinkers), this dash is more subtle, global, and elusive in its own way than either of the above mentioned philosophical (or sophistical) brand marks. In the name "G-d"—"in the name of G-d"—more than anywhere else, more than Derrida's "a" and Heidegger's "x," certainly, language bursts *and* bears more than it can bear. To catch this "sense," contemporary thought must free itself from the narrowness of its openness, to speak in seeming paradoxes. It must free itself, that is to say, of the avant-gardist prejudice for which all "burdens" are conceived within the opposition of slavery and freedom, and hence are alleviated only by more and more freedom, until freedom means nothing more than escape from slavery. But not all burdens are slavery. And freedom is not necessarily the highest value. In the name "G-d" language bursts *and* testifies, as it has always testified from time immemorial, to a glory it cannot contain but to which it is nonetheless subject.

But reason doubly protests and protects itself, denying the possibility of its rupture, ruling out higher claims beforehand, rendered their offensiveness merely "ostensive." Reason denies every chasm, abyss, and hiatus, denies them the very moment it must admit them, in the very instant it bears them witness. Negation, it declares, is its own, it own work, its very heart and soul—nothing but reason here. Beyond the genius of Hegel, beyond the immanent logic of negation, that is, the good or bad manners of reason would contend rather with myth, product of its own fancy, than with transcendence. One thus cannot rely upon traces, hints, glimmers, suggestions, however oblique or exquisite, of what reason must refuse to grasp, imperiously or politely. Words can be made to point beyond themselves, temporarily, but they will also be made to admit their finitude, their eventual exhaustion. The perseverance of the power of G-d's name to burst the bounds of language is perhaps an unremarked miracle in language, recalling the miracle—and only recalling?—of the perseverance of the Jews, which bursts the bounds of history.

I have written the name "G-d" with a dash, and a capital G, to indicate this rupture in language which raises it up, whether language wills it or no. The name "G-d" doubtless goes even farther. Fulfilling the dream of reason, but better than reason ever could (or would), it permits us to speak even more truly about language than can language, to again speak in seeming paradoxes. It suggests, per impossible, a manner of pointing at language from a vantage point exceeding all the resources and wherewithal of language. From where, for instance—contrary to the urbanity of a Hume and to the fulminations of a Nietzsche—can we ask ourselves, as we do and must: "Where art thou?" other than in the u-topian "space," the reverence, opened up by the name "G-d"?

Kantian respect respects the universal moral *law* in the other. But this law is the *same* law in the other as in myself. Reverence, in contrast, responds to the unique alterity of the other, in a moral responsibility to which even the law must be attached for its justification and hence for its justice. It is far more likely that it is to this reverence, rather than to an ecstatic temporality, as Heidegger thought, that Kant avers when he admits, at the core of his moral philosophy, the essential necessity and "incompetence" of human reason, as Kant conceives human reason, to justify human morality.

Is it only a blasphemy, then, at stake not writing G-d's name with an "o" or a small G? Perhaps for some. But philosophy has long since stopped worrying about blasphemy, except, in some thinkers, as a sought after stimulant. The issue which disturbs philosophers, in the dash and capital

G, is rather, to recall Derrida's "a" and Heidegger's "x," one of transcendence. Derrida and Heidegger stir up the utmost horizons of meaning, in Zarathustra's "stillest hour." But they have resolved, without admitting the presuppositions of their resolve, to never surpass the immanence of meaning itself, confining themselves to a world of signs relating to signs, ending always without the least sign, or perhaps only the sigh, of anything like "the sign." In their hands, transcendence, the "x," the "a," is vestigial or virtual, basking in the virtuosity of its virtuality. Their thought is ever on the alert to erase, to squelch the slightest hint of a genuine transcendence, with a vigilance equalled only by its agility in avoiding the erasure of transcendence in the manner of classical philosophy by *rational* dialectics. Thus thought strains and is strained to its utmost, whipped, stroked, teased, but only, to say it again, to *its* utmost. "It has never been more difficult to think."

With the term "G-d," capital "G" intact, "centered" on a dash which is not a sign, transcendence goes farther. The term harks back to a past too old, and heralds a future too distant, for the elasticity of ecstatic contemporaneity, within which contemporary thought plays. Higher than differ*a*nce and being-crossed-out, the name "G-d" does not signify its signified in a straightforward or oblique correspondence, or through a coherence, whether synchronic or diachronic or both, or through a correspondence and coherence delayed, deferred, or derailed. It leaves correspondence and coherence behind, or rather *beneath,* drawing them upward in its train, reaching higher, disturbing, giving pause, imposing too much, tracing what is already gone and not yet come, and as responsibility and obligation is both irreducibly present and beyond at once.

In this word-name-signal "G-d," indicated by a dash and capital G, there is a transcendence that transcends absolutely (holiness) and at the same time, as the sense we must make of this transcending movement, there is a transcendence that transcends *ethically.* They are one and the same upward movement, toward that which we cannot signify or know, but what, beyond contemplation, we are compelled to do, the good. One could write the name "G-d" as "G/d," with a diagonal slash rather than a horizontal dash, indicating the upward movement of moral rectitude, the ethical asymmetry Levinas names "one-for-the-other," being-for-the-other before being-for-oneself, which is how the movement which bursts through the name "G-d" signifies for human beings—"G-d who comes to the idea." Such is the central "theme," difficulty, exacerbation, elevation, in this volume.

The central theme, task, aim, or excellence, which brings together the chapters of this book is the articulation of the unique relation of two terms, "I" and "you," that do not reduce to one or the other, and do not both reduce to their relation. Neither one, nor the other, nor their "between" (however dialectical, differential, or chiasmic), but only the excessive and elevating pull of an ethics can "account" for such a relation, without letting loose the absolute priority of its claim. The aim of this book, then, is to expose the various manifestations of this "unrelating relation" at the heart of the thought of Franz Rosenzweig and Emmanuel Levinas. Its chapters present various ways, various significations, various historical links, in which these thinkers have attempted to make sense precisely where making sense is not good enough.

Like Socrates, neither thinker succumbs to the philosophical ceremonies of the day, to the decorous good manners, or the bohemian bad manners, which are today united in the wink of a knowing secularity. Overtly, consciously, without apology, both thinkers draw from the linguistic (and not just linguistic) treasure houses of ancient religion. It is indeed not just a question of language, or of religion in general. Levinas, and even more so Rosenzweig, invoke the wisdom of revealed religions, Judaism for the most part, but also, without contradiction, Christianity. They invoke the exalted language of creation, revelation, redemption, election, holiness, epiphany, glory, and the like. What entitles philosophers to rule out the G-d whose invisible authority has been admitted from the first? Is it so easy to decide who is acting and speaking like men asleep, and who like men awake? Who or what locked philosophy within the vast labyrinthine prison of being and nonbeing? Is an artificial intelligence of "on and off" to replace wisdom?

Rosenzweig and Levinas force *philosophers* to admit that there are more stringent demands than those of rigorous science. In facing the demands of their work one discovers that philosophical courage, fully sincere philosophical courage, admirable in its way, may also be . . . a cowardice. Has not Nietzsche taught us to be on the lookout for subterfuge precisely here, a subterfuge that would be the irony of all ironies: a sincerity, goodness, and rectitude, too sincere, too good, and too upright for philosophy, or a philosophy too uptight or too loose for sincerity, goodness, and rectitude? It is philosophy, then, that must learn to learn. Rosenzweig and Levinas teach that with no less rigor one must learn from the language, insights, and lives of the prophets, sages, fathers, mothers, kings, judges, psalmists, and rabbis of Israel, as well as the wise men, philosophers, sophists, scientists, and artists of Greek pedigree. Athens is too proud by itself to turn to Jerusalem, but it must be turned to Jerusalem nonetheless, for all our sakes. One comes to and goes from Athens as one likes, or as one can, or like the great Socrates one never leaves; but one must ascend or descend to come to and go from Jerusalem, where G-d's presence never departs.

That Socrates clothes were ragged and his feet bare was already a great lesson. That the Temple priests, climbing the sanctuary steps, wore long robes to not embarrass those below, was an even greater lesson. Pascal, in his *Pensées,* provides the explanation for both lessons: "All the splendor of greatness lacks lustre for those who seek understanding. The greatness of men of understanding is invisible to kings, the rich, leaders, to all who are great according to the flesh. The greatness of wisdom which has no existence save in God, is invisible to the carnal-minded and to the men of understanding. These are three orders, differing in kind." Or more succinctly, he writes: "The infinite distance between body and mind is a type of the infinitely more infinite distance between mind and charity, for charity is supernatural."

Despite its rigorous standards and intellectual heights, and despite its bravest, most Promethean struggles, philosophy by itself will never know its why or wherefore. In Jerusalem one does not beat one's head against that wall, one prays, in humility and gratitude.

Rosenzweig and Levinas, brilliant, cultured, university educated and educators, are too hard headed, too European, too Greek, to dare to pose a simple piety, however wholesome and wholehearted, against philosophy. (But why should we pretend to forget or ignore that both men regularly whispered the traditional prayers?) Instead, as moderns, complex spirits, they speak and write in two languages, of Greece and Israel, and of the church too. They have learned from Nietzsche yet another lesson, that there is no reason, other than the inertia of a centuries-old wishful thinking, to suppose that the true, the good, and the beautiful are united in harmony with one another. What is true, Nietzsche taught, could be very ugly indeed, and evil to boot. The dark times of our twentieth century have certainly confirmed his corrosive insight.

But if the true and the good and the beautiful are not necessarily one, that does not mean or imply, as Nietzsche erroneously thought, that the true, or, in his case, the beautiful, is *better* than the good. They never are and never can be better (without sleight of hand, heavy or light). What is good is precisely better than what is true or beautiful. Such is the specific difference of goodness, beyond any genus. Best of all, then, is to raise the true and beautiful to the good. Such is the "religious" task of sanctification, which Rosenzweig will call "redemption" and Levinas "sacred history," a spiritual vocation they both understand as the concrete historical work of instituting and maintaining social and political justice for humankind.

This volume is dedicated to the height of that good and, in its service, to the highest standards of scholarship. Whether it succeeds or not, at one or both, is for the reader to decide. My desire is for the words on these pages to set readers in the right direction: toward the writings of Rosenzweig and Levinas, but also toward the vision of a humanity whose spiritual destiny is oriented by goodness and justice, the vision, that is to say, which lies beyond and orients the writings of Rosenzweig and Levinas. These words aim at a vocation which, when properly grasped, cannot do without the rigors of scholarship and scientific thought, the rigors of the Greek academy, but one whose exigencies go higher still, toward a greater elevation and glory, better for all humankind: "to do justice and to love mercy and to walk humbly with thy God."

Acknowledgments

Portions of this volume have been given as talks or have been previously published in earlier, shorter versions as follows.

Parts of chapter 1 were given as a talk on June 3, 1990, at the Academy for Jewish Philosophy, Temple University, Philadelphia, Pennsylvania (and appear in the AJP 1990 Conference Papers on "Judaism and Chosenness," 2–59), and on July 15, 1990, at the Philosophy Workshop of the International Center for the University Teaching of Jewish Civilization, Hebrew University of Jerusalem, Jerusalem, Israel. Thanks to Norbert Samuelson, Zev Harvey, Raphael Jospe, and Aviezer Ravitsky. A shorter version of chapter 2 was given as talk on October 9, 1991, for the Philosophy Club of Birmingham-Southern College, Birmingham, Alabama. Thanks to Steve Henley. It appears in *Human Studies* 16 (1993): 111–28 (edited by Hwa Yol Jung) (Kluwer Academic Publishers). Part of an earlier version of chapter 3 was given as a talk on April 21, 1987, at the Religious Studies Colloquium of Franklin and Marshall College, Lancaster, Pennsylvania. Thanks to Annette Aronowicz. An earlier version appears in *Nietzsche-Studien* 19 (1990): 346–66 (edited by Ernst Behler). An earlier version of chapter 4 was given as a talk on December 19, 1988, at the Association for Jewish Studies, Boston, Massachusetts. Thanks to Alan Udoff. Chapter 5 appears in *Great Modern Jewish Thinkers*, edited by Steven Katz (Washington, D.C.: B'nai B'rith Books, 1992). A shorter version of chapter 6 appears as the introduction to my translation of Emmanuel Levinas, *Time and The Other and Other Essays* (Pittsburgh: Duquesne University Press, 1987), 1–27. Chapter 7 was given as a talk, in its French version, on October 6, 1987, at the Colloque sur Rosenzweig jointly sponsored by the Goethe-Institute de Paris, the College International de Philosophie, and the Bibliotheque Nationale de Paris. It appears in English in the *Graduate Faculty Philosophy Journal* 13, no. 1 (1988): 141–53, and in French translation by Jacques Rolland in *L'Herne: Emmanuel Levinas,* edited by Catherine Chalier and Miguel Abensour (Paris: Editions de l'Herne, 1991), 343–51. Deep gratitude to Jacques Rolland and Stéphane Mosès. A part of chapter 8 was given as a talk on December 17, 1990, at the Association for Jewish Studies, Boston, Massachusetts, and appears in the *Journal of Jewish Thought and Philosophy* 1, no. 2 (1992): 197–221. A part of chapter 9 was given as a talk at

Brigham Young University, Provo, Utah, on October 26, 1992; at the University of Utah, Salt Lake City, Utah, on October 28, 1992; and also for the Society for Philosophy in the Contemporary World, Estes Park, Colorado, on August 16, 1993. Thanks to James Faulconer, Darwin Thomas, Nancy Snow, and Jack Weir. Part of chapter 9 appears in *Contemporary Philosophy* 15, no. 4 (1993): 1–7. A version of chapter 10 was given as a talk given on July 20, 1988, at the Philosophy Workshop of the International Center for the University Teaching of Jewish Civilization, Hebrew University of Jerusalem. It appears in *Philosophy Today* 32, no. 2 (Summer 1988): 165–78. An earlier version of chapter 11 was given as a talk on March 14, 1988, at the College International de Philosophie, Paris, France. Thanks to Arno Munster. It appears in *The Truth Proper to Religion,* edited by Daniel Guerriere (Albany: SUNY Press, 1990), 175–201. Thanks to Ronald Goodman for improving an earlier manuscript. Chapter 12 was given as a talk on October 16, 1987, at the Society for Phenomenology and Existential Philosophy, University of Notre Dame, Notre Dame, Indiana, and also on October 22, 1987, at the Centre International pour Étude Comparée de Philosophie et d'Esthétique, Tokyo, Japan. Deep gratitude to Tomonobu Imamichi. A shorter version appears in *The Question of the Other,* edited by Arlene Dallery and Charles Scott (Albany: SUNY Press, 1989), 35–43. The kernel of chapter 13 was given as a talk on February 27, 1987 to the graduate student colloquium of the Department of Philosophy, Pennsylvania State University, State College, Penn. In its current form, the first half was presented on November 21, 1993 to the American Academy of Religion in Washington, D.C.; and the second half on October 22, 1993 to the Society for Phenomenology and Existential Philosophy in New Orleans. Thanks for Harold Brogan, Alphonso Lingis, and Peter Ochs. Parts of chapter 14 were given as a talk on December 17, 1991, at the Association for Jewish Studies, Boston, Massachusetts. Also thanks to: Bob Lechner of *Philosophy Today,* who was first to publish any of my work; Tom Rado, friend and physician, for kindness and companionship in the final months; Richard Allen of the University of Chicago Press, for editorial services and conversation above and beyond the call of duty; and Edith Wyschogrod, for her unstinting support.

Abbreviations

Levinas

CPP   *Collected Philosophical Papers*. Edited and translated by
Alphonso Lingis. Dordrecht: Martinus Nijhoff, 1987.

DF   *Difficult Freedom*. Translated by Sean Hand. Baltimore:
Johns Hopkins University Press, 1990.

EE   *Existence and Existents*. Translated by Alphonso Lingis.
The Hague: Martinus Nijhoff, 1978.

EI   *Ethics and Infinity*. Translated by Richard A. Cohen.
Pittsburgh: Duquesne University Press, 1985.

LR   *The Levinas Reader*. Edited by Sean Hand. Oxford: Basil
Blackwell, 1989.

NTR   *Nine Talmudic Readings*. Edited and translated by Annette
Aronowicz. Bloomington: Indiana University Press, 1990.

OBBE   *Otherwise than Being or Beyond Essence*. Translated by Alphonso
Lingis. The Hague: Martinus Nijhoff, 1981.

TI   *Totality and Infinity*. Translated by Alphonso Lingis.
Pittsburgh: Duquesne University Press, 1985.

TO   *Time and the Other*. Translated by Richard A. Cohen.
Pittsburgh: Duquesne University Press, 1987.

Rosenzweig

FR   *Franz Rosenzweig: His Life and Thought*. Presented by Nahum
N. Glatzer. New York: Schocken Books, 1967.

JDC   *Judaism Despite Christianity*. Edited by Eugen
Rosenstock-Huessy. Translated by Dorothy Emmett. New
York: Schocken Books, 1971.

JL   *On Jewish Learning*. Edited by Nahum N. Glatzer. Translated
by Nahum N. Glatzer and William Wolf. New York: Schocken
Books, 1955.

SR   *The Star of Redemption*. Translated by William W. Hallo. Notre
Dame, Indiana: University of Notre Dame Press, 1985.

USH   *Understanding the Sick and the Healthy*. Edited by Nahum N.
Glatzer. Translated by Nahum N. Glatzer and T. Luckman.
New York: Noonday Press, 1954.

Additional

BT   Martin Heidegger, *Being and Time*. Translated by John
       Macquarrie and Edward Robinson. New York: Harper and
       Row, 1962.
VM   Jacques Derrida, "Violence and Metaphysics: An Essay on the
       Thought of Emmanuel Levinas." In Jacques Derrida, *Writing
       and Difference*. Translated by Alan Bass. Chicago: University of
       Chicago Press, 1978.

PART ONE

ROSENZWEIG

ONE

Jewish Election
in the Thought of Franz Rosenzweig

It was not simply the zeal of the reformers to purge Jews and Judaism of their own distinct and socio-politically "embarrassing" nationalism, their peculiar status as a people among citizens, that led to the nineteenth-century denial of the election or "chosenness" of the Jewish people. It was in the spirit of enlightened universalism, representing the progressive forces of the nineteenth century, that such a denial was made. The French Revolution was not made in the name of France but in the name of equality, liberty, and fraternity. Hegel, too, in Germany had said the same thing in his own way. His was not a defence of the Prussian State per se, but of the Idea of the Prussian State, an idea realized in the Prussian State but not an essentially Prussian idea, an idea available and desirable for all states and hence all citizens. Citizenship would henceforth be based on the rights of man, on a universalism evident to any reasonable person. It would no longer be shackled by the particularities and particularisms—the parochialism—of the nations.

The election of the Jewish people, in contrast, best represented what enlightened universalism opposed. No better instance of parochialism could be imagined than this real one, the most ancient of them all, inaugurated and sanctioned by G-d Himself. Just as later Hitler was not at all irrational or misdirected to unleash his obsessive, fantastic, and murderous hatred against Jews and all things Jewish, because the Nazi program and Jewish morality stood and will always stand at the antipodes of good and evil, neither were the progressive forces of the nineteenth century mistaken in radically opposing the Jewish idea of election as the limit case of socio-political parochialism.

Napoleon's famous and obviously rhetorical questions of 1806, put to the "Great Sanhedrin" he convened in Paris early in 1807, sum up all that is at stake in the opposition to Jewish election. Concerning the sixth question, regarding national loyalty and Jewish law, Napoleon writes the following revealing instructions in a letter to his minister of the interior on August 23, 1806:

6. Do the Jews who were born in France and whom French law treats as French citizens regard France as their fatherland? Are they obliged by their laws to defend

France, to obey her laws, and to conform to all the provisions of the Civil
Code?—The Sanhedrin must declare that the Jews are obliged to defend France
as they would defend Jerusalem, since they are treated in France as they would
be in the Holy City.[1]

The question, then, for the Jews, is whether republican France is France
or Jerusalem, whether it is yet another false Messiah or the messianic
dream come true. Of course with hindsight we now know that France
remained France and Jerusalem remained Jerusalem. But for those Jews
and non-Jews alike who imbibe from the cup of French revolutionary
idealism, France becomes Jerusalem, and warrants here and now the loyalty and devotion that Jews traditionally gave in their prayers and hopes
to "Jerusalem"—the holy city and the world to come. The France of
Napoleon would no longer be one nation among others, but having shed
its particularism, its parochialism, in the guise of its new Civil Code, its
universalism would represent the real and final fulfillment of even the
deepest meanings intended in the ancient, long-held dreams and yearnings
of the Jews for Jerusalem.[2] Being a citizen of France would be equivalent
to being a citizen of the world, a universal human being, a person as
such—apotheosis. All this today . . . until the dream burst.

It is by no means an accident, then, that Napoleon's letter is followed
by an equally hard-headed (and hard-hearted) one just three months later,
at the end of November, concerning Jewish marriages:

Out of every three marriages in each of the administrative districts of the Sanhedrin or consistory, no more than two marriages between Jews and Jewesses are
to be authorized; the third must be a mixed marriage between Jew and Christian.
If this provision seems too difficult to carry out, it will be necessary to take steps
which will lead to that end by way of exhortation, education, incentives, and
command. . . . When out of every three marriages one marriage is a mixed French-
Jewish union, the Jewish blood will cease to have any distinctive characteristic.[3]

How happy Napoleon would be with America in the late twentieth century, where without exhortation or command Jews intermarry at a rate
estimated to be above fifty percent and rising. According to Enlightenment assumptions, Jews, too, should rejoice. A high intermarriage rate
indicates that twentieth-century America is even closer to the ideal of

1. *The Mind of Napoleon: A Selection from his Written and Spoken Words*, edited and
translated by J. Christopher Herold (New York: Columbia University Press, 1961), 114.
2. The Paris Sanhedrin for the most part gave Napoleon satisfaction, limiting the Mosaic
Law to the exclusive sphere of religion. The historian Howard Morley Sachar sums up the
result as follows: "When Portalis *fils,* one of Napoleon's Commissioners, wrote later that
'the Jews ceased to be a people and remained only a religion,' he perceived the Sanhedrin's
true significance perhaps even more accurately than did the Jews themselves" (*The Course of
Modern Jewish History* [New York: Dell, 1977], 63).
3. *Mind of Napoleon,* 115.

universal citizenship than nineteenth-century France, closer to if not actually realizing the messianic age. In this enlightened perspective the voluntary decrease and ultimate disappearance of the Jewish people is no tragedy at all but rather the very measure of universalism, the bright sign of a higher ideal coming to age, the increase and spread of equality, liberty, and fraternity, the realization of the true gifts and goals of Judaism itself. According to the grandeur of this vision, then, Judaism positively desires its own disappearance, its auto-emasculation, but only, of course, as a movement from parochialism to universalism.

To see the triumph of the great goal of a universal humankind, the greatest and most enduring of all the tribal bulwarks to be breached and overcome is precisely the most parochial of them all, the Jewish parochialism par excellence: the election of the Jewish people. Enlightenment and election, and hence emancipation and election, stand in deepest contradiction.

But the notion of election, so deeply associated with the Jewish people, so deeply ingrained in the consciousness of this people "from time immemorial," will not simply fade away, die out, be married off. The vision of enlightened universalism, supported today in America, Europe, and increasingly across the globe by powerful forces of "exhortation, education, incentives, and command," has not quite unhinged the Jews from their ancient election. Everywhere Jewish parents do not rejoice but wring their hands and weep over intermarriages in their own families. Everywhere Jewish organizations are haunted, and feel themselves to be *implicated* by the high and ever increasing intermarriage rate. Striking the same nerve, no issue in recent years has raised more venom within the Jewish community than the so-called "Who is a Jew?" question.

After two hundred years of Jewish emancipation, the Jewishness of the Jew has become the touchiest of all questions *for Jews*. After two hundred years of Jewish emancipation, Jews everywhere still believe that it is *better* for Jews to marry Jews than non-Jews, regardless of the various post diem rationalizations of intermarriage in the contemporary Jewish world. The judgment of the Jewish community today remains as it always has: the Jewish people must be preserved. But—and here is the rub—what resources do Jews today have to defend, let alone to promote, their unique election and continued independent existence based on that election? Is there a post-Enlightenment way for Jews to take seriously their own election, to take seriously the Jewishness of their election?

Franz Rosenzweig and the Jewish Election

Can Jewish election be defended? Can it be defended, or even defined, under or after the bright light of enlightened universalism? What can

Jewish election mean *for Jews as Jews* today, in today's world? Is the Jewish sense of the Jewish election an essentially pre-Enlightenment notion, and therefore no more than an antiquated, obsolete throwback? Or is there a new, vital, and still Jewish sense beyond enlightenment, a worthy resilience to the Jewish election? Or, finally, is there a Jewish sense of Jewish election vital and viable for Jews today despite and independent of the impact and import of the Enlightenment?

It is with these central and urgent questions in mind—questions urgent and central for the existence and survival of Jewish consciousness—that I turn to the thought of Franz Rosenzweig. I turn to Franz Rosenzweig in particular because his work is or is taken to be both *contemporary,* that is, thoroughly conversant with the whole range of the Western cultural and philosophical tradition from the ancient Greeks onward, including Christianity, *and Jewish,* that is, rooted in Jewish sources, fully committed to the existence and survival of Judaism and the Jewish people, *and,* one must add, because by general consent he is considered to be one of the three or four greatest and most original of contemporary Jewish thinkers.[4] Beginning with a basic question, a question basic to Judaism, it is in the spirit of inquiry that I turn to Franz Rosenzweig, to discover his answer and to learn from it. If anyone has managed to think both a post-Enlightenment sense of Jewish election *and* a genuinely *Jewish* sense of the Jewish election, it must be Franz Rosenzweig.

Even though the Jewish election is not the explicit title or topic of any long work by Rosenzweig, it is nonetheless, as the following will show, an all-important element of his thought, perhaps its most powerful undercurrent. To overcome the humanism of Enlightenment rationalism without belittling or underestimating its real worth *or* the real worth of Judaism, Rosenzweig conceives the Jewish election as contributing *more* rather than *less* than the universal, to Judaism and to humankind, as the very heart and driving force of the universal itself.

In the following, I am going to trace Rosenzweig's thoughts on the Jewish election in their chronological order, though in doing so I will examine only four documents. I begin first with the now famous letter of 1916 to Eugen Rosenstock, wherein Rosenzweig writes that he will not convert to Christianity but will remain a Jew. I turn second to Rosenzweig's magnum opus, *The Star of Redemption,* published in 1921 and written on the Balkan front in the war years after the above letter. I turn third to Rosenzweig's very beautiful and profound commentaries on a selection of poems by Judah Halevi, which Rosenzweig translated from

---

4. One could make various lists, but I think the following thinkers would have to be included: Hermann Cohen, Franz Rosenzweig, Martin Buber, and Emmanuel Levinas.

Hebrew into German and had published in 1924 (Konstanz) and 1927 (Berlin).[5] These commentaries were written just after the onset of the debilitating and ultimately fatal paralysis whose symptoms first appeared at the beginning of 1922. Fourth, I conclude with another letter, not as famous as the first, but, as we shall see, containing some of Rosenzweig's most important thoughts on the Jewish election. This letter was written to Rosenzweig's colleagues at the Jewish Lehrhaus in Frankfort am Main at the end of 1924, shortly after the appearance of the Halevi book and, again, in the midst of the progressive and ultimately fatal paralysis.

Letter to Rosenstock (1916)

Jewish election is given a central place in Rosenzweig's 1916 mid-October letter to Eugen Rosenstock, a Christian theologian, Rosenzweig's friend, and a converted Jew. "Should I 'be converted'," Rosenzweig writes, "when I have been 'chosen' from birth?"[6] This letter, wherein Rosenzweig defends his own ab-original Jewish identity against the spiritual claims of Christianity, is one of several such letters to Eugen Rosenstock written in 1916 (see *JDC* 77–170). These letters come after three years of Rosenzweig's intense study of and return to traditional Judaism, a return coming all the way from the verge of a decision to convert to Christianity in the summer and early fall of 1913, a decision and temptation exacerbated by argumentation with the older and at that time more religiously knowledgeable Rosenstock.

Rosenzweig's assertion that he has been "*chosen* from birth" is defensive. At one stroke it resists two linked temptations sorely felt by this well-educated German scholar of German philosophy: to convert explicitly and wholeheartedly to the Christian religious communion, with its millennial claim to being the true spiritual fulfillment of Judaism and hence in every way Judaism's superior, *and* at the same time to enter wholeheartedly into the secular German culture—one thoroughly permeated by Christianity, according to Rosenzweig's Hegelian thinking, and according to the real facts of German academic life—which also took itself to be in every way superior to Judaism. But the larger context of Rosenzweig's assertion shows that it is more than defensive, or that it is defensive in a fundamentally positive way.

5. Rosenzweig's Halevi translations and commentaries are to be published in English by the University of Alabama Press; the commentaries translated by Eva Jospe and Tom Kovach, the poems by Gerda Schmidt, in a volume edited and introduced by myself.

6. *FR* 347; *JDC* 115; Rosenzweig, *Der Mensch und sein Werk: Gesammelte Schriften*, vol. 1, *Briefe und Tagebücher* (The Hague: Martinus Nijhoff, 1979), 254: "Soll ich 'mich bekehren,' wo ich von Geburt her 'auserwählt' bin?"

Elsewhere in his letter Rosenzweig affirms the intrinsic worth and independence of the Jewish spiritual world. He characterizes Judaism as a "citadel," and as a "ship" in search of its own proper harbor, which is not, he makes clear, Christianity. This dual aspect of the Jewish election, that it maintains both a *separation from* Christianity, Germany, Western culture, and an *affirmation of* Judaism, of the independence of Jews vis-à-vis non-Jews, Judaism vis-à-vis non-Judaism, the affirmation of Jews qua Jews, Judaism qua Judaism, will remain the key to grasping the significance of election throughout Rosenzweig's subsequent thought. My terms "distinctive" and "distinguished," used to characterize an elect Judaism, combining descriptive and prescriptive senses, capture the negative and positive meaning Rosenzweig attaches to his own election as a Jew: "distinct from," "distinguished from" what is not Jewish, and "distinct as," "distinguished as" a Jew.

Already in the 1916 letter to Rosenstock the essential duality, the distinction, of election appears in a specific, historic Jewish-Christian form. That is to say, Rosenzweig understands that Jewish election means one thing to Christians and another thing to Jews. He sees in Christianity a theological commitment to the belief that Christians and not the Jews are G-d's chosen people, that they and not the Jews are elect, and have been the elect since the time of the life and redemptive death of Jesus.[7] According to this view, G-d once chose the Jews, to be sure, but that first chosenness has definitively ended. G-d's new choice is the Christian and Christendom, those alone who now keep true faith in G-d. But such a belief in election, so controversial regarding its visible signs and apportionment within the Christian communion, has never, vis-à-vis its relations to the real Jewish community (versus an idealized gloss, the "Israelites," the "Hebrews," always the Jew frozen in time), been sufficient for

7. To talk about theological commitment to supersessionism in nowise implicates what many or even most persons who profess Christian belief in our time think about Jews and Judaism. Rosenzweig is concerned with a certain logic of Christian belief vis-à-vis Jews and Judaism.

Regarding its logic or theology, there are alternative strains or options within Christianity itself. One might propose, for instance, a "dual covenant" view, where Jews and Christians are both chosen by God, not Christians instead of the Jews, but Christians after and alongside the Jews. One would emphasize New Testament references such as that made by Paul in Romans 11:25: "For if you were cut off from what is by nature a wild olive tree, and were grafted contrary to nature into a cultivated olive tree, how much more shall these who are the natural branches be grafted into their own olive tree?" The Christian theologian Paul M. van Buren, in his three volume *A Theology of the Jewish-Christian Reality* (San Francisco: Harper and Row, Publishers, 1980–88), attempts to understand Christianity and Rosenzweig along these lines. (Professor David Novak, however, has challenged van Buren's success, or really his logic; see note 10 below.)

Christians to overcome a fundamental, almost life-threatening irritation at the continued existence of Jews—Jews who continue to affirm, or whose very existence continues to confirm their claim to election.

That Jews exist poses no essential difficulty for the doctrine of the Christian election. G-d's shift in choice does not entail that He must obliterate His first chosen. But Jews must be abject. They must give witness both materially and spiritually to the poverty and error of their ways, to the sin and blasphemy of their rejection of the true Messiah. G-d's change of heart must be seen not to have been arbitrary, for the sake of the Christian's own faith in the Christian election. G-d's change of heart must therefore be premised on the error of the Jews, and hence only as erroneous, as at fault, as having failed G-d, in direct contrast to Christian faithfulness, can Jews be represented in Christian consciousness. According to this view, only an abject Judaism fits into the Christian scheme; a chosen, elect Judaism does not.[8]

Jewish consciousness of Jewish election as separation and affirmation is precisely what Christians call Jewish "stubbornness." In this way the dual Jewish consciousness of election is maintained in the Christian vision of Jewry, but with reversed value. Reversing the Christian reversal with which he began as an assimilated, i.e., Christianized, Jew, Rosenzweig writes:

But could this same idea (that of the stubbornness of the Jews) also be a Jewish dogma? Yes, it could be, and in fact it is. But this Jewish consciousness of being rejected has quite a different place in our dogmatic system, and would correspond to a Christian consciousness of being chosen to rule, a consciousness that is in fact present beyond any doubt. The whole religious interpretation of the significance of the year seventy is tuned to this note. (*FR* 345; *JDC* 111; *Briefe* 250)

Christian theology interprets the millennial wandering, alienation, and suffering of the Jews as confirmation of G-d's rejection of them owing to their (stubborn) rejection of Jesus as Messiah. The destruction of the second Temple in the year seventy serves as an especially dramatic piece of evidence for this Christian reading of Jewish suffering as divine punishment.

The "Jewish dogma" to which Rosenzweig refers, emphasizing the term "dogma," has to do with the same phenomena but read from a Jewish perspective. Jews agree that their wandering, alienation, and suffer-

---

8. Needless to say, Islam also insists that Jews be regarded as second-class citizens of a genuine, i.e., an Islamic state. Of course, a chosen, elect Christianity or Islam have never fit into the Jewish scheme, which does not mean, however, and in contrast, that Jews must see Christians and Muslims as second-class citizens. These relations are complex and in any event not symmetrical.

ing, and the destruction of the second Temple, are divinely ordained, are part of a theodicy. But the value Jews place on these events is entirely otherwise than the Christian one. True, Jews understand that their suffering, as with all suffering, is a punishment for various sins: the corruption of the High Priesthood, slander between Jews, Hellenization, an illegitimate monarchy, etc. (but *never*, to be sure, the rejection of Jesus, whose historical existence is all but ignored). But, at the same time, the theodicy of the Jews includes an understanding of its exile as a positive event, as a new stage in the preparation for the coming of the Messiah. For Judaism the dispersion of the Jewish people means, positively, either a retrieval of the divine sparks spread throughout the world at large, outside the Promised Land, or the spread of Jewish values to the non-Jewish world, or both.

Rosenzweig's 1916 thoughts on election—as separation and affirmation, meaning one thing for Jews and another for non-Jews—though not extensive, set the general tone for all his subsequent thinking on this theme.

The Star of Redemption (1921)

The matter stands differently with the *Star*. It is no exaggeration to say that the *Star* is so dominated by the notion of election that it can hardly be extricated for special examination. The life of the chosen people, the "eternal people," as Rosenzweig often calls the Jews, is the real goal of the book and nothing less than the guiding star of world history. Rosenzweig is still Hegelian enough for such grandeur.

Nonetheless, for all its sweep and grandeur, Rosenzweig's deep commitment to what turns out to be a rather traditional view of the world-historical significance of Jewish election does not appear at first sight to the reader scanning the *Star* for references to Jewish election. Explicit references are relatively few. Rosenzweig does not speak at all of the Jewish election in part 1, "The Elements or The Ever-Enduring Proto-Cosmos" *(Die Elemente oder die immer wahrende Vorwelt)*, which is on creation. This is not surprising, however, since part 1 is guided by questions of method and is the most philosophical part of the *Star*. Philosophy does not and can not know of a particular people's divine election. Neither does Rosenzweig explicitly raise the topic of election in the heart and center of the *Star*, part 2, "The Course or The Always-Renewed Cosmos" *(Die Bahn oder die allzeiter neuerte Welt)*, which is on revelation, always understood in terms of the nature and significance of the meeting of divine love and human love in the unique presence of face-to-face dialogue, a notion which forms the core of Rosenzweig's "new thinking."

But this too is no surprise when one considers that Rosenzweig's overall strategy in the *Star* is to move from the abstract to the concrete, from philosophical reflection to real social life. Thus Rosenzweig deliberately reserves what he takes to be the most concrete topic of his discussion, the role of Jewish and Christian communal life, for part 3, "The Configuration or The Eternal Hyper-Cosmos" *(Die Gestalt oder die ewige Uberwelt)*, which is on redemption. And part 3 is indeed where Jewish election is explicitly discussed.

Election appears several times in part 3 of the *Star*, but most prominently three times: twice in book 1, "The Fire, or The Eternal Life" *(Das Feuer oder das ewige Leben)*, which is on Judaism, and once in book 3, "The Star, or The Eternal Truth" *(Der Stern oder die ewige Wahrheit)*, which is on ultimate truth. It does not appear in book 2, "The Rays, or The Eternal Way" *(Die Strahlen oder der ewige Weg)*, which is on Christianity, but when election is discussed in book 3 it is intimately related to Christianity. I turn to these three appearances in order.

Sabbath Morning and Sabbath Afternoon

The first appearance of election in book 1 of part 3 is not a surprise, as I have said, both because Rosenzweig's thought is more concrete at this stage of the *Star* and because book 1 of part 3 is devoted to Judaism. Its first appearance is, nonetheless, very brief, but with a brevity that belies the importance of what is said. Election appears in relation to the Sabbath morning and the Sabbath afternoon services.

First, of the morning Sabbath services Rosenzweig writes: "On the eve of the Sabbath, expression is given to the knowledge that the earth is a creation; in the morning, we find utterance of the people's awareness of being elect through the gift of the Torah which signifies that eternal life has been planted in their midst" (*SR* 312). Here we find the link between the expressions "chosen people" and "eternal people." The Jewish people are the chosen people because they have been chosen to be given and to receive the Torah, which means "that eternal life has been planted in their midst." Here too is the deep connection between election and the schema of creation-revelation-redemption which structures Rosenzweig's thought and structures the *Star*. G-d creates the world for all, but He reveals Himself to the Jewish people, or so the Jews declare on Sabbath morning.

Because Rosenzweig's thoughts on the relation of the Jewish election to the Sabbath are bound to his broader and ruling architectonic of creation-revelation-redemption, that is to say, more specifically, are bound to the homology Rosenzweig sees between the evening-morning-afternoon series of Sabbath services and the series creation-redemption-revelation, the link between election and Sabbath morning and afternoon services is also, therefore, a link between election and revelation and redemption. We must turn to Rosenzweig's commentary on the Sabbath afternoon service to flesh out the significance of the Jewish election in the Sabbath morning services, where it was understood as G-d's having chosen the Jewish people alone to receive the Torah. Rosenzweig writes: "In the insert in this prayer [the afternoon prayer], Israel is more than the chosen people, it is the 'one and only' people, the people of the One and Only God. Here all the fervor which the praying Jew breathes into the holy word 'One,' the fervor which compels the coming of the Kingdom is at its greatest intensity" (SR 313). Let us understand what Rosenzweig means here by placing these thoughts within the context of his creation-revelation-redemption schema. Creation is created for all people, not just for Jews. Adam is a human being, not a Jew.[9] Judaism does not begin until G-d reveals himself to Abraham and assigns to Abraham and his progeny a special role. Revelation is revealed to the Jewish people, hence they are the chosen people. This is celebrated on Sabbath morning. Now, according to Rosenzweig, in the Sabbath afternoon service "Israel is more than the chosen people, it is the 'one and only' people, the people of the One and Only God." This is what the Jews fervently pray on Sabbath afternoon, and this is the fulfillment of their election. But what can this mean? How is being the "'one and only' people" *more* than being G-d's chosen people, as was already understood on Sabbath morning? The key to answering this question lies in the advance from revelation to redemption. Rather, the key to understanding the advance from revelation to redemption lies in understanding the significance of the difference between what is said in the Sabbath morning prayers and the Sabbath afternoon prayers, which is to say, in understanding the difference between the two senses of Jewish election enunciated therein.

Thus, to turn things around in order to get them straight, the significance of revelation and of redemption can be distinguished and understood precisely in terms of the difference between an *exclusive* and an *inclusive* election, the election of Sabbath morning and the election of Sabbath afternoon respectively. With this we begin to see the real importance of chosenness not only in Rosenzweig's life but in his thought as well. Exclusive election is the election of the Jewish people who are given and have the Torah, who fully live within the precincts of its eternality, when and while other peoples, the nations, do not have the Torah and hence do not fully live within G-d's eternity. This the Jews celebrate on

9. On this reading Abraham would be the first Jew. There are alternative Jewish readings whereby Adam is the first Jew. But according to these readings, he is then not the first human being, which leaves our original point unaffected.

Sabbath morning. But the exclusiveness of the Jewish election is only temporary, provisional, a propaedeutic. From being G-d's one chosen people, in the sense of being one nation among nations, separate *because* of their election, a divine people differentiated from the pagan nations who do not follow G-d's path, the Jews must become G-d's chosen people in the sense that all people, all nations, also come to follow G-d's path, and hence all enter into the state of being G-d's chosen ones. From one among many, election must come to mean one for all.

It is at this juncture that we see the important role of history in the redemptive process, in the movement from revelation to redemption. The work of history is precisely the eternalization of the peoples, bringing them into the purview of G-d's revelation, as exemplified by the Jewish people, the chosen people here and now. Sacred history is the progressive election of the nations. And this work of eternalization or election is performed, in Rosenzweig's view, by Christianity and by Christianity only. Which brings us to the last of Rosenzweig's explicit comments on election in the *Star*.

Indeed, the culminating and most concrete part of the *Star*, part 3, is entirely and essentially about election. At the end of history, when the Christian work of redemption is completed, and hence when not the election but the exclusiveness of the Jewish election is rendered obsolete because G-d's election has become all inclusive, then and only then comes the divine truth, which is neither Jewish nor Christian. The final truth is the whole truth, one and for all, neither a *true part* of the truth, as is Judaism in an unredeemed world, nor a *false* (because premature) *whole* of the truth as is Christianity in an unredeemed world. At the end of history lies the truth (book 3) which comes after the exclusiveness of an essentially exclusive Judaism (book 1) no longer excludes anything other, and hence also after an essentially incomplete Christianity (book 2) completes its mission. Then and only then everyone and everything will be included in G-d's election. At that time, and not until that time, there will be, as Jews say on Sabbath afternoon, "one and only" one people, namely *all* humankind, which will then also be subservient to the "One and Only G-d." Such, for Rosenzweig, is the true sense of the Sabbath afternoon election, the all-inclusive election.

The Jewish people will be and must remain the exclusive chosen people until the end of time, but only until the end of time. Time and history are redemptive processes, sacred history being the progressive redemption of the world, the spread of revelation. How do we know when time is at an end, when the world is redeemed? What is the nature of the redemption of the world? It is precisely all-inclusive election, when the whole world attains the eternality currently lived by the Jews. The world is redeemed when everyone becomes like the Jews, not in the exclusiveness of Jewish election but in the eternal truth that that exclusiveness harbors and protects until the end of time. The Jews, then, are waiting for the world to catch up. But the world does not catch up accidentally. Christianity is the sole agent or instrument of the eternalization, hence the redemption—which also means the *Judaicization*—of the world, at which time both the Christian mission and Jewish exclusiveness will be superfluous and only truth will reign.[10]

Because of the importance of these notions, though at the risk of repetition, I want to emphasize what has been noted. The election of the Jews means that today the Jews exclusively, the Jews alone, have the truth. Throughout all history only the Jews will be so blessed, which is their chosenness, their election. But the truth, to which today Jews alone exclusively cling, insofar as it is the truth, can and should be taken up by all peoples. Indeed it will be taken up, for this is G-d's plan. But it is not for Jews to spread the truth, except by their example. Actively spreading the truth, going out and persuading the nations to take it up and to abide by it, is precisely the task of Christianity, a task it performs in the service of G-d. At the same time this active spreading of truth, the expansion of

10. At the 1988 annual conference of the Association for Jewish Studies, in Boston, David Novak argued that despite an apparent and oft noted ecumenicalism in Rosenzweig, Christians who are persuaded by the *Star* should really choose to become Jews rather than remain Christians. By converting to Judaism they would individually achieve today what they strive as a religion to achieve for all humankind at the end of time. Conversely, I might add, by this logic Jews with a bent to missionizing might find their vocation in Christianity.

The difference between Christians who convert to Judaism and those who do not mimics the difference found in Buddhism between those sages, the Arhavats, who attain complete enlightenment today and those sages, the Bodhisatvas, who put off the complete enlightenment that is within their reach today for the sake of the eventual enlightenment of all humankind tomorrow. Jews would be the Arhavats and Christians would be the Bodhisatvas.

Conceptually it is no accident that these two terms and their irreconcilable difference—salvation for some today and salvation for all tomorrow—appear in all world religions. The explanation for it can be found by drawing out the implications of the two meanings of absoluteness found in the third of Kant's antinomies in the *Critique of Pure Reason*. For G-d as totality, *Elokim,* absoluteness means that His creation is perfect, already and always, every day a Sabbath. But for G-d as transcendent, *Hashem,* absoluteness means that his creation is imperfect, beneath Him, and hence in need of redemption, sanctification.

Even granting Novak's point, however, does not rule out a genuinely ecumenical dimension to the *Star*. See Ronald Miller, *Dialogue and Disagreement: Franz Rosenzweig's Relevance to Contemporary Jewish-Christian Understanding* (Boston: University Press of America, 1989). Rosenzweig, in any event, delegates the responsibilities of *mission*—redeeming the world—to Christianity. It is interesting to note that rabbinical Orthodox Judaism tends in practice to make the same general delegation. Ironically, the modern American Reform movement, with its great stress on the religious responsibility to engage in social and political activism, would, in Rosenzweig's view, be the least ecumenical form of Judaism.

Christendom, is the authentic or religious development of history, sacred history.

The progressive development of Christianity and the development of history are synonymous, just as this same process is the Judaicization of the world. When Christianity succeeds in its task, then and only then will the whole world be filled with G-d's glory, meaning that G-d will not only be One but His Name will also be one. This last expression, "on that day God will be One and His Name will be One," is well known to Jews, for it is not only taken from Zechariah 14:9, but it is repeated at least thrice daily at the conclusion of every prayer service (and not just on Sabbath afternoons).

What this vision of a complementary and dynamic relation between exclusive and inclusive election also means, however, and perhaps somewhat surprisingly for today's Jews and Christians, is that both Judaism qua exclusive and Christianity qua mission, that is to say, both Judaism and Christianity as they exist today as "religions," will have rendered themselves superfluous, no longer necessary, in a fully redeemed world. Indeed they would not only be superfluous; at some point—the end of time—Jewish exclusivity and Christian evangelizing would be positively counter to the spirit of redemption, and by persisting would stand in rebellion against redemption itself. Thus part 3 of the *Star* is Rosenzweig's religious revision and rendition of Hegel's philosophically oriented *Phenomenology of Spirit:*[11] the goal, truth, revealed to and practiced today by Judaism (book 1), is spread throughout the world by Christianity (book 2), and reaches its absolute climax, its divine form, in a post-Jewish and post-Christian but fully redeemed world (book 3). Absolute eternal truth, in and of itself, is neither Jewish nor Christian, but endures in-itself in Judaism in its eternal purity throughout time, and converts time to eternity, becoming for-itself in-itself, through the sacred history which is the mission of Christianity.

Let us note, too, that Rosenzweig's thesis about the relation between the ultimate redemption of humankind and the current election of the Jews says nothing against Jewish particularism, either in time or at the end of time. It only opposes, and only then at the end of time, Jewish exclusivity. And it only opposes Jewish exclusivity when that exclusivity comes to exclude nothing, when what is "excluded" is at the same time

11. There is certainly a touch of Nachman Krochmal's influence at work in Rosenzweig. For a brief account of Krochmal (1785–1840), especially his Jewish rereading of Hegel, see Shlomo Avineri, *The Making of Modern Zionism: The Intellectual Origins of the Jewish State* (New York: Basic Books, 1981), 14–22; for a longer account see Jay M. Harris, *Nachman Krochmal: Guiding the Perplexed of the Modern Age* (New York: New York University Press, 1991).

what is included. It is in this sense that the expressions "redemption," "eternalization," and "Judaicization" are ultimately equivalent within the Rosenzweigian perspective.

While the two references to Jewish election in relation to Sabbath worship which we have just examined do not have great textual prominence, their real importance should now be clear.

Two more prominent discussions of Jewish election in the *Star* occur elsewhere, again both in part 3. The first occurs exactly where one would expect it, in book 1, on Judaism; the second occurs in book 3, which is devoted to neither Jews nor Christians as such, but to the final redemption, the whole truth. That Rosenzweig discusses the Jewish election in this context should no longer be surprising, however, given what has been said above. These two longer discussions of election are linked, and occur where they do, because they both bear on the relation between Jewish election today, in the present, and the final redemption or election of all humankind in the future. Both discussions link the Jewish election to the coming of the Messiah. I will turn first to the discussion in book 1.

Judaism and Christianity

Rosenzweig admits a polarity or ambivalence in the Jewish perception of Jewish chosenness that plays a central role in the ecumenicalism (alleged or genuine) of Rosenzweig's thinking. The Jews are G-d's specially chosen people; they alone have been given the Torah. But G-d also loves the other nations, however much and often Jews, absorbed in their own election, may lose sight of this truth. Speaking of this peculiar concatenation in Jewish consciousness, of the outward blindness that its own election causes, the way the Jew overlooks G-d's positive relation to the other nations owing to the brilliant illumination of Israel's own divine revelation, Rosenzweig writes: "As the beloved of God, as Israel, he knows that God has elected him and may well forget that he is not alone with God, that God knows others whom he himself may or may not know, that to Egypt and Assyria too, God says: 'my people'" (*SR* 307). To be sure, the Jew knows of G-d's love for the other nations, so clearly enunciated by Israel's prophets. But G-d's love of Israel tends to make the Jew "forget" G-d's love for others. Since the Jews have been chosen to be given and to have received the Torah, and hence are already "the eternal people," a question and doubt arises within Jewry as to why they should, and in what manner they should, be concerned with the other less blessed nations. "He knows he is loved—so why concern himself with the world!" writes Rosenzweig in the next sentence.

The Jewish election, then, at least in the Jewish consciousness of it, has an inherent ambivalence. The Jews, however, are not ambivalent about which dimension of that ambivalence is of greatest significance to them. Rosenzweig does not cite, but he probably knew of the requests made by Moses to G-d, as explained in *Berachot* (7a): After G-d's anger at the Jewish people for the incident of the Golden Calf, Moses asks G-d first that the divine presence be eternally with the Jewish people, and second *that it not be with the other nations*. All the rabbis cited in this talmudic passage agree that G-d grants both wishes.[12] The inward positivity of an exclusive election, the treasures given and contained in a special relationship to G-d, the glory of a centripetal self-absorbed inward look, is what is most significant to the Jew according to Rosenzweig.

Even though the Jews know that the other nations are G-d's peoples too, that G-d rebukes his own angels, for example, when they rejoice in the death and destruction of Israel's Egyptian enemies, or that, as the prophets make clear, G-d uses Israel's enemies for divine purposes, the weight of the Jewish perception of its own election lies, quite naturally, with the Jewish nation's concern for and with itself. Rosenzweig writes:

He knows he is loved—so why concern himself with the world! In his blissful togetherness-alone with God, he may consider himself man, and man alone, and look up in surprise when the world tries to remind him that not every man harbors the same certainty of being God's child as he himself. Yet no one knows better than he that being dear to God is only a beginning, and that man remains unredeemed so long as nothing but this beginning has been realized. (*SR* 307)

We must not overlook that there is another side to this duality in Jewish consciousness, to the split between Israel's present eternity and the present unredeemed status of the world, thus far seen as the conflict between the favor G-d bestows on Israel and his love for the nations. This other side is Jewish consciousness of the Messiah. Directly following the statement above, Rosenzweig writes: "Over against Israel, eternally loved by God and faithful and perfect in eternity, stands he who is eternally to come, he who waits, and wanders, and grows eternally—the Messiah" (*SR* 307). The Jew today is indeed eternal, and his glance is directed inward, staying within a Judaism content with its election, but today also, adding a wrinkle of complexity to his apparent contentment, the Jew prays and yearns for the Messiah, for he whose coming will mean the redemption of the whole world.

Rosenzweig never underestimates this split in Jewish consciousness of Jewish election; the gift of eternity today on the one hand, and on the other hand an attunement to the as yet unredeemed character of the

12. Moses' third wish was to understand divine justice, the rewarding of good and the punishment of evil, which determinations often seem lacking in our world. This G-d did not reveal to Moses.

world. More than an ambivalence, Rosenzweig sees in this split a fundamental contradiction, one which runs through *all* of Judaism:

The Jewish world . . . is twofold and teeming with contradictions in every single thing. Everything that happens in it is ambivalent since it is related both to
this and the coming world. . . . As the contrast between holy and profane, Sabbath and workaday, "Torah and the way of earth," spiritual life and the earning
of a livelihood, this split goes through all of life. As it divides the life of Israel
into holy and profane, so it divides the whole earth into Israel and the peoples.
(*SR* 307–8)

This statement is important. We can see that for Rosenzweig the Jewish
election has three distinct results or meanings for Jewish consciousness
and life, each involving a fundamental unresolved split. First, election
unites the Jews as the holy people and separates them from non-Jews;
second, it divides the Jewish world from within, as, for example, between
Sabbath and workaday, Torah and worldly pursuits; and third, it unites
Jews with the non-Jewish world in a Jewish obligation to somehow see
the unredeemed non-Jewish world redeemed. This last point regarding
the Jewish obligation to redeem the world has, I think, multiple unresolved interpretations in Rosenzweig's thought; and it was also very likely
a sore point for the German Jewish intellectual Rosenzweig himself, a
man who turned from a highly promising university career to become
director and teacher at a Jewish adult education school in Frankfurt am
Main.

What is the *Jewish* obligation to the non-Jewish world? We must not
forget that the exalted status of the Jewish people, alone of all peoples
elected by G-d, tends to make the Jews "forget" the non-Jewish world.
This exaltation is the very "eternity" of the Jews, their election and glory
today, and at the same time, as Rosenzweig emphasizes, it poses a great
"danger" to Judaism, an inner-directed Jewish temptation, the danger of
a self-absorption purchased at the price of giving up care for the "outside"
world. But hasty or ill-considered responses to this danger will not do, at
least not for Rosenzweig. For Rosenzweig the redemption of the world
is specifically the task of Christianity, the Christian evangelizing mission,
the "good word." What then is left for Jews as Jews to do for the unredeemed world without losing the exaltation of the Jewish election? Because he did not have a single answer to this crucial question, Rosenzweig
gives three, each one putting Judaism into a different relation to the
Christian mission.

The first answer to the problem of a properly Jewish concern for the
non-Jewish world is, as indicated above, the Messiah. The Messiah's coming will solve the world's problems, will redeem the whole world. The

way for Jews to care for the "outside" world is for them to pray and yearn ever more fervently for the Messiah. By an odd twist, but one that already tells us something important about whether Rosenzweig has succeeded in developing the post-Enlightenment Judaism with which he is often credited, or whether to the contrary he has rather returned to a pre-Enlightenment Judaism, it is this very traditional solution, redemption of the world through the Messiah, that is perhaps the most ecumenical of Rosenzweig's three answers. By permitting the Jews a maximum of self-absorption, it gives most credibility to Christianity fulfilling the role of a more practical, world-historical mission—without fully succumbing to the "danger" of a Judaism entirely uncaring vis-à-vis the non-Jewish world. Here Jews do not at all ignore the world; they daily pray and yearn for the coming of the Messiah, the Messiah who will save the whole world, Jewish and non-Jewish.

Rosenzweig's second answer speaks to a somewhat more active and practical Jewish role in the redemption of the world, and consciously addresses the special relationship between Judaism and Christianity. But for all that it might actually require *more* of the Christian mission than the first answer. Once again Israel need not missionize to the gentiles of the world; this task still remains distinctively Christian. But Israel itself, nonetheless, saves the world. It does this through its suffering, a suffering inflicted upon the Jews by the non-Jewish world. How does Jewish suffering redeem the world? Here Rosenzweig understands Israel's election in the light of Isaiah's famous "suffering servant" image: Israel is the world's "suffering servant." Rosenzweig writes: "He has elected his people, but elected it to visit upon them all their iniquities. He wants every knee to bend to him and yet he is enthroned above Israel's songs of praise. Israel intercedes with him in behalf of the sinning people of the world and he afflicts Israel with disease so that those other peoples may be healed" (*SR* 307). Israel (like Jesus in Christianity) suffers for the sins of the world, and through its suffering it relieves the world of what would otherwise be its proper punishment. Rosenzweig is invoking the duel redemptive power of suffering expressed by the later Isaiah ("he was bruised for our iniquities"), a power which in our day has appeared most clearly in a Gandhian garb: the world beats Israel until Israel's afflictions force the world to recognize its own injustice. Or to express the same result from a different angle: Israel's affliction forces G-d, in his love for Israel, to reform the world's evil.

Since the suffering of Israel comes from non-Jews, from the non-Jewish world, the end of Jewish suffering depends, on the one hand, on the redemptive power of Jewish suffering, its ability to force G-d to redress evil, but then, on the other hand, it depends on the result of that spiritual power, the decrease of oppression against the Jews, the moral and spiritual improvement of the world. Here redemption depends not on Jews but on those who oppress the Jews, that is to say, on the non-Jewish world. It depends on the non-Jewish world becoming better, morally and spiritually better. Once again, as with the first solution, the Christian mission remains the all-important complement to the Jewish role as suffering servant.

It is therefore not the non-Jewish world in its Christian character, according to Rosenzweig, that oppresses the Jews, but the non-Jewish world in its pagan character. By "pagan" Rosenzweig means those persons, or that part of a person, not yet touched by love, or what in the *Star* he also calls "revelation." Since love for the Christian means imparting love rather than receiving it, the Christian, until the end of time, until the redemption of his entire self and the whole world, is never fully Christian, is always part pagan. To increase the Christian part, that is, to be successful in the Christian mission, in his own self and through the world, means both a decrease of paganism and a decrease of oppression against Jews. The redemptive enterprise, then, which the Jews elicit through their own unjust suffering, means that the world must be depaganized. This depaganization of the world, provoked by sympathy for Jewish suffering, is carried out by means of the Christian mission. Christians, by saving the world, save the Jews too—and in the process save themselves from their own atavistic, pagan, destructive impulses.

Rosenzweig puts hardly any weight on this second path, or, rather, he puts considerably less weight on it than on the other two paths of redemptive Judaism. Not only does Rosenzweig not develop this idea, but when he presents it he already has G-d Himself putting a damper on it. In the sentence preceding the one quoted above, Rosenzweig seems to withdraw this solution and offers a third one: "He [G-d] demands the visible signs of offering and prayer brought to his name, and of 'the affliction of our soul' in his sight. And almost in the same breath he scorns both and wants to be honored only with the secret fervor of the heart, in the love of one's neighbor, and in anonymous works of justice" (*SR* 306). What election requires of Jews in relation to non-Jews is concrete acts of neighborly love and the essentially anonymous works of justice.

Jewish election would thus require not only that Jews maintain their own inner circle of eternity but also that they spread to the world at large the ethics and justice which are essential elements of eternity, elements essential to the eternalization of the whole world. What the Jewish election demands of Jews in relation to the non-Jewish world is ethical behavior and the struggle for justice, and not only prayers for the Messiah and silent suffering for the sins of others. It demands ethics and justice within the Jewish community, to be sure, but also as the concrete realizable goals that Jews, as Jews, must insist upon and work for throughout the world.

This third redemptive path turns out, however, to be the least ecumenical, because it brings back into Judaism what for Rosenzweig seemed to be the exclusive and definitive task of Christianity: missionizing the good word. Following this third path, what would be best for Christians would be to become Jews, because even the missionizing which appeared to be a non-Jewish task (even though ultimately in the service of Judaism) from the point of view of the first two answers, would in the third perspective become an essentially Jewish activity.

Despite or more likely in lieu of this obvious result, it is clear that for Rosenzweig Jewish missionizing is not the key to the problem of Jewish election. For Rosenzweig, missionizing remains the exclusive, indeed the definitive *Christian* task. Whether Christianity be therefore understood as essentially different from Judaism, having a genuinely new sense of compassion (foregoing eternity today for the sake of the world's unachieved eternity) to contribute to world history, or whether Christianity is simply missionizing Judaism, the Judaicization of the world, without any new essentially non-Jewish component to add, what is clear is that for Rosenzweig it is Christianity and not Judaism which has the task of overcoming paganism and spreading the good word. Whether this division of labor is justified, in itself or in the *Star,* is another matter, but there is no question that it is Rosenzweig's preferred division of religious responsibilities.

Judaism is the "fire," Christianity the "rays." Judaism moves inward, is centripetal, Christianity is centrifugal, moving outward. Thus, in a genuine paradox, despite Rosenzweig's warning that self-absorption at the expense of the world is Judaism's special "danger," his famous ecumenicalism—the delegation of the project of world missionizing to Christianity—is precisely a central contributing factor to the quintessential danger of chosenness, Jewish self-absorption, love turned so inward that it ignores the unredeemed world at large.

Rosenzweig knows that it is Sabbath morning, that the Jewish election is exclusive, but he knows too that Sabbath afternoon follows the Sabbath morning, that a universal and all-inclusive "election" remains the goal. Such is the goal of Judaism even if it is not a Jewish goal, if by "Jewish" one means only an exclusive, separate Judaism. For his part, Rosenzweig's emphasis on the exclusivity of the Jewish election for the Jews does not blind him to an ultimate truth beyond Judaism. In the name of this final all-embracing truth, where everyone and hence no one will be elect, even Jewish election must be obliterated. He recognizes the presently unresolvable polarities of election, within the Jewish people, the contradictions between "Sabbath and workaday, 'Torah and the way of earth,' spiritual life and the earning of a livelihood," and between the Jewish people and the nations, "Israel and the peoples." He cannot deny these contradictions even though (for the sake of ecumenicalism?) he still places the weight of Jewish election on its exclusivity, on the unity of the Jewish people, on Jewish holiness, in contrast to the divisions and divisiveness of the nations, their profanity. It is not for Judaism but for Christianity to actively convert the nations, to spread the word. Judaism is an example, pristine, adamantine, polished but not shining.

Judaism Despite Christianity

With both Rosenzweig's emphasis and his ambivalence in mind, it is time to turn, though more briefly, to the second discussion of election and the Messiah in the *Star,* a discussion which occurs in book 3 of part 3. Here we find an entire section on the Jews entitled "The Man of Election" *(Der Mensch der Erwahlung)*. Its opening sentence confirms the duality and tension, the rift, between exclusive and inclusive election that is characteristic of Rosenzweig's account at the same time that it confirms the emphasis Rosenzweig places on Jewish exclusiveness, on the need of the Jew to "constrict himself for Jewish feeling." Rosenzweig writes:

Like God, man too constricts himself for Jewish feeling when this seeks to unite him into a unitary glow out of the dual consciousness, still flaming into one another, of Israel and the Messiah, of the gracious gift of revelation and the redemption of the world. One concept leads from Israel to the Messiah, from the people that stood at the foot of Sinai to that day when the house of Jerusalem 'shall be called a house of prayer for all peoples.' (*SR* 404)

It seems that even if France (or America) is not yet Jerusalem, France must one day become Jerusalem, or rather Jerusalem must one day include the whole world, including France. But until that glorious day the Jew must remain a Jew, holding firm to the exclusivity of his election, and leave to Napoleon, or rather, and the difference is important, leave to Christianity, rather than to the state alone, the task of transforming the world into Jerusalem.

What this means, too, is that the Jew must *resist* the transformative mission of Christianity, *for the sake of that very mission,* for the sake of its genuine completion. "I am not forgotten by *God,*" Rosenzweig had written to his converted cousin Rudolf Ehrenberg years earlier in November 1913, shortly after deciding to remain a Jew, and added "—that God whom one day your *Lord* too will serve" (*FR* 29). It seems that Rosenzweig was from the very beginning of his return to traditional Judaism cognizant that Jews must remain Jews not only for their own sakes, for the sake of Judaism, but also for the sake of Christianity too, for the sake of world redemption. The Jew must constrict himself, hold to his allotted eternity, and hold back against the allure of premature "redemptions." As we will see, Rosenzweig later develops this point further. Here he insists that "the man of election," despite his ultimate goals, despite, let us add, their greater or lesser institutionalization in the world, "constricts himself for Jewish feeling." Not until the Messiah comes, not until that miraculous transcending moment, simultaneously Jewish and non-Jewish, when Jews become like the nations and the nations like the Jews, that is to say, when both enter into the truth of a united humanity, a common language, when not only is G-d one but His name is one, not until then can the Jew relax the exclusiveness of Jewish election. Such is the very election of Jewish election, at once exaltation and affliction, holding forth by holding back, growing by conserving.

Judah Halevi (Spring 1924)

The complementarity between Judaism and Christianity that appears in the *Star* becomes a central theme and tension of Rosenzweig's commentaries on the poems of Judah Halevi, first published in the spring of 1924.

I will limit my remarks to two of the commentaries. One looks at Jewish election from the outside, from the Christian world. The other grasps the tension of election from the inside, from within the Jewish world. The tension, however, is the same though looked at differently. It is that between forces thought to be progressive and forces thought to be regressive, between what hastens and what delays the coming of the Messiah or redemption, between what expands the inclusiveness of divine election and what conserves its exclusiveness. The two perspectives differ from one another over the question of which is truly which, what progressive and what regressive, a question not for Christianity, which is certain of its answer, confidently spreading the good word, but for Judaism, torn and tempted by both its highest hopes and its deepest fears, hope for the future, fear for survival, here and there in moments of noble enthusiasm letting the idealism of its hopes get the better of the cautious self-protective realism of its fears, and suffering all the more for that.

Standing in the non-Jewish world, the redemptive enterprise measures its success (as was made explicit in Napoleon's letters) by the assimilation of the Jews. Redemption, in the modern period, is understood to be the progressive historical instuaration of a universal and necessary reason in place of parochial and contingent traditions. Individual Jews are often found supporting, even leading various movements in this wholly rational approach to the redemptive enterprise, contributing labor and money to its furtherance, both inside and outside of the traditional Jewish world. In his Halevi book Rosenzweig makes the following important statement about the complex relationship between Jewish separation, assimilation, and redemption, as seen from Jewish and non-Jewish eyes:

This people has a unique characteristic which, when one tries to dismiss it through the front door of reason, forces an entrance through the back door of feeling. It is evident in the paroxysms of an anti-Semitism that never found madder expression than in the hundred and twenty years during which everyone tried to prove that Jews were no different from other people. The unique characteristic of the people is this: that it looks at itself in about the same way as the outside world looks at it. A whole world asserts that the Jewish people is outcast and elect, both; and the Jewish people does not itself, in some assertion of its own, refute this dictum, but instead merely confirms it. Except that seen from the outside, the characterization assumes the form of external connectedness, while from within it represents an inseparable whole. (*FR* 335–36)

From the outside (in a Christian context, to be sure), Jewish exclusiveness is understood to be a result of both Jewish stubbornness and Jewish guilt. Because they rejected the Christ, the Jews are outcasts, deservedly so, especially when and insofar as the Jews themselves insist on their differences. Along this trajectory, the uniqueness of the Jews has been variously interpreted as a sign of divine rejection, genetic inferiority, social and political underdevelopment, bad breeding and manners, primitive mentality, orientalism, psychic disorder, and regression. All such interpretations must come from outside of Judaism (even if proposed by Jews), and all must claim to grasp Judaism better than Judaism grasps itself. All this is in keeping with Rosenzweig's earlier understanding of the supersessionist Christian interpretation of Judaism.

So, too, Rosenzweig's thoughts regarding the reverse side of Israel's exclusive election, the view from within the Jewish community, remain caught in the unavoidable tension between Israel's own genuine appreciation for the real advances made by the non-Jewish world in its striving toward redemption and the continued restraint Israel must nonetheless maintain in fulfilling its own unique and eternal destiny. What has changed is Rosenzweig's heightened sensitivity to and appreciation for the positive allure, the *Jewish* allure, that non-Jewish developments can have for the Jewish world. This change is doubtlessly influenced by Rosenzweig's personal decision to remain Jewish, his growth in Jewish knowledge and practice, and his new assessment of the power of the temptations that almost led him away from his birthright, as will become clearer in the following section. Whatever the cause, Rosenzweig is clearly renewing his attempt to understand the motivations for that movement which brought and continues to bring large numbers of Jews to lose their

Judaism, whether unconsciously, naturally, as it were a matter of course, or voluntarily, thoughtfully, reflectively, and hence to give up the millennial Jewish exclusiveness of election. He is renewing his attempt, in other words, to understand Jewish assimilation. He sees that many Jews who assimilate do so for what are taken to be very good reasons, giving up Judaism for the sake of "higher causes" such as Marxism, socialism, feminism, Christianity, humanism, patriotism, love, and the like.

To understand the attraction of assimilation, Rosenzweig now sees that there is an ambivalence, conflict, or contradiction in the very idea of the Messiah. He finds this tension expressed by the traditional Jewish distinction between "the true and the false Messiah." In one of the most important passages of his commentary on Halevi he writes:

The expectation of the coming of the Messiah, by which and because of which Judaism lives, would be a meaningless theologumenon, a mere "idea" in the philosophical sense, empty babble, if the appearance again and again of a "false Messiah" did not render it reality and unreality, illusion and disillusion. The false Messiah is as old as the hope for the true Messiah. He is the changing form of this changeless hope. He separates every Jewish generation into those whose faith is strong enough to give themselves up to an illusion, and those whose hope is so strong that they do not allow themselves to be deluded. The former are the better, the latter are the stronger. The former bleed as victims on the altar of the eternity of the people, the latter are the priests who perform the service at this altar. And this goes on until the day when all will be reversed, when the belief of the believers will become truth, and the hope of the hoping a lie. Then—and no one knows whether this "then" will not be this very day—the task of the hoping will come to an end and, when the morning of that day breaks, everyone who still belongs among those who hope and not among those who believe will run the risk of being rejected. This danger hovers over the apparently less endangered life of the hopeful. (*FR* 350–51)

Thus Rosenzweig understands that their own election—meaning the better world, the eternal world that it opens up to Jews and ultimately to the whole world, the prospect of redemption—splits the Jewish people internally between those who see the Messiah as having come in their own day, "those whose faith is strong enough to give themselves up to an illusion," *the better,* and those who still wait for the Messiah beyond the so-called progressive ideas of their day, "those whose hope is so strong that they do not allow themselves to be deluded," *the stronger*. So there is not simply an external conflict between Jews who say the Messiah has not come and Christians who say he has come, but rather within Judaism (and no doubt also at the origin of the Jewish-Christian split) lies an internal conflict between Jews who say the Messiah has not come and *Jews* who say he (or it, i.e., the "messianic age") has come. In our time, in contrast to the time of the Sabbatian heresy,[13] say, this internal Jewish conflict manifests itself in the division of Jews into those who religiously await the Messiah and those who have found and actively pursue the coming of the "messianic age" through Marxism, socialism, feminism, patriotism, etc.[14]

It is this inner tension coming from an exclusive yet globally redemptive telos, splitting the Jewish people from within, that explains why, as Rosenzweig had already written in the *Star,* the Jewish people develop and continue over time not by inclusion but by exclusion, excision, refinement, rejection, hardness, the shedding of a weaker if more "idealistic" periphery (see, e.g., Ezekiel 22:15–19). Judaism's miraculous survival over thousands of years depends not on expansion but on retraction, on the strength of a hard but faithful core of practitioners. Such has always been its historical experience, confirmed again and again, from the Egyptian exodus, where tradition teaches that four-fifths of the Jews did not go out into the desert, to the expulsion from Spain, where perhaps as many as half of Spanish Jewry chose to remain in an officially *Judenrein* Spain. Of this development through excision, Rosenzweig wrote in the *Star:* "Judaism, and it alone in all the world, maintains itself by subtraction, by contraction, by the formation of ever new remnants. . . . It constantly divests itself of un-Jewish elements in order to produce out of itself ever new remnants of archetypal Jewish elements. Outwardly it constantly assimilates only to be able again and again to set itself apart on the inside" (*SR* 404).

The irony, of course, is that it is not always or only the prudent, or the scoundrels and criminals, that Judaism must reject. Often, and especially in our day, Judaism must reject its idealists. Here are those who are "better" in the belief that Judaism itself has taught them, who embrace

13. Sabbatai Sevi (1626–76) was probably the most popular of all the false messiahs in the long history of false messiahs in Judaism. For a detailed account of his life and doctrines, see Gershom Scholem, *Sabbatai Sevi: The Mystical Messiah, 1626–1676,* translated by R. J. Zwi Werblowsky (Princeton: Princeton University Press, 1973).

14. For an excellent and more general account of the impact of messianism in European political history, see Norman Cohn, *The Pursuit of the Millennium* (New York: Harper and Row, 1961). For an account of the even broader question of the impact of religion on modern Europe, see Hans Blumenberg, *The Legitimacy of the Modern Age,* translated by Robert M. Wallace (Cambridge, Mass.: MIT Press, 1985). Blumenberg contests Karl Löwith's thesis that progress, the dominant idea in modern Europe, is a secularized version of, and hence in direct continuity with, the religious idea of eschatology. In this great debate one can only conjecture that Rosenzweig would stand against Blumenberg, seeing in modern Europe a secularized development of Christianity. This, in any event, as his correspondence amply attests, is what motivated his original intention to convert to Christianity: as a good German and a good European, Rosenzweig felt that he was already, except in name, a good Christian.

the higher and even the highest values, values which these idealists feel compelled to embrace today, even though their embrace, once again, and again and again, ends up empty handed, holding a false Messiah who slips away and vanishes, though leaving great wounds behind. It is these noblest, best, and brightest—but *ultimately,* as history has proven time and again, best and brightest *not* by Jewish standards—who are subtracted, divested, excluded from the Jewish people, and who must be excluded if Judaism is to continue until the kingdom of heaven reigns on earth. They, Rosenzweig has said, with great sympathy I think, are the lost sheep, "victims on the altar of the eternity of the people."

In contrast to these who are better, there are those who, because they are "stronger," do maintain the continuity of Judaism, and keep it alive through all the generations, through all persecutions, through all temptations. These, the stronger, have a quality Rosenzweig takes to be the great Jewish virtue: patience. Only these stronger Jews elect to cling to the exclusiveness of the Jewish election today, for the sake, whether openly admitted or not, or even considered, of a global eternity tomorrow. Indeed, these stronger ones must maintain an ever more severe and self-disciplined patience precisely as the world progresses toward its redemptive end. As the pressures from without decrease in this positive way, the restrains from within must proportionally increase. From within the elect community the moral and spiritual developments of a progressing world, laudatory though its advances are, mean negatively a heightened temptation, but positively they demand a steeling of the community's sights to a yet more distant future, a higher future, to an eternity the world, despite all its progress, has not yet equalled. In the *Star,* Rosenzweig writes:

In Judaism, man is always somehow a remnant. He is always somehow a survivor, an inner something, whose exterior was seized by the current of the world and carried off while he himself, what is left of him, remains standing on the shore. Something within him is waiting. And he has something within himself. What he is waiting for and what he has he may call by different names; often enough he may barely be able to name it. But he has a feeling that both the waiting and the having are most intimately connected with each other. And this is just that feeling of the "remnant" which has the revelation and awaits the salvation. (*SR* 405)

It is this patience—etched in the wrinkles of the old Jew's face[15]—that maintains the purity of the ancient faith, resisting the attractions, false and genuine, of more modern ways, held and holding to a commitment

---

15. See *SR* 408: "The type of the aged Jew is as characteristic for us as the youthful type is for the Christian nations. For Christian life de-nationalizes the Christian, but Jewish life leads the Jew deeper into his Jewish character."

to Judaism, an inner commitment that despite all the sirens' calls and all the just causes, "forces an entrance through the back door of feeling," even when "one tries to dismiss it through the front door of reason."

Letter to the Lehrhaus (November 1924)

Rosenzweig's thoughts on election were not changed in any radical way but rather were considerably sharpened and deepened, especially from a Jewish perspective, when in November 1924 he reconsidered his position in a letter to Martin Goldner, Nahum Glatzer, Hans Epstein, and Lotte Fürth, his colleagues at the Freies Jüdisches Lehrhaus in Frankfort am Main.[16] Rosenzweig now considers Jewish election in conjunction with Jewish law. Here is the true test of Rosenzweig's conception of election, for there is probably nothing more revealing about the nature and significance of a modern post-Mendelssohnian Jew's Judaism than his or her position regarding the nature and significance of Jewish law.

The letter is an extended meditation on the following words, which are taken from Nahum Glatzer but which Rosenzweig considers "his own ideas uttered by someone else," namely: "that only the election of the people of Israel came from God, but that all the details of the Law came from man alone." By reflecting on this claim, that election is from G-d but that the details of the law are from man, Rosenzweig is both meditating on his own thoughts and reinvoking his celebrated debate with Martin Buber, a debate to which his thought regularly returns.

Briefly and broadly, the debate with Buber concerns the significance of the divine-human relationship which lies at the heart of revelatory religion. Given the traditional Jewish view that revelation—"the" revelation—means the giving and the receiving of the Torah at Mount Sinai, meaning the giving and the receiving of Jewish law, halakah, written as well as oral, the Buber-Rosenzweig debate on the significance of the divine-human relationship centers on the question of the status of Jewish law in relation to revelation. Is Jewish law derived, directly, immediately, inseparably, as tradition has it, from G-d's unique revelation and from the elaboration of that revelation in the normative rabbinic tradition (Midrash, Mishna, Gemora, commentaries, codes, responsa, etc.), and hence is itself divine, unalterable, eternal, or is Jewish law a human contribution, a human invention, one but only one way humans have chosen to try to hold onto the truth of revelation, and hence a finite, changeable, and ultimately a voluntaristic way?

The answer to the above question concerning the divine or human

16. *FR* 242–47; *Briefe* 1001–5. All extended references in this section are to this letter.

status of Jewish law is linked to a prior question about the nature of revelation itself. Is revelation a unique once-and-done-for-event ("Mount Sinai"), an event which ends or lives in a biblical, talmudic, rabbinic canon and tradition, in the cautious, obedient, and fully faithful extrapolation of an always prior (meaning both "before in time" and "superior in quality") canon, or is revelation a continual event, eternally available, G-d's eternal presence, occurring today, at this very moment? Or, if it is in some way both of these, then in what proportion or dialectic? What does it mean to say, for example, that the Torah is a *living* Torah, or that the comments of a talmudic commentator are inspired by or with *holy spirit*, and that they too were given at Mount Sinai? This debate is usually formulated in terms of the meaning of Mount Sinai. Did G-d reveal Himself by revealing revelation, or did He reveal Himself by giving Himself over, revealing Himself in and through his Law, both written and oral, placed now in the loving, caring hands of pious and devoted interpreters?

It is easy to forget the forest for the trees in this debate, and to forget that Buber and Rosenzweig basically take the same position, a position concerning revelation that makes them both contemporary thinkers, post-Enlightenment thinkers. First, both answer the above questions by basing their thinking on a revelation that is not a unique event once-and-done-for ("Mount Sinai") but an event that is continually available. Second, revelation is not only continually available for both thinkers, but both understand that the very presence of the present, authentic presence, authentic engagement in time, the juncture of time and eternity, is a function of revelation. Third, both agree that the special locus of revelation is in the intimacy of the I-thou relationship, the intersubjective or interpersonal relation. We must not lose sight of the fact that it is on the basis of these three fundamental points of agreement, at very close quarters then, that Rosenzweig parts company with Buber.

The point of contention is, as I have indicated, the authority of traditional Jewish law. Buber turns against tradition with a vengeance. He not only rejects the divine status of Jewish law, but takes Jewish law to be an obstacle to divine revelation.[17] Hence Buber rejects Jewish law altogether, and he does so in the name of the intense revelatory presence of the divine in the I-thou relationship. Rosenzweig also understands revelation in terms of an intense revelatory presence manifest in the I-thou relationship. But in sharp contrast to Buber, Rosenzweig accepts Jewish law. How he

---

17. See Maurice Friedman, *Martin Buber's Life and Work: The Middle Years, 1923-1945* (Detroit: Wayne State University Press, 1988), chapter 3, "Rosenzweig and the Law." The first sentence of this chapter reads, in part (40): "The greatest and best-known divergence between Martin Buber and Franz Rosenzweig was in their attitude toward the Jewish Law. . . . "

is able to do this, how he understands the relation between Jewish law and divine revelation, is precisely the topic of his letter to his colleagues at the Lehrhaus.

Traditional Jewish law poses a problem for both Rosenzweig and Buber because it locates the divine-human relationship, or the normative authoritative occurrence of this relationship, in the past—as the written and oral Torah given at Mount Sinai in the Jewish year 2448 (1312 B.C.E.)—rather than in the present, in the I-thou. The authority of the Torah interpreted by the rabbis does not derive from their special engagement in the divinity of an I-thou relationship, though their piety, sincerity, and fair-mindedness must be unquestioned; nor does it derive from their entering into some variation of the divine I-thou relationship with texts, though the rabbis when they consult the texts to apply Jewish law always adjudicate each case according to its particular contours. Rather, for the tradition, the authority of Torah depends on its having been given by G-d once and for all in its entirely at Mount Sinai. Accordingly, contra Buber and Rosenzweig, revelation is over. Even if revelation is extended to cover the words of the prophets, prophecy too is definitively over. What was revealed once-and-for-all must today be interpreted, to be sure, but interpretation is valid only when performed in obedience to that once-and-for-all revelation ("Mount Sinai"). The Torah has been given, it is "no longer in heaven," but it was given as G-d's most precious gift and must be treated as such. Such a view precludes believing the Jewish law to be a human contrivance.

Buber holds to a clear and straightforward position, one which he held both in theory and practice: he rejects the authority of traditional Jewish law in the name of the continuous and ongoing presence of revelation here and now (in the I-thou). Rosenzweig, in contrast, came in his life to follow more and more of the traditional Jewish laws, to the point that he would neither reject nor denigrate a single one of them, however arcane or apparently antirational, claiming that the laws he did not follow were laws that he did "not yet" follow. Having come to the point of embracing the whole of Jewish law, in theory if not wholly in practice, Rosenzweig seems to be on murkier terrain than Buber, or than the traditionalists for that matter. The central question he must therefore answer is the question of the grounds or the justification for Jewish obedience to Jewish Law. And it is this question precisely that the letter of 1924 to his colleagues at the Lehrhaus addresses. Let us finally get to it.

Rosenzweig begins, as I have noted, by examining the statement, so seemingly congenial to him, that "the election of the people of Israel came from God, but that all the details of the Law came from man alone." Though in the letter Rosenzweig attributes the words to Glatzer, the position is actually Buber's. When Rosenzweig admits in his next sentence that "I should have formulated this—and have actually done so to my-self—in very much the same way, but when one hears one's own ideas uttered by someone else, they suddenly become problematic," he is not only confirming the value he has always placed on the back and forth exchange of dialogue, its revelatory character, but at the same time and in this very spirit, he is preparing himself to fundamentally reconsider, and in this reconsideration to reject, the truth of the position stated. To express this in terminology dear to Emmanuel Levinas: Rosenzweig confirms the saying, while he rejects the said. In 1924 Glatzer's words, which are claimed by Rosenzweig for himself, but in the subjunctive mood, and which in truth express Buber's actual position, have "suddenly become problematic."

Rosenzweig is no longer satisfied with "so rigid a boundary between what is divine and what is human." Such a dissatisfaction is understand-able in view of what Rosenzweig has already maintained about Jewish election. If choosing the Jewish people is G-d's action, but the law and its details are only a human action, then in what sense would the law be special or authoritative? If the Jewish law is completely human, then in what sense is it superior to other human laws, the laws of Germany, say, or the laws of America? What is Jewish, i.e., chosen, in Jewish law if the law is purely human? Rosenzweig has already accepted the idea that Jew-ish chosenness is not purely human but comes from G-d.

Precisely the untimeliness of the Jews is their election, an election com-ing only from G-d. The height of "Mount Sinai" is not an event once-and-done-for, but the priority of being ahead of time, a Jewish life lived in an eternity which exists in a real u-topian[18] (i.e. eternal) community prior to the full conversion of all time into eternity through the Christian eternaliz-ing (Judaicizing) mission. But Jewish eternity today, in the present, ahead of time, depends on adherence to Jewish law. If Jewish law were human, and not the product of a divine intervention in history, then it would lose its authority, just as Judaism would lose its eternity and the Jewish community its exemplary untimeliness. Even if one were to argue, in an effort to buttress and preserve Jewish law despite its human status, that by human standards Jewish law is the best law, because it is on a higher moral plane, even if this were true, which would certainly be hotly dis-puted, nothing would or could guarantee that Jewish law would always or even long retain its lead, and certainly nothing would or could guaran-tee its superiority all the way to the end of time. In other words, the

18. It is Karl Marx who has given a bad name to "Utopia." For a corrective, see Martin Buber, *Paths in Utopia* (Boston: Beacon Press, 1958).

eternity or election of the Jews and Judaism would be severed from Jewish law if the laws, in contrast to election, had a merely human origin, were merely timely, i.e., historical. But for Rosenzweig Jewish law cannot be severed from Jewish election. There would be no reason ultimately to retain Jewish law until the end of time if Jewish law were purely human. Other laws would in time doubtless become superior, if they have not already become so.

Rosenzweig responds to the humanist challenge to Jewish law by blurring the sharp division separating divine choosing and human legislation upon which the rejection of Jewish law depends, and by hitching Jewish law to Jewish election. He writes: "We must keep in mind the obvious fact that a law, that the law as a whole, is the prerequisite for being chosen, the law whereby divine election is turned into human electing, and the passive state of a people being chosen and set apart is changed into the activity on the people's side of doing the deed which sets it apart." Election itself is not passive. The divine election of the Jews means that the Jews must thenceforth live up to the standards of election.

What exactly does Rosenzweig mean when he writes "that the law as a whole, is the prerequisite for being chosen"? This can mean neither that G-d follows His own law in choosing the Jews nor, obviously, that the Jews must already have the law before being chosen. What it does mean is that the Jewish people are chosen because they, the Jewish people, agree to follow the law. The Jewish people are chosen from among the nations because, as the Midrash teaches, they are the only nation that agrees to accept the Torah, to follow it, to do its deeds, prior to having seen it: "We will do and we will hearken."

Let us also ask what the law is for Rosenzweig. "It is the prerequisite for being chosen," to be sure, but it is also, as this sentence continues, "the law whereby divine election is turned into human electing, and the passive state of a people being chosen and set apart is changed into the activity on the people's side of doing the deed which sets it apart." Accepting the law transformed the Jewish people from passivity to activity. On the one hand, when Rosenzweig writes that "divine election is turned into human electing," he is returning to a central idea of the *Star*, namely, the link joining revelation and redemption: "It is only in being loved by God that the soul can make of its act of love more than a mere act, can make of it, that is, the fulfillment of a—commandment to love" (*SR* 214). On the other hand, Rosenzweig is now explicitly raising the question of the relationship between the generalized divine imperative found in the *Star*, the "commandment to love," and the specific and particular imperatives of Jewish law, the "details of the Jewish law." Or, as he expresses this key question in his letter: "The only matter of doubt is whether or to what degree this law originating in Israel's election coincides with the traditional Jewish law."

This, then, is the crux of the matter. Where does Rosenzweig stand? That divine revelation and Jewish election mean the imposition of divine imperative, we know Rosenzweig believes. In the *Star* it meant the commandment to love, the command upon the beloved to return the miraculously given love of the lover (= the other = G-d), and then, further, for the beloved to give love in turn to the neighbor. But now the question has to do with "traditional Jewish law," with "the details of the Jewish law." In what sense and to what extent, if at all, are these, too, divinely commanded in the divine election of the Jews? In the *Star* Rosenzweig argued that the imperative of divine revelation, the redemptive enterprise, can only be fulfilled within the two living communities based on divine revelation: Jewry and Christendom. But in the *Star,* too, Rosenzweig did not explicitly link the authority of the numerous and detailed laws of Judaism's complex legal system, upon which the living Jewish community had traditionally been based and organized, to the direct authority of divine revelation. Rosenzweig took no position, neither for nor against. What becomes clear from his letter is that Rosenzweig has come to see a link between these two sorts of imperatives: the fundamental command to love and the detailed commandments of Jewish law, halakah. The issue for us is to determine more precisely the sense in which Rosenzweig understands this link.

Rosenzweig cannot bring himself to a straightforward espousal of the traditional justification for the Jewish law, namely, that it must be followed because it was given by G-d to Moses and the Jewish people at Mount Sinai. Revelation is also, and still, loving in the present, which is the very presence of the present. In the *Star* Rosenzweig already presented a "reason" for obeying the miraculous revelation of love, namely, that by being loved, one is in all fairness obligated to love in return, and (no doubt more to the point) one *has* the wherewithal, the model, the inspiration, to do so. Of course, one is not compelled to return love for love owing to either logico-deductive or physico-causal necessity, but rather out of ethico-spiritual obligation, i.e., election. So there is a reason for loving, because one is already loved, even though there is no reason or reasonable explanation for having already been loved, which is pure revelation, G-d's move. Maimonides too, articulated reasons for the divine commandments. Nonetheless, Maimonides, like all traditional Jewish thinkers, understood that the "bottom line" for obedience to a divine command was purely and simply because a divine command is a divine command. One must do G-d's will because it is G-d's will, whether one has a reason for obeying the law or even an understanding of the significance of the law.

Rosenzweig's position is different. In stating it, it will also become apparent why it must take so long to get to it. In place of the traditional justification for obedience, and *as* his own most positive alternative, Rosenzweig explains why he cannot explain what he means. That is to say, he explains precisely why it is essentially impossible for him or anyone else to articulate the precise connection between revelation and law. Precisely *this* inexpressibility is as far as expression can go. But instead of leaving off here, instead of making a fetish of inexpressibility, as has been done in much contemporary thought—"they now worship the question mark itself as God,"[19] wrote Nietzsche—the conclusion Rosenzweig draws is far more positive: the rest must be *done, the law must be followed.* Inexpressibility is not the point of divine command, but results rather from the transcendence (the "Messiah," and beyond the Messiah the one truth) toward which divine command clearly directs the Jewish people. Do, and *then* hearken if you can, to the best of your ability, but if you cannot hearken then *do* nonetheless.

But in calling for obedience to the Jewish law, in full view of the impossibility of expressing its justification, its precise link to divine revelation, Rosenzweig is not worshipping Nietzsche's question mark. Rosenzweig differentiates between "what can be *stated* about God and what can be *experienced* about God." The former, what can be stated about G-d, includes only one proposition: that G-d exists. This one knows from being loved. As to the latter, what can be experienced about G-d, Rosenzweig resorts to analogy because he cannot, for essential reasons, state directly what he means. He selects a very traditional Jewish analogy, one closely associated with the prophet Hosea: marriage, the marriage of the Jewish people to G-d and G-d to the Jewish people. But instead of saying simply, as is so often said in the Jewish tradition, that the relationship of the Jewish people to G-d is like the relationship of bride to groom, or wife to husband, Rosenzweig as a contemporary thinker is attuned also to the medium of his message, to the import of language, and focuses on the deeper significance of the need for analogy at just this point:

What we can thus state—or even prove—about God is related to our possible 'experience' in the same way that the empty announcement that two persons have married, or the showing of the marriage certificate, is related to the daily and hourly reality of this marriage; it is no one's concern and yet it is the only thing that counts, and the objective statement of the fact of marriage would be meaningless without this most private, incommunicable reality.

In other words, objective statements about experiencing G-d are neither equivalent to nor able to express the heart of what is experienced about G-d in actual obedience to Jewish law. Thus, contra Buber, Rosenzweig

---

19. Nietzsche, *On the Genealogy of Morals,* Third Essay, section 25.

is not simply referring to an ineffable but real experience of the divine in the I-thou relation between man and G-d, or more broadly between the Jewish people and G-d, *nor* is he simply referring to the ineffable but real experience of the divine in the I-thou relation between human and human—all of which one already finds in the *Star* and in Buber, and later in Levinas. Rather, Rosenzweig is here referring to the ineffable but real experience of the divine found in the relationship established by the Jewish people, or more exactly by individual Jews in the obedient performance of the Jewish *law*.

It is not that following the law is a blind and stupid obedience, but rather that following the law has an inner logic, one experienced in the obedience, and derives its divine authority, its link to election, in the light of this inner logic. But, like the experience of marriage, which transpires only between the married couple and is invisible to all the world, the inner logic of obedience to divine law is essentially incongruous with and hence hidden to objective explanation. Following the Jewish law, then, is what exceeds reason and yet manages to concretely bear the inexpressible in the inexpressibility of G-d. This is why, too, living life "beyond the book" is so important to Rosenzweig, and why, also, such an appeal is in no way an appeal to "naive experience." Rosenzweig explains his marriage analogy by extending it to other analogous experiences: "The matter of the details of the Law is analogous to the wealth of experiences, of which only that experience holds which is in the act of being undergone, and holds only for him who is undergoing it. Here too there is no rigid boundary in the relationship between God and man." Rosenzweig thus overcomes the emptiness, abstraction, or generality of a "commandment to love," which remains abstract in the *Star* despite its material base in physical or sensual love, and he overcomes the same emptiness, abstraction, or generality of the relationship of the Jewish people as a whole to the law as a whole. His concern turns out to be with the individual Jew's obedience to individual Jewish laws, and the essentially inexpressible way that that obedience, and only that obedience, *validates* the divinity of the Jewish law. Such is the concretude of Rosenzweig's "new thinking," and its risk for the old thinking. Like the reality of marriage experienced daily and from within, essentially invisible to outsiders,[20] the individual Jew's obedience to individual Jewish laws is the privileged way or access to an authentic experience of G-d. Only in obeying the law, as Rosenzweig himself increasingly came to do, does one witness the divine authority for Jewish law, its place in Jewish election.

20. One catches a glimmer of this invisibility made manifest, sad to say, in the complete surprise which is often the response of close friends and relatives upon hearing of the dissolution of what they and all the world otherwise took to be a happy marriage. Marriage in this sense is completely private, an affair for and between two people.

The inexpressibility of the experience of the divine in obedience to Jewish law does not rule out the coherence of alternative modes of explanation, such as those articulated by William James, Sigmund Freud, Julius Wellhausen, and Max Weber, whom Rosenzweig singles out for mention. It trivializes them. Compared to the experience of the divine which comes from obedience to the law, "these historical and sociological explanations" are not false, Rosenzweig writes, rather they "are of superficial and subsidiary importance." Thus without denying the limited validity of scientific psychological and sociological explanations of religious experience, explanations which do deny the divinity of Jewish law, Rosenzweig can defend the "immediacy" of the "experience of the theo-human reality" achieved through "doing," through obeying Jewish laws.

Rosenzweig thus affirms the religious or divine significance of even the most recalcitrant and scientifically improbable elements of the Jewish law. He makes these affirmations not, we must be clear, because science is false, but because its truths do not go far enough, are not deep enough, do not enter into what is operative in the Jewish election. Only through obedience to Jewish law can the Jewish election be experienced and grasped both in the first person singular and in its appropriate space and time, sanctified space, eternalized time. What is experienced and what can be stated objectively are not coextensive. I quote Rosenzweig's letter again:

In this immediacy we may not "express" God *(Gott aussprechen)*, but rather address God *(Gott ansprechen)* in the individual commandment. For whoever seeks to express him will discover that he who cannot be expressed will become he who cannot be found. Only in the commandment can the voice of him who commands be heard. . . . Not that doing necessarily results in hearing and understanding. But one hears differently when one hears in the doing. All the days of the year Balaam's talking ass may be a mere fairy tale, but not on the Sabbath wherein this portion is read in the synagogue, when it speaks to me out of the open Torah. But if not a fairy tale, what then? I cannot say right now; if I should think about it today, when it is past, and try to say what it is, I should probably only utter the platitude that it is a fairy tale.

Not only is objective expression inadequate, according to Rosenzweig, but the act of objective enunciation and the effort to know G-d inevitably fail and lead to G-d's disappearance. Rosenzweig turns the tables: the truly vicious circle lies in the attempt to know G-d objectively.

That objective accounts of religion are superficial and miss the heart of the matter was already Rosenzweig's criticism of philosophy and theology in 1921, in part 1 of the *Star*. It was against the disappearance of G-d that occurs in and for objective thought that Rosenzweig defended revelation as love in part 2. But there revelation was the revelation of revelation, the command to love, and as such it lacked content, lacked, despite appearances to the contrary, an inherent connection to the rich content found in Rosenzweig's account of Judaism in book 1 of part 3. The turn to the Jewish holy year in part 3 was, it is true, a genuine concretization of the contentless love of part 2, but it was nevertheless separate from it, an accidental or fortuitous concretization, because Jewish life in the *Star* is presented as nothing more than a historical necessity. That only these two religious communities, the Jewish and the Christian, happened to exist, was not based, however, on the inner demands of revelation. Or, to say this differently, the two communities authorized by revelation, a community of the beloved and a community of the loving, were only formally linked to the religious actualizations of being loved and loving in the Jewish community and Christendom respectively. Rosenzweig had yet to fully appreciate the role of law in Jewish life.

The lack of inherent connection between the rapture of love and the concrete practices of real communal life becomes apparent in Rosenzweig's inability to distinguish the Jewish turn from love to the Jewish eternal community and the Christian turn from love to the Christian missionary community, except that in the former case one is born Jewish, born for the Jewish community, and in the latter one becomes Jewish, as it were, chooses the Christian missionary communion. In both instances, regardless of the manner of initiation, the ultimate purpose of the religious community is the same: to turn from being loved to loving others. But in the sole directive in the *Star* which links revelation to community life, namely, "love thy neighbor," the Jew has as little reason in his or her community as has the Christian in his or her community to adhere to the specifics of the Jewish law. Buber, too, loved his neighbor, and saw no good reason to adhere to Jewish law.

In the 1924 letter to the Lehrhaus, Rosenzweig attempts to make the external connection between revelation-election and law an internal one. Revelation, being loved, entails more than a blanket imperative to love the neighbor; it requires, as can only be experienced from within, that the Jew follow the individual commandments of the Jewish law, mitzvot. Only thus does the Jew experience and preserve divine love, actualize God's eternity on earth. Thus the boundary between man and G-d, which is the topic of Rosenzweig's letter, a division settled in the *Star* by an external separation between G-d's revelation, which was the revelation of revelation,[21] and man's redemptive enterprise, love of the neighbor, spreading what was received in part to the whole, is here blurred by

21. Rosenzweig repeats this formula in the *Halevi* book too: "All that God ever reveals in revelation is—revelation" (*FR* 286). But he adds: "Whatever does not follow directly from this covenant between God and man, whatever cannot prove its direct bearing on this covenant, cannot be a part of it." What comes out of the Lehrhaus letter is that now Rosenzweig sees that Jewish Law can and does "prove its direct bearing on this covenant."

bringing G-d into the redemptive enterprise, as it were, by means of the Jewish law. The fulfillment of the Jewish law is for Jews the inner link connecting the eternal to the temporal, the sanctification of time ("on that day, in that very hour").

Thus Rosenzweig comes back from the brink of an almost complete assimilation, from the detached freedom of a universal reason, to the election of the Jewish people through obedience to Jewish law. Because he came from so far and returned so far, Rosenzweig's status as a returnee to Judaism, a *baal teshuvah,* is important and instructive. He is careful to qualify his thoughts on revelation, election, and law as "the beginning of our way," as "peculiar to our situation," that is, the situation of the Jew coming from the outside and moving into the center of Judaism, moving from a total disregard toward an ever greater obedience to the Jewish law, based on a total acceptance of the whole of it. The letter concludes with the affirmation of a distinction between Rosenzweig's circumstance and perspective as a returnee and "the situation of the Jew who never left the fold."

For Rosenzweig the difference between these two Jews, the one who comes back and the one who never left, has to do with the appreciation of the divine significance which comes from following Jewish Law. It is the difference between those who, like Rosenzweig, are still impressed with being impressed, and hence talk too much and must learn to be silent, must learn to obey and learn from obeying, and those who do not feel the need to explain themselves but who experience deeply, who do not talk "about" but enter into prayer and life within the eternity of a community regulated and guided by Jewish law. "So far as we are concerned," writes Rosenzweig in very telling words, the "*mitzvah* which leads from what can to what cannot be expressed is nearest our hearts." The letter concludes as follows:

Thus, I do not think the boundary between the divine and the human is that between the whole and the parts, but that between something whose origin we recognize with a recognition which can be expressed, communicated, and formulated, and something else whose origin we also recognize and recognize just as clearly, but with a recognition which cannot be expressed and communicated. I should not venture to dub "human" any commandment whatsoever, just because it has not yet been vouchsafed me to say over it: "Blessed art *Thou.*"

I will not here decide whether Rosenzweig has overestimated the difference between his situation and "the situation of the Jew who never left the fold." The point is that the living of Jewish life—the "INTO LIFE"—toward which the thoughtful and thought provoking words, the well-crafted words, of the *Star* propelled its readers, is now, in 1924, not just a life devoted to love for the neighbor, but a Jewish life of love for the neighbor, obedient to Jewish law.

Rosenzweig's Election

Too much ground has been covered in this chapter to permit ending with a simple concluding summary or review of Rosenzweig's thoughts on election. Instead, I will conclude with a final observation, a final overview. From the initial affirmation of his having been chosen from birth, made in his 1916 letter to Rosenstock, to his mature reflections on the special and positive significance of Jewish law *for him,* made in his 1924 letter to his colleagues at the Lehrhaus, Rosenzweig's return to Judaism did not occur as a series of intellectual and spiritual leaps and bounds, but rather as a sure and steady deepening, a sure and steady movement from the periphery to the center of Judaism. The specific line which we have attempted to follow, Rosenzweig's developing understanding of *and personal commitment to* Jewish election, mimics the very process of Jewish learning, of commentary, reviewing texts again and again, each time probing more deeply, grasping wider implications, recognizing tighter integrations and harmonies of meaning within and with the rest of Jewish tradition. Indeed, the ongoing development of Rosenzweig's understanding and commitment to Jewish election does not merely mimic the Jewish process of learning, it is precisely an instance of it.

TWO

Authentic Self and History:
An Alternative to Heidegger

One of the outstanding intellectual "events" in the spiritual and cultural life of continental Europe after the First World War was the publication of Martin Heidegger's *Being and Time* in 1927.[1] The work represented, reflected, and reinforced a major change in times, as it shifted intellectual concern from the time of eternity to the time of temporality and history. Thus it (and Heidegger's subsequent thinking) became a fulcrum for continental thought, a standard from which other thinkers, major and minor, measured their critical distances.

Whatever else Heidegger's monumental book was meant to be, whether a renewal of ontology, as Heidegger ever increasingly insisted in the course of his career, or a new existential epistemology, as it no doubt is, or an existential-historical redirecting of Husserlian phenomenology, which it also no doubt is, the bulk of its pages are devoted to the elaboration of an original conception of the self. *Being and Time* is about human subjectivity and the larger contexts within which human subjectivity plays a role.

Having said this, a qualification must be added, lest readers and devotees of Heidegger cry foul too soon. Precisely because the theses of *Being and Time* regarding human subjectivity are both radical and original, requiring a rethinking of the nature of human subjectivity from the ground up, to retain the term "human subjectivity" or its equivalents, "self" and "subject," as names for its subject matter is immediately suspect. One of the primary negative accomplishments of *Being and Time* is a radical rejection of "subjectivism," the interpretation of human being as "subject" opposed to "object," as the "subjective" opposed to the "objective," as a "self" within a "world." Heidegger finds this divisive point of view inher-

1. Edward J. van Buren has recently proposed a fascinating thesis regarding *Being and Time*. He argues that this text, which Heidegger published at the age of 37, must be seen as a late, reworked, "transcendentalized" version of Heidegger's earlier and potentially more fruitful thinking of the early 1920s. See "The Young Heidegger: Rumor of a Hidden King (1919–1926)," *Philosophy Today* 33, no. 2 (Summer 1989): 99–108. Interesting and thought provoking as is van Buren's thesis, we should not forget that *Being and Time* has an authorial imprimatur that earlier lecture notes, however carefully recorded, or made use of by another scholar or thinker, cannot have.

ent in the very words "subjectivity," "subject," and "self." To begin with such a division, Heidegger claims, is never to be able to bridge it. But that would be all right if the division were a legitimate or rather a fundamental one. The problem is that it is not. Hence one cannot begin with the split between "subject" and "object." Arguing in this manner, Heidegger makes one of the defining and fundamental moves of all twentieth-century continental thought.

The underlying aim of the spiritual project initiated in *Being and Time* is a renewal of ontology where ontology is to be thought back to its true origins and dimensions prior to the division of "reality" into "subjective" and "objective" in the modern epoch. To get to this unitary conception of being, Heidegger must begin with a unitary conception of the self. Thus the bulk of *Being and Time* is concerned primarily with elaborating just such a conception. But because the terms "self," "subject," and "subjectivity," are polluted, as it were, by the very split that *Being and Time* aims to undercut, what I have called Heidegger's "conception of the self" is instead named an "analytic of Dasein" or a "Dasein analytic."

The term *Dasein,* which most Heidegger translators now prefer not to translate, in German does not mean, or is not limited to meaning, "self," "subject," "subjectivity," "human being," or even "human existence." The *Da* by itself literally means "there." The *sein* by itself literally means "being." Hence Heidegger's preferred term means, literally, "there-being," or, to put it into slightly better English, it means "being-there." Thus subjectivity, thought more originally, thought beneath the modern division of "reality" into "subjective" and "objective," is "being-there." Although the English literal translation is obviously an invention, the original German term is not. *Dasein* in its more usual German usage would be translated as "existence." It is a term used in ordinary German, but it has also been used as a technical term by German philosophers prior to Heidegger, by Hegel to take a prime instance.

Heidegger uses the term *Dasein,* as I have indicated, for both short-term and long-term purposes. In the short term it is to reconceive selfhood, to see the unitary phenomenon of selfhood beneath the modern division of the self into "subject" versus "object." In the long term, it is to reorient selfhood to the larger context of being, itself rethought beneath the modern division of "reality" into "subjective" and "objective." The term *Dasein,* then, in precise contrast to such terms as "self," "subject," and "subjectivity," is perfectly suited to both of Heidegger's purposes because it invokes both the unitary being of the individual being that Dasein is, the *sein* that is *Da,* as well as the broader unitary world-giving *Sein* at large, epochal historical being, toward which Dasein is opened by first being open to its own individual sort of being.

The "Dasein analytic" of *Being and Time,* then, is a propaedeutic to the thought of being itself. As such, and perhaps despite its claims to originality, it rejoins a long philosophical tradition. To think selfhood as propaedeutic is one the most characteristic features of modern "post-Cartesian" thought. Perhaps even more broadly, it is a characteristic feature of the entire tradition of philosophy which seeks knowledge of the whole. Taking up this broader perspective, *Being and Time,* for all its radical originality, holds a place homologous in the structure of Heidegger's thinking to the place "The Journey" holds in the structure of Parmenides' theogony (propaedeutic to "The Way of Truth"), and to the place the *Phenomenology of Spirit* holds in the structure of Hegel's absolute philosophy (propaedeutic to the *Logic*). Serving as ladders to the absolute, Dasein and the "Dasein analytic" would have only relative value in the grander scheme of a more complete being/knowledge.

Nonetheless, and I emphasize this "nonetheless," whatever else its larger goals and wider horizons, and whatever be the real value of those larger goals and wider horizons, *Being and Time* is very much an account of the being and time of human subjectivity. It is as such that in this chapter it will be contrasted to the account of the being and time of human subjectivity found in Franz Rosenzweig's *The Star of Redemption.*

Though one would not know it from reading *Being and Time,* or from reading Heidegger's many later publications, or, for that matter (as far as I know), from reading the unpublished writings that are now appearing in his voluminous posthumously published *Gesamtausgabe,* six years *before* the publication of Heidegger's magnum opus, in 1921 another profoundly original and comprehensive book of philosophy had been published in Germany in German, *The Star of Redemption* by Franz Rosenzweig.[2] In stark contrast to the eager interest and acclaim with which *Being and Time* was received, and the ever widening audience which Heidegger's then rising intellectual star attracted, the appearance of Rosenzweig's *Star* was hardly noticed or noted. Rosenzweig himself, though also a young man, only one year older than Heidegger, died eight years after the publication of *The Star of Redemption,* in 1929, at the age of forty-three. A small group of his friends, all German and Jewish intellectuals, knew immediately the real importance of the *Star* and Rosenzweig's true

2. Should we doubt that the dark shadow cast by Heidegger's Nazism may in large measure, if not entirely, be responsible for Heidegger's total neglect of his fellow soldier's and fellow countryman's book, whose Jewishness was by no means hidden? Such a conjecture is, of course, already an indictment. See Victor Farias, *Heidegger and Nazism,* edited by Joseph Margolis and Tom Rockmore, French translated by Paul Burrell, German translated by Gabriel R. Ricci (Philadelphia: Temple University Press: 1989). See p. 320 n. 22 below.

stature as a contemporary thinker. But hardly anyone else realized it, certainly not Heidegger, at least as far as the published record indicates.

For many years *The Star of Redemption* has received little general notice.[3] Today it is receiving serious attention as a central text in the academic study of "modern Jewish thought," hence within the larger academic field of Jewish studies. Beyond this, it remains a text for the most part ignored in wider academic and intellectual circles. While there are many historical reasons why the *Star* has not found a wider audience or been recognized for what it is, a major and original text in contemporary thought—its difficulty, its Jewishness in a non-Jewish world, the general neglect of religion in contemporary academic philosophy, the mass murder of the German Jews (natural first readers), Rosenzweig's early death, Heidegger's preeminence, etc.—none of these reasons singly or together justify this disregard.

Among the many important and original insights in the *Star,* in this chapter I wish to focus upon Rosenzweig's conception of the self, and the link between self and history. Rosenzweig's conception is original and important in itself, and, like Heidegger's later Dasein analytic, it demands that one link human being, time, and history. As such, it takes its place within the issues and controversies which constitute contemporary thought. It is for this inner reason, then, that this chapter compares and contrasts the original conception of selfhood, and its intimate relation to history, found in Heidegger's *Being and Time* to that found in Rosenzweig's *The Star of Redemption.*

By rejoining two theories accidentally and hence uncritically separated at birth, my intent in this chapter is to make Rosenzweig's lesser-known contribution to a fundamental and contemporary understanding of self-

---

3. While the Heidegger literature, by Heidegger and about Heidegger, has become a veritable industry, attention to Rosenzweig is only now spreading beyond a small but devoted following.

The first major thinker to attend at length to Rosenzweig's thought was Karl Löwith. In 1942 Löwith published an article in English on Rosenzweig and Heidegger: "M. Heidegger and F. Rosenzweig on Temporality and Eternity," *Philosophy and Phenomenological Research* 3, no. 1, (September 1942). In 1966 this article was reprinted, but with a slightly modified title, "M. Heidegger and F. Rosenzweig: A Postscript to *Being and Time*" (in Karl Löwith, *Nature, History, and Existentialism,* edited by Arnold Levison [Evanston: Northwestern University Press, 1966], 51–78). The slight modification of the title marks, it seems to me, another quarter century of neglect of Rosenzweig and glorification of Heidegger. In 1942 it was sufficient to pose Rosenzweig's notion of eternity in opposition to Heidegger's notion of temporality; in 1966 Rosenzweig is but a postscript to *Being and Time.* This change is especially interesting inasmuch as in the article itself Löwith, who was Heidegger's pupil, defends Rosenzweig. My discussion in this chapter is indebted to Löwith.

hood both better known and more plausible, and at the same time to make Heidegger's better-known contribution more questionable.

Contemporary Thinkers

Before turning directly to selfhood, some background is useful. Because both thinkers reject the idea that selfhood can be defined independently of larger context, to understand the self one must also understand the larger context within which the self is situated. These larger contexts will, however, be elaborated alongside with, indeed as an integral part of, my account of the self in these two thinkers. It is not to these directly that I want to turn now. What I want to present first, is even larger, or perhaps only more abstract, namely, a brief (and incomplete) list of the major points of agreement and disagreement which unite and separate Rosenzweig and Heidegger. These points are interrelated.

Regarding agreements, first, both Rosenzweig and Heidegger reject the foundational status of cognitive, representational thinking, and hence they reject the general bias of the entire classical tradition of philosophy from Parmenides to Hegel. For Rosenzweig this means rejecting the unity of being, a unity based on the unity of being and thinking inaugurated by Parmenides. To do this Rosenzweig begins with three irreducibly separate "elements": G-d, world, and man. For Heidegger, in contrast, this does not mean breaking up the unity of being and thinking, heritage of Parmenides, but rather thinking this unity more deeply than is possible within the categories of representational thought.

Second, and following from the first, both Rosenzweig and Heidegger reject modern positivist science, and the essentially Comtean tradition of the philosophy of science, as a legitimate or radical alternative to the classical representational tradition of philosophy. For both thinkers, positivist science is seen as a rival to their own critical reappraisal of the tradition, and a rival to their own respective visions of what should replace that tradition as its radical corrective or superior alternative. For the critical intents and purposes of both thinkers, then, positive science (and "philosophy of science") and classical philosophy are birds of the same feather.

Third, both Rosenzweig and Heidegger ground their thinking in significations bound to concreteness, facticity, finitude, and existence, in contrast to the inherent abstractness of representational theorizing. They bind their thought to the requirements of temporality and history rather than to the requirements of eternity and pure logic. Hence, as I have already indicated above, for both thinkers authentic selfhood is inalienably linked to temporality, history, and death.

It is because they agree on these three points that the link between Rosenzweig and Heidegger is greater than the bonds of shared chronology, geography, and academic training. They are not merely contemporaries, but both contemporary thinkers. Nonetheless, based on these basic points of agreement, profound differences separate them.

First, for Heidegger, *thinking* remains the central concern of the West, its inner greatness. The most thought worthy matter for thought is thinking itself. The central question for philosophy is the philosophy of the question, the retrieval and revival of what has remained unthought in the history of philosophy, namely, the meaning of being. It is no accident that in his efforts to retrieve and revive a manner of thinking prior to and more original than the history of philosophy, Heidegger turns to poets, and no accident either that in his effort to think through what thinking gives itself to think, the poets he turns to are those for whom the subject matter of poetry is poetry itself.

What is special about human being, for Heidegger, and hence what prompts the writing of the Dasein analytic of *Being and Time* as the propaedeutic to genuine thought, is that human being is nothing other than the site of a self-reflexive relationship of being, the place or *Da* where being understands itself, where thought thinks itself. "Dasein," Heidegger writes in the famous fourth section of *Being and Time*, "in its being, has a relationship towards that being—a relationship which itself is one of being" (*BT* 32). Hence for Heidegger, as he writes in conclusion to the same section "the question of being *(die Seinsfrage)* is nothing other than the radicalization of an essential tendency-of-being which belongs to 'Dasein' itself" (*BT* 35). In a word, this radicalization is the central concern of Heidegger's entire thought. Human being is thought worthy only insofar as, and to the extent that it is "the issue of being."

For Rosenzweig, too, human being must move from misunderstanding to understanding, from the "sickness" of a self-understanding based on abstract concepts to the "health" of a common sense in touch with basic extra-rational elements, as he names the poles of this movement in his work of July 1921, *Understanding the Sick and the Healthy*. Because philosophy has hitherto endorsed a human self-understanding based on concepts which are inevitably abstract in relation to what Rosenzweig understands to be the more authentic and concrete self-understanding of a healthy common sense, Rosenzweig must also call philosophy into question. Thus he calls for a radical "new thinking."

In contrast to Heidegger, however, Rosenzweig's "new thinking" is not a more authentic modality of being, a rectification of the relationship between being and thinking that the history of philosophy has itself masked and distorted, but rather a complex recognition of the limitations of rational thought which is at the same time a complex acceptance and encounter with what is irreducibly other to rational thought. Though both Rosenzweig and Heidegger aim to displace subjectivity from the center stage it took in the modern period, Rosenzweig aims also to displace the alternative candidates from center stage: the world (being) and G-d. The starting point for a genuine appreciation of the status and stature of selfhood, in Rosenzweig, comes from an axiomatic acceptance of an irreducibly fractured "reality," where man is but one element alongside of and in relation to the world and to G-d, all three of which are fundamentally independent of one another and yet at the same time in relation to one another. To think precisely this sort of relationality, where the terms of the relations are both in and out of relation, exceeds the capacities of philosophy. To properly grasp them, Rosenzweig turns to the language and experience of religion.

There are three irreducible terms and three (or six, depending on one's perspective) essentially different relations. First, G-d stands in relation to world and man. His relation to the world is *creation*. As a worldly being, then, man is a creature, G-d's creation. The world relates to G-d, if one may so express it, also as created being. Second, having created the world with man in it, G-d relates to man qua man in an essentially different way than to the rest of creation. G-d's special relation to man is *revelation,* which Rosenzweig, taking up long Jewish and Christian traditions and focusing especially on the central theme of the Song of Songs, understands in terms of love, G-d's love for man. Man's relation to G-d, then, is as beloved, beloved of G-d. Third, and finally, man and the world are also in relation, one essentially different from creation and revelation. Man's relation to the world and to his fellow man is *redemption*.

Given Rosenzweig's starting point—three irreducible elements and three irreducible relations—his conception of the authentic self differs radically from Heidegger's. Selfhood will not be grasped in the context of an all-embracing unity of being and thinking, forgotten or originarily reappropriated, but rather in the context of Rosenzweig's schema of three independent elements (G-d, man, world) and their independent but interrelated relations (creation, revelation, redemption), hence as creature (G-d's creation), as beloved (of G-d), and as redeemer (of man). For Rosenzweig, then, the larger philosophical-existential project opened up by and for authentic selfhood is not the gift-giving of history, the epoch-making power which is the Seinsfrage, but, to express it in one expression, a "theomorphical"[4] orientation: a creaturely but human life with and for

4. For Rosenzweig's use and sense of this term, which I will take up later in this chapter, see Rivka Horwitz, "Franz Rosenzweig's Unpublished Writings," *The Journal of Jewish Studies* 20 (1969): 57–80; especially 74–75.

other humans and the whole of creation oriented by the inspiration of divine love and the ethical and juridical tasks of redemptive history. This conception, along with and in contrast to Heidegger's, must be unpacked.

Selves

For both Heidegger and Rosenzweig the self is first found in everyday life. It is first found *lost* in everyday life. In this, Heidegger and Rosenzweig agree with philosophical tradition. Nonetheless, about the significance of everyday life, and its inadequacy for selfhood, they disagree both with philosophical tradition and with one another. Against the tradition, obviously, they will not argue for a more *rational* conception of subjectivity, for the true life, the philosophical life, as a "rigorous science," for overcoming *doxa* through *episteme*, phenomena by reality, time by eternity, or any form of salvation through logic and higher reasoning. For both thinkers the fault of everydayness lies not only in its lack of anchor, in the evanescence of its opinions, its incomprehension in the face of change, but also in the abstractive impact of rationality itself. Rationality, for both, is part of the problem, not the solution. Very generally, everyday life distracts the self from a realization of the concretude, finitude, and genuine tasks constitutive of authentic selfhood.

For Heidegger "everydayness" means that the self behaves and thinks of itself as if it were one entity among other entities.[5] "Selfhood" is pictured according to the order of re-presentation, as an idea or object re-presented by the self to the self. The self is meant to be what the self represents itself to be. Hence selfhood is conceived as essentially no different than any other object, i.e., as a substance with attributes, but with human specifications (e.g., "rational," "making," "thinking," "tool-using," "upright posture"). Casting Heidegger's account of everydayness in this manner is still not quite right because such an approach treats it as a metatheory. What Heidegger proposes, instead, is a phenomenological-hermeneutical account of everydayness as lived. In practice, then, everydayness means that each self defines itself in terms of attributes. What makes one self different from another self, then, or, for that matter what marks the development of one self over time, is never a difference of essence but rather differences in attributes and their concatenations. The self is a "student," or a "lawyer," or a "blue-eyed lawyer," or was once a "student" and is now a "lawyer." But unbeknownst to such a self-

---

5. For an excellent account of this aspect of the inauthenticity of subjectivity in Heidegger, see Michael E. Zimmerman, *Eclipse of the Self: The Development of Heidegger's Concept of Authenticity* (Athens, Ohio: Ohio University Press, 1981).

conception, this sort of selfhood is not genuine, and this sort of self-definition never satisfies. Indeed, the helter-skelter running to and fro of everyday inauthentic or undifferentiating selfhood is a way of covering over its lack of depth. Heidegger's Dasein analytic is replete with penetrating phenomenological descriptions of the various ways the ersatz self, "the one" who is no different really than "the they," busies itself manufacturing and maintaining it illusory individuation, collecting and discarding attributes.

What the everyday self cannot see, because it is a *mere* representation of selfhood and not genuine selfhood, is that human being is essentially finite, at bottom a being-toward-death, opening out onto a future that is only possible, and already given over to a specific past in which it has already engaged itself, to which it is already inextricably committed. The everyday self, in succumbing to the illusions of a represented reality, represents itself *within* space and *within* time, as if selfhood, or individuation, were a point on a Cartesian grid. For represented time the future is already there, laid out, like next year's calendar. The self merely goes into it. So, too, the past is what has already happened, like last year's calendar. The self merely remembers or forgets what is done and over with. Space and time are a framework within which the self, essentially independent of the framework, takes on and sheds attributes. But for Heidegger such representations are in truth only an escape from a deeper, more troubling self-awareness, an evasion of authentic self-appropriation, which concretely means a flight from death.

What is truly inalienable about selfhood are not unique attributes or unique concatenations of attributes. Rather, what is inalienable or autochthonous about selfhood is death, being-toward-death, mortality, and all the implications that finitude has for the kind of being that the self truly is. For one, no one else can die for the self. The self is irreplaceable in its death. In this lies the beginning of true individuation, irreplaceability, inevitability. Not, to say it again, that the self comes to see itself as having unique attributes, but rather than the self, as mortal, sees itself as engaged in this reality here and now and no other. Not only is the self individuated as dying its own death, it is individuated as the zero point of meaning. Individuation, then, is to "be-there" in being more deeply, to be engaged in being in the manner appropriate to a mortal being, Dasein in a particular historical place and time, ultimately in relation to epochal world-historical Sein.

The authentic self, Dasein, "being-there," no longer lives *within* an allegedly pre-set, objectively given, independent framework. It now sees such a representation to be illusory in the abstractness and fixity of its independence and predetermination. Rather, it comes to recognize itself *in* and *through* the particular setting wherein and whereby it dwells, in the significance of the world and time in which it lives, that is to say, engaged in history. Authentic Dasein, authentic being of the there that is, in contrast to the everyday self, is not within the world, but is the very unity or opening of being-in-the-world *(In-der-Welt-sein)* itself, this world, now: being there in reality not elsewhere in fantasy.

There are thus two levels in Heidegger's conception of selfhood, though more than two meanings are associated with these two levels. There is authentic selfhood, which is Dasein made aware of its essential being through being-toward-death, engaged in this time and space, in history. And there is inauthentic selfhood, which is Dasein fleeing from being-toward-death by escape into the represented reality of an objective space-time framework, where it is "one" like "they," but with different attributes. Of course, it is only *after* the everyday self comes to its true self, through the shock of being-toward-death and by hearkening to the "silent" promptings of the "voice of conscience" *(Stimme des Gewissen),* that Dasein can differentiate between inauthentic and authentic selfhood. In a whole lifetime, not every self is so enlightened. Thus there are three "stages," occurring in the following order, in the development of self-hood: (1) *undifferentiating* everyday re-presented selfhood, the self qua "subject" in the bad sense, a thing with attributes, an entity among enti-ties; (2) authentic Dasein, being-toward-death, being-in-the-world, en-gagement in the hermeneutic circling of being which Dasein is, the pro-cess of an ever-more concretized engagement in being (= history = language);[6] and (3) regular intermittent fall from, and loss of sight of, the level of authenticity achieved, hence a return to undifferentiating ev-eryday life, but a life which now stands in dialectical relation to the au-thenticity of Dasein already achieved, and hence an everyday life which increasingly recognizes itself as *inauthentic* selfhood. Thus, once the break-through has been first made, from the free-floating busyness of undiffer-entiating everyday life to authentic Dasein, to enrootedness in being, the rest of Dasein's life occurs as a more or less deep, and a more or less intermittent, dialectic of falling away from and return to the authentic self-appropriation of Dasein.

One final point needs to be added. It is hard not to get the impression (and it is not only a matter of tone or style) from Heidegger's pronounce-ments that to achieve the deepest appropriation of being, the deepest authentic being-there, all the way to the fount of the self-revelation of historical-epochal being itself, is a blessing, or a state of grace, reserved

6. See my article, "Dasein's Responsibility for Being," *Philosophy Today* 27, no. 4 (Winter 1983): 317–25.

for the few, for those with the rarest of rare sensitivity to being's slightest yet deepest movements, to a handful of poets and philosophers throughout all history. What Heidegger has found, then, at the heart of subjectivity, is what every fundamentally aesthetic reading of subjectivity and history must always find: the solitary poet as fount of world-historical truth, the solitary poet as legislator of the world. It is the oracle who bespeaks and enters more deeply into world-reality, not the prophet who speaks for G-d to uplift humankind. For the one humanity is sacrificed on the alter of the great individual, for the other the great individual sacrifices on the alter of humanity.

Rosenzweig also begins with everyday life, but his descriptions of it are not Heidegger's. It is not a matter of treating oneself as an entity among entities, of failing to differentiate between authentic and inauthentic being. Nevertheless, there are token similarities between their two conceptions of everyday life. Rosenzweig calls the everyday self the "personality" *(Personalichkeit)*. Like Heidegger's undifferentiating everyday self, the self as "personality" is determined superficially by social roles. Also like Heidegger's undifferentiating everyday self, the self as "personality" lacks an inner relation to its own death.

The central difference, however, is that the insubstantiality of personality for Rosenzweig does not derive from rootlessness, alienation, monadicism, worldlessness, or detachment from being, as does the inauthenticity of the undifferentiating everyday self and inauthentic Dasein for Heidegger. The inadequacy of selfhood qua personality comes rather from the reverse, from over-attachment to the world. The personality is content to wear the masks of the world, to play a role on the world's stage, to be projected out into the world, dispersed in it, to take up one or all names in history. But in all this, which is obviously not equivalent to Heideggerian authenticity, it is precisely not itself.

Again like Heidegger, for Rosenzweig the shattering of the everydayness of personality means a new appreciation for the significance of death. But the significance of death as Rosenzweig's conceives it is quite different from that appreciated in Dasein's being-toward-death. For Rosenzweig the ownmost character of death, that one dies one's own death, that no one can die anyone else's death, does not open the self up to its ecstatic relationship with (and of) being, but rather closes the self more firmly upon itself, ties the knot of selfhood tighter, seals the self more hermetically, and thus breaks with the apelike role-playing of personality. What the self's fear of death does, according to Rosenzweig, is open the self up to the givenness and unalterability of its worldly nature.

What the personality faces in facing death is what Rosenzweig names its "character" *(Charackter)*, its ownmost non-relational selfhood, which is so isolated from history that for all intents and purposes it is timeless. As character, the knot of selfhood is tied as tight as possible, down to an unalterable nugget of ownmost being. What the personality encounters in its character is the givenness of *created* being, isolated, alone, individual, creaturely being: not creating, not free, but created, given. "Fear of death" (*SR* 3)[7] breaks the self of its representational self-deceptions, as with Heidegger, but not for the sake of a deeper engagement in the ecstasies of historical being. The character represents that inalienable, unalterable hard core or nugget of selfhood impervious to history. It is that which is given, or created, and not made.

In this notion Rosenzweig contests the idea that selfhood is fully constituted by exterior relations, or that the self is infinitely malleable in the manner proposed by "existentialist" philosophers.[8] Obviously Rosenzweig cannot "prove" or "derive" this claim, because if he could it would at the same time be proven false. The givenness of character is simply given, breaking the individual's tie to "humanity," "ethics," and other universals or substitutes for universals. Rosenzweig can only acknowledge it. This, as Nathan Rotenstreich has pointed out so clearly, is precisely the sense of the "meta" of Rosenzweig's "metaethical" account of man: one must begin grasping the self *outside* of ethics. We shall see later that this exteriority is no less important in grasping the role that the individual plays *in* ethics. Rotenstreich is also doubtlessly correct in seeing here Rosenzweig's more or less "hidden polemic against Kant's or [Hermann] Cohen's identification of the human individual and the human ethos that led them to the primary reference to mankind at large."[9]

The contrast and comparison with Heidegger is striking. Breaking out of everyday selfhood in Heidegger means a deeper appreciation for Dasein's embrace of the world and history. For Rosenzweig, in contrast, it means the opposite: a greater detachment from the rest of the world owing to a harder, firmer, and nearly impenetrable attachment to one's own unique created being. For Heidegger authentic Dasein, rooted in history, can "choose its hero" (*BT* 437) to emulate. For Rosenzweig, the character, rooted in its own unique created nature, can find its proper detachment from all the world, can itself become a "hero," a being so fully grounded in its own unique resources, in its own unique self, that it can make a stand in defiance of the whole world, unto death. What is

---

7. The *Star* begins with the words "From death" *(Von Tode)* and ends with the words "into life" *(Ins Leben)*.

8. See chapter 3 in this volume.

9. Nathan Rotenstreich, "Rosenzweig's Notion of Metaethics," in *The Philosophy of Franz Rosenzweig,* edited by Paul Mendes-Flohr (Hanover: University Press of New England, 1988), 82–83.

similar, however, in both conceptions, is that the break with everydayness in response to death leads to a sphere of individuated immanence. In Heidegger's case this sphere includes all of being, because Da-sein is ultimately the Seins-frage. In Rosenzweig's case, in contrast, it includes only the isolated, solitary individual—a point of similarity and difference to which I shall shortly return.

Karl Löwith articulates the difference separating Heidegger and Rosenzweig in terms of the difference between "temporality and eternity."[10] This time discrimination cuts to a core difference, and it is helpful especially in comparing Rosenzweig's notion of character to Heidegger's conception of authentic being-there (though its usefulness goes even farther, as we shall see, insofar as Rosenzweig's conception of the self extends further than character). Everything in Heidegger follows from Dasein's timeliness, first its appropriation of its own ecstatic temporality in being-toward-death, and then and consequently its appropriation of the historicity of being itself, the Seinsfrage. For Heidegger the shift from inauthenticity to authenticity is a shift from pre-tense, the pretense that one is within a pre-established time framework, as it were, to what has no pre-tense, but is Da-sein, the temporalizing of being. The dimensionality of time is thus no longer a function of *representing* time, but is rather the very manner in which Dasein is *Da* or ex-ists.

In breaking from everydayness to face its own futural death, Dasein is being "called from itself to itself," anxious about nothing other than having to be its *own* basis, realizing at the same stroke that it is too late to be its own basis. Dasein must be its own basis because its basic being—toward death—is non-relational. This does not mean that Dasein becomes isolated, closed in upon itself like a hermit or hero, but rather that it is the self-relationship of being, being related to being, being faced with nothing other than being, that is, faced with itself.

Dasein is nonetheless always too late to be its own basis. It comes to its authentic self-recognition *after* having lived in an everyday manner, that is to say, after its ownmost non-relational self-relationship has been concretely determined with regard to both place and history. Deathbound Dasein is in each case totally "mine" *(Jemeinigkeit)*, says Heidegger, and at the same time the self cannot be itself from the ground up for it is already German, Hungarian, violinist, mathematician, female, orphan, aunt, prisoner, poor, soldier, etc. Precisely these determinations "throw" Dasein, or make Dasein "thrown" *(Geworfen)*, because Dasein *in truth* wants to be only itself, wants only to return to itself completely, without residue or debt, to be itself from the ground up. Struggle in Dasein is therefore the struggle to end all struggle, the struggle to return to oneself

10. See note 3 above.

completely, even if this quest for identity in ex-istence is an impossible dream, essentially interrupted and indeed constituted by a history which surpasses each and every Dasein. But, and this is the point toward which I have been driving, authentic Dasein can only come to itself *through* and *as* history, as "historicizing." Ultimately, temporalizing being-there is historicizing being-there. Heidegger makes this move, linking Dasein and history, across the notions of Dasein's fate (*Schicksal*) and destiny (*Geschick*), in the fifth section of division 2 of *Being and Time* (*BT* 424–55). I cite only the following: "Dasein's fateful destiny in and with its 'generation' goes to make up the full authentic historicizing of Dasein" (*BT* 436). It is to this line of thought, explicating with great care and sensitivity the historical character constitutive of Dasein, that Heidegger subsequently dedicates his thought.

Owing precisely to the above dynamic in the Heideggerian analysis, a constitutive dynamic within Dasein and in Dasein's relation to history, Löwith makes an observation that Rosenzweig too could make, namely, that "Heidegger's analysis, despite its starting point in facticity, still moves within the idealist framework."[11] It moves within the idealist framework not, obviously, because of any attachment to objectivizing thought, but rather, more profoundly, because of its insistence that what is authentic or ultimate is—per impossible—undisturbed, undistracted self-relatedness, being fully in relation to itself. It is this movement of self-identification, *even if now understood across facticity, existence, and history,* that links Heidegger to Parmenides and Hegel. To be oneself one must appropriate the epochal manifestation and manifesting of what is.

Heidegger, as we know, considers his own thought a radical break with all philosophy. His response to the charge being made here, namely, that his is a narrow and therefore a vicious circularity, would be, of course, that it is not so, and that it is not so precisely because of Dasein's tie to history. But Rosenzweig and Löwith cannot be satisfied by Heidegger's globalizing move to history precisely because globalization is not the solution but rather the intensification of the problem as they see it. Dasein's tie to history, insofar as it is also ontological—Dasein as the manifestation or mouthpiece of the self-reflection of being, which is how Heidegger determines this tie, genuine history as opposed to objectivizing historiography—is nothing other than the history of being revealing itself. As such, it remains a part of the problem, indeed is but an extension, an exasperation, of the problem, because for Rosenzweig the problem is precisely the totalization of the ontological, the ontological grasped through thinking, no matter how concrete.

The problem of idealism for Rosenzweig is not simply that it is repre-

---

11. Löwith, *Nature, History, and Existentialism,* 62.

sentational, objectivizing, which is the problem for Heidegger, but also and crucially that it is totalizing. This is why, again, Löwith is correct in seeing that Rosenzweig would charge Heidegger with idealism *despite* Heidegger's starting point in facticity. Because Dasein's ecstatic being, its ex-istence, is not freed from everydayness just for the sake of its own temporalizing, its own being-toward-death, but as deathbound temporalizing is also thrown into a broader engagement in the world, a world constituted by being through history—a private farce shattered by a personal fate rising to a historical destiny—the Dasein rooted in its own being is rooted in all being. In the end, as Heidegger says repeatedly in his later writings, Dasein is itself the Seinsfrage, which is something he had already said in *Being and Time* (see citation above) in 1927, though without laying out all the consequences.

The authentic self is an appropriation of a history into which it has always already been thrown. Thus resoluteness *(Entschlossenheit)* turns out to be nothing other than release, letting go, letting be *(Gelassenheit)*. Authenticity is the spiraling movement from time to temporality to historicity, a movement which Heidegger himself sums up with the term "appropriation" *(Ereignis)*. Authentic Dasein *is* temporalizing, *is* historicizing, hence *is* the Seinsfrage. Dasein's shift from inauthentic to authentic existence is now conceived as nothing less than the shift from "the end of philosophy" to the "task of thinking."[12] Dasein is itself the "task of thinking," what the later Heidegger calls the destruction/retrieval of the epochal revelations of being.

One can hardly imagine a more grandiose, exalted, or *philosophical* status for human being. Yet Rosenzweig would find it far too limiting. It is not enough to be, and certainly not enough to be the thinking of being, regardless how one interprets its genitive. The whole of his criticism is already contained, *in nuce,* in the notion of self as *character,* in the rupture with all representations and ecstasies that this "permanent," "static," and "daimonic" (*SR* 216, 212, 213) aspect of subjectivity brings about. But this rupture is only the beginning, the beginning of genuine subjectivity, and the beginning of Rosenzweig's break with all the later post-Husserlian ecstatic conceptions of subjectivity, such as Heidegger's, that he did not live to contest (and which, for their part, managed to overlook Rosenzweig's *Star*).

12. I have deliberately appropriated the title of one of Heidegger's late articles, first published in 1964, which is intimately linked to his earlier work. It appears in English in a book all of whose contents contribute to establishing the same inner link between the early and the later Heidegger. See Martin Heidegger, "The End of Philosophy and the Task of Thinking," in *On Time and Being,* translated by Joan Stambaugh (New York: Harper and Row, 1972), 55–73.

Rosenzweig also ends up in history, but by a route and in a manner quite different than Heidegger's. Though both Heidegger and Rosenzweig eschew theory dependency, history as Rosenzweig conceives it is not therefore either the epochal unfolding of being or some other variation on the theme of being's ontological conversation with itself. Rather, as we shall see, what is at play in history is something Rosenzweig believes is even more serious than being, if one can imagine such a seriousness beyond the ponderousness of Heidegger's rhetoric of "essence,"[13] something more important: the story of man's redemption in and of the world, *holy* history.

History *begins* and *ends* with G-d, *beyond* being, but is throughout the work of man. Here the self is charged with an entirely different exigency than the ontological destiny of Heidegger's Dasein. But we are getting ahead of our exposition. To see how Rosenzweig gets to history, and why he characterizes its progress in religious terms, let us return first for a closer look at the self as personality and character.

As we have seen, the self in Rosenzweig begins as it does in Heidegger, already caught up in everyday life. But instead of developing through two stages, from inauthenticity to authenticity, or simply from personality to character, there is a third and higher development, which Rosenzweig names the "soul" *(Seele),* which is beyond personality and character and reorients their significance.

The first two sorts or stages of subjectivity in Rosenzweig in some

---

13. Professor John D. Caputo, in a number of recent studies, has begun to "deconstruct" the basic rhetorical strategy of Heidegger's (phenomenological-philosophical) *Denken*. See "Thinking, Poetry and Pain," *The Southern Journal of Philosophy* 28, Supplement (1989): 155–81; "Heidegger's Scandal: Thinking and The Essence of the Victim," in *The Heidegger Case,* edited by Joseph Margolis and Tom Rockmore (Philadelphia: Temple University Press, forthcoming); and "Hyperbolic Justice: Deconstruction, Myth and Politics," *Research in Phenomenology* (forthcoming).

Caputo's disaffection with Heidegger remains "deconstructive" because he sees in Derrida (not Levinas) an openness to alterity which breaks out of the (immoral) confines of Heidegger's blinding and reductive use of "essence." For my part, I question whether this route does not rather lead more subtly into the Heideggerian essence. Indeed, regarding the question of radical alterity, I argue that Derrida is, as Habermas calls him, "an orthodox Heideggerian" (see Jürgen Habermas, *The Philosophical Discourse of Modernity: Twelve Lectures,* translated by Frederick G. Lawrence [Cambridge, Mass.: The MIT Press, 1991], 165). See also chapter 14 in this volume.

The basic rhetorical strategy of *Denken* works like this, in a hushed and commanding voice: "Let us, we few, we few great and genuine thinkers, not be distracted by, and therefore dispense with considering ——— [fill in the blank: "starvation and hunger," "pollution," "death camps," etc., all treated as mere particulars], and go deeper, further, more profoundly, to what is more worthy of thought, to genuine thinking, which whatever anyone else says is and always has been what is *really* at play: 'the *essence* itself.'"

ways resemble, as we have seen, Heidegger's distinction between everyday inauthentic selfhood and authentic Dasein. The agent of everyday life, the personality, is a nexus, juncture, or node of socially determined roles. "As the origin of the term already implies," Rosenzweig writes, "personality is man playing the role assigned to him by fate, one role among many in the polyphonic symphony of mankind" (*SR* 68). The personality, like Heidegger's everyday self, is a superficial determination of human individuality, a *mere* persona, an impersonation.

The superficiality of the personality becomes apparent retrospectively, again as in Heidegger, when it gives way to character (which Rosenzweig often simply calls "self" *[Selbst]*). Character, like Heidegger's authentic Dasein, is non-relational. It is non-relational because it is a self-relationship. But quite unlike Heidegger's ecstatic-projective Dasein, the self-relationship of character is, as I have already indicated, a self-enclosure. Though one can say of both Dasein and character that they are totalizing, character is inward directed, centripetal, daimonic, while Dasein is outward directed, centrifugal, ecstatic. "The self," Rosenzweig writes, "is solitary man in the hardest sense of the word." In contrast, he continues, "the personality is the 'political animal'" (*SR* 71). Taking up Rosenzweig's allusion to Aristotle's characterization of the human being as a political animal, the contrast with Heidegger can be sharpened as follows: in becoming authentic Dasein changes from one sort of political animal, slave to small politics, absorbed in "private" willfulness, to another sort of political animal, a master of grand politics, a releasement *(Gelassenheit)* to what is; Rosenzweig's shift from personality to character, in contrast, means a break with the political altogether. Character is the self inwardly turned, feeding on its own resources, on its own nature, the unique self. "The self," Rosenzweig writes, "lacks all bridges and connections; it is turned in upon itself exclusively" (*SR* 78).[14] When conceiving the character in its independence from personality, Rosenzweig names it *daimon*—"the *daimon*, the character as distinct from the personality" (*SR* 213).

Let us note right away that in sharp contrast to Heidegger, self-referentiality, inward in the case of character, outward in the case of authentic Dasein, but always *immanent*, a *totality*, whether global or insular, is for Rosenzweig a *limitation* to be overcome rather than a field of meaning to be appropriated. For Rosenzweig, created being is too small,

---

14. Just as the "reasons" or motivations which determine the distinctive character of each Dasein's particular way of being-toward-death must remain shrouded in mystery or particularity in Heidegger, so, too, the origin of the distinctiveness of each person's character remains a mystery, or too particular, in Rosenzweig. All one can say is that character is a consequence of creation, it is one's created being.

as it were, only one element of three. In coming to one's own "authentic" created being, plunged into one's unique character, the self is still in isolation, indeed it is most in isolation.

Very much like the shift from inauthentic selfhood to authentic Dasein, the shift from personality to character entails a retrospective recognition of the inadequacy and superficiality of everydayness. Rosenzweig likens the initial relation of the self as character to the self as personality to that of an armed thief: "the self assaults man like an armed man and takes possession of all the wealth of his property" (*SR* 71). Beyond the initial shock, the second aspect of this relation, the character's reappropriation of what has been "gained" through personality, is analogous to authentic Dasein's retrieval of its "thrownness," its reappropriation of the being with which inauthentic Dasein is willy-nilly already enmeshed. For Rosenzweig, character and personality stand in inverse proportion, the former, the private self, or the singular style of the self, displacing the latter, the public self, the self as node of relations, in an ongoing process which is the very process of maturation. It is possible that at the end of a lifelong development, "the aged," Rosenzweig writes, "no longer have a personality of their own; their share in the common concerns of mankind has paled to a mere memory. But the less they are still individualities, the harder they become as characters, the more they become self" (*SR* 72).

For Rosenzweig, again like Heidegger, the more authentic individuality, the character, unlike the less authentic one, personality, is intimately related to death. Besides conceptual representations of death, the only "death" personality knows is metaphorical, its own collapse in having to give way to the truer self, character. Character, on the other hand, is moved by fear of death, real death, death as terminus. Indeed it is precisely the self as character, the unique self, its interiority, that dies and is forever lost at life's end. The attributes which make up personality, in contrast, have no essential relation to death. They are mobile and plastic, and, like Groucho Marx's eyebrows, eyeglasses, and mustache, they can "live on" attached to this or that person in this or that new combination. Character, on the other hand, is the original unalterable core of an individual, the ownness and inalienability of the self. "There is no greater solitude," Rosenzweig writes, "than in the eyes of a dying man, and no more defiant, proud isolation than that which appears on the frozen countenance of the deceased" (*SR* 72).

Important as are the differences that already separate Rosenzweig's discrimination of personality and character from Heidegger's discrimination of inauthentic and authentic Dasein, the key difference, the one which reveals the limitations of personality and character, and the limitations, from a Rosenzweigian perspective, of the entire Heideggerian Dasein analytic, emerges with the third sort or stage of selfhood in Rosenzweig's account, the self as soul *(Seele)*. A point of clarification about the term "soul" should probably be stressed right away to avoid possible distractions and confusions. In using the term "soul" Rosenzweig may well be alluding to, but he is certainly not referring to, the notion of a peculiar spiritual substance with which each person is meant to be endowed that somehow endures intact after death. "Soul" is indeed both "spiritual" and an endowment which comes through contact with exteriority, but for Rosenzweig it is the term of a relation rather than a substance in and of itself. "Soul" is precisely the self that emerges, and only emerges, at the intersubjective level. Intersubjectivity, for Rosenzweig, but in sharp contrast to Heidegger, introduces a new and irreducible level of significance to subjectivity.

Heidegger, following Husserl, assimilates intersubjectivity to the existential structure of Dasein. Far from a transformative encounter with alterity as such, something like Dasein's encounter with its ownmost death, encountering the other is at bottom a "being with" *(mitsein)* the other, a "being with," that is, that is a constitutive structure of Dasein's own being. Being-with others does not transform Dasein in any essential way but rather is itself transformed in Dasein's authenticating encounter with its ownmost death.[15] Inauthentic Dasein merely drifts along with others, indifferent to their ultimate concerns as it is indifferent to its own ultimate concerns, in a world seemingly pre-established. Authentic Dasein, in contrast, which aims resolutely at the issue of being, released into the historical truth of being, relates to another Dasein by "leaping in for him" or "leaping ahead of him" (see *BT* 158–59), either taking over or steering another Dasein toward the one thing needful, that Dasein's self-appropriation of its historical epochal being. In this capacity, however, even though Heidegger refers to intersubjectivity as a "positive mode" (*BT* 158), that is, not the idle surface relations of inauthentic selves, Dasein's "being-with" others means no more and no less than that

15. See *BT* 308: "The non-relational character of death, as understood in anticipation, individualizes Dasein down to itself. This individualizing is a way in which the 'there' is disclosed for existence. It makes manifest that all Being-alongside the things with which we concern ourselves, and all Being-with Others, will fail us when our ownmost potentiality-for-Being is the issue. Dasein can be *authentically itself* only if it makes this possible for itself of its own accord. But if concern and solicitude fail us, this does not signify at all that these ways of Dasein have been cut off from its authentically Being-its-Self. As structures essential to Dasein's constitution, these have a share in conditioning the possibility of any existence whatsoever. Dasein is authentically itself only to the extent that, *as* concernful Being-alongside and solicitous Being-with, it projects itself upon its ownmost potentiality-for-Being rather than upon the possibility of the they-self."

one Dasein plays the role for another Dasein of what is at best and properly that other Dasein's *own* "voice of conscience."

Even when authentic, one Dasein relates to the alterity of another Dasein not face-to-face, in a frontal encounter with alterity, but on the basis of the difference or similarity in the depth and resolve of their respective appropriations of their ontological enrootedness in being. The deeper Dasein can "leap in for" the less-deepened Dasein, taking over what lies ahead of or beneath the less-deepened Dasein. Or, better, the deeper Dasein can "leap ahead of" the less-deepened Dasein in order to steer that other Dasein toward its own appropriate appropriation of being. In either case, whether one Dasein dominates another or liberates another for its own proper being, being functions as the "third term" or the "neutral" terrain around which both Daseins—indeed, all Daseins—are gathered. Daseins are linked to one another laterally, side by side, in the depth and resolve of being, as part of the "destiny" of a "generation" (*BT* 436), assembled by the same horizon, which is ultimately the horizon of world-historical being. What this means, then, is that whether authentic or inauthentic there is no frontal relation between one Dasein and another. All relations are relations of being, whether in flight from being or in a more or less resolute appropriation of being, regardless of the hermeneutical depth achieved. It is Sein that organizes Daseins. In his later thought, which assumes all the detailed phenomenological labors of *Being and Time,* this same totalizing structure continues to prevail, though taking on a more "poetic" form. Heidegger now crystallizes the whole of his earlier analytic of Dasein into the single term "mortal," gathers mortals with "earth," "sky," and "gods" in a resplendent "fourfold," where each figure comes to play an integral role in the drama of several epochal acts which is at one and the same time the temporal-historical revelation of being.

Rosenzweig's account of the "soul" is designed precisely to avoid the totalization Heidegger achieved in two steps by reducing intersubjectivity to subjectivity and then by reducing subjectivity to a part in the world-historical ontological drama. So great is the significance of the alterity encountered frontally in the intersubjective encounter, as Rosenzweig sees it, that it has the power to open up the hard core, the hard nugget, the very fixity, of character. The subjectivity awakened in intersubjectivity, the "soul," opens up a new level for the self, indeed, a whole new way of life, one constituted by moral and social demands—demands which begin with and remain inextricably linked to the ultimate commander, G-d. To use Rosenzweig's broadest terms: the self is not merely beyond being by being beneath it, as a "meta-ethical" character, G-d's creature; it is also "meta-logical," subject to G-d's revelation; and "meta-physical," charged with the task of redemption; both of which relations exceed what can be totalized within the confines of ontology, however ecstatic, or, if you will, within the confines of theology or secular politics.

The "human soul," Rosenzweig writes, "is the soul awakened and loved by God" (*SR* 199). This same soul "awakened and loved by God," is also the human "I" addressed by the human "thou."[16] "The love of the human, the earthly lover—that was a counterpart, nay more than a counterpart, it was a direct likeness of divine love" (*SR* 212). Rosenzweig's point is that the impenetrable and imperturbable self-sufficiency of the character which enters into the intersubjective encounter, the character which as character and only as character, in contrast to the personality, cannot be absorbed or dissipated by the term of that encounter, *is* nonetheless pierced and perturbed in that encounter. The very paradox of such an impossible disturbance, however, is indicative of its non-ontological (despite the use of the verb "to be") reverberation.[17] Only a religious language is sufficient to its excess. But this excess is at the same time bound to a specifically intersubjective register of significance.

This excessive significance, breaking through and opening up the impermeable character, emerges in and as love,[18] the "beloved soul," and supports all the registers of social life developing out of and built upon this original encounter with what overwhelms the self: in ethical obligation, in communal life, and finally across history. The "I" of the "I-thou" is en-

16. This dialogical account of selfhood, so totally at variance with Heidegger and the tradition of German idealist philosophy, is at home with another set of contemporary German thinkers: Hermann Cohen, Martin Buber, Hans Ehrenberg, and Eugen Rosenstock, and in France with Emmanuel Levinas.

For a closer and more sustained exposition of the role and significance of the personal pronouns constitutive of Rosenzweig's relational conception of selfhood, especially in relation to time, see chapter 4 in this volume.

17. Jacques Derrida, Heidegger's heir in France, follows Hegel in insisting (in *VM*, responding to Levinas, among other places) that the necessary use of the verb "to be" in any attempt to exceed being is a sufficient and telling sign that such attempts are essentially misguided, impossible, and hence doomed to failure. For Derrida all such abuses of language are forms of non-philosophy masquerading as philosophy. But Rosenzweig is a master of Hegel. Knowing of these difficulties (not impossibilities, or perhaps only "impossibilities" for philosophy) in language geared to ontology, Rosenzweig turns to "religious" language, which from the start ("In the beginning . . . ") exceeds the language of being.

18. See also Stéphane Mosès, for example, in his superb book on the *Star*, *System and Revelation: The Philosophy of Franz Rosenzweig*, translated by Catherine Tihanyi (Detroit: Wayne State University Press, 1992), 42, 113, 130–31. "It is in itself the shattering of man's autonomy, the instituting, in a consciousness already opened up to the horizon of otherness, of an affective relation toward the absolutely Other, toward that which precisely invests it from the outside. It is this relation that Rosenzweig calls love" (113).

gaged and beholden—obligated and responsible—to the interlocutor, because the alterity presented as the very presence of the other pierces the self beyond any and all resources of selfhood alone. Such an "I," stunned in being "beloved," is what Rosenzweig means by the "soul awakened and loved by G-d." Rosenzweig characterizes as "theomorphic" the movement through which and within which the soul is constituted from the outside, the movement from the other to the self, because of the transcendence to which it is witness, and because its orientation is a coming from above to the below.[19] The assimilation of this orientation of above and below to the interhuman orientation (as divine-human orientation), in other words, G-d's love for the beloved soul, is entirely lacking in Heidegger's analytic of Dasein and in the larger ontological historical horizons upon which that analytic opens up.

A question immediately arises: What is Rosenzweig's reason for asserting a homology between the human "I-thou" and the relationship between G-d and the soul? Whence this isomorphism and theomorphism? Rosenzweig's first answer is historical: "Up to the threshold of the nineteenth century," he writes, "one simply knew that the I and thou of human discourse is without more ado also the I and thou between God and man" (*SR* 199). The isomorphism between human love, human discourse, and G-d's relation to the individual, was self-evident—"without more ado"—to individuals living in an age of religion. Such was precisely the concrete, existential sense of "religion" in that age.

But how do those persons who live after the nineteenth century, *we* for whom this homology is far from self-evident, how do we verify it? Again Rosenzweig appeals to a superlative self-evidence, but this time one found in a widespread human "phenomenon": the human experience of love, love between lovers. Rosenzweig's "argument" lies in the claim that what is experienced in the love of lovers, "true love," love in the sense extolled in the Bible's Song of Songs, is necessarily more than just human. There is no *reason* for one human to *love* another. To use another, or to use one another, yes; to gain pleasure from another, or to gain pleasure from one another, yes; to aim together at the same good or goods, yes; but love? It is inexplicable—for the one beloved. "Love," Rosenzweig writes, without further ado, "simply cannot be 'purely human'" (*SR* 201). Philosophers and others who claim they "do not believe in love" always explain it away, as a form of use, or pleasure, or biology, or something or other; but they precisely never explain it, never explain

---

19. See chapter 11 in this volume for an account of the Jewish origins and the wider implications of this theomorphic orientation from above to below. Mosès, in *System and Revelation*, writes: "Revelation precisely means the vision of an *oriented* universe" (34).

love as love. And love, love for the one beloved, remains inexplicable; such is the "reason" it can only be understood, to the extent that it is "understood," as divine, as G-d's love. Love, the inexplicable transcendence experienced in love, the excessive contact with the other person undergone in love, suffered in love, where one suffers for the other, feels for and with the other, is the root of the "I-thou" relation that breaks the character of its isolation, splendid or tragic.

What Rosenzweig is looking for and finds in the direct human encounter of love is a way of radically linking individuals without one or the other giving up their independence. The "character" profoundly moved by the "thou," turned inside out into a "beloved soul," nonetheless remains transcendent relative to the "thou," never is completely or finally turned all the way inside out. So, too, the "thou," the "lover," transcends the "I," with a transcendence like nothing other than G-d's, indeed with the transcendence of G-d.

The whole argument with Heidegger, then, comes down to differing interpretations of *transcendence*. Heidegger's rejection of an atomized account of time and beings, an account reflecting objectivizing consciousness, representation, hinges on his positive doctrine of Dasein itself *as* transcendence, Dasein as an *ecstatic* being, a being whose *ecstasies,* whose possibilities, extend unto death and ultimately through all history, to its source in the self-revelation of being. But this transcendence, as Levinas will later show with great care, is really only a vast extension of immanence, not a true transcendence where the transcendent *breaks* with what it transcends. It is this latter line, of genuine rupture, breaking the unity of the universe, that Rosenzweig pursues in challenging the very unity of being, the Parmenidean essence of philosophy. Being itself, the whole of being, is conceived by Rosenzweig, as we have seen, to be but one element of a triad of irreducible elements. Being, then, is an element whose true sense does not derive from itself, from its internal relations, no matter how far-reaching they be, including Heidegger's fourfold of "earth," "sky," "mortals," and "gods." Rather its true sense comes from its nonassumable relations to other elements which totally exceed its very possibilities. Only a "religious" language is adequate to these sorts of "relations," which by nature exceed the bounds of a philosophy which is bound to bind thinking and being together. Being is *created* by a G-d beyond being. Being is *redeemed* by man, for man, too, qua soul, is metaphysical, beyond being.

These relations, this very sort of relationality, where being and thinking are not linked to subsume all terms, cannot be found in Heidegger's Dasein analytic, just as it cannot be found in Heidegger's Seinsfrage. For Rosenzweig, however, the self undergoes such a relationality in order to become itself, undergoes it in love, in the poignant coming together of what must remain apart, the unity and irreducible duality of an inexplicable being-loved, and in all the discourses and aims of the "I" and the "we" whose source lies in the "I-thou," in this exceptional non-imperial contact.

Love is the linchpin of Rosenzweig's conception of the self, and indeed, as is indicated by its very position in the text, in the heart of the center, in book 2 of part 2, it is the linchpin of the entire philosophical-theological worldview of *The Star of Redemption*. It is the goal of creation, both of man directly, as the one to whom revelation, qua love, is possible, and of the world, indirectly, as that which man, qua loved, can love in turn, i.e., redeem. For Rosenzweig, love cannot be accounted for within the confines of the unity of being and thinking, and yet it expresses a higher sense rather than some ineffable suprapersonal mystic annihilation of self or of all dualities. Hence Rosenzweig turns to the language of religion, of divine love, to give account of authentic selfhood and its world-transforming role.

This means that contra Heidegger authentic selfhood is not some Promethean enrootedness in the very rocks of the earth, but rather the most far-reaching uprootedness. First the self is torn from is superficial drifting, the personality, to enter into the individuation of character, isolated solitariness, uniqueness, the givenness of its being, created being. Then the insular existence of character is overturned, pierced, by an otherwise inexplicable penetration—it can only be *love*. The character is pierced by the other's love, where the other remains other and the self is introjected to a new realization, as a beloved being. The self is *somehow* beloved, such is the continuous miracle, the revelation of love. It cannot be made sense of in ontological or in human terms without denying its character of pure exteriority and unearned bestowal. "Love simply cannot be 'purely human'" (*SR* 201), Rosenzweig writes.

But the "beloved soul" is only half the story of the intersubjective renewal of selfhood as soul through love. The other half is the "loving soul," the soul which having "learned" love by being loved can now love in turn. "Man loves because God loves and as God loves. His human soul is the soul awakened and loved by God" (*SR* 199). Having been loved, the soul can now break out of the overwhelming one-way presence of the relation of being beloved. Having learned the excess of love the soul can now bring that excess to its relation to others and to the world. Such indeed is redemption. From being loved to love of the neighbor—this is Rosenzweig's formula for a new politics.

From the "soul beloved" to the "loving soul" is the movement from revelation to redemption, from G-d's love of man to man's love of man: love of the neighbor. It is only in being loved, oriented by love, that man learns of commanding and commandments. The first commandment is the following and from it all others follow: "As he loves you, so shall you love" (*SR* 204). "Only the soul beloved of God can receive the commandment to love its neighbor and fulfill it. Ere man can turn himself over to God's will, God must first have turned to man" (*SR* 215). Rosenzweig's new politics will be humanistic without being humanist. Social and political life will be driven by man's love of man, by the ideal of universalizing love, by man's active and concrete redemption of humankind and the world, but its source point will not be man but G-d, G-d's love for man.

In the first inexplicable but necessary moment of love, as a "beloved soul," the self learns the worth of *love*, undergoes it, is opened by it, in a one-on-one relationship with another that is like nothing so much as the grace of G-d's love, *and thus*, in a nonphilosophical and nontheological deduction, in love, now as a "loving soul," the self learns *to love*, and learns the worth of loving others, the neighbor, and beyond the neighbor, the stranger. Thus as soul, the character, created being, is charged with the elevated task of redeeming all humankind, out of a depth, therefore, of which Dasein is not even cognizant let alone capable.

Character and soul, the one fixed and the other penetrated by and penetrating with transcendence, go together and mutually require one another; the character requires the soul to keep its impetus, its *conatus essendi* toward isolation and complete monadic separation incomplete, and the soul requires the character to keep its love from completely devastating or devouring its own site, to keep the self burning bright with love, being loved and loving, without being blinded into the mystical indifference of oblivion. Levinas, decades later, will use the image of the burning bush for just this interdependence between non-relational selfhood, the fixed character, whose resources he will describe in terms of a "passivity more passive than all receptivity," and the relational self, the loved and loving soul, bound to an intersubjectivity caught up from the first in ethics and justice. Character is the bush, which is never consumed, soul is the fire, which burns with an imperative and divine voice, demanding goodness and justice.

The basic unit of Rosenzweig's conception of human reality is neither the atomistic individual (character without soul), as it is in the Lockean tradition of liberalism, nor a nexus of social relations (soul without character), as it is in the Hegelian and Marxian historicist tradition, nor, furthermore, is the basic unit an updated "existentialized" version of either of these two theories of the self, the monadic self-enclosed Sartrean self or the ecstatic historical Heideggerian Dasein. For Rosenzweig the self that is simply given, the character, is an analytic component of authentic selfhood. Character is a component or moment of selfhood. One is only fully character, only character, wholly character, if ever, at death. A full conception of selfhood, rather, requires that a self with such an orientation, such a givenness, the self with character, be the self "miraculously" loved and as such capable of love. Such is the vulnerable and responsible self, a self called higher than being to a vocation better than being: to the vocation of ethics and justice.

When Rosenzweig comes to describe community life in part 3 of the *Star,* where he discusses the imperative to redeem one's fellow man and the world in greater detail, the two aspects of the soul, beloved and loving, become two forms of communal life: the Jewish community, beloved of G-d, elected, chosen, an eternal people; and the Christian community, loving with G-d's love, proselytizing, missionizing, a historical people. The self of intersubjectivity and social life, the soul, is grasped in its wider and more concrete context, deepening the processes first understood in terms of personal love, extending its transcendent beginnings to transcendent ends, still characterized in "religious" language. Beginning in being-loved, the chosenness of the Jews, who remain chosen, i.e., beloved, and as such eternal, leads to loving in turn, to Christianity, to Christian love which is a mission, the conversion of heathens, widening the circle of love through a holy history, which cannot end until all humankind has been redeemed, i.e., "knows" love.

History is never the impersonal affair of being revealing itself to itself, using man as a mouthpiece, as it was repeatedly conceived by German idealism up to and including Heidegger. Rather, history is the deepening and widening of love, that is to say, of the interhuman relationship, the "I-thou." This history, the invisible becoming visible, the spread of goodness and justice, is holy history. For Rosenzweig the ultimate sense of history must be understood in terms of love, both the exemplary community of love present now in the Jewish community, and the love communion actively being spread throughout the world by Christian missionizing; that is to say, history must be understood as redemptive or holy history.

I will end this chapter with a brief sketch of the steps that have brought us to this conclusion. The personality, which lives lost in its purely social roles, is stunned one day to find its deeper character. Its ownness then consists of moving toward its own unique character, its true self, its nature. But its coming to itself, which is not a hearkening more deeply or carefully to being, as is self-retrieval for Heidegger, is diverted and redirected by love. Through the "miracle" or "revelation" of love the character is reconditioned by its soul, authentically, that is, lovingly and ethically engaged in dialogue with others: to hear the other and to speak to the other in turn. Only as first given in character can the soul enter into the penetrating love, the exigencies, of the "I-thou," without being torn up by the master-slave dialectics so well described by Hegel and Sartre, who base their philosophies on the freedom of consciousness rather than a human-divine love. The excess of being loved finds its outlet, in turn, in loving others, which is the first imperative of political life and the goal of history. In this way Rosenzweig can acknowledge the crucial importance of history for humanity, indeed, the deeply historical dimension of humanity, without at the same time sacrificing humanity on the altar of history, as does Heidegger, and as is all too usual in much of today's social and political thought and planning. Instead, Rosenzweig holds a historical humanity to the higher standard of a redemptive mission, launched by love and aiming for love, a love that cannot be "purely human."

THREE

Rosenzweig versus Nietzsche

Nietzsche needs no introduction. It is doubtful whether a philosopher today can write, or even think, without consciously or unconsciously referring to themes that belong under the heading "Nietzsche." Indeed, Nietzsche's importance was recognized very early, before his death, already by the end of the nineteenth century. It is otherwise with Franz Rosenzweig. Owing to the difficulty of his style, the destruction of the German and European Jewish world, the inability to fit his thought within familiar classifications, his Jewish *and* Christian religiosity, the real and spiritual proximity of Heidegger—he is barely known, more than half a century after his death.

In this chapter I cannot hope to rectify this neglect. What I propose to do, however, is to present the central elements of Rosenzweig's appropriation of Nietzsche. I say "central" because this chapter does not set itself the task of elucidating the full range and complexity of Rosenzweig's reading of Nietzsche.[1] I use the neutral term "appropriation" because Rosenzweig's relation to Nietzsche is, at the least, ambivalent. Rosenzweig both praises and buries Nietzsche. It is the latter move, Rosenzweig's criticism of Nietzsche, however, that is perhaps of greatest interest in our day, which is so fascinated, often uncritically, with Nietzsche. For it is undeniable that much of what passes for the "progressive critical spirit" of our time, when individualistic and self-centered rather than socialist and other-directed, can well be called Nietzschean. Intellectuals, in any event, often find themselves "in a world," to cite Emmanuel Levinas's pointed words, "where infidelity to Nietzsche . . . is taken as blasphemy" (*OBBE* 177). My aim, then, in presenting Rosenzweig's reading of Nietzsche, is precisely to awaken this paradoxical blasphemy, to hammer away at the philosopher who philosophizes with a hammer.

This account of Rosenzweig's Nietzsche will also be limited to Rosenzweig's great theologico-philosophical work, *The Star of Redemption*.[2]

1. Many broad issues—for example, a Nietzschean response to Rosenzweig, or an account of the Nietzsche that Rosenzweig misses—cannot be raised here.
2. Rosenzweig wrote much of the *Star* on postcards to his mother when as a young man he served on the Balkan front as a German soldier during World War I. One can hardly help noticing that the effect of World War I on Rosenzweig, as on so many of his generation, was quite unlike the effect of the Franco-Prussian War of 1870 on Nietzsche, who also served in the German army, as a medic. Recognizing the truth of Hegelian political philosophy in

Rosenzweig is not fascinated with Nietzsche. Unlike Shestov, Bataille, Mann, Löwith, Jaspers, Heidegger, et al., he does not devote a long study to Nietzsche. Rosenzweig's work in philosophy was for the most part done in German idealism, primarily on Hegel and Schelling.[3] What he later called his "dues paid to the German nation" was a two-volume dissertation tracing the development of Hegel's changing conception of the state, published in 1920.[4] It should come as no surprise, therefore, that Nietzsche does not figure *prominently* in the *Star*.[5] But for all that, Nietzsche does figure *importantly* in this work. He appears precisely at the book's three pivotal points, in the introductions to its three parts.[6] Nietzsche's first appearance in the *Star* is positive, his second appearance is both positive and negative, and his third appearance is nega-

---

the long European conflict, Rosenzweig learned, according to Stéphane Mosès, "that the bankruptcy of the European states is at the same time the bankruptcy of universal history and, even more generally, the bankruptcy of a concept of reason which, from the first Ionian thinkers to the idealism of Jena, has ruled over Western philosophy" ("Politique et Religion chez Franz Rosenzweig," in *Politique et Religion: Actes du XXe Colloque de Intellectuels Juifs de langue française* [Paris: Gallimard, 1981], 286, my translation). Whatever his bad opinion of Germany and German imperialism, Nietzsche's writings are shot through with a militarist style—"Militante mais pas militaire," Henri Birault would proclaim in his lectures on Nietzsche at the Sorbonne, referring to Nietzsche's style—and even more than a matter of style, they consistently glorify the strengthening power of strife and conflict in terms of war, in contrast to what Nietzsche saw as the mediocrity and weakness that result from peace, which he equated with sleep.

3. For an examination of Rosenzweig's relation to Schelling's later thought, see Else-Rahel Freund, *Franz Rosenzweig's Philosophy of Existence* (The Hague: Martinus Nijhoff, 1979).

4. Franz Rosenzweig, *Hegel und der Staat*, 2 vols. (Munich and Berlin, 1920).

5. Stéphane Mosès, in *System and Revelation*, limits his comments on Rosenzweig's relation to Nietzsche to two sentences. Else-Rahel Freund, in the work mentioned above, avoids Nietzsche's name entirely.

6. In the introduction to part 1, entitled "On the Possibility of the Cognition of the All," see the sections entitled "Nietzsche" (9), "Man," (9–10), and "Metaethics" (10–11); in the introduction to part 2, entitled "On the Possibility of Experiencing Miracles," see the sections entitled "The Point-of-View Philosopher" (105–6) and "The New Philosopher" (106); in the introduction to part 3, entitled "On the Possibility of Entreating the Kingdom," see the sections entitled "The Magic of Prayer" (270–71), "Tyrants of the Kingdom of Heaven" (271–72), "The Sinner's Prayer" (273–74), "The Fanatic's Prayer" (274–75), "Goethe and Nietzsche" (286–87), and "Revolution" (287).

Regarding the great importance of these sections, and the introductions to each of the three parts of the *Star* more generally, I am in agreement with Steven S. Schwarzchild, who has written: "The Introductions to each of the three parts of *The Star of Redemption*, which present a historical summary of the main subject to be dealt with in each part, crystallize the most striking element in each part, and constitute the transition from one part to the next; Rosenzweig himself described them as 'possessing a style of their own' "(*Franz Rosenzweig [1886-1929]: Guide of Reversioners* [London: The Education Committee of the Hillel Foundation, 1960], 16).

tive.[7] The contents of this chapter will be limited to Rosenzweig's first and third appraisals of Nietzsche, with emphasis on the latter, Rosenzweig's criticism.

Rosenzweig's complex evaluation of Nietzsche can be briefly summed up as follows: while Rosenzweig applauds Nietzsche for escaping the empty abstractions of Hegelian philosophy,[8] for posing a philosophizing subjectivity against philosophical objectivity, he criticizes Nietzsche for escaping Hegelianism in the wrong way, or, rather, for escaping Hegelianism in the right way but insufficiently, both because Nietzsche's individualism, qua pagan, is inferior to Goethe's pagan individualism, and because the entire pagan option, including both Nietzsche's and Goethe's paganism, is inferior to the revealed religious alternative offered by Christianity and Judaism.[9]

7. A word about the *Star*'s architectonic: Rosenzweig has been accused of having imposed an artificial and obtrusive structure onto his thought. There is some truth to this charge, both with regard to many of the tripartite divisions which are found in the text, and with regard to its overall structure. One must be cautious regarding the systematic character of Rosenzweig's "system." The charge should not be taken too far, however. Most of what Rosenzweig has to say, even within what can sometimes be a awkward structure, is *not* the product of a misguided attempt to lend consistency to an artificial construction. It is rather the product of a genuinely new way of thinking. Rosenzweig's thought, especially in its most Shellingian moments (e.g., in part 1 of *SR*), is convoluted and difficult enough as it is; I hesitate to say whether its structure alleviates or compounds the difficulty. In any event, I mention the artificiality of Rosenzweig's architectonic so that the neat symmetry of his evaluation of Nietzsche in the three introductions of *SR*—first positive, then positive and negative, and finally negative—not be dismissed as a function of external architectonic factors.

8. For Rosenzweig, author of *Hegel und der Staat* (1920), "Hegelian philosophy" represents the essential summation and conclusion of the entire tradition of Western philosophy which began with Parmenides. Thus, while perfectly aware of the differences, Rosenzweig will equate Hegel's system with German idealism and with philosophy from Parmenides to Hegel.

9. It might seem, then, from a purely logical point of view, that Rosenzweig's criticism of Nietzsche would be effective whether or not one further agrees with Rosenzweig's commitment to Christianity and Judaism (see *SR* part 3.) One would argue that even if, unlike Rosenzweig, one did not accept the revealed religions, then one could still accept Rosenzweig's argument that Nietzsche's nonbelief is inferior to Goethe's nonbelief. That is, it seems as if one could embrace Goethe against Nietzsche *and* against Judaism and Christianity.

But this will not work, at least for Rosenzweig. Rosenzweig's criticism of Nietzsche in the name of Goethe depends on the proximity Rosenzweig sees between Goethe and Christianity. Rosenzweig reckons Goethe a thoroughgoing pagan, but at the same time he is "the first" father "of the Johannine Church" (see *SR* 283–88). Rosenzweig's Goethean argument against Nietzsche in no way undermines or can avoid his argument for Christianity and Judaism over both Goethe and Nietzsche.

The Goethean argument, nonetheless, which is an argument for the intensity or vitality of life in its temporality, a thankful artistry without Nietzschean excess, is still, Rosenzweig

Nietzsche against Hegel

Traditional philosophy "from Parmenides to Hegel" or "from Ionia to Jena," as Rosenzweig expresses it, is the quest to know, to cognize, to represent, to formalize, to conceptualize the all, the whole, the totality of the real. From Parmenides' notion of the one changeless being to Hegel's fully determinate, systematic, and dialectical notion of natural, historical, and spiritual being, the *eros* of philosophy has always been the same: the desire for total comprehension of the all, the desire for absolute comprehension, the desire to comprehend all of being through thought.

Rosenzweig will agree with many other close readers of Hegel that the philosophical *eros,* the quest for absolute knowledge, is successfully satisfied with Hegel's system of absolute idealism. Hegel's idealism concludes philosophy because it not only knows all but knows itself to know all. Being and thought are finally brought together without significant residue. But Rosenzweig also believes, nonetheless, or paradoxically, that idealism pays too high a price for its success—one must die to life. Yet to grasp Rosenzweig's point one must return to the death that philosophy does know, for philosophy has not been ignorant of death.

Philosophy, Socrates taught, is a learning how to die. Rosenzweig's point, however, is that rather than learning how to die by learning how to live, philosophy has learned how to die to death itself. Philosophy knows death through a kind of suicide. Rather than face the fearful and bleak realities of mortality, it kills off life, or, since it must somehow live, swaddles life tightly within ideas. For real life, it substitutes a "life" of eternal immutable *deathless* ideas, a "life" prior to life, an a priori life, a "life" always in the past, the "life" of knowledge, the owl's life, for the mortal and existential immediacy of life itself. Philosophy would rather know the "itself" of life than life itself; it substitutes essence for reality. Against this flight into the past of knowledge, the philosopher's flight into philosophy, the flight into the deathlessness and the totalization effected by philosophical comprehension, Rosenzweig counterposes the fact of death and the fear of death.

Just as *The Star of Redemption* ends with the words "into life," it begins with the words "from death": "From death, in the fear of death, all cognition of the all originates" (*SR* 3).[10] Connecting the first and last words

---

notwithstanding, quite attractive on its own. For even if one is persuaded on Jewish or Christian grounds not to embrace Nietzscheanism, it does not follow that one is persuaded to embrace Judaism or Christianity in their historical specificity. Goethean love of the moment and the earth may well remain, and in our day may have become even more popular as an independent and creative alternative to Nietzscheanism, Judaism, and Christianity.

10. I have altered and rearranged the Hallo translation of this sentence to bring the word "death" as close to its beginning as it is in the original.

of the *Star* one discovers what may be the briefest possible summary of Rosenzweig's thought: from death to life.[11] In Rosenzweig's estimation the tradition of philosophy from Parmenides to Hegel has taken exactly the wrong direction, moving steadily from life to death. The task of thought today, then, is to move instead from death to life, hence to recovery from philosophy and the civilization which is its reflection. Philosophy has made a fetish of death, a fetish of suicide, instead of providing aid to life. Now that philosophy has finally completed its march to the grave in Hegel, the philosophy of absolute inescapable self-inflicted death, Rosenzweig argues persuasively for a new eros, a "new thinking," for a movement "from death to life," a movement from the protective and defensive rigor mortis of philosophical autonomy to the succoring commitments of community life.

But how can death overturn or reorient philosophy? Precisely because it escapes the philosopher's philosophy. It is an all too simple truth for the philosopher who is enthralled with his or someone else's philosophy, but a truth nonetheless, that regardless of his philosophy the individual philosopher dies. Death is not merely conceptually necessary; it is existentially inexorable. Death is never equivalent to the cognition of death. Real death, the disappearance that looms beyond the last gasp, is not equivalent to the philosophical concept of negation, and it is certainly not assuaged by it.

Rosenzweig's claim is stronger yet: not only is death lacking to philosophy, as everyone would readily agree that innumerable facts and details—"particulars"—have been and are always lacking to philosophy, without serious consequence, but, lacking death, philosophy lacks its own *origin*. Such a lack is then of the greatest possible consequence for philosophy, for it punctures philosophy's greatest pretense, undermines what has always made for its very greatness, its alleged greatness—it destroys the very possibility of absoluteness. To pose death against philosophy, therefore, is not merely to oppose one concept to another, as when the philosophical critic opposes a more comprehensive conception to a less comprehensive conception (of whatever), and the former destroys or sublates the latter. Such opposition is perhaps philosophy itself, the movement of negation.

11. Else-Rahel Freund begins her book on Rosenzweig by commenting on the connection between the first and last sentences of the *Star*. Perhaps she has gone even further than I have regarding the significance of these few words: "Taken together—'from death into life'—they comprise the entire meaning of Rosenzweig's philosophy" (3).

In a pamphlet of 1920 entitled "Towards a Renaissance of Jewish Learning," Rosenzweig writes: "Literature is written for the sake only of those who are in process of development, and of that in each of us which is still developing. . . . Books exist only to transmit that which has been achieved to those who are still developing. While that which is between the achieved and the developing, that which exists today, at this moment—life itself—needs no books" (*JL* 58).

To pose death against philosophy, on the other hand, is to oppose a mortal life, the life of the individual person, the one who dies, life in the first person singular, to a system of concepts now understood to be deathless and not absolute. If philosophy is the search for origins—which is traditional philosophy's way of comprehending the all, by digging, by going to the roots, finally by grounding itself—then death, at the "origin" of philosophy, makes a mockery of philosophy itself. It is as if, Rosenzweig is suggesting, beneath the *archê* of comprehension, which includes negation, lies the *an-archê* of death, more radical than negation, and the latter, rather than the former, gives rise to thought. Thought, then, by nature, cannot be philosophical if by philosophical one means self-grounding.

The *Star* transcends textual closure, moves from the black and white page to variegated life, to end with several cleverly triangulated final sentences (see p. 297 below) which seem graphically to depict the passage from reflective discourse ("the book") into communal life with others. The discourse disappears neither into a pumped up conceptualization of the abstract nothing of traditional philosophy, which was rejected at the outset, nor into the solitude and subjectivism of the individual's ownmost death, which at first jolted the abstract nothing from out of its escapist daydreams. Rather it moves into temporal, moral, and religious life beyond the book, a life whose essential elements, structures, and movements, the book itself has painstakingly characterized.

Many if not most books, however, aspire to transcend the condition of textuality, to refer to the "concrete," to "move" the reader, to "incite" action, to "change" behavior, or in some way or other to go "beyond the book" or "beyond the word." Even consciousness dreams these dreams, inventing for itself a world of prereflective naivete or instinct. What is perhaps most interesting in such thought, and in each case most characteristic, is the precise manner in which language transcends itself.

After the first three sections of the introduction to part 1 of the *Star,* which pose the singularity and unassimilability of death against what must now be seen as the *rationalization* of death—suicide through intellect—in Hegelian philosophy, Rosenzweig then introduces Kierkegaard, Schopenhauer, and Nietzsche as the three thinkers who effect the break with Hegel. Rosenzweig does not say anything of particular importance about Kierkegaard, and what he says about Schopenhauer he says more directly about Nietzsche.[12] It is Nietzsche, in any event, rather than Kierkegaard or

---

12. Given the Hegel connection, and given both their deep religious commitments, it is hard not to see that Kierkegaard gets a very short shrift from Rosenzweig, and not only in the *Star.* One would be well advised, I think, not to overestimate the significance of this dismissal, however. My own (unproven) suspicion is that Rosenzweig, unlike Heidegger, was simply not especially familiar with Kierkegaard's work.

Schopenhauer, who he takes to have first effectively broken with Hegelian philosophy.

Why does Nietzsche stand out as the first true opponent of the Western philosophical tradition? What does he represent? In a word, Nietzsche stands out because he represents, for the first time in the history of philosophy, a man who philosophizes. That is to say, he represents a man who remains a man while being a philosopher. Nietzsche is a man who philosophizes rather than a man who loses himself to become the manifestation of a concept, or the instantiation of a type, or the representative of an idea, or the cipher of an ideology, or the surface effect of a deep structure, or the example of a generalization, or the specific difference of a genus, or any of the many ways in which life turns to death in traditional philosophy. This may not seem like much—to be a man and a philosopher at the same time—but it is enough, in Rosenzweig's view, to break with Hegelian philosophy.

Rosenzweig freely admits that prior to Nietzsche poets and saints made their own souls the objects of their spiritual lives, but he maintains that Nietzsche is the first philosopher to do so. Unlike philosophers of the past, who tolerated their own prephilosophical individuality only so far as and until they gained the philosophical strength of mind to leave it behind, trading singularity for the autonomous and universal "life" of the mind, Nietzsche brings his own soul along in his mind's adventures. Indeed, for the first time the mind experiences *adventures* rather than inductions, deductions, or dialectical developments. "Thus," writes Rosenzweig, "man became a power over philosophy—not man in general over philosophy in general, but one man, one very specific man over his own philosophy. The philosopher ceased to be a negligible quantity for his philosophy" (*SR* 9–10).[13]

What is important for Rosenzweig about Nietzsche in the overcoming of classical philosophy is not Nietzsche's philosophy, his specific doctrines, but Nietzsche's way of doing philosophy, his personalization of philosophy. We can say that Nietzsche represents the start of philosophy's return from knowledge to wisdom. Such a return can only be a jolt for knowledge, for the "philosopher" who sacrifices himself for what he knows, the "philosopher" whose *who* becomes a *what*, whose present becomes a past. At this early point in the *Star*, Rosenzweig is concerned to stand philoso-

---

13. Rosenzweig is certainly aware of Max Stirner's *The Ego and Its Own*, but considers it a mere book in relation to the tragic singularity *lived* by Nietzsche. He writes: "Now something else, the living man, independently took a stand opposite the cognitive world, and opposite totality there stood the singular, the 'unique and his own,' mocking every All and universality. This novum was then thrust irretrievably into the riverbed of the development of conscious spirit, not in the book so headed, which in the last analysis was only that—a book—but in the tragedy of Nietzsche's life itself" (*SR* 9).

phy back on its feet in real life, in the life of the philosopher who really has feet, arms and legs, a head, and a heart. He opposes Plato's beautiful image of the dying Socrates, the talking head saying first and last things, the philosopher par excellence. But to oppose traditional philosophy cannot be a matter of more doctrines. Indeed, in the case of Nietzsche, the man Nietzsche who philosophizes without losing himself, Rosenzweig is not in the least interested in doctrines, perhaps erring thereby in the opposite direction: "What he [Nietzsche] philosophized has by now become almost a matter of indifference. Dionysiac and Superman, Blond Beast and eternal return—where are they now?" (*SR* 9) he asks rhetorically.[14] Nietzsche, not Nietzscheanism, overcomes Hegel.

But the quick dismissal of Nietzsche's doctrines in part 1 of the *Star* also alerts the reader to a shift that occurs in parts 2 and 3, a shift in who or what Nietzsche is for Rosenzweig, concomitant with the shift in Rosenzweig's appraisal of Nietzsche. As Rosenzweig's evaluation of Nietzsche moves from positive to negative, so, too, does Rosenzweig's Nietzsche move from being a real, three-dimensional, flesh and blood person, the first philosophizing man, to becoming an abstract, two-dimensional, aesthetic image, a set of fictional characters posturing and declaiming within a literary text, the script of a theatrical drama. Although Nietzsche criticizes *theoria*, he offers only theatre instead, again only a book, another spectacle and not life itself. Rosenzweig's flattening portrayal of Nietzsche already appears to some extent in the introduction to part 2, but it is especially pronounced in the introduction to part 3, where Rosenzweig returns to Nietzsche to contrast him negatively with Goethe. In part 3 the issue is no longer Nietzsche the person, the man who first combines soul and mind philosophically, but the doctrines and figures which appear in Nietzsche's *Thus Spoke Zarathustra*, particularly the figure of Zarathustra and his doctrines of the overman and eternal return. In part 3, interestingly enough, where criticism of cognition is no longer the question, it will be Goethe the *man*, representing the highest pagan *life*, who will be contrasted positively against Nietzsche's literary-philosophical characters and the doctrines espoused by his creations.

This shift from a three- to a two-dimensional Nietzsche is a symptom

---

14. Rosenzweig is able to dismiss the ideas of the blond beast and the overman even while he is a German soldier in the trenches of World War I. One might speculate whether he would have been equally cool to the content of Nietzsche's doctrines had Rosenzweig lived just a few years longer. But such speculation would be premature and, as it turns out, unfair to Rosenzweig. As we shall shortly see, Rosenzweig does respond quite specifically to Nietzsche's doctrines, especially to the doctrines of the overman and the eternal return. He directly addresses precisely the question of the split between Nietzsche and his doctrines, Nietzsche the man versus Nietzsche the doctrinaire.

of the inadequacy of the Nietzschean break with Hegel. Subjectivity is only a start, only a way out of philosophy. It is not, however, a step forward, or even a step into life. Unwittingly true to a philosophy he rejects absolutely, Nietzsche does not understand that love is the way beyond philosophy into life. The same critical wedge Rosenzweig drives against Hegel he drives against Nietzsche: philosophy must somehow "take account" of love, somehow face up to the *revelation* of love. It is not enough to oppose philosophy with subjectivity, which is still too caught up, will it or no, in negating a negation.

Love

Is it not a hopeful sign that philosophy itself has always opposed revelation, in which it sees no more than "heteronomy"? Against the heteronomy of revelation, which like all heteronomy philosophy takes to be sheerly arbitrary, philosophy desires autonomy. What philosopher has not secretly or openly desired to be like the gods? Whatever is revealed must be rejected, no matter how attractive the message or uplifting the gifts— such is the hardness and hardiness of philosophy, its classical courage and rigor. Philosophy must begin with and within itself if it is to be fully reasonable. And perhaps also, though at first unconsciously but finally with German idealism explicitly, it aims to be fully reasonable precisely in order to remain with and within itself. Unique events are indigestible, and hence no matter how momentous, such as the giving of the law to Moses at Mount Sinai, they must be reduced to allegory or metaphor. Philosophy, sufficient unto itself, will tell the truth about these visions and dreams. Their bestowal will no longer be needed because from the first, in truth, they were never necessary, never necessary truths. A human philo-sophy precedes and lies at the core of every allegedly divine philanthropy.

For Rosenzweig revelation is not only, or not originally, limited to the revelation of the law to Moses at Mount Sinai, or the revelations of the life of Jesus as recorded in the New Testament. Rosenzweig is neither a traditional philosopher nor a traditional theologian; he does not begin with the authority of the Bible. Posing the Bible against philosophy is as stale and fruitless as posing philosophy against the Bible. Rosenzweig's notion of revelation is not opposed to the specific revelations of the Old and New Testaments, but neither is it equivalent to them—it conditions them.[15] What has made it *possible* to take up revelation, heteronomous

15. The term "conditions" here is not meant in the transcendental sense familiar to German idealism, where it refers to the conditioned's a priori possibility *for knowledge*. One

though it be, has been the break-up of classical philosophy, the break-up of the philosophy which falsely claimed to contain its own origins within itself. What interests Rosenzweig in part 2 of the *Star,* where revelation is the literal and spiritual center of the text, is neither the pure possibility of revelation (which was the topic of part 1) nor the specific revelations of Judaism and Christianity (which will be the topic of part 3). Rather, it is the question of what makes revelation revelatory.[16]

What makes revelation revelatory, for Rosenzweig, is not the authority of a dogma but the authority of an event, the very eventfulness of the present, its presence: the event of love. Revelation, for Rosenzweig, is the individual's recognition of being loved, the fully positive experience of heteronomy. To be loved is to be in relation with what exceeds the grasp of classical philosophy; it is to be in relation with transcendence without integrating or incorporating its alterity. Only on the basis of *this extra-ordinary relation, where the terms of the relation are both in relation and out of relation,* does one transcend philosophy into life. Only on the basis of this extra-ordinary relation, furthermore, can one love one's neighbors in turn, or, as Rosenzweig expresses it, can one *redeem* one's neighbors. Love for the neighbor expresses hope for a global community of love—the kingdom of G-d. Furthermore, to be a being that is both in relation and out of relation is to be a *created* being, a being given to itself before choosing or constructing itself.

Revelation maintains itself in its extra-ordinary relation because unlike knowledge it appears as personal command, in the first and second person,

---

could say that the whole contribution of Rosenzweig's thought is to undo the idealist meaning of conditioning, and therefore the idealist philosophical project. To speak of conditions, for Rosenzweig, is to refer not to knowledge but to social life, to the concern for others and for justice. Levinas, who shares Rosenzweig's perspective here, makes use of a disjunction—"the condition or the non-condition"—to emphasize this new sense of conditioning. But the prefix "non" only helps if it is understood outside of the oppositions of formal and dialectical logic.

16. Like all contemporary philosophers, time is of crucial importance to Rosenzweig. I am here emphasizing the temporal dimensions of the *Star*'s three parts since they play a significant role in Rosenzweig's reading of Nietzsche. For Rosenzweig, knowledge and creation concern the past, love and revelation concern the present, and prayer and redemption concern the future. The error of traditional philosophy has been to reduce time's three dimensions to the past in the name of eternity, but really for the sake of an abstract nothingness. Nietzsche throws the gauntlet of the present (eternal return) and future (overman) against philosophy's obsession with the past. But Nietzsche's error, as we shall see, is not to properly appreciate the presence of the present, the presence of revelation and love, or the relation of the present to the future, the redemptive love of the neighbor, or the relation of the present to the past, created being. Goethe, who unlike Nietzsche does appreciate the presence of the present, only partially does so, missing out however on a genuine appreciation for the future.

rather than as impersonal proposition, in the third person. Revelation appears in the face of the other, which is from the first imperative rather than indicative. In the face of the other person one is commanded "to do justice and to love mercy and to walk humbly with thy God" (*SR* 424, quoting Micah). The command of revelation is the command to love G-d; or, we can say, along with Rosenzweig—in a shift of emphasis whose importance cannot be overestimated—the command to love, when fulfilled, by loving the neighbor, is the command to love G-d. By loving the neighbor man loves G-d.[17] Rosenzweig takes this to be the sense of the *Pesiktha deRav Kahana*'s comment on Isaiah 43:10: "If ye acknowledge me, then I am" (*SR* 182). The idea here is that "love simply cannot be 'purely human'" (*SR* 201), if by the "purely human" one means the efforts at attaining autonomy. Traditional philosophy has tried to be purely human, whether escaping finitude (creatureliness) in the deathless immanence of ideas, in objectivity, or embracing finitude in the pagan bowels of nature, in subjectivity. Neither direction discovers love.

Such is the "religious dimension" of Rosenzweig's thought: against Hegelian and post-Hegelian philosophy he affirms the non-affirmable— love. To arrive at love, the rigor of philosophy, now in a new subjective key, must join with the revelation of theology, also in a new key. The product of joining the new philosophy with the new theology is what Rosenzweig calls "the new thinking." And the new thinking is not thinking in the sense of contemplation but precisely life in the living community of one's fellows. G-d's love, that man is beloved by G-d, the command to love G-d, finds fulfillment in the command to love one's neighbor. Loving one's neighbor (including the institution of the material, juridical, and political conditions for such love) is G-d's presence in history.

It is in answering the question of where to fit Nietzsche not just into the criticism of Hegel but into the positive movement from cognition to community, in the shift from knowledge to love, that Rosenzweig's ambivalence emerges. Nietzsche to his credit is beyond old philosophy, but to his detriment he is not quite the new philosopher. Nietzsche represents something beyond Hegelianism, beyond classical philosophy, to be

17. By loving man we love God. This is certainly also one of central ideas in the work of Emmanuel Levinas. Levinas has several times acknowledged his enormous debt to Rosenzweig. See chapter 10 below.

According to Levinas, who was born into the traditional Judaism of Lithuania, in Kovno, where both orthodox and liberal Judaism could be found side by side, rather than into the assimilated Jewish upper-middle class culture of Rosenzweig's Germany, this idea is one of the central themes of Rabbi Hayyim of Volozhyn's *Nefesh Hahayyim*—a text probably unknown to Rosenzweig.

This idea, however, must not be confused, according to Rosenzweig, with Abraham Geiger's ethical humanism. See *FR* 240.

sure, but because he rejects love he not only represents an open horizon but a horizon that is too open. Rosenzweig writes:

The new concept of philosophy at least has the merit of making any kind of philosophizing possible after Hegel. All its peculiarities come down to one: the old type of philosopher, impersonal by profession, a mere deputy of the naturally one-dimensional history of philosophy is replaced by a highly personal type, the philosopher of the *Weltanschauung,* the point of view. And here the questionable aspect of the new philosophy steps into plain view, and all serious philosophical efforts are bound to be accosted by the questions put to Nietzsche: Is this still science? (*SR* 105)

Is Nietzsche's philosophy scientific? Is his philosophy philosophy? Rosenzweig answers in the negative. But Rosenzweig faults Nietzsche's thought not because it is insufficiently rigorous or strict, insufficiently logical or precise—charges and demands which have so often been heard against Nietzsche. Rather, Rosenzweig rejects Nietzsche's thought because Nietzsche rejects love. How strange to philosophers' ears: it is because Nietzschean thought rejects love that it is not scientific or philosophical enough! Rosenzweig remains sympathetic to the homeopathic power of the Nietzschean refusal of concepts, sympathetic to Nietzsche's lived break with the abstractions of classical philosophy, but Nietzsche gets caught in the negative. He fails and then glorifies his failure to construct a new philosophy.

Nietzsche fails, paradoxically, because he is still *too* respectful of the philosophical tradition. He says, in effect, adhere to the old ways of knowledge, bend to the old philosophical *eros,* or leave it—and then he leaves it. He leaves philosophy leaving philosophy intact. To accept objective truth—or, worse, to accept the superstitious form of truth, religion—is to be a slave. To give up the notion of truth altogether is be free. Since Nietzsche no longer accepts objective truth he gives up the notion of truth altogether. But then, as I think Nietzsche would be the first to agree, one can no longer do philosophy. Nietzsche's aim rises above—beyond—even the highest of the "higher men." For Nietzsche there can be no compromise with truth: one can only go under or over it.

Thus any attempt to preserve philosophy, that is, to preserve philosophy from and beyond Hegel, will necessarily be against Nietzsche. To preserve philosophy Rosenzweig demands a *new form* of objectivity, an objectivity open to what the tradition called "revelation." For it was in a struggle against the heteronomy of revelation, which the philosophical tradition could not distinguish from the anarchy of opinion, that the objectivity of the old philosophy was forged. Rosenzweig demands that philosophy rethink itself from out of its roots, that it be more radical than it ever thought possible. Of the Nietzschean break with old philosophy and the requirements left outstanding for new philosophy, but which, contrary to Nietzsche, must be met by the new philosophy if there is to be philosophy at all, Rosenzweig writes:

> Its new point of departure is the subjective, the extremely personal self, more than that: the incomparable self, immersed in itself. To this and to its point of view it must hold fast and *withal* attain the objectivity of science. The most extreme subjectivity, one would like to say deaf and blind egotism, on the one hand, on the other the lucid clarity of infinite objectivity—where is the bridge between them to be found? (*SR* 106; my italics)

For Nietzsche there is no bridge between subjectivity and objectivity; the healthy and the sick must be segregated.[18] Rosenzweig finds the bridge in the ethical and juridical imperative in communal life and in the other person's face to which the final sections of the *Star* are devoted.

Nietzsche brings classical philosophy to its finale, but no further.[19] Nietzsche would rather break than bend, rather condemn than compromise. In this failure Nietzsche pays a high double price: he not only misses Rosenzweig's new post-Hegelian sense of objectivity, i.e., revelation as love, but he misunderstands subjectivity, misses the genuine subjectivity that comes with revelation—the para-doxical meeting of heteronomy and autonomy. Thus, ironically, it is precisely in the name of subjectivity that Nietzsche misses subjectivity. In the name of a radical subjectivity divorced from the old and the new truths, divorced from truth altogether, Nietzsche inevitably misses the truth of subjectivity. His failure, however, is no mere personal quirk, for it represents a danger ever present to contemporary thought, the temptation of radical subjectivism.

Love is by nature social. Love occurs most intimately in the society of two, the sensual lovers, the lover and the beloved; it occurs in the family, between husband and wife, between parents and children, between brothers and sisters, between grandparents and grandchildren, between aunts,

18. For an entirely different point of view of health and sickness, authentic subjectivity and the role of objectivity, one which challenges the kind of intellectual expertise that both Hegel and Nietzsche valued, and contrary, perhaps, to the very distinction between knowledge, opinion, and revelation valued by all philosophers, see Franz Rosenzweig, *Understanding the Sick and the Healthy*.

19. Heidegger also takes Nietzsche to be the conclusion of traditional Western philosophy, the final form of the willfulness that drives philosophy from its beginnings, willfulness come to self-recognition, the "will to will," and thus the high-point of metaphysics rather than its overcoming. As the maximum subjectivization of being Nietzsche represents the maximum forgetfulness of being. For a closer look at the differences which separate Rosenzweig and Heidegger, and a more detailed exposition of Rosenzweig's conception of the self, see chapter 2.

uncles, nieces, nephews, cousins; it occurs beyond blood in friendship, in a variety of communities, in the neighborhood, in various groups, in society at large, in humanity; and perhaps beyond human society it joins humans to the society of living creatures, and to all of reality. But to love others it is not enough to love oneself. That self-love is the basis of other-directed love has become a cliche in our time, and it has always been a philosophical point of honor. To love others one must love oneself, yes. But this cliche overlooks another love, a love necessary even to loving oneself. To love others or oneself one must first experience love, one must first be loved. This is Rosenzweig's message: only the self (creation) that is loved (revelation) loves others (redemption).

The above brief sketch of revelation and love will permit us to understand why the Nietzschean philosophy expressed by Zarathustra in *Thus Spoke Zarathustra* represents, for Rosenzweig, a danger rather than a positive option in the post-Hegelian context. One last word about Rosenzweig's theory of the self must be added. The "self" of classical philosophy, for Rosenzweig, is an artificial construction, the product of a flight from mortal life. Rosenzweig calls this self "personality" to distinguish it from the "character" that one discovers when the constructed self is shattered by love or death. Beyond the self as character, however, lies the self as "soul." That is to say, beyond the self which is flesh and blood—pagan— rather than abstract, beyond the self touched by love, lies the loving self, the self participating in the two communities of love given to Western civilization, the Jewish and the Christian communities. Rosenzweig obviously locates Nietzsche at the pagan level, the level of real love and death beyond the abstract *eros* and eternity of philosophy, but he also locates Goethe there.

Superior to Nietzsche, at the pagan level, Goethe represents the blessed self, the self thankful for itself, knowing itself beloved, the self freed of the time consuming and distracting surface play of social roles, of personality, the self open to all of its capacities. This is precisely the self that Nietzsche misses. Yet Nietzsche rejects the Hegelian construction. It is Nietzsche, then, who is truly in a no-man's-land. Refusing philosophy, he refuses religion and real life too, mistaking the latter two for the former's versions of them. To extricate himself from his untenable situation Nietzsche succumbs to mythologizing, and even makes a pose of it. In the name of Zarathustra, he stalwartly demands—and makes a demand of this very demand—a self that he himself can create. Thus instead of the Goethean self which is thankful for its gifts, Nietzsche feels only a deep emptiness within and a deep emptiness without. Facing these two deep voids with courage—the pagan virtue par excellence—he strains to fill them with life, but only succeeds, from Rosenzweig's point of view, in painting them over. In a whirlwind, Nietzsche lacquers his needs with seductive but two-dimensional figures: the ego of the eternal return to fill in the present void within, and the figure of the overman to fill in the futural void without. Rosenzweig will name these pagan options with quite different names and give to them quite a different value: "sinner" and "fanatic."

Nietzsche's Egoism: The Sinner

The sinner is he who values himself more than he is worth. Rather, he values his freedom more than his self. Like a god, the sinner ignores his true self, indeed denies its existence ("a grammatical fiction") in order to create himself. The deed is futile and dangerous, however, because the self is already created.

The sinner is he who values what he takes to be his *own,* which is his own freedom, more than anything or anyone else, even though the self is not equivalent to its freedom, or, as Rosenzweig says (as does Levinas after him), even though a genuine freedom is finite. To maintain freedom at all costs means denying death. This was precisely what cognitive philosophy did in the name of eternal ideas. On the existential plane, however, it means fabricating not a system but a self. While seeming to gain the self by strenuously valuing itself, the self loses itself by overvaluing itself, by overlooking its own mortality, its vulnerability, its very ownness. "The I can simply not conceive its own death; what it fears is its own corpse" (*SR* 273). What is sinful is not the fear of death but the fearless response whereby the self attempts or aspires to constitute itself by itself. In truth it is but idealism in an existentialist guise, the shadow of idealism, or the "appearance" about which idealism pretended to be "the truth."

To avoid one's true self, the self that is given, one's character, all alterity must be denied. The personality must have no cracks. Immortality has always been the pagan ideal. "Oneself would like to be self, awakened to a life of one's own, the survivor *par excellence,* the survivor of all that is eternally 'Other'" (*SR* 274). For Nietzsche, what is other par excellence is truth. In distancing himself from truth, which in its traditional conceptual form would take the self from itself in the name of a deathless and abstract system, Nietzsche errs in the other direction, distancing himself from all alterity, and hence from the only alterity left to him, his own alterity and the alterity of other people.

Attentive to the dialogical philosophies of Eugen Rosenstock-Huessy and Martin Buber,[20] Rosenzweig will say that the sinner is the self that can only say "I" and "he," but cannot say "you." It is in this failure, this insistence on ownness *by itself,* that the pagan self denies revelation and redemption—"for what is redemption," Rosenzweig writes, "other than that the I learns to say thou to the he?" (*SR* 274).[21]

Whatever the sinful self asks for the present, or for the future, falls on deaf ears, because the sinful self speaks to no one but itself, and its own talking keeps it from hearing. By nature it is therefore murderous. The sinner's future is, like its present, *only* its own. It always only prays to itself and thus for the other's death, regardless of what words the sinner actually uses in his concern for the present and future. "Thus the prayer for the death of the Other," Rosenzweig writes, "is fulfilled prior to any praying, for from eternity on man is already on his own" (*SR* 274). Character is given; it need not be asked for. But to ask for it, to be obsessed with gaining what one already has, one must deny that one has what one has, and deny that other's have what they have. The egoist subject, like the idealist subject, is monadic—even if it must subdue the entire world lest its monism be challenged.

The pagan prayer of the self by itself—always "the prayer for the death of the other"—is always *too late,* since it prays for what has already been granted, asks for a self which is in fact given from the beginning, created. It is myopic, to the point of overlooking itself. It confuses the future with the present, wanting what it has, demanding what it should be thankful for. It is too late and too close for its own self, missing what it cannot see far enough to see. It asks for that for which it should already be thankful: the self. One does not in truth make oneself, constitute oneself, create oneself; one finds oneself, through death and love. The other loves me not as the individual of a genus but in my uniqueness, in my singularity—and only in view of that love is my singularity brought into its own. Rosenzweig writes:

What is sinful in the prayer is that man, rather than treating this content as already fulfilled and therefore thanking God for his own-being which is conditioned by the human, the creaturely otherwiseness of all the others, instead requests it and thus treats it as something as yet unfulfilled. For thereby he prays at the improper

20. Rosenzweig had profound personal and intellectual relationships with both Rosen-stock-Huessy and Buber. His conversations and correspondence with Rosenstock-Huessy, in particular, were quite important in his own early development; see *JDC*. Already in 1916 Rosenzweig was in possession of a rough draft of Rosenstock-Huessey's *Applied Psychology* (1924), and later thought of *SR* as its complement.

21. Compare this with Levinas, who writes: "The relationship with the infinite then no longer has the structure of an intentional correlation. . . . A you is inserted between the I and the absolute He. Correlation is broken" (*CPP* 73).

time. He should have requested it before his creation; once created, he can only thank for his own. (*SR* 274)

For Rosenzweig, Zarathustra is a sinner, indeed, the sinner par excellence. Zarathustra teaches love of self in opposition to love of the neighbor. He teaches, contrary to Rosenzweig, that love of neighbor is the product of not loving the self enough or rightly: "Your love of the neighbor," says Zarathustra, "is your bad love of yourselves. You flee to your neighbor from yourselves and would like to make a virtue out of that: but I see through your 'selflessness'."[22] Of course, Rosenzweig thinks of love of the neighbor not as selflessness but as the very soul of the self, the rupture of a constructed personality and the rupture of the natural self's self-enclosure. The true self, for Rosenzweig, is given, but given in relation to the alterity of death and love. It combines heteronomy and autonomy—which is beyond the resources of traditional philosophy and pagan life.

The mirroring between Nietzsche and Rosenzweig in relation to their views of self-love and love of the neighbor is uncanny—and of course only Rosenzweig could read Nietzsche. Rosenzweig answers Zarathustra's challenge. Zarathustra says, as if mocking Rosenzweig: "The *you* is older than the *I*; the *you* has been pronounced holy, but not yet the *I*; so man crowds toward his neighbor" (172). Rosenzweig would agree, but only by correcting Nietzsche, to say that it has precisely been the *I* that was declared holy by the philosophical tradition culminating in German idealism. The holy *I* of idealism has been declared holy by becoming empty, a negativity. Exalting the individual *I* over the abstract *I*, the "unholy *I*," as Nietzsche would say, over the holy *I*, the egoist *I* over the idealist *I*, as Rosenzweig would say, does effect a break with old philosophy, but it can not by itself be a path to genuine holiness. It is rather a path to unbridled egoism, but at the same time an empty egoism. Such is Rosenzweig's general critique of Nietzsche's subjectivism: it is less than philosophical.

Zarathustra's egoism, while it bravely resists the egoism of German idealism, does so by cutting the very smallest of figures indeed, the very smallest of circles: the self infatuated with itself, the self of and by itself. It escapes the conceptual abstractness of idealism, true, but it does so by

---

22. Friedrich Nietzsche, *Thus Spoke Zarathustra*, translated by Walter Kaufmann, in *The Portable Nietzsche*, edited and translated by Walter Kaufmann (New York: Viking Press, 1967), 172. Hereafter, page references to *Zarathustra* will be cited in parentheses. See also Nietzsche, *Beyond Good and Evil*, section 201, where Nietzsche writes: "In the last analysis, 'love of the neighbor' is always something secondary, partly conventional and arbitrary-illusory in relation to *fear of the neighbor*" (Kaufmann translation [New York: Random House, 1966], 113).

too great a retreat into the privacy and opacity of a self-obsessed and self-sensing existence. With so little material left to its resources, it futilely attempts to build what is already built, vainly attempts to create what is already created, deceitfully attempts to give itself what is given: the singular, the unique, the ownmost self. Egoist freedom succeeds only in exhausting itself and others with much sound and fury.

Zarathustra's Overman: The Fanatic

But Nietzsche, despite or really because of his egoism, is not indifferent to his neighbors.

In the Prologue to *Thus Spoke Zarathustra*, Zarathustra leaves his mountain retreat and enters the forest to return to the world of human society. He encounters an old man, a saint[23] who recognizes him and demands to know why Zarathustra is returning to mankind after having gained enlightenment. Zarathustra answers simply: "I love man" (123). But Zarathustra's love is pedagogic; he is returning to men to teach: "Behold, I am weary of my wisdom, like a bee that has gathered too much honey; I need hands outstretched to receive it." Because Zarathustra is overfull with wisdom he "goes under" to men; he has a doctrine to spread. His love of men comes not from intermingling with them, or participating in a joint enterprise, but from having found a gift in his "many years"[24] of solitude and wanderings, a gift to give, the gift of the overman. Through the rest of *Thus Spoke Zarathustra* there will be no give and take with Zarathustra; he comes complete, sculpted in solitude, a many faceted but self-made diamond. Like a sun, Zarathustra wants only to shine forth, to illuminate; he wants only to teach but has nothing to learn; he wants only to give but never to take. Zarathustra's sadness comes because he cannot find adequate takers. His generosity burns because it is excessive.

Zarathustra's first words to the villagers he meets in the marketplace of the first village he enters are the following: "I teach you the overman. Man is something that shall be overcome. What have you done to overcome him?" (124). Zarathustra is the self-proclaimed "herald" (128) of the overman, of he who surpasses man as much as man surpasses the ape. If Zarathustra cannot find his proper student, he who Zarathustra can mold in the image of G-d, then he will, like G-d, create his student: the overman.

Nietzsche has obviously—in style and content—cultivated parallels be-

23. Schopenhauer?
24. The time assessment is the saint's upon recognizing Zarathustra: "No stranger to me is this wanderer: many years ago he passed this way. Zarathustra he was called, but he has changed."

tween *Thus Spoke Zarathustra* and the New Testament. Zarathustra is to the overman what John the Baptist was to Jesus: herald and preparer. The important difference, however, is that Jesus actually follows John the Baptist in the New Testament, while the overman does not—and cannot—arrive to follow his herald. The key issue in both cases—and a key issue by itself—has to do with the relation of the present to the future, more specifically, with any attempt in the present to hasten the arrival of a desired future. The fanatic is he who wants to hasten the future, but wants so much to hasten the future that he only succeeds in delaying it.

In contrast to the sinner's prayer, which is always too near and too late to appreciate the present, too self-absorbed to be itself, too self-absorbed, really, to be concerned with the future, the fanatic's prayer is concerned with the future, but it is focused too far away, is impatient with the present with which the future must be connected, and is thus always too soon to hasten the future. While the sinner was so wrapped up in what he took to be himself, the self he had to create by himself, that he could only say "I" and "he" and not "you," the fanatic is so outside himself in what he wants himself and others to be, that he, too, can only say "he" and "I" and not "you." But whereas the sinner cannot say "you" because his vision is nearsighted, too caught up in an image of the "I," the fanatic cannot say "you" because his vision is farsighted, too caught up in an image of the "he." Zarathustra's *doctrine* of the overman is the result of fanatic prayer.

The problem with Zarathustra's overman, very simply, is that he is a figure too distant for man to achieve. The overman is at best a cartoon character, a "Superman" for innocent childhood fantasies. For Nietzsche, however, the *fact* that man cannot achieve the overman means only that man must be sacrificed to the overman. Man's highest aim, as a supplement to love of self, becomes not love for the neighbor but love for what is beyond the neighbor, for what is beyond man altogether. Zarathustra proudly admits as much: "What is the ape to man? A laughingstock or a painful embarrassment. And man shall be just that for the overman: a laughingstock or a painful embarrassment" (124). No wonder, then, that unlike John the Baptist's prophecy, the prophecy of Zarathustra remains unfulfilled, and unfulfilled in principle. Zarathustra demands too much, he demands the impossible—the very impossibility of demand. By aiming too high—too far—Zarathustra calls for the total breakdown of the give and take of human community, the total abrogation of the commands and services of the inter-human, the destruction of all old tablets, and as such he is a false prophet.

By demanding too much, by remaining always and only a herald, Zarathustra not only does not hasten the future, he delays it. "He seeks to capture the kingdom forcibly," writes Rosenzweig, "at the point which the searchlight of his prayer shows him as the next one but which never is closer than next-but-one" (*SR* 275). The overman is never concerned for the neighbor, never concerned for those near him, but is only absorbed in distant horizons, in distances, always only concerned for the next-but-one. The only figure—beside his animals—that Zarathustra cares for in *Thus Spoke Zarathustra*, not surprisingly, is the *corpse* of the tightrope walker who has fallen in the first village. Zarathustra does not teach man the bridge from subjectivity to objectivity, the bridge from the presence of the self to itself—character—to the truth of the other—love. Rather he teaches that man himself is a bridge that must be overcome: "Man is a rope, tied between beast and overman—a rope over an abyss. . . . What is great in man is that he is a bridge and not an end: what can be loved in man is that he is an *overture* and a *going under*" (126–27). For the sake of the next-but-one, Zarathustra cannot stand—let alone love—the next one, the neighbor. The future will come when today, man's today, is obliterated. Hence it will never come. Nietzsche began writing in the mid-1870s insisting on the *untimeliness* of his meditations *(Unzeitgemasse Betrachtungen)*[25] and of all genuine thought; in 1887, in the *Genealogy of Morals* he reiterates: "We philosophers need to be spared *one* thing above all: everything to do with 'today'."[26]

When Zarathustra speaks explicitly of "love of the neighbor"—to denounce it—the despair he feels at the inadequacy of the flesh and blood neighbor and the love he feels for the one who is not near and who can never be near, the next-but-one, are even more apparent:

Do I recommend love of the neighbor to you? Sooner I should even recommend flight from the neighbor and love of the farthest. Higher than love of the neighbor is love of the farthest and the future; higher yet than the love of human being I esteem the love of things and ghosts. (173)

"Things and ghosts"—Zarathustra's own words. Precisely Rosenzweig's criticism. Having escaped philosophy's ideas, Nietzsche retreats to images, to a private mythology.[27] Moving from the one-dimensionality of ideas to the two-dimensionality of images still does not yield the three dimensions of life.

25. See Nietzsche, *Untimely Meditations,* translated by R. J. Holingdale (Cambridge: Cambridge University Press, 1983).

26. Nietzsche, *On the Genealogy of Morals,* essay 3, section 8; 109.

27. See chapter 11, note 9, regarding Yeats's *Vision.* And what of Judge Schreber's visions? Each to his own—the ultimate Nietzschean maxim (a "subjective maxim," of course).

Narcissism: Nietzsche's Imagination

We should take note again, in concluding, that Rosenzweig's reading of Nietzsche ends not with Nietzsche, the person, but with Nietzschean figures. What Rosenzweig applauded in part 1 of the *Star*, in the conflict with old philosophy, was the man Nietzsche, philosophizing in the first person singular. But Nietzsche gets no further. Because he mistakes his protest for his message, Nietzsche cannot and does not want to escape his subjectivity; he produces not a thought for life, as Rosenzweig wants, but *images* of living figures. It is as if the only way away from the blinding sun outside of Plato's cave were back in the cave, as if the only alternative to the contemplation of ideas were the contemplation of images. But beyond ideas and images is the face of the other person, real life rather than imaginary or ideational life. The abstractness of philosophy's concepts is only incompletely overcome by the images of a solitary philosopher. Zarathustra remains, after all, but a "character" in Nietzsche's work. Worse, from Rosenzweig's perspective, a perspective which moves from death to life: the overman is but the "character" of a "character"! It is no accident that when Rosenzweig speaks positively of paganism—positively because paganism, unlike idealism, does enter real time—he speaks not of a figure but of the harmony of the life and work of Goethe.[28]

Nietzsche's part, then, in the *Star* follows a path inverse to Rosenzweig's. Nietzsche first appears in part 1 as a person, and ends in part 3 as an image, a "character." The *Star*, however, begins with the negative form of the invisible, that is to say, with the abstract concepts of old philosophy, and concludes with the positive form of the invisible, that is to say, with the incomparable directness which shines in the face of the other, the other's ethical claim on the self, and finally, beyond the text entirely, the *Star* concludes with an exit from the book into life.[29] Thus it moves from the abstract to the personal to the communal, to real life—beyond the book—in the community.

Nietzsche is too young and too old for Rosenzweig. He is too young in his rebellion against philosophy, which is a rebellion too insistent on

28. One wonders, in the light of what Rosenzweig says about first and last names in the *Star* and in *The New Thinking*, whether to make anything of the fact that Rosenzweig never refers to Goethe by his full name.

29. Readers unfamiliar with the *Star* may not be aware of just how graphic is Rosenzweig's conclusion. Each line of the last few sentences (of part 3) is centered and becomes progressively shorter to form a triangle whose bottom point is made up of the words "INTO LIFE" *(INS LEBEN)*. Part 2 concludes with a similar configuration whose bottom words are "to enlightenment" *(zur Erleuchtung);* part 1 concludes the same way, but with "into the miracle" *(in das Wunder)*. See p. 297 below.

himself and himself alone. Peter Pan. But he is too old for life and the love of the neighbor, too demanding of a future far far away, a leap and not a bridge, lightning and thunder but not light and wisdom. This excessive youth and excessive age, the double impatience of the "too late" and "too soon," are rooted in Nietzsche's narcissism.[30] His self-infatuation can only survive through fantasy: the myth of self-creation within the self-created myth. Nietzsche does not get lost in ideas but lost in images, a Pied Piper to himself.

Such a reading of Nietzsche sheds a new and dark light on the subtitle of *Thus Spoke Zarathustra:* "A Book for All and None." It is for *none* because it is for Nietzsche alone, expresses his "I," the subjectivity which has broken from abstract philosophy, but only for itself.[31] It is for *all* because everyone, in Nietzsche's vision, should create themselves, distance themselves from everyone else, become "he"s rather than "you"s to one another, become distant ones, those always farther away than neighbors, each and everyone a brightly shining sun not in the community of neighbors and humankind but at the farthestmost periphery, away from all others and all genuine alterity. Atoms in the void, so it rather seems to

30. It is perhaps interesting to note in this regard—without confusing the following with Rosenzweig's critique of Nietzsche—what Freudian psychologists say of "melancholia" or "secondary narcissism." The *Diagnostic and Statistical Manual of Mental Disorders* (3d edition, 1980) of the American Psychiatric Association describes the "narcissistic character" as a "disorder in which there are a grandiose sense of self-importance or uniqueness; preoccupation with fantasies of unlimited success; exhibitionistic need for constant attention and admiration; characteristic responses to threats to self-esteem; and characteristic disturbances in interpersonal relationships that alternate between the extremes of overidealization and devaluation, and lack of empathy" (315). Further, in terms of uniting sinner ("self" over other) and fanatic (sacrifice of next one for next-but-one), we quote the following: "The exaggerated sense of self-importance may be manifested as extreme self-centeredness and self-absorption. Abilities and achievements tend to be unrealistically overestimated" (315). And: "Interpersonal exploitativeness, in which others are taken advantage of in order to indulge one's own desires or for self-aggrandizement, is common; and the personal integrity and rights of others are disregarded" (316).

31. If Nietzsche is not a philosopher, then in what sense, to go back to part 1 of the *Star,* does he break with Hegel? Was it not as a man *and* a philosopher that Nietzsche escapes Hegel? There are, I think, two ways to answer this objection. First of all one could maintain that Nietzsche *is* a philosopher but a bad one, one who fails to work out an adequate epistemology. But more deeply, one would have to point to the difference between Rosenzweig's new thinking and the traditional sort of philosophy that raises the above objection. The Nietzsche of part 1 does not have to be the Nietzsche of part 3 owing to what has transpired in the development from part 1 to part 3. For Rosenzweig the notions of creation, revelation, and redemption, not being concepts, or notions really, are not simultaneous but make up a *sequence.* To explain this difference, which has to do with the irreversibility of time, goes beyond the confines of this chapter. See *SR* 188–89; and also 95–98, 104, 170 below.

us, beautiful atoms perhaps, but still each alone in the void. Speak loudly or quietly, there is no one to hear, except oneself. One is compelled to ask who it is, to turn Nietzsche's own words against him, who really "fears the neighbor"[32]—he who faces the greatest alterity in the risk which is love, love of the other as other, or he who has courage only for those differences which are always circling within the orbit of the same, variations on a solitary theme?

For Rosenzweig, Nietzsche's Zarathustra "illustrates . . . how one can become a sinner and a fanatic in one person, an immoralist who smashes all the old tablets, and a tyrant who overpowers his neighbor as well as himself for the sake of the next-but-one, his friend for the sake of new friends" (*SR* 286), but never for his friend's sake. There can be no doubt that Rosenzweig is referring here to the section entitled "On Love of the Neighbor" in Nietzsche's *Thus Spoke Zarathustra*. In recommending "love of the farthest," in contrast to love of the neighbor, Nietzsche, who is afraid to see the "farthest" in his neighbors, or to find neighbors who are farthest, offers instead the "friend." This is precisely the move Rosenzweig characterizes as having a friend not for the friend's sake, as in true friendship, but having a "friend for the sake of new friends." Nietzsche's "beyond" seems more daring, but it is still flight from real obligations and responsibilities. Zarathustra says:

I teach you not the neighbor, but the friend. The friend should be the festival of the earth to you and an anticipation of the overman. I teach you the friend in whom the world stands completed . . . the creating friend who always has a completed world to give away. (173–74)

Yet Zarathustra's friend is another Zarathustra, another herald of the overman, a giver who has had his fill of man, ripe only for the overman, sick of real men and women.

In the desperation which comes from the unreality of his quest for the immanent equivalent of genuine transcendence, Nietzsche falls prey to an existential version of the "third man" argument, attempting to fill the chasm which his own thought and will have created between man and overman with the friend. But there would still be a chasm to be filled between man and friend, and between friend and overman, etc. Love of the neighbor presents a far far greater challenge, but one to which Nietzsche adamantly refuses to rise. In it, however, Rosenzweig leaves Nietzsche behind, and opens a path for a new thinking.

32. See note 22.

Rosenzweig contra Buber:
Personal Pronouns

Starting with Buber's *I and Thou*

The I-Thou relation has, of course, been made famous by Martin Buber's *I and Thou,* published in 1923. Buber writes:

When I confront a human being as my Thou, and speak the basic word I-Thou to him, then he is no thing among things nor does he consist of things. He is no longer He or She, limited by other Hes and Shes, a dot in the world grid of space and time, nor a condition that can be experienced and described, a loose bundle of named qualities. Neighborless and seamless, he is You and fills the firmament. Not as if there were nothing but he; but everything else lives in *his* light.[1]

Despite its by now many detractors, *I and Thou* is an impressive book, founded on Buber's evocative insights, often beautifully expressed, into the significance of intersubjective experience.

Like Buber, Franz Rosenzweig and Emmanuel Levinas are often called "dialogical" philosophers. This means that they accord a great, even a primordial status to the significance which emerges uniquely from the encounter of one subject with another subject across language. They see a root "grammar" (Rosenzweig), or a radical "concreteness" (Levinas), and a "directness" in the face-to-face encounter. By extension or dilution all other orders of meaning are more or less affected by, and effective though, these qualities. Close though Rosenzweig and Levinas are to their celebrated dialogical colleague, they are nonetheless neither of them "Buberians." Indeed, like all thinkers who are particularly close to one another, they are especially critical of Buber, and even more especially they are critical of his conception of the I-thou relation. Rosenzweig contests the very existence of the Buberian I-thou, while Levinas accepts it only within severely restricted parameters.

Rosenzweig and Levinas agree with one another that Buber's account must be either revised or reoriented in the light of a deeper understanding of the nature and dynamics of intersubjectivity. Rosenzweig and Levinas

1. Martin Buber, *I and Thou,* translated by Walter Kaufmann (New York: Charles Scribner's Sons, 1970), 59. I have modified Kaufmann's translation, using "Thou" in place of "You" for the sake of consistency.

are Buberian in spirit (or at a certain level of generality) to the extent that they too have centered their thought on intersubjectivity. But they also are anti-Buberian in the letter (or at a more specific level) to the extent that both thinkers raise severe criticisms of Buber's particular account of the structure and significance of intersubjectivity. Because they are both more attentive to the implications of language in human encounter, one can even say that Rosenzweig and Levinas are more "dialogical" than Buber in *I and Thou*.[2]

The aim of this inquiry, however, is not to compare and contrast Rosenzweig and Levinas to Buber. It is rather to clarify the significance of the "I," "thou," "he," and "we" in Rosenzweig and Levinas. It is to clarify these terms in the one philosopher in the light of the other because Rosenzweig and Levinas, despite their many differences, are in fundamental agreement about the role and significance of these personal pronouns (excluding certain significations regarding the "we"). In view of this aim I have begun with Buber because Rosenzweig's careful response to Buber's *I and Thou* provides an excellent entrance to Rosenzweig's and Levinas's own thoughts on the I-thou relation.

Scholars are fortunate with regard to Rosenzweig's response to Buber's *I and Thou*. His fundamental criticisms were articulated immediately, indeed, prior to the publication of *I and Thou,* in letters written to Buber in September 1922,[3] responding to the page proofs which Buber, his teacher (and student), collaborator, and friend, had sent to him for comment. The basic criticism is incisive and total: Buber is guilty of making the I-thou bear too great a burden, a burden it cannot by itself bear. Or, to put the same criticism from a different angle, Buber's opposition between the I-thou and the I-It is far too narrow, the issue is more complicated, more nuanced. "With the I-It," Rosenzweig writes in his letter, "you give the I-thou a cripple for an opponent." In place of the simple one-on-one opposition between the reductive objectifications of the I-It (which manner of thinking, Rosenzweig continues, is "less than three

---

2. This is certainly Rivka Horwitz's general thesis with regard to Rosenzweig, and Rosenzweig's influence on Buber. See the two concluding chapters, "Franz Rosenzweig and *I and Thou*" and "September 1922," in her *Bubers' Way to "I and Thou"* (Philadelphia: Jewish Publication Society, 1988), 193–218.

3. The letter most important for this chapter, an undated letter, is found in English translation in *Martin Buber: A Centenary Volume,* edited by Jochanan Bloch and Haim Gordon (New York: KTAV, 1984), 157–59. It is also found in Appendix B of Rivka Horwitz's *Buber's Way to "I and Thou",* 226–29, where four letters from Rosenzweig to Buber, and two letters from Buber to Rosenzweig, written from August to September 1922, are published. A reproduction of the original handwritten version can be found in Franz Rosenzweig, *Der Mensch und sein Werk: Gesammelte Schriften,* vol. 1, *Briefe und Tagebücher,* Band 2, 1918–1929, 827.

hundred years old in Europe")[4] and the infinite meaningfulness of the
I-thou, Rosenzweig proposes three (or four, or perhaps five) intersubjective relationships, each of which is intimately bound to the others and all
of which are opposed to the idealist reductions of what Buber calls the
I-It.

The relations Rosenzweig proposes are: he-it, I-thou (which has two
sub-forms, *I*-thou and I-*thou*), and we-it.[5] I would like to note two peculiarities that have, as far as I know, been overlooked when considering
Rosenzweig's response to the page proofs of *I and Thou*. First, Rosenzweig capitalizes some of the personal pronouns and not others. Second,
he sketches the pairs in a graphic configuration. What Rosenzweig wrote
in his letter to Buber looks as follows:

ER-Es, Ich-Du, Wir-ES

ICH-Du

Ich-DU[6]

Both of these gestures, the capitalized words and the configuration, are
far from accidental or careless, and are in fact interrelated, as I shall show.
To express this positively, they are deliberate and charged with significance, and hence reward a closer consideration.

For Rosenzweig (and for Levinas also) the first person "I" and the
second person "thou" have a special significance not simply because of
the relationality, dialectic, or *gestalt* of the I-thou encounter. Although
both terms are relational, they also have a special significance because of
the way in which the "I" of the I-thou is related to an absolute "he," a
"HE" which for the human "I" is never an "I" or a "thou," and because
of the way in which the "thou" of the I-thou is related to an absolutized

---

4. Three years later, in 1925, in his essay "The New Thinking," Rosenzweig calls the
worldview invoked in Buber's I-It "a prejudice of the past three centuries" (*FR* 195). Also
cited in Horwitz, *Buber's Way to "I and Thou"*, 212.

5. *Three* relations, then, would be: He-it, I-Thou, and We-It. *Four* relations would be:
He-it, *I*-thou, I-*Thou*, and We-It. *Five* relations, finally, would be: He-it, I-Thou, *I*-Thou,
I-*Thou*, and We-It. These possibilities will be explained in the body of this article.

For an account of the "I" and "Thou" treated more literally as the personal pronouns
of a dialogue between G-d and man, and based on relevant passages in the *Star* other than
those which I cite, especially Rosenzweig's appropriation of G-d's "Where art thou?" said
to Adam (Genesis 3:9) and G-d's dialogue with Abraham (Genesis 22:1), see, Stéphane
Mosès, "Franz Rosenzweig: Le Je et le Tu dans l'expérience de la Révélation," *Revue de
l'Institut Catholique de Paris* 28 (October/December 1988): 31–44.

6. *Martin Buber: A Centenary Volume*, 158; also see note 3 above for original manuscript. The *Centenary*, unlike the Horwitz volume, reproduces the configuration of Rosenzweig's sketch, but it makes two unfortunate errors regarding the we-it relation: (1) emphasis
has mistakenly been reversed, capitalizing the "we" rather than the "it"; (2) the "it" is printed
without the final "t." Thus in the *Centenary* the we-it relation appears incorrectly printed
as "WE-I," rather than "We-IT," following the German.

"we," an "IT" which for its part is also never the "I" or the "thou" of the I-thou encounter experienced today. Thus the "I" and the "thou" of the I-thou are not exclusively or even reciprocally relational; they are not exhausted by the relationality of the I-thou, and *as such* they are engaged in the I-thou encounter. Buber has missed all this. The relations of he-it and we-it, though irreducible to the I-thou and essentially exterior to it, transcendent, are equally and nonetheless in crucial relationship to it. In a nutshell, this is Rosenzweig's criticism of Buber.[7]

Unlike Rosenzweig, Levinas did not, of course, have the opportunity to write a letter to Buber commenting on the page proofs of *I and Thou*.[8] He did, however, know both Buber's published text and Rosenzweig's alternative reading of intersubjectivity laid out in *The Star of Redemption* (which Buber apparently also had some knowledge of before the publication of *I and Thou*).[9] He also had the possibility of knowing the criticisms of *I and Thou* Rosenzweig sent to Buber in September 1922.[10] Levinas nowhere criticizes Rosenzweig's criticisms of Buber. Indeed, for that matter, he nowhere even mentions them. His own criticisms of Buber cover different territory than Rosenzweig's, though, as I will show, the territory Rosenzweig did cover could just as well have been Levinas's own. Still, this having been said, Levinas's explicit criticism is slightly less harsh or total than Rosenzweig's.

Levinas agrees that Buber's account of the I-thou is indeed distorted, and that it is distorted because it is too general, thereby claiming to account for more than it actually does account for. But unlike Rosenzweig, Levinas finds a place for a restricted version of the Buberian I-thou: it describes the erotic relation. It describes not intersubjectivity, or genuine intersubjectivity, in toto, or in general, or at bottom, as Buber thinks,

7. In his letter to Buber, Rosenzweig writes, parenthetically, of his relational pronouns: "with you, surely, I can be thus formulaically brief." Horwitz, *Buber's Way to "I and Thou"*, 228. Where Rosenzweig was formulaically brief, I will expand and expound.

8. Levinas did, however, correspond with Buber regarding Levinas's critique of Buber's "I-Thou." See the two letters of 1963 published in the pages following Levinas's 1958 article (sent to Buber in German for response in 1963), "Martin Buber et la theorie de la connaisance," in Emmanuel Levinas, *Noms Propres* (Montpellier: Fata Morgana, 1976), 52–55. For an English translation of Levinas's article and Buber's reply of 1963 (to which Levinas's letter to Buber is a reply), see, "Martin Buber and the Theory of Knowledge," in *The Philosophy of Martin Buber*, edited by Paul Arthur Schilpp and Maurice Friedman (LaSalle, Illinois: Open Court, 1967), 133–50 and 723.

9. I accept Rivka Horwitz's evidence for her claim that "Buber must have had some knowledge of Rosenzweig's *The Star of Redemption*" prior to the publication of *I and Thou*. Horwitz also brings evidence to show that the exact timing of Buber's reading of the *Star* is difficult to sort out. See, Horwitz, *Buber's Way*, 166–67, especially note 19 on page 166.

10. The 1922 correspondence between Buber and Rosenzweig, in the original German, was first published in Grete Schaeder, ed., *Martin Buber: Briefwechsel aus sieben Jahrzehnten* (Heidelberg, 1972–75), 2:112–39.

but the warmth, closeness, and enclosure of two persons within the private world of erotic intimacy, where the intensities of a sensual mutuality and reciprocity between two persons vie with the ethical responsibilities of an irreducible separation and asymmetry. Buber's error, then, would be to have mistaken part for whole. (We will see that what Rosenzweig means by "love" is not equivalent to, or limited to, what Levinas means by the "erotic encounter," and hence Levinas's restriction of the Buberian I-thou does not apply, equally, to Rosenzweig's I-thou of love.) For Levinas— and for Rosenzweig—the key to intersubjectivity is not the mutuality or reciprocity of its terms, but their nonreciprocity, their asymmetry, the *emphases* of the one or the other which make of the face-to-face encounter a "diagonal" and "diachronic" relation rather than a horizontal or synchronic relation.

To better grasp the sense of this last claim, we must leave Buber and return to Rosenzweig's three relationships. But first a methodological statement: I say *Rosenzweig's* three relationships, but I will also mean Levinas's. Rather than first presenting Rosenzweig, followed by Levinas, and then comparing and contrasting them, Levinas will be present throughout my exposition, looking over Rosenzweig's shoulder as it were. To bring Rosenzweig and Levinas together in this way is to suggest neither that Rosenzweig is "Levinasian," as if my presentation were an idiosyncratic or forced reading, an "interpretive violence," as one says today, nor that Levinas is but a epigone of Rosenzweig, as if one would be better advised to dispense with the pupil and get on with the master. It means, rather, that Rosenzweig and Levinas are like father and son, and at the same time both are patriarchs.[11] Each without the other would be the less for the loss.[12] Each illuminates the other.

"I," "Thou," "He," and "We" in Rosenzweig and Levinas

The pattern Rosenzweig sketches in his 1922 letter to Buber is intended to bring to mind, and essentially depends upon, the sequential structures

11. To see just how far Levinas's account of intersubjectivity is Rosenzweigian and not Husserlian, that is to say, to see how far Levinas has strayed from the "rigorous science" approach of a strict descriptive phenomenology, I recommend that the reader compare Levinas with Alfred Schutz. I am thinking particularly of the brilliant pages of phenomenological analysis Schutz wrote in 1932, entitled "The Dimensions of the Social World," translated by Thomas Luckmann, in Alfred Schutz, *Collected Papers,* vol. 2, *Studies in Social Theory,* edited by Arvid Brodersen (The Hague: Martinus Nijhoff, 1964), 20–47.

12. Perhaps another analogy for their relationship, if taken with a rather large grain of salt, is that of Moses and Rabbi Akiva in the celebrated story in which Moses finds himself learning his own Torah sitting in the class of Rabbi Akiva—Rosenzweig playing Moses to Levinas's Akiva. Meaning: it is all in Rosenzweig, but we learn it from Levinas.

which dominate *The Star of Redemption,* published one year earlier. There are three sub-sequences which appear in a larger sequence of three in the *Star:* G-d-world-man, creation-revelation-redemption, and Judaism-Christianity-truth. The three sub-sequences form the three books which make up each of the three main parts of the *Star.* The middle sub-sequence, creation-revelation-redemption, does not merely structure part 2, however, but also structures the whole of the *Star.* This means that the entire part 1, with its sub-sequence of G-d-world-man, must be understood under the heading Creation (which intensifies the account of the Creator G-d in book 1 of part 1); the entire book 2, with its sub-sequence creation-revelation-redemption, must be understood under the heading Revelation (which intensifies the account of revelatory love in book 2 of part 2); and the entire part 3, with its sub-sequence Judaism-Christianity-truth, must be understood under the heading Redemption (which intensifies the account of absolute truth in book 3 of part 3). This is very important, as we shall see, since perhaps what is most original about Rosenzweig's *Star* is precisely (1) the way it grasps G-d, world, and man as givens or "elements," prior to the unity effected by rational or systematic thought; (2) the way it lays out the significance of Judaism, Christianity, and truth in relation to a final redemptive communion; and (3) the manner in which it links creation and redemption through revelation, the latter understood as *love.* It is precisely all this, and more, that Rosenzweig is packing into the interrelations of personal pronouns, the "I," "thou," "he," and "we," and especially the I-thou relation that brings them together, which he has so carefully sketched in his letter to Buber.

The central sub-sequence, creation-revelation-redemption, which is not only a sub-sequence but is also the overarching sequence of the entire *Star,* and hence structures not only the three books of part 2 but the three parts of the *Star* as well, evidently has the greatest impact on the significance Rosenzweig finds for the "he-it" and the "we-it" in relation to the "I-thou" (and thus also for his dissatisfaction with the Buberian account). The first sub-sequence, G-d-world-man, under the sign of creation, is most important to understand the significance of the HE of the HE-It (i.e., of the ER-es). The third sub-sequence, Judaism-Christianity-truth, under the sign of redemption, is most important to understand the significance of IT of the We-IT (i.e, of the Wir-ES).

The *Star* has a triadic architectonic quite unlike, and radically opposed to, the triadic structure of Hegelian thought. As I have indicated, part 2 stands in a special relation to parts 1 and 3, and is the fulcrum upon which the whole volume rests. Even more precisely, book 2 of part 2, on revelation, is the fulcrum of the entire *Star.* Revelation, the center of the *Star,* is a relational term. It brings together G-d and man, and at the same time it brings together man and man. But Rosenzweig does not proceed dialectically. Elements such as G-d and man (and world) must be grasped not only in relational terms, but also, and more deeply, in their own independence. Such an approach is, very broadly, Rosenzweig's way of overcoming the philosophical idealism which inevitably results when ideational synthesis is left to its own more or less sophisticated devices. Hegelian philosophy, in contrast, represents what is no doubt the most sophisticated version of ideational synthesis taken at its word.[13] The prime *elements* of the *Star* are G-d, world, and man, as delineated in part 1. The work of part 1 consists in wrenching these three basic elements out of the ideational contexts within which they are inevitably grasped by the thought Rosenzweig calls "Idealist," by which he means mainstream ontology "from Parmenides to Hegel." Rosenzweig cannot just *posit* these terms to establish their independence, for all positings, all givens for consciousness, succumb to the rejoinder idealism ever and always throws at what it calls "empiricism": naivete, a pretending to discover what the mind has in truth constructed. Rather, Rosenzweig takes these elements as *creations,* in the case of the world and man, and ultimate *creator* in the case of G-d. This explains the neologisms of part 1. Because Rosenzweig uses the suffix "meta" to indicate an elemental independence from the synthesizing logic of rational thought, he uses the term "metaphysics" to refer to a transcendent G-d, "metalogic" to refer to the independence of the (created) world, and "metaethics" to refer to the independence of (created) man.[14] This also explains, though retrospectively, the sense in which all of part 1 is under the sign of divine creation.

It also explains the basically religious language of the *Star.* The prime *relations* of the *Star* are creation, revelation, and redemption. Delineated in part 2, these link together the elements of part 1 *without* undermining their fundamental independence. But at the same time, insofar as the sub-sequence creation-revelation-redemption of part 2 structures the entire *Star,* making of its three main parts a sequence, then revelation is the term that joins together not only creation and redemption, but also the sequence of elements, G-d-world-man, from part 1, and the sequence of redemptive communions, Judaism-Christianity-truth, from part 3. The

13. On Rosenzweig's and Levinas's overcoming of Hegel, see chapter 7 in this volume.

14. See Nathan Rotenstreich, "Rosenzweig's Notion of Metaethics," in *The Philosophy of Franz Rosenzweig,* 69–71. Rotenstreich writes (71): "The notion of *meta* is introduced in order to save the irreducible ontological position and thus the uniqueness of the respective sphere to which it refers (viz., God, world, and man)." Levinas understood that to call the irreducible independence of each element "ontological," without qualification, is once again, and already, to give priority to the world over G-d and man; and to call it a "position" is to give priority to man over G-d and world.

whole of the *Star,* in other words, is brought together by and rests upon revelation. Revelation, the point of utmost intensity where divine and human meet, is for Rosenzweig nothing other than *love,* including the erotic love between a man and a woman. This, the literal center and spiritual heart of the *Star,* is also the I-thou. The full significance of revelation, and hence the full significance of the I-thou, in contrast to Buber's "crippled" version, can thus only come into view at the end of the *Star,* when all the pieces of Rosenzweig's vision are in place, when all that revelation calls forth and calls for has been brought into view.[15] Thus it is in book 3 of part 3, on truth, that Rosenzweig is able to write the following synoptic statement, regarding revelation:

Only in the immediate vicinity of the heart and center of the all, of the revelation of divine love, is the Creator and Redeemer too manifested to us, to the extent that such manifestation is vouchsafed at all. Revelation teaches us to trust in the Creator, to wait hopefully for the Redeemer. Thus it allows us to recognize Creator and Redeemer too only as him who loves. (*SR* 382)

I have invoked the architectonic of the *Star* because of its relevance vis-à-vis the pattern of personal pronouns Rosenzweig sketches in his 1922 letter to Buber. The whole critical force of that pattern lies in its invocation of the complicated and interrelated significations of the configurations which structures Rosenzweig's just published *The Star of Redemption.* That is to say, specifically, the order of the top row, the sequence of "HE-It, I-thou, We-IT," relates to the overarching sequence of the *Star,* creation-revelation-redemption. This global sequence is at play in the significance of interhuman encounter. Clearly, Rosenzweig links the meaning of the first and second person singular, of the I-thou, to the third person singular and the first person plural. But further, Rosenzweig makes the following correlations: the "HE-It" with creation, hence with G-d; the "I-thou" of human encounter with divine revelation and love; and the "We-IT" with global redemption through both Judaism and Christianity—as all these implied terms are articulated and related in the *Star.* Thus in his "formulaically brief" sketch of interpersonal relations, Rosenzweig is correcting Buber's conception of the I-thou in *I and Thou* with the entire "new thinking" of the *Star.*

15. Although Rosenzweig calls his book *The Star of Redemption,* emphasizing its highest reach, *redemption,* it is for reasons of centrality, as I have been discussing, that permit Stéphane Mosès to emphasize *revelation* in the title of *System and Revelation,* his own book on the *Star.* It is for the same reason, too, that Paul Ricoeur risked a "backwards reading" of the *Star* moving from redemption to revelation to creation, in his talk entitled "Reading Rosenzweig: The 'Figure' in the *Star of Redemption,*" given at the Rosenzweig symposium held at the National Library of Paris, October 5, 1987.

I have reserved articulating Rosenzweig's temporal interpretation of the sequences in the *Star,* and hence the temporal significance of the I-thou encounter, until this point. The importance of time in Rosenzweig's (and—I will say it for emphasis—in Levinas's) conception of the I-thou can hardly be overestimated. Time is one of the fundamental structures of the interhuman encounter, a way as profound as those above, and integral to them, to grasp the significance and necessity of the relation of the "he" and "we" to the "I-thou." Very simply: G-d's creation has occurred in the past; the world's redemption will occur in the future; divine-human revelation occurs in the present. Or, to reverse these predications, the fundamental sense of "past" is G-d's creation, of "future" is the world's redemption, and of "present" is divine-human revelation or love.

For Rosenzweig and Levinas the I-thou is precisely the presence of revelation for man, and it takes on all the acuity of a *divine and human love* precisely because, as part of a unidirectional sequence, it is open to and broken by both the irrecuperable past of G-d's creation, the G-d who is the "HE" of Rosenzweig's "HE-It," and the unattained (and unknown) future of the world's redemption, the "IT," of Rosenzweig's "We-IT." In this compact claim we find expressed the whole "dialogical" philosophy of Rosenzweig and Levinas. What follows will be clarification and, in one importance instance, qualification.

The correlations expressed are no doubt intellectually exciting and suggestive. As philosophers, however, as seekers of wisdom, we must know the reasons why Rosenzweig characterizes intersubjectivity in terms of just these correlations. Why, in contrast to Buber's simple opposition between I-thou and I-It, must the I-thou be understood in terms of a he-it and a we-it? Why, furthermore, must the I-thou be understood in terms of *I*-thou and I-THOU (ICH-Du and Ich-DU)? Why, in addition, are these three human relations, these personal pronouns and pronouncements, correlated to the obviously religious sequence of creation-revelation-redemption? More generally still, what need has philosophy for religion, for a relation to G-d and a belief in His providential goodness?

Contra Parmenidean Philosophy

To answer these several questions we must first recall precisely what Rosenzweig is striving to overcome. On this point Rosenzweig is quite clear. His philosophical opponent is idealism. By "idealism" he does not only mean modern German philosophy from Kant to Hegel, or even the whole of modern European philosophy from Descartes to Hegel (the objectifying thinking of Buber's I-it, which is "less than three hundred years old"), but rather the entire history of philosophy, philosophy "from Parmenides to Hegel."

Parmenidean philosophy is driven by the quest for an absolute which is consonant with reason. It is reason seeking an immanent or self-grounding absolute. From the start reason knows being to be one, and as such absolute, sufficient unto itself, but its problematic through the history of philosophy, "from Ionia to Jena," is to reason its way through the "apparent" multiplicity of beings to demonstrate that beings and being form an unbreakable whole, a totality.[16] Philosophy, then, is the struggle to understand appearances in terms of reality, diversity in terms of unity, changes in terms of permanence, temporality in terms of eternity, opinions in terms of reason. Rosenzweig periodicizes the history of this quest, which is the history of philosophy, as the successive working out of three select absolutes, which are each taken in turn and by necessity as the one and only absolute: the world (or being) in the ancient period; G-d in the medieval period; and man in the modern period. In each period an immanent principle—world, G-d, or man—is taken to be the one self-starting and self-standing ground and unity of all.

The modern period of Parmenidean philosophy initiated by Descartes (Buber's I-it), is constituted by the recognition that the thinker is also an integral part of the all. Therefore, for being to be an immanent absolute, self-starting and self-grounding, as it must be for reason, the being of thinking, understood in the modern period as objectifying representation, cannot be excluded from the thinking of being. It is in this sense that the modern period of philosophy is essentially "subjectivist." For modern thought the true subject, i.e., the *thinking* ego, the *cogito,* is understood to be not my "I" or your "I," the "I" that I speak as the particular individual that I am, or the "thou" whom I address or who addresses me as the particular individual I find in front of me, but rather a third term, *that* from out of which all differences are generated, including the "I" and "thou." In this fashion being itself becomes a sort of super- or supra-ego. As a self-generating origin that thinks, the absolute resembles nothing so much as the human rational faculty writ large, or what has been variously called: "cogito," "transcendental ego," and "absolute ego," or, by shifting from an interpretation of thinking based in reason to one based on will (or on an admixture of reason and will), it has been called "Geist," "world will," and "will to power." Particular egos, subjectivities, including others,

16. It is interesting to note that the protagonist of Parmenides' theogony only enters the realm of the Truth Goddess after having passed *though* "the gates of day and night," leaving mundane oppositions such as day and night behind. Jews, on the other hand, every morning in their prayers thank G-d especially for "giving the heart understanding to distinguish between day and night."

are only *relative* origins, more or less superficial manifestations of the origin of all origins, the all-inclusive absolute. Human subjects are no more than "thous" to an absolute "I," which in reality talks to itself through us, and only speaks truly when it speaks rationally, or world historically, or willfully (depending on how one characterizes the absolute supra-subject). Years after the publication of Rosenzweig's *Star*, Heidegger too, attempting to reverse Nietzsche's willful reversal of Schopenhauer's pessimism, still conceives of authentic Dasein as a "letting be" or "releasement" *(Gelassenheit)* through which world historical be-ing thinks itself. It is because the absolute is conceived as a self-generating origin that the reasoned quest for such an absolute—rational philosophy "from Parmenides to Hegel"—finally concludes in the idealism of the absolute subject, the idealism for which, to take up Hegel's famous formula, "subject [the relative "I," *my* I] is substance and substance [the absolute "I," world spirit] is subject."

Such is Rosenzweig's formidable philosophical opponent. There is only one way to radically challenge this opponent. One must show once and for all that the absolute is not and can not be absolute. One must show that the entire project of determining the one as all and the all as one is not only unending, for then it might well be continued as an "infinite task" with an indefinitely deferred conclusion,[17] but that *here and now* the philosophically conceived one is not one. It must be shown, duly noting the priority of thinking in the modern period, that: (1) thought and being are not the same, or if they are the same that they are not the all; and (2) that which escapes or exceeds thought (or thought-and-being) is not merely a residue of thought, thought's residue, as if thought called all the shots; thought (and being) must be exceeded, and the exceeding of thought must not be yet another thought (or being).[18] Thought's other must be genuinely other than thought, having its own meaning and dignity, its own significance, independent of thought. To capture this independence, Levinas will say of such an alterity that it is "otherwise than being or beyond essence." Of course, by its own lights thought is not inclined to endorse such independence, nor can thought be expected to ever endorse it. Thought "by nature" or "in principle" or "in itself" or "by essence" is inclined to think only itself, which is to say that it thinks otherness in terms of itself. It declares its other "pre-philosophical," or "content," or "dialectical partner," or when especially frustrated, thought will excommunicate its other as "irrational," "mad," "weak," or "sick."

17. Deferral can be serious (Husserl) or playful (Derrida).

18. Levinas writes of obviating the seemingly inescapable hegemony of Aristotle's dictum that "not to philosophize is still to philosophize." See, Emmanuel Levinas, "God and Philosophy," in *CPP* 153.

Given the logic of its natural disinclination, thought must not merely be convinced of its own insufficiency, per impossible, but must be positively undermined. Thought must be diverted or disrupted from its natural unfolding "in the name" of the *otherwise* than thought. The movement of elevation, thought in religico-ethical terms, is precisely such an irrecuperable disruption for thought.

Thus, it is to effect a positive disruption of the Parmenidean equation of thought and being that Rosenzweig introduces the language of religion into the discourse of philosophy. It is for this reason, too, that he insists, against Buber, yet remaining on the plane of contemporary thought, on the most concrete of living relations, intersubjectivity, and on the separation of intersubjectivity into its three irreducible yet interrelated dimensions of "he-it," "I-thou," and "we-it." Where reason would unify, revelation can bring together while holding apart. Not reason but revelation joins these three dimensions together without reducing one to the other. The "event" of this separation and conjunction—elevation—is impossible and invisible to philosophy, which knows only analysis and synthesis and the relative heights of thought, yet is nevertheless always presupposed by it.

The text of *The Star of Redemption,* nonetheless, does not begin with the "I-thou" encounter. It begins with philosophy and death. Death, and hence life, is the excluded other of philosophy. The "fear of death," which is the flesh-and-blood human being's response to the inescapability and presence of death as an unknowable and unwanted eventuality, is a powerful instance of "something" escaping thought and thereby undermining the wholeness constitutive of Parmenidean philosophy. Think however grandiose a philosophical system one will, death refuses to become wholly a concept. But Rosenzweig does not stop here. Were it only the individual's fear of death that exceeded philosophical comprehension, then Rosenzweig's voice, no matter how eloquent, would be but one more lonely howl in the cacophonous night chorus of existentialist despair. Rosenzweig's *Star,* however, unlike Heidegger's *Being and Time,* published six years later, only starts with death. Death serves only to crack the facade, as it were, of idealism. Death gets a foot in the door to life, but does not enter the palace. Death is subjective enough to undermine philosophy's pretensions, but too subjective to move beyond, or above, in the confidence of a higher truth.

Rosenzweig's thought starts with death but is centered on love, on being loved and on loving, on the pacific, specific, and caring relation between two flesh-and-blood persons. Only here can we find the "grammar" of Rosenzweig's "new thinking," the I, thou, he, and we, whose concreteness, immediacy, and orientation undermine and surpass philosophy's traditional resources and resourcefulness. The concrete encounter and exchanges of the I-thou, and not the relation of one reason to another, or the individual's fear of death, forms the heart of Rosenzweig's positive thought, the pragmatics of *das neue Denken*. This encounter undermines and surpasses idealism precisely because of the way in which its terms and their relation resist unity and unification. The "I" and the "thou" of the I-thou are neither centered in themselves *nor* in one another, and yet, or as such, they are in the most profound relation to one another. Such a relation, each time unique—"an 'unrelating relation' which no one can encompass or thematize," Levinas writes *(TI 295)*—exceeding philosophy, is the most concrete and direct of all events: the face-to-face encounter.

Rosenzweig insists on the language of religion because it provides him the force of resistance, the corrosive effect, as it were, to undermine the unity of Parmenidean philosophy. And, to put the matter positively, at the same time it provides him the affirmative language of hope, faith, and community, the affirmative language of compassion, morality, and justice, which surpasses Parmenidean philosophy and better accounts for what is truly at stake in face-to-face encounters and the true basis of signification. What is truly at stake in the face-to-face encounter is not just a set of truths, but obligations and responsibilities. This is why what is true "truly"—"dare at every moment to say truly to the truth" *(Wahrheit Wahrlich zu sagen)*, writes Rosenzweig *(SR 395)*, the "saying of the said," to invoke Levinas's expression, is higher than the truths *contained* in true propositions. What is at stake and what lies at the base of significance is an excess Rosenzweig calls "love," at once divine and human, hence also "revelation."

I-thou and Revelation

In contrast to a philosophy whose center is the self-grounding Greek "know-thyself," Rosenzweig's thought is oriented by what does not have its own center: the person who is loved and who loves in turn. Not surprisingly, this is precisely what one finds at the center of the *Star,* in book 2 of part 2: revelation as love, love as revelation. The *Star* is centered on the de-centered "I" and the de-centered "thou" of the I-thou, since Rosenzweig understands revelatory love—the meeting of divine and human—to be that which joins and separates the "I" and the "thou" of the I-thou. Revelation, love, the I-thou, join together what at the same time remains separate, linking terms which are and can be understood variously as two lives, creation and redemption, or the absolute HE and the absolute IT.

The "unity" of the I-thou meaning complex, which is at once being loved and loving, revelation and presence, is effected not by means of an immanent principle, but rather in the "presence" (Rosenzweig) or "proximity" (Levinas) of a bimodal intensity, an intensity not tensed with itself, like an anxiety, but intensified by inordinate obligations and responsibilities which come from within and outside, but in both cases from beyond. Revelation, for Rosenzweig and Levinas, is neither a mediation nor a meditation, but the claim of alterity.

To grasp the separation/connection which makes up the intensity of the I-thou, to grasp how a relation can link what remains irreducibly separate, we must appreciate the relation of the HE-it to the *I* of the *I*-Thou, and of the We-IT to the THOU of the I-THOU. Appreciating this twofold relation is precisely revelation, is precisely what is revealed in revelation. What this means is that the I-thou relation cannot be determined from a safe vantage point, however elevated, as if it were a spectacle. The "I" of the I-thou is always an "I" in the first person singular, my "I," me. The "thou" of the I-thou is always "thou" in the second person singular. Nothing is more invisible from the outside; it is more invisible than what one cannot see, even than what one cannot see in principle, the horizon of vision. It is invisible to outsiders precisely in the way the intimate bonds of marriage are invisible to outsiders. One only appreciates or "sees" the I-thou from within the I-thou, as an "I" saying "thou," from within the zone of its claim, with the breathless voice of its responses, for personal pronouns are without force if they are not pronounced (though they need not be actually enunciated, a look or glance will do). From within one is torn by the more or less fierce blasts of divergent zones of intensity, torn by unassimilable relations to the he-it and the we-it, irretrievable relations to creation and redemption, superlative relations to G-d and world. The proper "perspective," then, is a punctured one, a personal one, not subjective in a pejorative willful sense, but in a selfhood beset by prior and posterior alterities. Rosenzweig repeatedly reminds his readers that the "seeing" he demands is "beyond the book," a saying of the truth *truly,* in the meeting of transcendence and immanence which is neither one nor the other but a continually uplifting approach to both. The I-thou as such *is* revelation.

This exposition, then, only clarifies, or makes sense, if it not only points to revelation but at the same time invokes and appeals to revelation, to an "I" saying and a "thou" saying. It does not articulate, however, as it would regarding Buber, a special experience, whether "the *mysterium tremendum* that appears and overwhelms" or "the mystery of the obvious,"[19] always extraordinary and intermittent. Rather, everyday encounters and the ongoing life which they constitute are, for Rosenzweig and

19. Buber, *I and Thou,* 127.

Levinas, exalted and special, revelatory. One "verifies" this thought in life and not in thought alone.

I-Thou and HE-it

For humans, love begins not with loving but with being loved. This is perhaps the most crucial insight of all of Rosenzweig's "new thinking," the basis upon which everything else lies. Revelation is not love, but that one is loved. To start with being loved is to begin *before* man's *origin*. The *beginning* precedes the *origin*. Levinas calls this structure the "anterior posteriorly" (*TI* 170). Because of it, part 1 of the *Star*, on creation, remains a lifeless abstraction, an intellectualization, *until* part 2, where one discovers that creation has all along been real, has "always already been." The impact of the transcendence of creation, in other words, is fully felt in revelation. One discovers this—this is revealed—in recognizing the precedence of being loved. One might think here of the famous "first cause" argument for G-d's existence, but transformed and transposed onto the register of love, of personal rather than causal relations. Love is hence always miraculous, received before given, and hence divine.[20] The very structure of the *Star* mimics man's lack of mastery in love. For Levinas, this means that all of human *eros,* regardless of biological sex traits, falls under the sign of the feminine. The loss of *origin* is the constitutive moment, the positivity of love: one must first be loved before one can love in turn. Here again *sequence* is not an accident of time to be overcome by thought, like a ladder or raft discarded after use.

To love, one is always too late, always already having been loved. All the risk and acuity of love comes from what seems to be the very opposite from risk: one loves only when one has been loved. The sense of this can be glimpsed when we realize that for all its apparent romance, love unrequited is beyond human capacity, is G-d's privilege alone. For humans, love unrequited is finally not love at all but soliloquy, poetry, display, melancholy, and finally, in the extreme, suicide.[21] Love requited, on

20. Though I am limiting myself to Rosenzweig's letter to Buber and to an explanation of it based on the *Star,* the importance of the antecedence of being-loved before loving, i.e., the priority of G-d's love for man, is given great emphasis in Rosenzweig's commentary to his translation of Judah Halevi's poem entitled "With You" *(Bei Dir)*. See, Franz Rosenzweig, *Der Mensch und Sein Werk: Gesammelte Schriften,* vol. 4, Band 1, *Sprachdenken— Jehuda Halevi (Jehuda Halevi: Funfundneunzig Hymnen und Gedichte)* (The Hague: Martinus Nijhoff, 1983), 96. In the same commentary, Rosenzweig also gives credit to Rabbi Nehemiah Nobel, "my unforgettable teacher of Torah," for having spoken on this topic in a sermon given on Nobel's "fiftieth, and last birthday."

21. Is this not the theme of Goethe's *The Sufferings of Young Werther* and precisely Werther's youth?

the other hand, love as human's know it, is too late, and thus always a return *(teshuva)* to the lover, and only as such is it true love. The greatest risk and all the acuity of love is in the infinitesimal moment which separates the declaration (origin) of love from the confirmation (beginning) of love. Because there is no human way to guarantee a bridging of this gap, reaching back to what has already been given, the beginning of love precedes the beloved absolutely. That the beginning of love can never be recuperated is what makes love possible for man.

Such a *beginning* which precedes the origin is what Rosenzweig calls *G-d's* creation. It is not, as Nietzsche thought, a human creation, since human creations are always relative, and hence revert back to positings, origins, recuperations. Humans are themselves *created* beings. Levinas, too, will call the human "created." In the terminology of the personal pronouns we are examining, the created human is the It of G-d's HE-It. It is important to acknowledge, for this is the ultimate "sense" of being created, that the relation between the HE and the It, the HE-It, is, *from the point of view of the HE,* absolutely beyond human comprehension and experience (though it has often been made the subject matter of "negative theology"). However, humans do "know" G-d—in love. They experience G-d essentially in the mode of the irretrievably "too late," in the ever-renewed astonishment at their own ungrounded but real ability to love, based on the "miracle" of having been loved. One loves even though the very capacity to love exceeds one's capacities! In contrast to such true love, whatever *humans* create by themselves (which in the modern period includes everything) can be traced back, as I have indicated, to man himself, to his own origin, to "his own"[22] quite simply. To speak of "true love" beyond self-love, as do Rosenzweig and Levinas, is to risk the scorn of both philosopher and sophist alike.

Only G-d, the creator G-d, can have made humans in such a way that they can love, can receive what is given absolutely. Any other *relative* source of love, that is to say, any source other than a pre-original or transcendent G-d, would eventually become, as Hegel has shown, absorbed by the subject, become a form of self-love, Greek eros, immanence, substance-subject. Only a personal G-d, an absolute HE—who *creates* what for Himself is an "It" but what for man is the "*I,*" which Rosenzweig in the *Star* calls the "emphatic I," the "I, however" (*SR* 174–75), the

---

22. The pure "ownness" of whatever is taken to be a human creation is precisely the point that Max Stirner, in *The Ego and his Own,* insists upon ad nauseam. This book is necessarily Stirner's one and only book. Unlike Nietzsche, Stirner did not dream the impossible dream of creating a nonhuman creative source (the "overman"). Stirner, of course, as an early visionary of modernity, sees nothing but human creation, hence nothing but "ownness."

beloved self who is eternally separated from the source of its love—can produce a creature that can love in turn.

Hence the "I" of the *I*-thou is the "I" created by G-d, the it of G-d's HE. G-d's HE remains always in the third person, an absolute HE, meaning that for humans G-d can never be "I."[23] A person can never stand in G-d's place. One's "I" is created. Before one can say "I" in the "I-thou"—an "I" that encounters the other without reducing the other to the same, or without the other reducing the "I" to the same, to use Levinas's terms—one must first be the it of the HE-it. One must first be G-d's creation. Lacking this inexhaustible *beginning* prior to any *origin*, subjectivity turns into a tyranny, whether it is totalized or totalizes, whether in the usurped or substitute name of G-d, or in the blindness of an all too human vanity, crude or sublime.

Levinas recognizes this passivity or emphasis, this *it* of the "I" of the *I*-Thou, in the biblical term *hineni*,[24] "Here I am," which expresses the vulnerability, irreplaceability, and inexhaustibility of the self in the face of the other. The I of the "*I*-Thou," the it of the HE-it, is for Levinas a "passivity more passive than any receptivity," permitting an unsurpassable readiness and availability in the face of the other. That the self is created guarantees the inviolability of the subject without at the same time underwriting its tyranny. It is the irreducible and irrecuperable condition for the "I" to do and to suffer *for* the other and not for oneself alone. The irrecuperability of this element of selfhood comes from its relation to the absolute antecedence of the other qua "he," third person singular, in the "thou" one addresses.

On the sense of third person singularity, the "he" that precedes the "I" of the I-thou and makes the *I*-Thou possible, and necessitates a reference to G-d, Levinas writes:

He preceded all presence and exceeded every contemporaneity in a time which is not a human duration, nor a falsified projection, nor an extrapolation of duration, is not a disintegration and disappearance of finite beings, but the original antecedence of God relative to a world which cannot accommodate him, the immemorial past which has never presented itself . . . beyond being. (*CPP* 73)

The "I" that willfully refuses to stand in relation to the "he" beyond the "thou," in contrast, an "I" attempting to stand solely upon its own more

---

23. Commenting on Judah Halevi's poem "Homecoming" *(Heimkehr)*, Rosenzweig writes: "In his [man's] mouth the divine 'I' that stands behind everything God says must be transposed into an acknowledgement of the 'He'." Franz Rosenzweig, *Der Mensch und Sein Werk: Gesammelte Schriften*, vol. 4, 51. Translation by Eva Jospe. (This translation is superior to the one found in *FR* 288).

24. On the "here I am," see also *SR* 396.

or less hidden origin, precisely the philosophical "I," whether interpreted as substance (Cartesian cogito) or as history (Nietzsche's "I am all names in history"), or as some combination of substance and history (Hegel's "world spirit"), would be, for all its heady courage, tyrannical, shameless, and alone.

It is likely that Rosenzweig's "argument" for creation is a variant of the traditional transcendental argument. He reads the divine HE back from the otherwise inexplicable capacity of the actual living "I" to love a "thou." Or has Rosenzweig perhaps discovered the divine HE in a personal and direct mystical "I-G-d" experience?[25] In the absence of any evidence for the latter, I am inclined toward the former "transcendental" interpretation, which does not, in any event, exclude the more direct route. Levinas, for his part, "deduces" the third person singular, which he calls "illeity,"[26] from the face-to-face encounter. Like Rosenzweig's HE, this "he" precedes, as we have seen in the above citation, the face-to-face encounter it conditions. "A you," Levinas writes, "is inserted between the I and the absolute He" (*CPP* 159).

I-THOU and We-IT

But G-d does not create the "I" solely to have the "I" acknowledge an infinite debt, praising and adoring the creator G-d in gratitude, honoring its parent. Though such praise, adoration, and gratitude are no doubt fine, as far as they go, the "worship" of G-d will have another more demanding and adult route. To begin with being loved is not only to begin before the origin, "anterior posteriorly," it is also, and for the same reason, to begin before the ending. The term of G-d's love, the beloved, man as the concrete particular who is too late, is not the end or final goal of love. For each individual and in each instance love is miraculous, to be sure, but G-d also loves all that is, His entire creation. G-d's *it* is not only the "I" but also the "thou" of the "I-thou," which is to say that it is all humanity and the whole world, right up to their desired perfection.

In being loved man is called upon to live up to G-d's love, to complete G-d's creation, to emulate G-d by loving otherness in turn. This means, concretely, that the I must love the neighbor ("thou") and redeem the

---

25. Was it the experience during World War I referred to in his letter to Buber of August 22, 1922? Rosenzweig writes: "I found it while stumbling at night over a horrible prickly plant on the way from the front to Prilep in Macedonia; then I knew 'everything'. It was the moment of conception for my book (not yet as book); I knew the relationship between creation and revelation." In Horwitz, *Buber's Way to "I and Thou"*, 225.

26. "The detachment of the Infinite from the thought that seeks to thematize it and the language that tries to hold it in the said is what we have called *illeity*" (*OBBE* 147).

world ("we"). Rosenzweig and Levinas are in complete agreement (along with Buber and much of Jewish tradition) that the proper way for man to return G-d's love is not simply or solely by loving G-d directly and exclusively in return, but to love *as* G-d loves and what G-d loves, i.e., man's fellow creatures, who are also G-d's creations (created in the "image" and "likeness" of G-d). Only he who begins before his origin, as a beloved being, and hence only he who knows of the love that sustains the "I" of the I-thou, can and *should* love the "thou," the other, and ultimately all others, in turn.

To love in turn is the very commandment of G-d's love. G-d's central command, for Rosenzweig, is to love: "I" (G-d) love you, so you (the "It" of "HE," G-d's creation) as a human "*I*" (man) in your own right (the "*I*" of the "*I*-thou") are thereby ordered to love your neighbor (the "THOU" of the "I-THOU). This is why Levinas speaks of the subject of intersubjectivity as at once "ordained" and "ordered." Such is a person's, and a people's, *election*. One is elected to be for-the-other before oneself. This is the meaning of being chosen by G-d: chosen through love for loving service to humanity.

G-d does not command the "I" to love all mankind at once, as if G-d's command were a universal principle, an abstract law. Nor does He command that the subject's love end with this or that proximate and special neighbor, husband, wife, offspring, or parent, as if G-d's vision were limited or He played favorites. Between these two kinds of love, one particular and too narrow, the other abstract and too diluted, G-d's command to love commands that the "I" love the neighbor as such, what Rosenzweig calls "the nearest one." If everyone were to love the nearest one, then love would be concrete and universal at once, and the world would be redeemed. Then and only then would saying "thou" and saying "we" be equivalent. This is the "IT," the final truth and divine height, the perfection, toward which every I-Thou is moving. Precisely this, to say it again, is redemption, of which Rosenzweig writes:

For the world of redemption, absolute factuality derives from the fact that whoever be momentarily my neighbor represents all the world for me in full validity. . . . Now they unite in the mighty unison of a "we." This "we" always means "all of us," or at any rate "all those of us assembled here." . . . It can only be narrowed down, not expanded, whereas the singularity of the I and its companion, the Thou, can only be expanded. (*SR* 236)

When "we" means " 'you' and everyone else" at once, then the world will be redeemed, and all reality will have been transformed into G-d's IT. Nonetheless, *our* everyday world, here and now, today, does not yet bear this universal love, is not yet, to use Rosenzweig's language, an "absolutely factual" world. *Our* world, the world we live in here and now, today, is as yet unredeemed.

The "We-IT" which Rosenzweig associates with the call to redemption is the ultimate height toward which the height of the other person encountered socially drives. It is the very exigency of moral demand, the call to rise above a reality which is as yet lower than G-d; it is G-d's "be holy *because* I am holy." Just as my "I" is not the origin of itself but stands (qua it) in an irrecuperably prior relation to a transcendent HE, the "thou," without being a means, is not an end in itself but drives toward a divine perfection unachieved as yet here on earth. In putting the other first, the other-before-the-self, the "I" takes a step in the right direction, a step toward a universal "we," the "we" of a completely redeemed world, a world of complete love and justice. Step by step, neighbor by neighbor, the world is redeemed. It is when every "I" of every *I*-thou is oriented toward each and every other's welfare, when every "thou" is faced as an "I-THOU," upholding a face-to-face ethics in a world of historically institutionalized justice exclusive of no one, that the "I" and the "thou" will at the same time be a "we."

Before concluding a discussion of the "We-IT," we must be careful not to carry our reading of Rosenzweig's letter too far, or to join Levinas and Rosenzweig where they part company. Just as the I-thou has two emphases, *I*-Thou (the "I" as a created being, the it of HE-it), and I-THOU (the "thou" as appeal to final redemption, aiming at the IT of We-IT), for Rosenzweig there are two different emphases regarding the unredeemed "we" which moves toward absolute redemption. One constitutes the Jewish community, Israel, and the other constitutes the Christian community, Christendom. In this, Rosenzweig diverges from Levinas (or, to speak chronologically, Levinas diverges from Rosenzweig), for whom the appeal to universal goodness and justice never hinges (or never seems to hinge) on a distinction between Jew and Christian and everyone else.

It is well known that the *Star* provides a redemptive role in the sacred scheme of things for the Jewish and Christian communities, to the exclusion of all other religions and communities. In contrast, even an ecumenicism limited to Christianity, such as Rosenzweig's, is rarely found in the authoritative texts of the Jewish religious tradition, not at all because salvation is alleged to be found only within Judaism, but quite the reverse, because Judaism has never excluded righteous non-Jews, of whatever persuasion, from finding complete salvation outside of Judaism. On this point, then, in finding a sacred role for Christianity specifically and exclusively, Rosenzweig is a Jewish exception. Rosenzweig defines the Jews as the community of eternity now, the community which through its rites and holiday calendar lives eternity within time. As such, Israel provides a model of eternity for the world at large to emulate, serving as a "light unto the nations." In Rosenzweig's imagery: the Jews and Judaism are the "fire"; Christians and Christianity are the "rays." Whereas Jews are born Jewish, Christians are born pagan, and hence have become and must continue to become Christian (*SR* 407). Hybrid, Christians are thus only partially "eternalized." They rise to G-d's eternity by "Christianizing" pagan being, in themselves and in others. What this means, for Rosenzweig, is that the fundamental and necessary role of Christianity in the sacred scheme of things is to missionize, to spread the eternal truth, to convert whoever and whatever is pagan into eternal being. What follows from this division is that until final redemption is achieved, at which time, as we have seen, every "thou" will also be a "we," there must be two separate and different communities of the "we": the community of "we" Jews, Israel, eternal today and a model for all humanity, and the community of "we" Christians, ever spreading Christendom, eternal tomorrow and a mission today.

In the first chapter of this volume, entitled "Jewish Election in the Thought of Franz Rosenzweig," I have shown various ways in which one can understand Rosenzweig's conception of the relation of the Jewish community to the Christian community (and vice versa). Here my concern is with the "we," and its relation to the I-thou. It is important to see that part 3 of the *Star*, on Judaism-Christianity-truth, develops out of book 2, centered on revelation, the I-thou which is at once divine and human. What is it, let us ask, about Rosenzweig's conception of the I-thou, which is the very fulcrum of the *Star*, that permits him to differentiate two different forms of "we," one Jewish and the other Christian, providing divine sustenance, as it were, to the redemptive aspect of the I-THOU?

The answer lies in the two sides or types of love: being loved and loving in turn. The "I" must first be loved in order to love in turn. This is Rosenzweig's great insight, the hinge upon which all else rests. It explains, as we have seen, his religious language, the language of creation and revelation. To be loved first is to be a *created* being. To experience love is *revelation*. To love in turn, based on the revelatory wisdom of being loved, is to enter into the *redemptive* project, to aim for a universal "we." In part 3 of the *Star*, then, Rosenzweig distinguishes Judaism (book 1) and Christianity (book 2) on the basis of the two sides or types of love elaborated in part 2. Judaism is the community of being loved, the beloved of G-d, preserving and nurturing G-d's love, the "fire." The Jew is the it of G-d's HE-it. Judaism is oriented toward the past, by G-d's love given at Sinai once and for all. The type of the Jew is the old, hoary bearded, learned Jew.[27] Christianity, in contrast, and as a complement to Judaism, is the community of loving in turn, the "rays," spreading G-d's love to all of mankind, missionizing the world through the power of loving. Hence Christianity is oriented toward the future, toward G-d's second coming, toward the messianic end of time which is yet to come.

Just as there are two sides to love there are two types of community. The "we" of the Jewish community here and now is an eternal "we," but it is not yet universal. The Christian "we" of today, unredeemed, striving, spreading, growing, missioning, strives to make the eternal "we" at one and the same time a universal "we." Then and only then will the sacred roles of the Jewish community and the Christian community have been fulfilled. Then and only then will the eternal and universal "we" of all humankind be neither Jewish nor Christian, not truly or partially true but absolute *truth* (book 3 of part 3), the "IT" of the divine "We-IT."

Conclusion

The "I" of the I-thou is "in the middle," between the HE-it of G-d's creation, the absolute past, and the We-IT of the world's final redemption, the absolute future. The pre-original and the post-original meet in the I-thou, in love, without losing their transcendence. "I" remains "I," and "thou" remains "thou," but "we" meet as G-d's beloved creatures charged with eternity (as life or mission). The "I" and the "thou" of the I-thou are also and both "in the middle," between the HE of G-d's pure love and the IT of the world's perfection, between two eternities. "To live in time," Rosenzweig writes, "means to live between beginning and end" (*SR* 420).

27. See *SR* 408: "The type of the aged Jew is as characteristic for us as the youthful type is for the Christian nations."

PART TWO

LEVINAS

FIVE

Emmanuel Levinas:
Philosopher and Jew

Emmanuel Levinas was born on January 12, 1906, in Kovno, Lithuania, where his father owned a small bookshop and stationery store. Kovno was the district center, with a population of about one hundred thousand people, more than a quarter of them Jews. Though second to Vilna in fame for its Torah scholarship, in Kovno traditional self-absorbed yeshiva-oriented Lithuanian Judaism flourished. Here also Jews met with modern European influences. The Levinas home, the life, and finally the ethical philosophy of Emmanuel Levinas are a manifestation of this fateful encounter of Judaism and modern Europe. Two examples from his childhood reveal this combination of old and new. From the age of six Levinas was tutored in Hebrew, but his tutor used Hebrew-language textbooks rather than the traditional Jewish sources. When he was able, Levinas read the Bible in Hebrew, but his text was not a *Mikraot Gedolot,* an "expanded Scripture" containing the authoritative rabbinical commentaries which he later came to see as essential.

In May 1915 the Jews of the Kovno district were expelled by order of the Russian government. By 1916 Levinas's family had settled in Karkhov in the Ukraine. At age eleven, Emmanuel was admitted—with great family celebration, as one of the five Jewish children permitted, by competitive examination, to enter—to the public high school in Karkhov. By now Levinas was reading the great Russian authors, Pushkin, Lermontov, Gogol, Turgeniev, Dostoyevsky, and Tolstoy, in Russian. They provided the first stimulation for his philosophical thinking.

His first year in high school coincided with the final months of the czarist regime and the first months of the Russian Revolution. In the disruptions of the Russian Civil War, Ukrainian anti-Semitism broke out in all its unspeakable horror. In 1919–20 alone, more than one hundred thousand Jews were murdered under the "socialist" government of S. Petlyura. Levinas's family survived, but as Jews and petite bourgeois they suffered harassment that made them decide to leave the Ukraine at the earliest possible opportunity, which came in July 1920, when they returned to Kovno. In comparison with the Ukrainian interlude, Levinas remembers his days in the Kovno Jewish community as ones of "happiness and harmony."

The Judaism of Levinas's childhood was not a religion or an ideology or a system of beliefs; it was a way of life, a manner of living and thinking that permeated every aspect of a Jew's life, like the very air one breathes. Seventy years later, trying to describe this Judaism of his boyhood days in Kovno, Levinas said: "The spiritual essence—and this remains a quite 'Lithuanian Judaism'—rested for me not in mystical modes but in a tremendous curiosity for books."[1]

Levinas's second stay in Lithuania lasted only three years. In 1923, at the age of seventeen, he set out with his family's blessings for France to obtain a university education. At that time for Jews everywhere France was the land of Captain Alfred Dreyfus. True, it was France—its ruling elite, its military, the church—that had conspired to make of Dreyfus a scapegoat, falsely to accuse and convict him of treason, to send him to Devil's Island. But France was also the land of liberty, equality, and fraternity, where the clarion call of Emile Zola was heard and where after much travail and suffering Dreyfus was finally exonerated—in the very year of Levinas's birth, 1906.

Levinas enrolled at the University of Strasbourg, geographically the closest French university to Kovno. His first year he studied Latin. Independently he learned French and German. Beginning his second year, Levinas turned to philosophy. In all his published recollections of this period Levinas singles out four of his Strasbourg teachers for special appreciation: Maurice Pradines (1874–1958), professor of general philosophy; Charles Blondel (1876–1939), professor of psychology ("very anti-Freudian"); Maurice Halbwachs (1877–1945), sociologist (martyred in deportation to Buchenwald); and Henri Carteron (1891–1929), professor of ancient philosophy.[2] Levinas was impressed by these four men, by their characters as well as by their knowledge, seeing in them the embodiment of Western learning and humanism. He became personally close to Professor Blondel, "a man to whom I could say everything."[3]

In addition to the study of the established philosophical curriculum, Levinas was drawn to contemporary philosophy. He was especially attracted to the thought of Henri Bergson and Edmund Husserl, both of whom were still teaching at the time. The influence of these two philosophers, both born Jews, both assimilated, both making significant contributions to the highest intellectual levels of European culture, Bergson in France and Husserl in Germany, is unmistakable in Levinas's own thought. From Husserl Levinas learned a scientific method, phenomenol-

1. Interview with Levinas, March 1986, in Francois Poirié, *Emmanuel Levinas: Qui êtes-vous* (Lyon: La Manufacture, 1987), 67. My translation.
2. For more information about Levinas's professors, see *EI* 25, n. 1.
3. Poirié, *Levinas,* 70. My translation.

ogy, and through this method a philosophical appreciation for the existential conditions of intellectual life; from Bergson he learned a variety of
profound philosophical insights, especially regarding time and existence.
In Strasbourg Levinas also began his lifelong friendship with Maurice
Blanchot, a fellow student who would later become what he is still today,
one of France's leading literary critics.

The 1928–29 academic year was a special one for Levinas. Like the
many German students who would travel from university to university to
attend the classes of the greatest professors of their day, Levinas traveled
to Freiburg to learn phenomenology at its source, from Husserl. In this
brief time he became close to the almost legendary founder of phenomenology, who had just the year before retired from his university professor-
ship but who still directed students and was still reviewing and reformulat-
ing his own thought. Levinas became Mrs. Husserl's French tutor, an
employment that was one of Professor Husserl's discreet ways of providing support for his less affluent students. Levinas quickly entered into the
circle of phenomenology's elite students, and as early as the next year he
published articles in France reviewing Husserl's latest ideas and those of
his leading students.

During the same 1928–29 academic year Levinas attended the lectures
of Husserl's successor at the University of Freiburg, Martin Heidegger.
Heidegger's reputation in German academic circles had already begun to
surpass Husserl's. Just two years earlier, in 1927, Heidegger's *Being and
Time* had been published. This book, more than any other, not only
redirected phenomenology but altered the course of twentieth-century
thought. Forty years later, after having worked out and published his own
original (and anti-Heideggerian) philosophy, Levinas did not hesitate to
write, in a now famous passage, that henceforth "all philosophy must pass
through" Heidegger's *Being and Time*. We must not forget that these
carefully considered words of praise for Heidegger's philosophy were said
in the teeth of Levinas's fundamental and uncompromising criticism of
Heidegger's personal commitment to Nazism. To this day Levinas rigorously maintains this separation between Heidegger's thought and Heidegger's life, speaking at conferences on the former and refusing all invitations
to celebrate the latter. In his Freiburg days Levinas learned from Heidegger's penetrating phenomenological studies without becoming a Heideggerian, unlike so many of Heidegger's other students. Levinas was one of
the privileged few to attend the now famous Kant seminar held in Davos
in 1929, where Ernst Cassirer, philosopher of science, disciple of Hermann Cohen, and editor of Kant's complete works, debated Heidegger
on Kant. It was during this period too that Levinas began his study of
the rabbinic texts, a study he continues to the present day.

After his year in Freiburg, Levinas moved to Paris. He quickly completed his doctoral dissertation under Professor Jean Wahl. In 1930, when Levinas was only twenty-four years old, his thesis was published as *The Theory of Intuition in Husserl's Phenomenology*. It won the Prix de l'Institut from the University of Strasbourg and is still in print today after four French editions. The first book in French entirely devoted to phenomenology, according to Simone de Beauvoir's published account it inspired the young Jean-Paul Sartre to leave Paris for Freiburg to learn the new phenomenological philosophy. It was also the first of Levinas's books to be translated into English, appearing in 1973.

Levinas obtained his French citizenship. In 1931 his translation (along with Gabrielle Pfeiffer) of Husserl's *Cartesian Meditations* appeared. At the same time, Levinas began working as an administrator at the Alliance Israelite Universelle, a French Jewish organization dedicated to increasing the political rights and education of Jews throughout the Mediterranean basin. During the prewar years Levinas continued to study philosophy and to publish articles on Husserl and Heidegger. He also began publishing essays in Jewish thought and on Jewish current events. In 1934, for example, he published an article entitled "Some Reflections on the Philosophy of Hitlerism" in *Esprit*. It warned the French of the dangerous "awakening of primitive feelings" across the German border, subtly linking this movement to Nietzschean and Heideggerian reflections. In the early 1930s Levinas attended the celebrated Saturday night gatherings of the philosophical avant-garde at the home of the philosopher Gabriel Marcel, where he met Jean-Paul Sartre and Jacques Maritain among others. During this period he also met another future leading French philosopher, Paul Ricoeur.

Around this time Levinas married Rachel Levy, a childhood friend from his earliest Kovno days who had lived on the same block. In 1936 their daughter Simonne was born. She later became a physician. Their son Michael was born in 1948. He is a composer and concert pianist.

In 1939, as a French citizen, Levinas was drafted into the French army. Shortly thereafter, along with the entire French Tenth Army, he was captured at Rennes and made a German prisoner of war. After a few months of detention in France, he was transported to a prisoner-of-war camp near Hanover, Germany, for Jewish French soldiers. Here, like other prisoners of war elsewhere, he was forced to do manual labor, chopping wood in a nearby forest. Again the meeting of Judaism and modern Europe was fateful: Levinas's Jewish life was saved by his French uniform. It is a little-known fact that Hitler adhered to the provisions of the Geneva Conventions regarding prisoners of war for signatory nations such as France. Levinas's wife and daughter survived the war hidden at the Saint

Vincent de Paul monastery near Orleans. In their escape from Paris they were aided by Maurice Blanchot. Though imprisoned and cut off from the awful and awesome social, political, and military events of the day, Levinas found time to read some of the prison library books, notably works by Hegel, Diderot, Rousseau, and Proust, and "many things which I had not had the time to read otherwise."[4]

After the war Levinas rejoined his family in Paris. He was appointed director of the Oriental Israelite Normal School, a position he retained until 1961, when he took his first academic post as lecturer in philosophy at the University of Poitiers. In the 1946–47 academic year Levinas gave a series of four lectures at the Philosophical College of Paris set up by Jean Wahl in the lively and bohemian postwar Latin Quarter. These lectures, which form the first outline of Levinas's own thought, were published under the title *Time and the Other* in 1947 (English translation, 1987). The same year also saw the publication of another book-length expression of Levinas's own thought, *Existence and Existents* (English translation, 1978). These two relatively short books, whose theses were for the most part developed in isolation from the rest of contemporary French intellectual life, represent the first sustained articulation of Levinas's distinctive philosophy. Then and henceforth Levinas would propound an ethical and dialogical metaphysics grounded in a careful phenomenological description of the human situation in both its individual and its social moments. From the pain, horror, and confusion of political, social, and ethical upheavals on a scale unprecedented in European history, Levinas would forge a philosophy grounded in the highest demands of personal ethics and social justice. From the unparalleled extremity and incongruous juxtaposition of this historical and historic contrast of good and evil, war and peace, culture and barbarism, justice and injustice, Levinas created a philosophy infused with the highest moral teachings of Judaism.

From 1947 to 1951 Levinas entered into an intensive study of the Talmud under the firm guidance of the brilliant, demanding, and mysterious R. Mordachai Chouchani. Independently and unknown to each other, Elie Wiesel was at that time also in Paris learning from this same extraordinary talmudist. (For more on R. Chouchani see "The Wandering Jew" in Elie Wiesel's *Legends of Our Time*.) Though in his many "talmudic" lectures and publications Levinas has never named this teacher, to this day he speaks of R. Chouchani with only the highest of high praise, indeed, with reverence.

From the late 1940s to the present, Levinas published a great many

---

4. Ibid., 86. My translation.

articles, most of which have been republished in various collections. Based in part on these later collections, one can roughly divide Levinas's articles into four categories. First, there are articles developing and deepening his own philosophical thought, his ethical and dialogical metaphysics. The articles in this category can be further subdivided into two groups: first, those which, with revisions, come from or make up Levinas's two major works, *Totality and Infinity* (1961; English translation, 1969) and *Otherwise Than Being or Beyond Essence* (1974; English translation, 1981), and second, the rest. These latter do not link up to form integral books like *Totality and Infinity* and *Otherwise Than Being or Beyond Essence* but are gathered into four collections: *Humanism of the Other Man* (1972), *Of God Who Comes to the Idea* (1982), *Between Us* (1991), and *Freedom and Commandment* (1994). There are also two short volumes, each containing one important essay: *Of Evasion* (1982), reproducing one of Levinas's earliest articles, first published in 1935, and *Transcendence and Intelligibility* (1984). In the second category are the many essays and secondary articles that analyze and comment on the work of various modern and contemporary philosophers, critics, writers, and poets, confronting perspectives more or less close to Levinas's own thought and concerns: Agnon, Blanchot, Buber, Celan, Derrida, Heidegger, Husserl, Kierkegaard, Rosenzweig, Sartre, Wahl. These articles are now collected into five volumes: *Discovering Existence with Husserl and Heidegger* (1949, 2d ed. 1967), *Proper Names* (1975), *On Maurice Blanchot* (1975), *Outside the Subject* (1987), and *Unforeseen History* (1994). In the third category are the more than twenty "Talmudic Readings," Levinasian commentaries on talmudic *aggadah,* given as invited lectures since 1957 at the annual colloquia of French-Speaking Jewish Intellectuals, sponsored by the World Jewish Congress. Nineteen of these pieces have been collected into four volumes: *Quatre lectures talmudiques* (1968), *Du sacré au saint* (1977), *L'au-delà du verset* (1982), and *A l'heure des nations* (1988). The first two of these collections have been translated into English in one volume entitled *Nine Talmudic Readings* (1990). In the fourth category are the many brief and occasional pieces on topics of general Jewish and religious interest such as Israel, Jewish-Christian relations, monotheism, assimilation, and the Bible (plus Levinas's three earliest talmudic readings), which have been gathered together into the two editions of *Difficult Freedom* (1963, 2d ed. 1976; English translation, 1990).

One can see that despite his duties as director of the Oriental Israelite Normal School (1946–62) and despite the teaching responsibilities of his academic posts at the University of Poitiers (1961–62), the University of Paris at Nanterres (1962–73), and the University of Paris-Sorbonne

(1973–76), Levinas has been a prolific, an engaged, and, in my estimation, a profound writer.

Before moving on to Levinas's philosophy, there are some further words, simple but important words, that must be said about the man. Levinas has lived through interesting times, and he has been spiritually productive. He has tasted some rewards for his efforts, concluding his career as a distinguished and now an emeritus professor of philosophy at the Sorbonne. But through all this objective history and beyond the brilliance of Levinas's works, one still wants to know more about him. What is his character? How does he treat those near to him, his family, friends, colleagues, and students? Perhaps these questions are too personal and can only be answered by those persons who have known Levinas each according to his or her own unique experiences. But if I may venture an answer that I think those of us who have been privileged to know Levinas personally would endorse overwhelmingly, I would put it as follows: Levinas is and has been a good person, an exceptionally good person. It seems so simple an appellation, but it is a great one. Goodness does not only mean avoiding evil, it means positively doing good, reaching out to others, helping. Levinas's is not at all the case of an "abstract" intellectual, whose creative works have been purchased at the price of hypocrisy, pain, and hurt for those "behind the scenes." Quite the contrary. Beyond the generosity and probity of Levinas's public work, his book reviews, secondary articles, prefaces, contributions to Jewish causes, direction of an important Jewish educational and cultural institution, university teaching, dissertation supervision, a global correspondence, lectures every Sabbath morning in the synagogue, and the like, not to mention raising a family, there shines Levinas the man, his outgoing friendliness, his real concern for others, his genuine modesty and personal dignity, and always a warm and ready sense of humor. The ethics of Levinas the man and the ethics of Levinas the thinker are, in a word, at one. This too is in the oldest and best tradition of Judaism's spiritual leaders.

Philosophy

Levinas's major achievement is to have created an original, profound, and comprehensive philosophy, a dialogical ethics. Two basic moves characterize his thought, one negative or critical and the other positive. Negatively, he opposes the primacy which philosophy quite naturally accords to ontological and epistemological interests, the hegemony to which it raises the quest for truth. Positively, he proposes the higher priorities of ethics, the obligations and responsibilities that one person has for another person encountered face-to-face and that ultimately each person has for all humanity. For Levinas the absolute alterity of goodness takes precedence over the relative alterities of the true and the beautiful. Those who are familiar with the many layers and the long history of Jewish thought will see in Levinas's philosophy not only a thought in dialogue with the whole history of philosophy but a thought at the same time thoroughly consonant with many of Judaism's most significant beliefs and practices. There are few if any other philosophies about which the same can be said.

The titles of Levinas's two major works offer clues to his criticism of traditional philosophy: *Totality and Infinity* and *Otherwise Than Being or Beyond Essence*. Both titles are striking in their wide range and dramatic contrasts. In one, infinity is contrasted with totality; in the other, being and essence are contested by an "otherwise" and a "beyond." Although Levinas's ethics is concrete, elaborating the significance of flesh-and-blood human encounters, influenced by the descriptive analyses of phenomenology and existentialism, these titles are abstract. More than just abstract, they contain an essential and deep enigma: the alternatives contested are fundamentally incontestable.

Totality, being, and essence do not constitute a "side." In the Western philosophical tradition they are terms used to express the whole, the all—the whole of reality, all that is. Such terms are meant to be immune to opposition in principle. Does it even make sense, then, to speak of an *otherwise* than being? Anything that is, anything that is a "what" in any sense whatsoever, has being, is. Just *saying* "being" already affirms being, however nominal. As for totality, it means everything. How can everything have an alternative, an other, an exteriority? "Totality" and "being" are as all-encompassing as terms can be, which is precisely their value for philosophers. If Levinas's titles make sense, then, that sense is enigmatic, paradoxical, and challenging.

The titles are indeed paradoxical and enigmatic. Levinas's critical aim is to disturb and challenge rational thought. His terms and locutions are carefully chosen to upset reason at its most rational. They aim to upset reason *in the way that the obligations of ethics upset the telos of reason—from outside and above*. The issue is not one of titles, of course, but of thought and life. To appreciate what is at stake in Levinas's oppositions, one must appreciate the nature of reason and the role it plays in the West.

Basically "the West" is a will to truth, the quest for universal knowledge of the real, reason. This determination is what unites "being," "totality," and "essence." That Levinas sees in the West the will to universal truth is hardly a new insight. Hegel saw this and then saw himself fulfilling the Western telos. Nietzsche saw it and then strove to reverse or disperse it. Levinas, however, wants neither to fulfill nor to reverse or disperse the

Western telos. Without disparaging the genuine achievements of reason, he wants to reorient the West to a higher vocation. Above the will to truth Levinas discerns the call of goodness, a call whose appeal is not that of another truth but of a height that makes truth possible.

Attentive to the links between thought and temporality uncovered by contemporary philosophy, especially by Bergson, Husserl, and Heidegger, Levinas understands the Western telos in a yet more precise way. Its distinctive characteristic, its will to truth, is founded upon the equation of being and being-present. It is because being is first determined as what must be-present that the truth of being is then determined in terms of totality and essence. What is is what is true, justified. But what is true and justified is what is based on evidence that can be brought to the presence of mind, however broadly or "existentially" one conceives mind. The rational quest for being qua totality and essence, the very project of reason, science, is the ongoing quest for complete presence of mind, absolute knowledge. There is a great deal at stake, then, in Levinas's philosophical criticisms, for his oppositions strike at the core of the Western spiritual adventure begun by the ancient Greeks: the love of wisdom qua reason, science, objectivity, universality, absolute knowledge, total self-presence. Levinas attacks this core at its core, by upsetting the self-presence of reason.

There is an enormous if not insuperable difficulty, however. Because the West is essentially a scientific civilization, is determined by the will to truth, it leaves no room, as it were, for a criticism that strikes at the roots of critical thought. One cannot challenge the comprehensiveness of being, the totality of what is, the absolute, in other words, when there is no vantage point or place from which to make the challenge. From the point of view of reason, Levinas's oppositions are then not even false, they are *less* than false. Neither are they possible, because "possibility" is itself an integral part of the totality Levinas claims to oppose. If Levinas's oppositions were possible, so reason reasons, then they would be impossible, encompassed by what they claim to exceed. By the same token, so reason must also reason, Levinas's oppositions cannot be impossible either, because "impossibility" is also included within the unity of being, totality, and essence. Neither possible nor impossible, outside the excluded middle, neither contradictory nor noncontradictory, such is the conundrum, the impasse, the exasperation, but also precisely the transcending inspiration that motivates and is activated by Levinas's thought—*otherwise* than being, *beyond* essence. It escapes a thought that it astutely recognizes as having no exits.

Levinas's opposition to the circumspection of reason is not, however, only a negative enterprise; it is neither a "negative dialectics," to use

Adorno's expression, nor a "deconstruction" to use Derrida's. There is a completely positive side to Levinas's criticism: the positivity of the good. The positivity of goodness, however, is precisely what exceeds the positivity of positive science. The peculiarity and exasperation of Levinas's challenge to reason, then, is the sign of the entry of another dimension, the ethical, which remains other while yet intervening in what is not itself. The ethical orientation, its up and down, cannot be directly stated, said, explained, articulated, thematized, because knowledge is not its proper arena. If the good is to be thought in its goodness, and not thought as the thought of goodness, then it must be "thought" beyond thought itself.

The positivity of goodness is recalcitrant to thematization not because of some lack but because its positivity is too extreme, *too exigent* for reason alone. The good is both *farther* and *closer* than presence, hence invisible to reason. It is farther because the good remains transcendent, irreducibly other. Reason can reason as far as the transcendental but not as far as the transcendent. It is closer because its exigency is greater than the circuits of self-presence, imposing demands more pressing than the self could ever impose on itself by itself. The way of goodness is, in a word, *better* than the thematization of being, more glorious. This "better" is emphatically more important and serious than being; its "more" is immeasurable because its force lies outside the calculus of making-present. Not truer, of course, but better. Everything lies in an *emphasis* that breaks through the confines of a language and a reasoning unavoidably self-obsessed.

But all the above is still too abstract to capture the heart of Levinas's ethical philosophy. For Levinas the excess of ethics is anything but abstract; indeed, it is an excessive immediacy and concreteness. It is the excessive immediacy and concreteness of human relationship, the face-to-face encounter. Levinas is careful not to say that humans first relate to one another and *then* can relate to one another ethically. Ethics is not a gloss on a prior reality, is not a second-order experience. What Levinas is saying, to the contrary, is that the *human* first emerges in the ethical face-to-face. The human emerges not as a genus or as the specification of a genus, but as responsibility for the other. Only in the ethical relation does one encounter the other person as *other* and not as a role or mask in an historical play of behaviors. Thus the *real* also emerges from the ethical relation. The distinction so dear to philosophy between reality and appearance emerges not as philosophy supposes from the distinction between truth and opinion but rather from the source of this distinction, from the more primitive difference between sincerity and ceremony, between ethics and the refusal of alterity. The otherness that constitutes the other person as an other person is, for Levinas, not something true or false or beautiful or ugly, but a moral force, an obligation, a putting of the self into question.

Ethics exceeds reason, then, without being deduced from the limitations of reason. Ethics is not a consolation for reason's failure. Rather, ethics comes first, to the point that reason's capacities derive from the ethical relation. In this perspective Levinas has only admiration for the accomplishments of reason, that is, for an ethically responsible Western civilization. The priority of ethics does not come from choosing the right theory or from choosing to be good. Rather, ethics comes first because *the other person comes first.* The priority of the other person, which legitimates any putting of the other before the self, is what constitutes ethics in the first place and is the source of all priority—in all registers. Here is the positivity of Levinas's ethical philosophy. One does not know ethics, one undergoes it. And one only undergoes it in the first person singular, in the face-to-face relation with the other person, responsibly.

In linking ethics to the I-Thou of interpersonal relations, Levinas follows Buber's lead. But there is an important difference. Levinas felt that Buber did not fully appreciate the fundamental asymmetry of intersubjective relations. It is not the mutuality or reciprocity of the self and the other person but the priority of the other that makes for the *height* proper to ethics. Unless the rectitude of the other's alterity is maintained in its absoluteness, in its irreducible exteriority, the height of ethics will sooner or later be sacrificed, Levinas believes, to the horizons of ontology and aesthetics. For Levinas the face of the other person is from the first a moral height and destitution, imposing obligations on the self, disturbing its equilibrium. No gloss can ultimately smooth over this disturbance, and no ethics is secure without recognizing its insecurity.

Although Levinas's ethics prolongs certain Kantian themes, especially by locating ethical relations outside the historical totality, it does not begin with a self freely legislating its moral obligations and responsibilities. Against Kant, Levinas argues that it is precisely the *autonomy* of choice that makes it inadequate to the transcendence of moral demands. All decisions of the self remain precisely that, the self's. Levinas's philosophy is oriented by a different direction: from the other to the self. Only in the face of the other does the self come to feel its own natural capacities as potentially murderous. Animality is truly surpassed and a genuine humanity arises in the experience of shame, an experience coming out of the face-to-face. "Thou shalt not murder" is not for Levinas a command written on tablets of stone; it is the very apparition of the other as other, the epiphany of the other's face and the beginning of the self as moral agent. Moral agency is higher than will to power.

Nothing could be more serious, then, than the ethical relation, though no scale can measure the weight of the responsibilities it imposes. Responsibility, for Levinas, extends all the way to the other's death, which is to say, to a responsibility for the other's life. For Levinas the self is its brother's keeper; the other's material requirements are the self's spiritual requirements. Responsibilities, unlike ideas, increase in the "measure" that they are assumed . . . to infinity. Precisely this structure escapes reason, being better than the calculations of rationality.

Justice, for Levinas, grows out of ethics and remains bound to it. Responsibility for the other leads to responsibility for all others. Ethics and justice are nonetheless distinct for Levinas. Ethics comes from the inequality of the other's priority over the self, whereas justice requires equality before the law and the establishment of this equality through enduring institutions. For Levinas the call for equal treatment before the law derives from the inequality of the face-to-face relation, from responsibility for the other; without this connection justice itself becomes tyrannical. Just as the ethical self is not the specification of a genus but the uniqueness and exigency of an irreplaceable responsibility for the other, humanity for Levinas is not the genus of which individual human beings are the specification. Humanity is precisely the exigency for justice which shines in the face of the other person, for the other who faces is also the other of others who do not face. Thus in the face of the other, beyond its absolute transcendence, as it were, lies the transcendence of all humanity, of all others.

Moral life transpires not in the reference of word to thing or word to word but in the infinite rectitude of each face and every face. All of Levinas's published works attempt to express, by means of careful, nuanced descriptions, the ethical trace of movements recalcitrant to the light of reason, hidden to knowing, yet higher. They show the transcendence of moral force in all the registers of human life: in the warmth of the home, in shared work, in the voluptuousness of eros, in the face's expressiveness, in language, in the priority of peace over war, in the suffering of a humanity that demands justice. In each case Levinas shows the movement and priority of a superlative transcendence breaking up the seamless unity—and complacency—of being's presence.

Judaism

Levinas draws on many Jewish sources for his thought. But Jewish sources can be found for almost any thought, especially when the thinker is Jewish. Levinas's thought is deeply rooted in Judaism, but it is important to remember that what is basic about his creative work is its philosophical character. Despite his radical criticisms of the hubris of knowledge, Levinas's work remains philosophical. Philosophy is, of course, "Greek" rather than Jewish. *As a philosophy* the work of Levinas stands or falls independently of its relation to Judaism and Jewish thought. In this sense, Levinas's work is not vital to Judaism. But Levinas has throughout his work (and life) remained true to his Judaism. His work shows, then, to what extent Jewish sources can be made vital to global "Western" civilization.

One way to characterize the "Jewishness" of Levinas's thought at the broadest level is to see its opposition to philosophy as the most recent avatar of the ancient and perhaps eternal opposition between Jerusalem and Athens, the Bible and Homer, Jew versus Greek. Jews are reminded of this conflict every year on the holiday of Hanukah, celebrating the origin of their continual and miraculous triumph over the universalism which is Hellenic. Levinas's revival of this struggle occurs on a refined intellectual plane, in the most advanced terms of contemporary continental philosophy. In his work, as we have seen, it takes the form of an opposition between the absolute transcendence of the other person encountered ethically and the relative transcendence of the truth of being determined as presence, especially as found in the phenomenologies of Husserl and Heidegger. Opposing the primacy of knowledge, Levinas opposes all that is Greek. Against intellectual history's various formulations of the Socratic dictum that "one must know the good to do the good," the ethical priorities of Levinas's thought recall the altogether different priority expressed in the famous response of the Jewish people at Mount Sinai: "We will do and we will listen." Thus Levinas's entire philosophy can be understood as but another layer of meaning attached to Sinai, another interpretation—the priority of the other, conscientiousness before consciousness, ethics before reason—exalting and penetrating to the heart of one of the greatest moments in the religious history of the world.

But Levinas willingly concedes much to the genius of Greece in his contest with Greek hubris. Indeed, as a philosopher his very medium, his basic vocabulary, is Greek. The "Jewish" side of Levinas's thought is "enlightened," that is, it is a Judaism made universal, though not universal in the way of Greek science. Levinas opposes philosophy with an externality, to be sure, but not with the ethnic externality of a Jewish particularism. Rather, he opposes philosophy externally with the absolute or pure exteriority of ethical transcendence—philosophy can undergo opposition this far and no farther. But even if this opposition is not exclusively Jewish, it leaves room for Jews in their difference.

The Judaism that Levinas taps, then, is one that speaks to Jews, opens the space of their difference, but does not speak only to Jews because as a philosophy it can at best open the space of a pure difference and not only the space of Jewish difference. It is a Judaism, then, that speaks to all humanity, that teaches humanity its humanism, the absolute transcendence that opens up between people united ethically.

Whether a dialogical ethics expressed in the language of philosophy is Levinas's vision of all that Judaism is and can offer, equating Judaism and universality as did the early German Reformers, or whether this ethics is just what Levinas has to say as a Jew speaking in the forum of European intellectual life, is a question that cannot be decided on the basis of texts alone. The "Judaism" Levinas invokes in his publications, in any event, is one that teaches the whole world. The extent to which Levinas's ethics is "Jewish," then, is that wherein the Jewish message is a message for all mankind. "Whenever one sees 'Israel' " in the sacred texts, Levinas writes, "one can substitute 'humanity'." And, let us add in fidelity to Levinas's thought, in substituting "humanity" one need not erase "Israel." Perhaps one can say of Levinas what Levinas says of Moses Mendelssohn: "He did not forget in his universalism the singularity of the Jewish people and its universal meaning, which results from that very singularity."

The Holocaust is, of course, a unique historical event, the merciless and systematic murder of six million Jews, as well as many others, from 1933 to 1945, by the Nazis and their all too many collaborators, both active and passive. Its meaning for Jews and Judaism is just beginning to be grasped, more than half a century afterward. But however Jewish the Holocaust is and however much it is a specific historical event, its meaning for Levinas is not just Jewish or for Jews alone. And this is the case not simply because non-Jews were also murdered, or because all historical events are open to public scrutiny and evaluation. Rather it is because this specific violence against Jews, like all things in Jewish history, has implications and lessons extending to the whole of humanity for all times. The Holocaust teaches in detail the real workings of totalitarian politics, the empirical horror that results from ideology dominating man. People are often heard to express their ignorance about the nature of evil. Henceforth one can point to the Holocaust, in all its gruesome detail, as the "textbook" par excellence of how evil acts in the world. It also teaches the end of naive theodicy.

Interpreting the Holocaust this way, through universalization, recalls the traditional Jewish reading of Amalek.[5] The rabbis understood that Amalek was not just a desert tribe that once viciously made war on the Jews long ago when they left Egypt. Rather, Amalek's war, so the rabbis taught, teaches Jews how all radical evil operates, shows concretely the

---

5. See the comments of R. Shlomo Yitzaki (Rashi) on Exod. 17:16.

extreme, virulent, active, unprovoked hatred of Jews, an evil that recurs again and again in Jewish history, as Haman in Persia and as Hitler in Germany. Thus for the rabbis a particular event in Jewish history becomes paradigmatic for Jewish experience eternally. For Levinas all the particulars of Judaism and Jewish history are paradigmatic not just for Jews as Jews but for all humanity. Everything in Judaism, right up to the most Jewish elements so seemingly "for Jews only," the discussions in the Talmud about details of Jewish observance, the fringes of prayer shawls, the donning of tefillin, Hebrew prayers tacked onto doorways, all teach universal and not merely Jewish lessons.

What makes the Bible and the Talmud important to Levinas is not their Mosaic eponym—about which he says little and in whose defense he says nothing against higher criticism—but the unity and concreteness of their moral lessons. "I have always thought," Levinas said in 1981, "that the great miracle of the Bible lies not at all in the common literary origin, but, inversely, in the confluence of different literatures toward the same essential content. The miracle of this confluence is greater than the miracle of the unique author. Now the pole of this confluence is the ethical, which incontestably dominates this whole book" (*EI* 115).

The discourses and activities of the sages, personages, and rabbis of the Bible and Talmud are not quaint but expendable "examples" or "illustrations" subordinate to an abstract moral theorizing, as they would be for philosophy. Nor do they offer "proofs" in a rigorous philosophical sense. They are the sources to which humanity is turned and turns to learn its ideals in the first place. This perspective permits Levinas his talmudic readings, where, for example, he enters into a meticulous study of *Bava Mesi'a* 83a–83b, of the Babylonian Talmud, to discover a lesson on modern revolution. Or, in the same tractate, he finds that in the words of R. Simeon ben Lakish (Resh Lakish) "the notion of an American or industrial society is thought out to the end." The ethics Levinas finds in the Jewish texts is, of course, the face-to-face dialogical metaphysics that he elaborates in his properly philosophical works. The question as to whether he finds this ethics or introduces it is not Levinas's question. Levinas says very little directly about method.[6] The meaning, the ethics, however, is at once thoroughly and authentically Jewish and given to all humanity. Even if this be put into question, one thing remains certain: it

---

6. In his "talmudic reading" of *Baba Metsia* 83a–83b, Levinas asks regarding his own approach: "Commentary or interpretation? A reading of the meaning in the text or the text in a meaning? Obedience or boldness?" (*NTR* 96). But Levinas does not answer his question; he rather proceeds with his reading. Years earlier, regarding certain efforts in phenomenological studies, Levinas wistfully rued all the phenomenology that had not, alas, been written because of a prior concern for method.

is the same ethics—the face-to-face, the priority of the other, the obligation to respond—that is found in both Levinas's philosophical works and in his Jewish works.

It is not a simple matter, then, to separate the philosophical from the religious in Levinas's work. Properly religious or Jewish terms—"revelation," "election," "glory," "G-d"—are found throughout his writings, though always cast in an ethical light.

Levinas does not deny the idea of election, for example, but in his hands it becomes the individual's election to moral agency. The irreplaceable self, the self confronted by the other, put into question by the other, made responsible for others, is the elected self.

Revelation, for Levinas, is not limited to a specific event with specific commands, oral and written, given to Moses at Mount Sinai in the year 2448. Rather, revelation is the epiphany of the face, the face of the other person, a bursting through being, a nakedness more naked than bare skin.

Prophecy is not once and for all sealed in the words of the major and minor prophets recorded in nineteen books of the Bible. These words are prophetic for Levinas, and he often quotes the biblical prophets, especially Isaiah, but so too is all speech that calls forth the interlocutor's responsibility to respond. Levinas finds prophetic speech in Dostoyevsky, in Shakespeare, and in his contemporaries.

Levinas does not deny the holy; he interprets it ethically. Holiness is neither an attenuated or otherworldly sanctity nor an adherence to ancient laws. It is precisely and concretely love for the neighbor, food for the hungry, shelter for the unsheltered, a kind word, a door held open, an "after you." The material needs of the other are my spiritual needs—such is holiness.

And G-d? Levinas does not deny G-d, to be sure, but he does deny that the issue regarding G-d is one of affirmation or denial, belief or disbelief. It is the presence and not the existence of G-d that concerns Levinas. And for Levinas, as one might guess by now, G-d Himself appears in the ethics and justice of the relation of one person to another, in the one for the other. "A You," Levinas writes, "is inserted between the I and the absolute He."

Given his ethically and socially responsible linking of Jewish specificity and humanist universalism, as well as his appreciation for the advances of scientific knowledge, not to mention his European culture and his intellectualism, what does Levinas say about Judaism's traditional religious observances? Nothing in his philosophy makes specific ceremonial and ritual observances necessary, but neither does anything rule them out. Indeed, "direct" relations between Jew and G-d, what Levinas calls "ritual practices," including the most private of ritual observances, never lose their communal character as *mitzvot,* commandments from G-d incumbent upon all Jews. But the social link is even deeper. Ritual practices provide the self with opportunities for penitence, for purification of moral conscience, for the continual work of *Teshuvah.* This "internal work," however, is not merely required by social ethics but at one remove, such that it could be dispensed with, but rather is already and always an integral part of communal life. Jewish ritual practices must not, Levinas insists, be confused with the idea or ideal of a purely inner life. Private prayer, communion with God, is never wholly or only private. "This interdependence of inside and outside is also part of Jewish wisdom," Levinas comments (*NTR* 16). Levinas refuses, therefore, to sacrifice ritual practices to universal social values, and even denies the validity of the latter without the former. Further, Levinas's own practice of delivering a lecture at his Paris synagogue every Sabbath morning and remarks like the one that follows indicate that, like most religious Jews outside of the United States, Levinas sees the veritable worth, beyond any nostalgia, of maintaining traditional Jewish observances. In his preface to the 1982 French translation of Mendelssohn's *Jerusalem,* on the question of assimilation, Levinas writes:

Without doubt one still finds in Judaism today the unwavering minority of strict observance where—is there need to recall it?—the ceremonial and ritual law is not only a conduit intended to uphold, without distortion, certain representations of rational theology. It is, to the contrary, the very mode according to which the thought of the believer is dedicated to a God whose will is expressed through this law. Here the practice of the law, like its study, is not a simple expression of faith, but the ultimate closeness to a God who is revealed in History. Through all the ventures of dejudaization, it is in these groups, indifferent to the variations of the epochs and as if cut off from every relation to History, which have preserved the energy of the tradition and its invisible influence.[7]

Here is perhaps the place to name Rabbi Hayyim of Volozhyn and the high regard that Levinas has for his work, *The Soul of Life* (first published posthumously in 1824; translated into French in 1986 with a preface by Levinas). What attracts Levinas to this text are not the many Kabbalistic references, since Levinas eschews overt mysticism. Rather, it is Rabbi Hayyim of Volozhyn's basic thought that the Above and the Below, the divine and the human, are linked through human ethical behavior. Human ethical behavior has cosmic implications. What humans do, according to Rabbi Hayyim, is divinely "caused," insofar as humans learn how to behave by having been made in the image of G-d, *imitatio dei,* but what

7. Emmanuel Levinas, "La pensée de Moses Mendelssohn," *A l'heure des nations* (Paris: Editions de Minuit, 1988), 165–66.

they do also has divine "effects," having unlimited consequences that reverberate throughout all creation, from the lowest to the highest realms. Thus, as in the philosophy of Levinas, the good takes priority over the real, and G-d Himself, who created humans in His image, requires human goodness—ethics and justice—for His own redemption.

Levinas thus takes up the intense ethics of Judaism. His readings of the Talmud are not traditional or rabbinic, for they do not conclude with halachic rulings. But if his readings were only scientific or literary, then we could not understand why he so favors the sacred Jewish texts. Levinas's readings are aggadic rather than halachic, to be sure, but more specifically still they are *mussar*, morally instructive, teaching ethical lessons. Perhaps one must say that Levinas is engaged in a double task: teaching Jewish ethics to the non-Jewish world and teaching non-Jewish philosophy to the Jewish world. For Levinas Judaism is a "religion for adults." This means that it is a religion committed to interpretation, intellection, discussion, understanding, and commentary, where alternative and divergent views are expected, taken seriously, and have their respected place within the unifying and personalizing frame of an absolute transcendence present in the exigencies of ethics and justice. It is perhaps this vision that allows Levinas to speak as both a philosopher and a Jew, as a Jew to philosophers and as a philosopher to Jews.

On Temporality and Time

Radicalizing Alterity

Contemporary philosophers invariably take stands—explicitly or implicitly—regarding the structure and significance of time. It is on this count, one might go so far as to say, that a philosopher has or has not a fundamental position in ontology or metaphysics. Time is as central in contemporary thought as was eternity in ancient and premodern philosophy. Hegel's historical and absolute *Geist,* Nietzsche's doctrines of amor fati and eternal return, Bergson's intuition of duration and his critique of clock time, Husserl's detailed phenomenology of protentive and retentive internal time-consciousness, and Heidegger's phenomenology of the ecstatic temporality of Dasein are all names for fundamental, and fundamentally differing, approaches to and visions of time. Here lie the Ur-visions. Without such an approach and vision of one's own, one will end by being a Heideggerian, Nietzschean, Hegelian, Bergsonian, Husserlian (or perhaps not a contemporary thinker at all), all appearances to the contrary notwithstanding.

To this list of great contemporary thinkers, we must add the name Emmanuel Levinas. In full view of Hegel, Nietzsche, Bergson, Husserl, and Heidegger (and behind Heidegger, Kierkegaard), Levinas has laid out his own fundamental approach and vision regarding time, his own unique account of its structure and significance. To give this approach and vision an abbreviated name, as I have done above with these other contemporary thinkers, it can be called "ethical intersubjective time." The fundamental structure and significance of time, for Levinas, is both ethical and intersubjective, rooted in the unequalled directness of face-to-face encounter, and as such the fundamental structure of being.

It is because Levinas first begins to work out the details of his ethical intersubjective theory of time in *Time and the Other,* first given as a series of four lectures in Paris in 1946 and 1947, and published in 1948, that this work must be included alongside *Existence and Existents* (1947) as his two seminal works. These lead in a direct line to his mature philosophy, as it is expressed in *Totality and Infinity* (1961) and *Otherwise than Being or Beyond Essence* (1974).

Time and the Other has what phenomenologists call a "genetic" structure, which is to say that it begins at primitive levels of meaning (which are not necessarily foundations) and works upwards through levels of meaning each of which is built upon the prior ones. In this instance, Levinas begins at the beginning, with "existence without existents"—a sort of *apeiron* which he calls the "there is" *(il y a)* and "describes" analogically. He then describes the origination of a distinct existent, the subject. The text then moves to progressively more complex constitutive layers of subjectivity—its materiality and solitude, its insertion in the world, its labor and representation, its suffering and mortality—to conclude with the subject's encounter with the other person, dealt with specifically in terms of eros, voluptuosity, and fecundity.

Unlike the march of the Hegelian phenomenology, however, these stages mark a progression toward alterity rather than toward totality. They are driven by a desire to break out of the circuits of sameness rather than a yearning for the closure of a complete comprehension. Thus the descriptive analyses begin with what so lacks alterity that it is anonymous, existence without existents, the "there is," and ends with what is so radically and irreducibly other that it is the very paradigm of alterity, what Levinas here calls the "mystery" of the other person.

Comparison of Levinas's design with Hegelian phenomenology is instructive. For both thinkers the end of thought bears on its beginning. For Hegel, because the end provides the beginning with its truth, each stage between beginning and end is only partially true. Notions such as "being," "nonbeing," and "becoming," with which Hegel's phenomenology begins, are inadequate and surpassed because they are insufficiently articulate to account for the complex reality whose truth the Hegelian quest seeks to express. These most broad and basic terms trip on themselves, stutter, because they want to express, they mean to say, they yearn for a truth which is more than they can relate in their own terms. Only the fully filigreed and articulate concept, the fully self-reflective concept, absorbing into one comprehensive unity all interim "truths" even as they unfold across history, wholly realized only at the end of the phenomenological voyage, can adequately say what thought all along was trying to say, yet was all along only saying partially, stammering, slouching toward Jena and Berlin, and which is finally said in all its purity in Hegel's *Logic:* the absolute all-inclusive truth.

The contrast between Levinas's phenomenology and Hegel's does not result, then, solely from the former adhering to Husserlian phenomenology, the attempt to faithfully describe the origin and constitution of reality in all its manifold and interrelated layers of meaning, without presuppositions. Rather, the two phenomenologies are driven by entirely different, indeed antithetical ends. Hegel's phenomenology is driven by a yearning for the total truth, the truth which knows all and knows itself to know all. Levinas's phenomenology, in stark contrast, is driven by a desire for an exteriority which remains irreducibly exterior, and therefore it aims for a *liberation* from rather than the *realization* of totality, unity, closure, the identification of difference in the self-same. For Hegel, like Spinoza, truth alone sets us free because freedom consists in strict adherence to the true. For Levinas, like Plato, truth must be tempered by a wisdom which stands in relation to what truth alone cannot comprehend.

Levinas's itinerary is not a reverse Hegelianism, however, ending in indeterminate being. In Levinas, too, the "end" which moves the "beginning" becomes increasingly complex, determinate, and meaningful. Nothing is less determinate than the "there is" with which Levinas's phenomenology begins. But the end in Levinas is neither a finality nor a comprehension. Levinas's thought ends with what has no end: alterity, the infinite, the wholly other. Thus it breaks the noetic-noematic confines of Husserlian phenomenology at the same time that it rises to a more glorious height than the Hegelian phenomenology.

Levinas's itinerary in *Time and the Other*—from anonymous existence to the emergence of subjectivity, to subjectivity's practice, theory, and mortality, to its shattering relationship with the alterity of the other person—is essentially the same itinerary as was found in Levinas's immediately preceding work, *Existence and Existents*. However, the earlier work concluded with a section entitled "On the Way to Time," and *Time and the Other* progresses a few steps further in this very direction. The repetition and difference expressed in the relationship between these two texts, the way the analyses of *Time and the Other* retrieve and overlap the analyses of *Existence and Existents*, and push them further along, is indicative of the movement of all of Levinas's thought, and it indicates as well the remarkable continuity exhibited by the development of his thought as a whole. The movement of Levinas's thought is like that of waves, as Derrida was the first to say, but we must think of the waves as those of an approaching high tide, each wave pushing a bit further than the last, each venturing a more radical interpretation of alterity. Each new wave first appears almost subliminally, is seen fleetingly here and there while one is immersed in the wave closest at hand, and then looms larger until it too comes to crash at the always turbulent forefront of Levinas's thought.

The genetic or developmental design of the two early texts is again followed in Levinas's first major work, *Totality and Infinity* (1961).[1] There the stages unfolded in the early works are brought into an even closer focus, the analyses and descriptions are more complex and nuanced, the interrelations are more tightly woven, and in some instances they are

---

1. This developmental structure appears after section 1 of *TI*, which presents a broad thematic overview of the entirety of Levinas's thought.

altered. *Totality and Infinity* is a mature work, and again progresses further toward alterity, or, rather, is moved by a greater alterity, now in the choppy domain of ethics, with regard to the infinite obligations and responsibilities of social life. Levinas's second major work, *Otherwise than Being or Beyond Essence,* represents the next wave after *Totality and Infinity,* pushing Levinas's conception of the other person's radical and irreducible alterity into the domain of language, into the saying *(le dire)* which disrupts and gives sense to the said *(le dit)*. It is not that *Totality and Infinity* neglected the import of language and its relation to the alterity of the other person. Not at all. But in *Otherwise than Being or Beyond Essence* language becomes a central concern, the wave which crests. Finally, a recent collection, entitled *God Who Comes to the Idea* (1982), as well as the article "Diachrony and Representation" (included in the English edition of *Time and the Other*), focus upon the manner in which the other's alterity stands in relation to the absolute alterity of G-d. The relation with G-d was always at work on the horizon of Levinas's thought, which has never shied away from the term "religion," but with these later texts it crashes on the beach, gains a full hearing.[2]

To summarize and simplify these developments, to describe the oncoming waves with single words, Levinas's thought progresses through descriptive analyses of the alterity of *existence* in *Existence and Existents;* of *time* in *Time and the Other;* of *ethics* in *Totality and Infinity;* of *language* in *Otherwise than Being or Beyond Essence;* and of *G-d* in *God Who Comes to the Idea* and "Diachrony and Representation." Just as in each work one sees a development from sameness to the alterity which disrupts sameness, in Levinas's work as a whole one sees a progressive radicalization of the sense of the otherness of the other person. But there is a cumulative effect at work also, an undercurrent. Levinas does not drop the topic of time after *Time and the Other,* or ethics after *Totality and Infinity.* Not at all. With the analyses of ethics in *Totality and Infinity* the previous analyses of existence, existents, world, representation, and time, too, are radicalized. With the analyses of language in *Otherwise than Being or Beyond Essence,* the analyses of existence, existents, world, representation, time, and ethics are radicalized. And so forth with the analyses of G-d in relation to all the prior analyses. The image of waves, like all images, is limited. Perhaps a better image is that of a voice getting louder and louder, or better still, receiving commands of increasing importance and weight,

---

2. Already in *TI,* Levinas wrote: "We propose to call 'religion' the bond that is established between the same and the other without constituting a totality" (40). He further states: "Religion is Desire and not struggle for recognition" (64). On G-d, see subsection B6, "The Metaphysical and the Human," pages 77–79 of section 1 of *TI.*

commands which do not override previous commands but place them in an increasingly more glorious perspective.

Given the forward and backward movement of Levinas's works, one of the virtues of *Time and the Other* (and *Existence and Existents* for that matter) is that, because it is a basic text and at the same time an early work, it provides a clear sketch of most, though not all, of the main and lasting outlines of the whole of Levinas's thought, while being relatively free of the later complexity. It is, in a word, a good introduction to the whole of Levinas's thought, accurate and representative but accessible to the beginning reader of Levinas.

While the topic of time is central to *Time and the Other*, this book does not represent Levinas's final word on the subject. Rather, each of Levinas's works presents or assumes a distinctive analysis of time, and each of these analyses is progressively more radical than the ones before it. This is because Levinas links time to the alterity of intersubjectivity; as his theory of intersubjectivity becomes progressively radicalized in his work as a whole, so does his theory of time.

"The Old and the New" (1982) and "Diachrony and Representation," (1985), which are both included as the "Other Essays" in the English edition of *Time and the Other*, represent a more explicit return to the theory of time first developed in *Time and the Other*. The important difference is that in these articles the meaning of time is deepened in the light of Levinas's more mature reflections on existence, world, subjectivity, ethics, language, and G-d. Beginning with *Existence and Existents*, then, a work very close to *Time and the Other* in chronology and content, it is possible to trace the progressive "alterization" of time as it unfolds across the development of Levinas's entire work. This is the route I will take in the following, thereby locating Levinas's theory of intersubjective time, first developed in *Time and the Other*, within the context of his entire thought.

Existence

In *Existence and Existents* Levinas is concerned primarily with the time of the solitary subject, beginning with the time of the emergent existent, the instant. Following Bergson's lead, Levinas rejects the foundational status and relevance of the traditional view of time, where time is conceived as a series of tightly compressed instants. Time and instants conceived in this fashion are abstractions, more the product of the limitations of representational theorizing than genuine discoveries of reason. In classical thought, Levinas explains, an abstract time frame, a formal time "line," spreading out into infinite and symmetrical "befores" and "afters," is conceived first, and instants are afterwards placed within it as its content. Each instant is the same as all other instants, and each excludes all the others.

Levinas utilizes the notion of the instant to understand the time of the existent in its initial emergence from anonymous existence. From the classical view he retains the idea that instants exclude one another, are separate, monadic, but against the classical view he conceives the instant concretely, as the "accomplishment of existence" (*EE* 76). That is to say, Levinas appropriates the notion of an instant to grasp the first moment of origination, which he characterizes as an instant of primal sensation or materiality. This is the instant Husserl names the *Urimpression,* though Husserl also admits that at this level of "absolute subjectivity . . . names are lacking."[3] It is an originary self-sensing, where the sensing and the sensed are one and the same, yet are nonetheless, paradoxically, noncoincident.

The Levinasian instant is not a product of knowledge or causality. To think it is such a product is the error of classical thought. Rather the instant must be understood existentially and with a double edge, for it is both an original or primal "conquest," escape from the flow of a completely anonymous existence, escape from the "there is," and an original or primal "fatigue," the subject inescapably burdened with itself, weighed down by its own materiality. "What is absolute in the relationship between existence and an existent, in an instant," Levinas writes, "consists in the mastery the existent exercises on existence, but also in the weight of existence on the existent" (*EE* 77). This early notion of the existent as an atomic instant, as primal self-sensing, existence caught up with itself, materiality mired in itself, and hence no longer pure existence but the movement of an inescapable and instantaneous "hypermateriality," will remain throughout Levinas's thought.

The instant, first analyzed in *Existence and Existents,* will be the basis for what in *Totality and Infinity* is once again the first moment of subjectivity, described there as the subject's primordial "enjoyment" (*jouissance),* which is again both an independence, a happiness, and a dependence, a burden. The instant will also serve as the basis for what in Levinas's later writings, from *Otherwise than Being or Beyond Essence* onwards, is the increasingly important role played by passivity in the constitution of ethical subjectivity. The material instant lies at the base, as it were, of the superlative

---

3. Edmund Husserl, *The Phenomenology of Internal Time-Consciousness,* edited by Martin Heidegger, translated by James S. Churchill (Bloomington: Indiana University Press, 1964), par. 36, p. 100.

passivity, the extremity of inwardness, demanded of a subject in response to the extremity of the transcendence of the other person.

Time

The instant is again found in part 1 of *Time and the Other*. Once again Levinas characterizes the emergence of subjectivity in terms of hypermateriality, the intimate and paradoxical self-relationship and noncoincidence of self-sensing, like Hume's "perpetual flux" without habit or memory.[4] But he also takes up, critically, another sort of time, which he began to analyze in the concluding sections of *Existence and Existents,* namely, ecstatic or projective time, what Heidegger in *Being and Time* calls temporality or temporalizing. And it is in *Time and the Other* that Levinas begins to develop his most innovative and far-reaching idea about time, one hinted at in *Existence and Existents,* namely, the inextricable link between time and intersubjectivity.

At the end of *Existence and Existents* Levinas began to speak about time not merely in terms of the instant within which and as which subjectivity first emerges, but in terms of an escape from the instantaneousness of subjectivity. Levinas spoke of the subject's desire to get out of itself, to rid itself of itself, to "save" itself from the narrow confines of its material self-relationship, to disburden itself of itself. The instant has no past or future, it is fragile, evanescent, worldless, and thus it sees in a past and future as worldly horizons an exit from itself. It sees in projection, in being-in-the-world, an escape from its narrow confines. But the escape proves not to be genuine; it is an improvement of the conditions of confinement, as it were, but not a genuine liberation. Thus already in *Existence and Existents* Levinas expresses a proleptic criticism and suggests an astonishing alternative to temporality:

If time is not the illusion of a movement, pawing the ground, then the absolute alterity of another instant cannot be found in the subject, who is definitively *himself.* This alterity comes to me only from the other. (*EE* 93)

Instead of seeking alterity in the world, in representation, say, or, as in Heidegger, in temporal ecstasies, Levinas asks in the next sentence:

Is not sociality something more than the source of our representation of time: is it not time itself? . . . The dialectic of time is the very dialectic of the relationship with the other, that is, a dialogue which in turn has to be studied in terms other than those of the dialectic of the solitary subject. (*EE* 93)

---

4. David Hume, *A Treatise of Human Nature,* edited by L. A. Selby-Bigge (London: Oxford University Press, 1973), book 1, pt. 4, 252.

Articulating and elaborating the significance of the link between time and intersubjectivity is precisely the line of study Levinas does pursue, linking time's dimensions to the alterity of the other person and progressively radicalizing the sense of the other's alterity and thus the sense of time.

In *Time and the Other,* however, under the influence of Heidegger's brilliant analyses of being-in-the-world, this venture toward the other's alterity first passes though a necessary detour: time as a relative rather than an absolute escape from the immanence of subjectivity. That is to say, Levinas examines the time of ecstasis and the time of representation. Thus a later wave, the time of the other person, time as intersubjectivity, already appears on the horizon of worldly time, ecstatic temporality, to which Levinas first attends.

To characterize time solely in terms of the subject's originary self-relationship, the materiality of the instant, with its self-mastery and fatigue, is insufficient because the subject is not only mired in itself, an island unto itself, but is also ecstatically projected into the world. Inasmuch as Levinas has already caught sight of the subject's desire to escape itself, in *Time and the Other* the subject's ecstatic projection into the world is characterized as "salvation." The subject saves itself from its intimate self-enclosure, escapes itself by being-in-the-world, "loosening the bond between the self and the ego" (*TO* 62).

Still, even in this early work Levinas is dissatisfied with Heidegger's interpretation of the subject's ecstasies in terms of praxis, the use of tools, the instrumentality of the "in-order-to" (Heidegger's *das Um-zu*). Levinas finds that the subject is first *nourished* by the world, first *enjoys* the world, before using it. Enjoyment is prior to theory, to be sure, but it is also prior to practice. The more relevant point regarding time, however, is that the subject is not only monadic, an entity within the world, enclosed within itself, even if that enclosure is one of sensations rather than representations, but a being-in-the-world, a subjectivity whose abilities are extended out into the horizons of a future and a past.

Nonetheless, as I have indicated, for Levinas being-in-the-world, whether in the ecstasies of enjoyment, labor, or knowledge, does not truly break the immanence of subjectivity. The ties of self to ego are loosened but not undone. The subject always finds *itself,* its enjoyment, its labor, its knowledge, in the ecstatic movement which seems to offer the promise of an escape outside of itself. Despite their differing overall interpretations, and despite their differing evaluations, Heidegger and Levinas agree about the reference of worldliness back to subjectivity. Heidegger is explicit in stating that the "in-order-to" structure of praxis, the "referential totality" (*Verweisungsganzheit*) of the world, ultimately refers back to Dasein.[5] The temporality of ecstatic time delays but does not disrupt the time of subjectivity. Temporality effects a postponement or extension of immediacy but does not depose the circuits of immanence. Levinas's objection is clear and will be repeated in many contexts: the ecstasies of temporality, like all projections, are insufficiently other.

Levinas's objection forces him into confrontation with the great moment of alterity in the Heideggerian ecstatic theory of time, namely, being-toward-death. What opens up the horizons of temporality, the horizons of futurity and pastness, is death, Dasein's ownmost death, its death-boundedness. All the significations of the referential totality of the world ultimately refer back to Dasein, because only for Dasein is being, including therefore being-in-the-world, an issue. And being is an issue for Dasein because Dasein is backed up against the finitude of its own being, against its mortality. Dasein is the only being that dies rather than perishes or breaks. Heidegger takes death to be the "possibility of impossibility," which means that it alone opens Dasein up to possibilities as possibilities, possibilities, that is, of a finite subject, a subject whose every futural moment *may no longer happen*. The future, then, is not laid out in advance, as it is for representational thought, but rather it is what is only possible, projects projected by a being destined to die.

How can Levinas claim that ecstatic time, temporality, is merely a relative escape from the circuits of immanence rather than an absolute break from immanence, when precisely death seems to shatter the subject's immanence absolutely, and as such indicates that Heidegger has indeed understood the role of absolute alterity in the constitution of Dasein? The question is not intended to undermine the modern appreciation for finitude, to return to the classical tradition which overlooked death, or which took death to be a fall, punishment, or failure. It is rather a question of the proper interpretation of the essential mortality of finite being, for Levinas too recognizes the essential mortality of human being. Levinas is struck not so much by the alterity of death in Heidegger's analysis, but by its "mineness" *(Jemeinigkeit)*. Death for Heidegger is not only Dasein's *own*, it is that which is precisely *ownmost* about Dasein, its uttermost or authentic possibility of being. The alterity of death does not *shatter* Dasein

---

5. See, e.g., *BT* par. 18, pp. 117–18, where Heidegger writes: "But the totality of involvements itself goes back ultimately to a 'towards-which' in which there is *no* further involvement: this 'towards-which' is not an entity with the kind of being that belongs to what is ready-to-hand within a world; it is rather an entity whose being is defined as being-in-the-world, and to whose state of being, worldhood itself belongs. This primary 'towards-which' is not just another 'towards-this' as something in which an involvement is possible. The primary 'toward-which' is a 'for-the-sake-of-which.' But the 'for-the-sake-of' always pertains to the being of Dasein."

but shatter's Dasein's inauthentic possibilities, its misrepresentations of itself to itself, its escape from itself into the third person plural, the anonymous "they." Death does not break Dasein but rather individualizes Dasein, shakes Dasein from false pictures of itself, to make Dasein truly be its being.

For Levinas, in contrast, the separation of the self from anonymous being is effected not through death but through enjoyment and, building upon enjoyment, labor, dwelling, and representation. Individuation and separation, however, are not the same. The individuation of subjectivity, as will be made even clearer in *Totality and Infinity* and *Otherwise than Being and Beyond Essence,* comes not through the alterity of death but through the alterity of the other person, through intersubjective encounter. The irreplaceability of individuation is not, then, as it is in Heidegger, the irreplaceability of one's own mortality, the fact that no one can die anyone else's death, but rather the irreplaceability of responsibility. Already in *Time and the Other,* Levinas argues that death, too, is not my own, is not Heidegger's "possibility of impossibility," but rather the "impossibility of possibility" (*TO* 70, n. 43). Levinas notes that "this apparently Byzantine distinction has a fundamental importance." That is to say, against what Levinas describes as the "supreme lucidity and . . . supreme virility" of Heideggerian being-toward-death, Dasein's resoluteness, its courage to be the being it is, Levinas attends to another signification of death, the emasculation and suffering which mortality brings to subjectivity. He writes: "Death in Heidegger is an event of freedom, whereas for me the subject seems to reach the limit of the possible in suffering. It finds itself enchained, overwhelmed, and in some way passive" (*TO* 70–71). Suffering, not death, makes one be one's own being.

What, then, does Levinas make of death? In *Time and the Other* what Levinas finds of greater importance about death than the irreplaceability of the one who dies is rather its movement, its countermovement against subjectivity. It is in this countermovement, rather than in Heideggerian projection, that he sees the glimmer of a deeper sense of time. The future is not what comes from out of Dasein's ownmost being its being-toward-death, its resoluteness regarding its futural projections, but what comes toward the self, ungraspable, outside its possibilities. It is not the mastery of death that Levinas emphasizes but its *mystery,* the exteriority of the death which always comes to take me, against my will, too soon.

Death escapes the subject not because the subject flees into a superficial everyday existence, into the avoidance of self which is the everyday world of Heideggerian inauthenticity, but because the futurity of death, its unforeseeability, its ungraspability, overwhelms the subject's powers. Levinas writes: "The fact that it deserts every present is not due to our evasion of death and to an unpardonable diversion at the supreme hour, but to the fact that death is *ungraspable,* that it marks the end of the subject's virility and heroism" (*TO* 71–72). Such a relationship with an alterity outside my possibilities is a relationship with a future which can in no way be reduced to self-presence. Here Levinas is following in the footsteps of Bergson, for whom futurity and the signification of *surprise* and *novelty* were essentially linked.

But there is yet another significance to the alterity which threatens in death. Levinas writes that to relate to a future which is not part of the subject's horizon but comes toward the subject "indicates that we are in relation with something that is absolutely other, something bearing alterity not as a provisional determination we can assimilate through enjoyment, but as something whose very existence is made of alterity. My solitude is thus not confirmed by death but broken by it" (*TO* 74). The being "whose very existence is made of alterity" is the other person. Thus Levinas discovers the alterity of the future not in death as possibility, which would be insufficiently other to escape the subject's self-presence, its powers of assimilation, and is even the very dynamism, courage, resoluteness, and mastery of self-presence, but in death as *mystery,* and mystery as the alterity of the other person. Thus *Time and the Other* concludes with an examination of the "mystery" of the other person.

In *Time and the Other* Levinas has not yet interpreted social life in the ethical terms he later introduces in *Totality and Infinity.* The time of alterity is situated concretely in terms of the relationship with the other person encountered erotically, in the voluptuosity of the caress which caresses what withdraws and escapes presence into an alterity Levinas calls the "feminine other" (a type of alterity which applies to male and female genders).[6] Such a futural relationship to personal alterity is held open by a futural alterity so future as to be finally—in a finality which is peculiar because it is without end—in relation with another other person beyond the otherness of the feminine other, with another person altogether, the child, engendered in fecundity. To mark the extraordinary rupture and conjunction in being that such a relation effects, Levinas calls it "transubstantiation" (*TI* 271).[7] "The return of the ego to itself . . . is thus not without remission, thanks to the perspective of the future opened by eros" (*TO* 91). The child, engendered yet beyond even the alterity of the other who faces, is the ultimate sense of futurity.

At the stage of his thinking found in *Time and the Other,* the erotic

---

6. For a closer look at this issue, and a detailed exposition of Levinas's account of eros, see chapter 9 in this volume.

7. In *TO* Levinas writes: "I do not *have* my child; I *am* in some way my child" (91).

relationship serves as the prototype of relationship with alterity. This is because it involves relationship with the most radical alterity of all. Levinas will return to the erotic relationship at greater length only once more in his intellectual career, in section 4 of *Totality and Infinity*, entitled "Beyond the Face" (*TI* 251–85). But Levinas elaborates a more radical sense of the encounter with alterity, not in terms of erotics but as ethics. The encounter with alterity in the erotic relationship, from voluptuosity to fecundity, is henceforth understood to be the material condition for the ethical alterity which holds center place in Levinas's thought.

It is noteworthy that in *Time and the Other* Levinas analyzes only the future of time: "voluptuousness is the very event of the future," he writes, "the future purified of all content, the very mystery of the future." The erotic relationship with alterity, the caress which caresses what withdraws into "the feminine" (a withdrawal that constitutes the erotic signification, to say it again, of both male and female), constituting the voluptuosity of eros, the acuity of its duality,[8] constitutes time as a relationship with a future that escapes presence absolutely, the other's future, and beyond the other the child's future. This emphasis on the future, to the apparent exclusion of the past, figures quite strongly in Levinas's early works.

How is it to be explained? The obvious answer is to see in it Heidegger's residual influence, however unwelcome that influence would be for Levinas explicitly. Levinas's emphasis on futurity would come, then, from the priority Heidegger attributes to Dasein's futural projection, its being-toward-death, over its two other "equiprimordial" temporal projections, pastness and presence. But tempting as this explanation is, Levinas could not be more clear about his rejection of the Heideggerian interpretation of death. It is noteworthy, too, that unlike *Existence and Existence* and *Time and the Other*, Levinas's later works tend to emphasize the past,

---

8. Levinas opposes the entire tradition of eros understood as fusion, Aristophanes' position in Plato's *Symposium*. "To say that sexual duality presupposes a whole is to posit love beforehand as fusion. The pathos of love, however, consists in an insurmountable duality of beings. It is a relationship with what always slips away. The relationship does not *ipso facto* neutralize alterity but preserves it. The pathos of voluptuousness lies in the fact of being two" (*TO* 86).

One of the most original and thought provoking consequences of Levinas's view is that all of eros must be understood under the sign of the feminine. The entire realm of love is feminine, just as the entire realm of work, for Levinas, is masculine, regardless of the biological gender of those in love or at work.

The issues at stake here are surely complex and controversial. In 1947, in *Time and the Other*, Levinas wrote: "I do not want to ignore the legitimate claims of the feminism that presupposes all the acquired attainments of civilization" (*TO* 86). For more on this issue, see *TO* 84–85, translator's footnotes nos. 68 and 69; and, to note it again, chapter 9 in this volume.

almost to the exclusion of the future. One might still think of this as a gradual liberation from Heidegger. Or one might attribute the different emphases to Levinas's biography, to the different outlooks of youth and age, one forward looking, the other nostalgic. This must be mentioned because Levinas takes seriously the aging of subjectivity. His different emphases would be consistent with this concern and with its phenomenological basis, which would include the aging of his own subjectivity. But both of these suggestions, for all their obviousness, are facile, and explain very little in any event.

As to Heidegger's alleged influence, I think there is some truth to it, but it is a truth whose sense must be reversed. That is to say, Levinas's early emphasis on the future shows precisely and starkly just how distant Levinas is from Heidegger, indeed just how profound is Levinas's critique, going right to the heart of Heideggerian thought, to the central conception of Dasein as a temporalizing being, which lies at the basis of Heidegger's later vision of historicity and epochal being. By presenting a different account of time, especially of futurity, Levinas is, in a word, challenging Heidegger's most basic insights.

I think a deeper explanation for Levinas's early emphasis on the future and his later emphasis on the past hinges not at all on his relation to Heidegger but on the inner development of his own thought. I think Jacques Rolland has got it right when he argues, regarding the transition from *Totality and Infinity* to *Otherwise than Being or Beyond Essence,* that there is a movement in Levinas's thought from a focus on the astonishing surplus of the other's alterity, the other's transcendence, to a return focus on the effect that that alterity has on the subjectivity of the subject. It is this shift, I think, that accounts for the early almost exclusive emphasis on the future, the other as surprise and the unforeseeable, and the later almost exclusive emphasis on the past, on what has already passed, both in the other and in the passivity of the self. But emphasis is not exclusion; the radical future of *Time and the Other* requires the radical past of the later works. As Bergson said, one must wait for the sugar to melt in one's coffee; Levinas's thinking and writing develop over time, extending, elaborating, and locating the significance of earlier thoughts in the spaces opened up by an ongoing and later exposition.

The essential point is that time must be conceived in its full dimensionality, in its unity and difference. Indeed, precisely what Levinas comes to grips with is the way time breaks reality up into past, present, and future. The reality that is "all at once" is a pure concept, abstract being, being without becoming, which was precisely the route and goal of Parmenidean philosophy. But reality is not "all at once," and becoming is not pure illusion, nor is it reducible to being, even being-in-difference. Time is the break up of reality, absolutely. And, as all post-Hegelian thought has understood, and as we saw with Rosenzweig, the failure of the Parmenidean tradition of philosophy, and hence the recognition of the irreducibility of the difference between the real and the rational, has to do with the irreducibility of time, time liberated from the concept, hence with the break up of reality *otherwise* than through rational thought.

Though the link between a new characterization of time and a new vision of subjectivity was seen from the first, already by Kierkegaard, the problem is how exactly to characterize the alterity that breaks reality up as both time and subjectivity. In rejecting purely conceptual solutions to this problem, Levinas, like all of his contemporaries, was powerfully influenced by the work of Bergson, from whom he learned the "deformalization" of both time and subjectivity, whose major works he acknowledges at the end of "Diachrony and Representation" (*TO* 119–20), and whose thought he thematizes and criticizes in "The Old and the New" (*TO* 121–38). In Levinas's ability both to appreciate and to reject the influence of rational conceptualization on a proper understanding of time, one can also hardly overestimate the influence of Husserl's theory of "internal-time consciousness" and the project, though not the determinate results, of the existential-hermeneutical appropriation of Husserl's theory that Heidegger carried out in *Being and Time*.

To put the matter of influence succinctly: Bergson freed Levinas from rationalized time, time as a series of instants, which Bergson understood to be a spatialized *image* of time. Rather, Bergson linked time to subjectivity through his idea of duration. Husserl developed an alternative idea of subjective time by linking time to the "rays" *(Blickstrahlen)* or intentions of consciousness. Heidegger took this development, freed it from Husserl's rationalist commitments, most especially from subjectivity understood as transcendental consciousness, and reinterpreted subjective time in existential ontological terms as ecstatic or projective temporality. Levinas took the further step of discovering the alterity of time not merely in an existential subjectivity conceived as projective or ecstatic but across the rupture of the more radical (because irreducible) alterity of an existential and ethical intersubjectivity.

The liberating influence of Bergson was decisive for Levinas. One of Levinas's earliest philosophical labors, in 1935, was his little-known translation of an article by a Russian thinker, N. Khersonsky, entitled "La notion du temps."[9] The Khersonsky article reproduces the Bergsonian critique of the classical conceptualization of time, attacking the latter for

<hr/>

9. N. Khersonsky, "La notion du temps," translated by Emmanuel Levinas, *Recherches Philosophiques* 5 (1935–36): 41–51. The original is in Russian.

its spatialization and abstraction. The cognitive, judgmental representation of time is rejected because "the act of judgment's own logical force consists precisely not in separating the subject and the predicate by time, but in attributing simultaneity to them both." The time of knowledge is simultaneity, contemporaneousness. Concrete "living time," to the contrary, the translation continues, "flows from one instant to another without delaying with any one of them." Throughout the development of his thought, Levinas will always adhere to the critical perspective of this early position, characterizing the time of representation as the time of simultaneity, the contemporaneity of subject and predicate. It does not and cannot sufficiently account for the break up of reality. For his own part, however, Levinas does not affirm Bergsonian duration, the continual creation of novelty, as a satisfactory alternative to abstract time. The newness of duration is still an insufficient alterity, still too much a product of consciousness, albeit an intuitive consciousness, consciousness bound to imagination.

For Levinas, the classical conception cannot account for the fact or event which is the core of his own theory of time, the break up of contemporaneousness, indeed, the *rupture* of contemporaneousness. Here, too, is the reason for his rejection of the Husserlian-Heideggerian projective theory of time. Whether projected by a transcendental ego or an essentially temporalizing being, projected dimensions, even when named "future" and "past," always remain the synthetic projects of the projector. They are extensions of self-presence, not implosions of it.

In contrast, Levinas's great insight is to have realized that the other person encountered face-to-face is not the subject's contemporary. The I and the you do not meet one another "at the same time." The time of intersubjectivity is not simultaneity. Only subject to the alterity of the intersubjective encounter does the I encounter the irrecuperable break up of reality. The time of the other and my time, the times of mineness, ecstatic temporalities, do not occur at the same time. *Veritable time,* time in Levinas's sense, is the effect or event of the disjointed conjunction of two different temporalities: the other's time disrupts my time, and in this disruption Levinas discovers veritable time. "My time" and "the other's time" are expressions for temporality. Veritable time, however, is neither mine nor yours; it is the extraordinary juncture of I and other. It is this upset, this non-integrateable insertion of the other's time into mine, that breaks up time and maintains the alterity required by a genuine or veritable time, neither the other's nor mine.

The problem with time classically conceived has to do with the limitations of the rational conception of negation (see *TI* 40–43). Approaching time from the point of view of judgmental knowledge, the ancients characterized time's break up of reality in terms of predicative negation: the future and past are *not* present, thus in some sense they *are not*. Becoming could only be understood in terms of nonbeing. Caught within this logic of judgmental propositions, the classical tradition was led inevitably, in the name of rationality, to sacrifice time (as nonbeing) to eternity (as being). It made this sacrifice first by means of external negations, the Parmenidean way, where only the pure unity of being is affirmed, and finally with Hegel and Marx, true sons of Parmenides, by means of internal negations, where a historically evolved unity of being can be affirmed through a dialectic of being and nonbeing.

The whole of contemporary philosophy, then, and certainly not Levinas alone, has rejected the sacrifices made on the way, the reduction of plurality to unity, the reduction of reality to being and nonbeing, of time to eternity. This rebellion defines and sets the tasks of the contemporary epoch of thought, and thus again points out the central importance of time and how much is at stake in Levinas's innovations. Levinas goes to the root of the matter and declares that nonbeing is not sufficiently other to account for time. That this is true can hardly be denied regarding Hegelian thought, which precisely prides itself for its ability to integrate nonbeing into being as being's dialectical partner, indeed as the very motor of being, where what is ultimately true is neither identity nor difference apart from one another, but the "higher" identity of identity and difference. This is what satisfies rational thought, but it does not account for reality.

Heidegger, following and moving beyond Husserl, also rejects the classical tradition and its representational model of knowledge and time. But for Levinas, as we have seen, Heideggerian temporality, while not sacrificing time to the abstract and unified present of propositional knowledge, nonetheless sacrifices time to the ecstatic self-presence of an existential or ontological unity, to the prepredicative fore-structure of understanding. The problem, one must always keep in mind, is how to account for rather than reduce the break up of reality that time effects. The later Heideggerian "thought of being" means to be being's thought, but it cannot escape the ablative, the thinker's thought about being. And even if it does, as Heidegger's partisans insist, even if it does overcome subjectivism, alterity is nonetheless absorbed into being's move, into being's revelatory and epochal unfolding of reality. Heideggerian temporality, whether Dasein's or being's, does not go far enough for Levinas.

More than any other contemporary thinker, Levinas has understood that for time to be time the radical alterity of its dimensions must be respected. The only way to guarantee the irreducibility of time's dimensions, and hence to account for veritable time, is to recognize that time itself is nothing other than the rupture effected by the alterity of the other person upon the subject. Time is neither an abstract difference in contrast to identity, which would entail the obliteration of existential alterity, nor is it the concrete identity of difference and identity, which would entail the integration of alterity, its totalization. Rather time is the *non-in-difference* of one person to another, the proximity of the other which opens up an infinite distance without distance: obligation to the other.[10]

Ethics

In *Totality and Infinity* the time that Levinas had bound to the irreducible alterity of the other person, the time whose alterity was not only beyond the reach of the syntheses and identifications effected by both epistemology and ontology but was the very disruption of these syntheses and identifications, their non-return, the time which was precisely the non-in-difference of one person to another, is now explicitly recognized to be the time of morality. Veritable time is moral time, the time of obligation and responsibility to and for the other person.

Epistemology and ontology, whether precritical, critical, dialectical, or structural, in various ways reduce the alterity necessary for veritable time to the sameness of the present or presence, to temporality or to the representation of time. The irreducible alterity beyond the syntheses, identifications, correlations, and coordinations of both epistemology and ontology is a non-in-difference of one to another, an *ethical* alterity, an alterity encountered in and as the good it inspires.

To name the extraordinary ethical excess of the other and the relation that is the encounter with it, Levinas is fond of recalling Plato's expression, "the good beyond being" (*agathon epekeina tes ousias; Rep.* 6, 509b), among other similarly explosive formulations in the history of Western thought. He wants, thereby, not only to lend a philosophical dignity to this break with Parmenidean philosophy, to a thinking beyond being, a thinking based on a paradoxical relationality between terms that maintains their absolute separation even while maintaining their relation, but to emphasize the ethical character of the relation as well. Only as the height of the good can radical alterity, and hence veritable time, make sense. To conceive of intersubjectivity solely in ontological or epistemological terms (even admitting their insufficiency), to approach the otherness of the other person as the "problem of other minds," say, or the problem of accounting for the constitution of the sense "other person," is to forever miss the true or positive import of its surplus.

10. On non-in-difference as the key to Levinas's thought, see chapter 7 in this volume.

When Levinas explicitly acknowledges the ethical character of the relation with the alterity of the other person, and thus the inextricably ethical
character of the alterity constitutive of time, he can no longer remain
content to understand, as he did in his earlier works, the rupture time
effects as the "ungraspable," the "unknowable," "mystery," or as erotic
"withdrawal" and fecund "transubstantiation." Characterizations such as
ungraspable, unknowable, mystery, etc., though not incorrect as far as
they go, give an undue pride of place to grasping and knowledge. They
start and remain in precisely the orientation philosophy has always insisted
upon, starting from the ground up, seeking origins, principles. Even the
set of terms taken from the language of eroticism, "voluptuosity," "paternity," "maternity," "fecundity," are also misunderstood if the ethical significance of the break with ontology is excluded or overlooked.

Philosophy is the courage to get to the final ground, the ultimate
reason for all and everything. Because it did not begin with the finality it
seeks, it must turn around from its treasure trove, if and when it finds
one, and ground what at first lacked ground. Thus philosophy is first
philosophy in the double sense that it seeks the ground, foundation, origin, *archê,* and it then anchors, grounds, founds, everything upon that
origin. Philosophy converts opinion and appearance to truth and reality,
or discards them, by revealing opinion and appearance *as* opinion and
appearance by uncovering their true or real grounds, if they have them,
in ultimate truth and reality. Philosophy is thus synonymous with first
philosophy. Firstness is the *alpha* and *omega,* the *archê* and *telos,* of philosophy.

In contrast—and it is precisely this contrast, or the shock of it, or its
emphasis, which indicates how much and what is at stake in Levinas's
"philosophy"—the alterity of the other person demands to be approached
in terms of that which *surpasses* understanding absolutely, that which is
superior to the horizons of being and the truth of being, that which exceeds
or precedes the grounds of philosophy: the *excellence* of ethical command
and the infinite responsibilities called forth. The alterity of the other person is not simply recalcitrant to knowledge and caresses, like a stubborn
ignorance or a brutish power; it is a positive force. The force of its positivity, however, is moral rather than ontological or epistemological: it lies
in the command to be good, which means the command which commands
pacifically, eliciting moral response.[11]

---

11. Inasmuch as the moral force of ethics is pacific, Derrida's accusation that Levinas's
ethics is a violence is all the more poignant or nasty, as Derrida well knows. For a Levinasian
response to Derrida's charges, see chapter 14 in this volume.

Because philosophy is rooted in the firstness of first philosophy, in the quest for origins, origins which are inadequate to the excellence of morality, Levinas's propositions, in order to express both this excess and its excellence, shift back and forth from negative to positive, from the inadequacy of philosophy to the excellence of ethics, to the height of the other and the election of the self. To attempt to say straightforwardly that goodness exceeds being would be to fall prey to the synthesizing and identifying powers of being. What is said is thematized, grasped, understood, conceptualized. But the good makes greater demands than knowledge. The subject that is subject to the moral demand of the other person is traumatized, put out of balance, loses its moderation, its recuperative powers, its autonomy, is shaken out of its complacency and contemporaneousness with the world and others. Such is the impact of moral force, the asymmetry of the "height and destitution" of the other.

Death, too, which Levinas had already grasped in terms of the alterity of the other person, must now be understood ethically, at the limit, as murder. Indeed, in a certain sense every death is a murder, a life taken too soon, a life at the mercy of others and at the same time a life still for others. It is this last point which is important for Levinas. No matter how individualized, death cannot be removed from its social context, hence from its moral context, hence, at the limit, from murder. The link between time and intersubjectivity is not broken by the individuation of subjectivity effected, as Heidegger thinks, by the priority of the ownmost quality of death, its "mineness," where death is the spark that turns existence back upon itself, back upon the issue of being, ultimately upon the *Seinsfrage*. Rather the link between subjectivity and intersubjectivity, and hence veritable time, is confirmed even by death. Levinas writes in *Totality and Infinity*:

Murder at the origin of death, reveals a cruel world, but one to the scale of human relations. The will . . . exposed to death but not immediately, has time to be for the other, and thus to recover meaning despite death. This existence for the other, this desire of the other, this goodness liberated from the egoist gravitation . . . retains a personal character. . . . The desire into which the threatened will dissolves no longer defends the powers of a will, but, as the goodness whose meaning death cannot efface, has its center outside of itself. (*TI* 236)

One does not choose death. Death comes and takes one away, like a thief in the night—like a murderer, a grim reaper. Here is a new turn of meaning to the Epicurean formula: Where the self is, death is not. For its part, the egoist will, autonomy, always threatened by death because mortal by nature, need not respond by gathering itself into a greater strength, a more personal resolve—no strength or resolve can, in any event, resist death. Indeed, the will, seeing itself as a power in the face of the other's mortal vulnerability, can come to recognize itself as potentially violent, potentially murderous. Thus shamed, the self would rise to the moral responsibility and obligations of goodness.

The transformation or reorientation of the egoist will into good will is not an ontological or epistemological necessity, however, even if it can be linked to death, because no one has to be good. One does not have to respond to the other. Rather, Levinas will say, shifting from nominative to prescriptive language, it is *better* to do so. Goodness is an election, an election to moral status. The I is elected the moment it is "capable of seeing the offense of the offended, or the face" (*TI* 247). Only a moral response can respond to the radical alterity of the other person, hence only in moral terms is time "constituted," or rather, undergone. Death takes on a new sense where the self is concerned for the death of the other even *more* than its own. "Goodness," Levinas writes, "consists in taking up a position in being such that the other counts more than myself. Goodness thus involves the possibility for the I, exposed to the alienation of its powers by death, to not be for death" (*TI* 247). Thus in death, on Heidegger's grounds, as it were, Levinas discovers the ethical alterity of the other, the responsive passivity of goodness, and a possible concern for the other that knows no limits, rather than the individuation of a Dasein opened onto and more firmly rooted in being. Radical exposure is exposure to the other, not to being. Radical exposure is being uprooted by the other.

Exposed to the alterity of the other person, the I's egoist capacities, the synthesizing which has hitherto defined the ego (whether the subject's or, as in German idealism, the world's) for philosophy, are "reconditioned," "put into question," overexposed, such that the I is now *first* for-the-other *before* the firstness of its being for-itself. It is in this ethical reversal, the peculiar time of an "anterior posteriorly,"[12] that Levinas finds the ultimate—or most glorious—sense of time. Beneath all origins, it is a beginning, a priority, a "first," which for ontology and epistemology must come second (or third, after appearance, after reality). It is like the freshness of rebirth, or the purification of pardon. It is a beginning whose priority emerges out of the bursting structure of overexposure, excessive vulnerability, for-the-other before being for-oneself, hence overturning being for what is better than being. Time thus involves not only the superlative alterity of a nonencompassable future, the infinite. But also,

---

12. *TI* 170. Cf. 54.

in response to that alterity, time involves an anteriority prior to representation but only revealed "posteriorly," hence an irrecuperable past. Levinas will call this past "created," since it is prior to the cause and effect sequence constructed by representational consciousness, and thus also prior to freedom, the dialectical partner of causal necessity.[13] Created being would be a *superlative passivity*—brought out of me by the other, where the I is chosen rather than chooses. The pastness of such passivity would be deeper than the recuperative power of syntheses which hitherto had seemed to come first, and which otherwise define themselves as the power of coming first and hence serve in one way or another as the grounds for any first philosophy. "No memory," Levinas wrote in 1963, "could follow the trace of this past. It is an immemorial past."[14] The past beyond the ken of *my* memory becomes my past, *as* my responsibility. It is the other in me. Just as the other is always yet to come, the other has always already passed. As we saw in chapter 4, Rosenzweig argued that Buber's I-thou lacked precisely these two dimensions of radical futurity and pastness.

Precisely the obligation introjected by the proximity of the other into subjectivity, a subjectivity subject to the other, an obligation which is at once the election of the self, its responsibility to respond to the other, is suffered by subjectivity as always already having passed into the self, as having *already* put the self into question, an-archically—to the extent, that is, that the ego is put into question, to the extent, in other words, that the ego is good. Time as moral beginning, as response to alterity, precedes temporality as originary thinking, as response to being.

Thus a radical *passivity*, a radical exposure, prior to all the syntheses which have hitherto defined temporality, subjectivity, being, representation, and truth for philosophy, and a radical *alterity*, again beyond all the syntheses which have hitherto defined temporality, subjectivity, being, etc., for philosophy, are related by means of ethics, and thus by means of a time liberated from self-presence, liberated from synthesis and self-sameness. The alterity of the other impinges on the subject's temporal syntheses from the outside, disrupting its unity with what comes from on high, from above. And in the same extraordinary moment of nonsimultaneity with the other, the other's height is an appeal calling forth a subjectivity subject to the other, for-the-other-before-itself, that is to say, a subjectivity which "fears murder more than death." The ethical subject

13. For the contrast and the importance of creation in relation to causality, see the section "Fecundity, Paternity, and Filiality" of chapter 9, "The Metaphysics of Gender."

14. See Emmanuel Levinas, "The Trace of the Other," translated by Alphonso Lingis, in *Deconstruction in Context*, edited by Mark Taylor (Chicago: University of Chicago Press, 1986), 345–59.

recognizes its powers as murderous and the other as vulnerable, the object of actual or potential violence, irresponsibility, and injustice. In this ethical "deformalization" of the self and other, excessive alterity and excessive passivity, a future and a past never present, Levinas uncovers the ultimate structure of time.

Language

The ethically elected ego is both already obligated and never sufficiently obligated. In the fractured structure of these excessive obligations Levinas finds the structure of time: A past already in force, a moral force, putting the ego into question, "despite itself" *(malgré soi)*, against its synthesizing nature, more passive than its agency, without ever having been present— obligation to the other; a future which never becomes and never can become present—the other's command. Such is the structure of ethics and time, disrupting the self-presence of being and knowledge. But such is also the structure, as Levinas's use of the terms "trace" and "expression" indicates, of language, of the significance of signification.

In his 1963 article "The Trace of the Other," Levinas characterizes the extraordinary relationship between the I and the other, a relationship between terms which remains outside of relation while yet being in rela-tion, the non-in-difference of one to the other, proximity, in terms of signification (and, on the concluding pages of "The Trace of the Other," let us note the approach of an oncoming wave, in terms of G-d). Over the next several years, in a series of articles which were to be collected together to become the core of *Otherwise than Being or Beyond Essence,* Levinas focuses on the ethical alterity of the other person and the ethical exposure of the subject, thus on the alterity constitutive of time, in terms of language and signification. It is a matter of elaborating more precisely what is meant by "the *trace* of the other," the way in which meaning is elicited by the moral force of the face, how it arises in expressivity and through moral imperative, the manner in which language is a calling forth and a beginning in responsibility to and for the other.

As early as *Totality and Infinity* Levinas conceived the other's face as equivalent to expressivity, laying emphasis on the relation of sign to per-son signifying rather than the relation of sign to thing signified:

Expression manifests the presence of being, but not by simply drawing aside the veil of the phenomenon. It is of itself presence of a face, and hence appeal and teaching, entry into relation with me—the ethical relation. And expression does not manifest the presence of being by referring from the sign to the signified; it presents the signifier. The signifier, he who gives a sign, is not signified. (*TI* 181–82)

Thus Levinas distinguishes the relation of sign to signified, which is an epistemological and ontological relation, from the extraordinary relation of both the sign and the signified to the signifier, the other.

In *Otherwise than Being or Beyond Essence,* language and signification are understood in yet a more complex fashion. Levinas realizes that signification at the phenomenal level is not simply a matter of signs referring to what they signify. In our century there have been many critics of a straightforward correspondence model of signification and truth. In France the criticisms of Heidegger and Derrida have had greatest sway, as have their alternative noncorrespondence models of signification and truth. Derrida leveled his attack first against Husserl,[15] showing that the signification of a sign depends more on the meaningful absence of other signs than on any ostensively direct intuition of the signified beyond the sign. A fully intuited meaning would in fact be impossible or, more precisely, forever deferred, because signs depend on other signs, absent signs, for signification. For a sign to be significant, Derrida argues, it is sufficient that it stands in relation to other signs that are absent. Language is meaningful not because it touches base here and there in a one-to-one correspondence with things, but because it is a historically shifting network of signs, signs which not only refer to one another but defer to one another, playing between themselves in various historically determined configurations, where the presence of one sign is meaningful owing to the absence of other signs. This play is equivalent to what Heidegger, in his later work, called the "verbality of the verb." "Language," Levinas writes in *Otherwise than Being or Beyond Essence,* commenting on this line of thought, "issued from the verbalness of a verb would then not only consist in making being understood, but also in making its essence vibrate" (*OBBE* 35).

But it is not in semiotic play or in verbality, in the vibration of absence and presence, that Levinas finds the alterity constitutive of meaning and time. Such a play, despite its inevitable deferral of meaning, despite its vibrancy and essential undecideability, remains an economy, the economy of what is *said (dit).* But what is said depends, in its turn, on another more radical "absence," the irreducible absence of what in *Totality and Infinity* Levinas called the "signifier," he who speaks and at the same time

15. See Jacques Derrida, *Edmund Husserl's "Origin of Geometry": An Introduction,* translated by John P, Leavey, Jr. (Stony Brook: Nicholas Hays, Ltd., 1978); and Jacques Derrida, *Speech and Phenomena: And Other Essays on Husserl's Theory of Signs,* translated by David B. Allison (Evanston: Northwestern University Press, 1973). But as a stiff scholarly corrective Derrida's Husserl interpretation, that is, for a careful unmasking of Derrida's misreading Husserl, see J. Claude Evans, *Strategies of Deconstruction: Derrida and the Myth of Voice* (Minneapolis: University of Minnesota Press, 1991).

commands ethically, putting the self into question. "The very essence of language," Levinas wrote in *Totality and Infinity,* foreshadowing the later analyses of *Otherwise than Being or Beyond Essence,* "consists in continually undoing its statement by the foreword or the exegesis, in unsaying the said, in attempting to restate without ceremonies what has already been ill understood in the inevitable ceremonial in which the said delights" (*TI* 30).[16] This movement of language is one Levinas now sums up in the term *saying (dire),* which is the ethical condition of what is said. Of saying and time, in *Otherwise than Being or Beyond Essence,* Levinas writes: "It is the impossibility of the dispersion of time to assemble itself in the present, the insurmountable diachrony of time" (*OBBE* 38).

It is because language depends first on one-for-the-other, in saying, the exceptional command of the other evoking the subject's responsibility to respond, that there is meaning, the said, and time, past, present, and future. The said, what can be represented, tends toward the present, toward simultaneity, contemporaneousness, the economy of self-presence, even if it always "fails" to close upon itself, as Derrida points out, even if it endlessly vibrates, is subject to endless reconfiguration, and manifests an irreducible equivocation in being. These deformations in language are nonetheless not the "deformalization" to which Levinas points. Saying is never present in the said, for the said is both too late and too early, is already caught—no matter how subtle, brilliant, or perverse its vibrancy—within the economy of truth and self-presence. Saying enters the said otherwise than the vibration or play of the said: it is traced in the said as an overdetermination, both as the possibility of unsaying or resaying the said—the pure future—and as a disruption, undercutting, or undermining to which the egoist subject must passively submit, in patience, in suffering, in an undergoing of what has already struck the egoist subject in a vulnerability it can never ground or recuperate—the immemorial past. The time structure of such a relation, one which is both ethical and the source of all significance—the face-to-face relationship, proximity, non-in-difference, the one-for-the-other, the saying of the said—is the time Levinas names "dia-chrony."

In his 1982 paper entitled "Diachrony and Representation," Levinas again focuses on the inner links of the triple signification—ethics, language, and time—of a dynamic and asymmetrical intersubjectivity. He begins as he has so often begun before, with a condensed and schematic recapitulation of his entire itinerary. The new step Levinas takes, however,

16. Citations such as this one confirm my thesis that there are no significant breaks or ruptures in the development of Levinas's own thought, after, that is, he has shaken off the early and very brief bout of a Heideggerianism that helped him take his first existential steps beyond Husserl. See chapter 10 below.

is to articulate the paradoxical alterity of dia-chrony, the prototype of all time, in contrast to the time of re-presentation and presencing. For time to be thought as the break up of reality into the irreducible dimensions of past, present, and future, it must finally be thought in terms of a *past which was never present* and a *future which will never be present*. Such, as has by now become clear, is the other's future and the other's past for the subject subjected to the other despite itself. Time bursts upon the subject through the other's saying, the other's command, but only for an ego which rises to its goodness, the ego *first* for-the-other, for-the-other-before-itself, elected to its better self. Levinas employs the term "dia-chrony" in opposition to the term "synchrony," just as earlier he has posed "mystery" against "possibility"; "infinity" against "totality"; "otherwise than being" against "being"; "beyond essence" against "essence"; "saying" against "said"; and the "other" against the "same." The terms are not on the same plane. Time and ethics effect a "curvature." Time, which is at once the structure of intersubjectivity, language, and ethics, effects the very singularization of the first person, wherein subjectivity, as we have seen, is elected to goodness, indebted to the infinite demands of the other, a donation, an inexhaustible reserve, even if what is given are "only" words of comfort or a silent "presence." The ethical fission of subjectivity is deeper than self-presence. The seriousness or significance of significa-tion, language, meaning, is precisely the introjection of a future and a past, genuinely transcendent dimensions, alterities, not one's own. Meaning, goodness, and time are a fissuring of the self by and for the other.

G-d

The last stage of Levinas's thought, the alterity of the "to God" (*à Dieu*), extends the significance of the other's otherness to its furthest reaches. In *Totality and Infinity* Levinas had already characterized the intersubjective relation as "religion," the insatiable desire for the absolutely desirable, in contrast to the complacencies and satisfactions of ontology, epistemology, and theology. The central term of that text, "infinity," is explicitly bor-rowed from Descartes' *Meditations,* where it referred to the divine which "dazzled" the Cartesian ego. Levinas has always been concerned with and committed to Judaism, the religion of his birth; *Totality and Infinity,* however, marks the beginning of what comes to be a more and more explicit and extensive insertion of G-d into his properly philosophical writings. Nonetheless, Levinas's G-d does not appear like a tidal wave to obliterate the work of all the earlier waves. G-d appears as an integral part of the ongoing body of work it extends but does not undo.

As indicated by his attachment to the religious writings of Franz Ro-

senzweig, especially *The Star of Redemption* (1921), and his attachment to
the Lithuanian rabbinic tradition, particularly as found in the celebrated
work of Rabbi Hayyim of Volozhyn (1749–1821), the *Nefesh Hahayyim*
(*The Soul of Life,* published posthumously in 1824), G-d for Levinas is
neither an absolute power nor the object of mystical or dogmatic belief.
G-d, too, is encountered in the alterity of the other person. G-d Himself
"comes to the idea" in proximity, in the non-in-difference of one to another.

The glory of the wholly other G-d is found in the face of the other, in
the priority of the other over the self, in a subjectivity subject to the other
in a subjection which is precisely moral election. "The subjection that
precedes deliberation about an imperative, measures, so to speak, or attests
to, an infinite authority" (*TO* 117), Levinas writes in the section entitled
"To-God" in "Diachrony and Representation." The height of G-d is "measured" in the depth of obligation. The appearance of G-d, then, is not
the unique appearance of a set of absolute rules or a privileged text, backed
by thunder, lightning, and a cloud of smoke; it is rather the very excellence
of ethics, the command beyond commandments, the love for the other
prior to the love for oneself. "Love," as Levinas describes it, recalling
Pascal, is "without concupiscence." Revelation is the moral epiphany of
the face.

Hence G-d is the ultimate support for the dimensions of time. "The
futuration of the future," Levinas writes, "is not a 'proof of God's existence,' but 'the fall of God into meaning'" (*TO* 115). Thus to care for
one's neighbor more than oneself, to take on responsibility for the other,
ethics, and to take on the other's responsibilities, justice, is to enter into
a *sacred* rather than an ontological or epistemological history. "The existence of God," Levinas has said in a recent interview, "is sacred history
itself, the sacredness of man's relation to man through which God may
pass."

Because the moral demands of the other draw the subject out into a
future and past never reducible to the present, into the broader demands
of justice, both time and history are sacred, infused by the divine. Sacred
history, the ethical time and significance of sociality, is not, according to
Levinas, "the voyage of an Odysseus" who ventures out courageously but
only in order to finally return home. Rather, it is the journey of an Abram,
who leaves his ancestral home for good, who never returns and has not
yet arrived at his final promised destination, who encounters and is subject
to the absolute alterity of G-d, who overthrows idols and is transformed
to become his better self, Abraham. Thus time and the articulation of
it in Levinas's works become "consecrated," as Levinas writes of Rabbi
Hayyim's *The Soul of Life,* "to a God who claims to be dependent on

humans, on the persons who, since they are infinitely responsible, support the universe."[17]

In-conclusion

Thinking time in relation to the other person, and hence in relation to the moral obligations of social life, means exceeding the categories and structures which have thus far determined thought itself. It means exceeding the *necessity* of thought's necessary categories and structures, for the sake of a greater and more glorious necessity, and exceeding the *priority* of thought's a priori conditions and transcendentality, for the sake of a greater and more glorious priority. Not, certainly, to enter a wild no-man's-land where anything and everything is permitted, where thought becomes radically otherwise than thinking, a vertiginous leap toward "action," "dance," or "violence," where the rupture of thought makes all names possible by making them all equally unintelligible or silly;[18] but, as Levinas would have it, to be awakened to an even more vigilant thinking, to a more attentive, alert, sensitive, sober awareness, to a thinking stripped of its formality and ceremonies, stripped to the rawest nerve, to an insupportable but inexhaustible and inescapable suffering and vulnerability, a thinking which *thinks otherwise* than thought itself, because suffering the inversion and election of being for-the-other before itself.

To think otherwise, for Levinas, is to undergo the *emphasis,* the *hyperbole,* the *superlative,* the *excellence,* which escapes thought while determining it. It is to recognize the dative, the "to the other" and the "for the other," which overdetermines the nominative. It is to enter into a disorientation which is neither an opinion, a prejudice, a dogma, nor a truth, but the wonder proper to ethical significance.

This perpetual dis-orientation is responsibility. But the responsibility Levinas has in mind is paradoxically a *greater* responsibility than the already infinite responsibilities set by *ratio* in the quest for the truth of being, in its call for sufficient reasons and historical enrootedness. The responsibility Levinas discerns in thinking, then, is not just another *more rigorous* attention to method and evidence, another epistemological duty

---

17. Emmanuel Levinas, "Preface," to Rabbi Hayyim de Volozhyn, *L'Ame de la vie,* translated into French by Benjamin Gross (Paris: Editions Verdier, 1986), viii.

18. In his now famous postcard to Jacob Burckhardt dated January 6, 1889, Nietzsche writes: "What is disagreeable and offends my modesty is that at bottom I am every name in history" (in *The Portable Nietzsche,* 686). Though these words were written during the last moment's of Nietzsche's lucidity, to dismiss them as sheer "madness" is a judgment that must be qualified by the rejoinder that if they are indeed the product of madness, then all of Nietzsche's work is mad (which, of course, it is not, at least in the sense intended).

added to the responsibilities which guide and give reasons for reason, the autonomy of the measured life. Rather, there is an *other* responsibility, an unmeasured and unmeasurable responsibility, one directed from and toward the *outside* of thought, from and toward the irreducible alterity of the other person.

There are obligations greater than the infinite responsibility to think and be on one's own, greater, then, than all the traditional philosophic responsibilities, greater because *better*. The alterization effected by the intersubjective encounter, which is time itself, breaks up reality into an irrecuperable past and an unreachable future, disrupts the natural complacency of being, overloading subjectivity, charging the subject with a greater responsibility than its capacities can handle. This will mean that less than a hundred years after its existentialist liberation from twenty five centuries of servitude to the categories of knowledge, from the alleged *eternity* of *essential being*, time must be rethought beyond its recent tutelage to the structures of existential understanding, freed from its tutelage to existential and structural conceptions of *history* and *temporality*. Time must be liberated from its liberators, for time is not a matter of freedom.

Levinas demands further thought, demands that thought go further than it has ever gone or *can* go. Yet his thought is not another nuance in hyperconsciousness. In our day we are all too familiar with disorientation and disorder. They have lost their glamour. We live, Levinas writes in a recent article, in "the century which in thirty years has known two world wars, the totalitarianism of right and left, Hitlerism and Stalinism, Hiroshima, the Gulag, the genocides of Auschwitz and Cambodia."[19] Ours is an age of dis-aster, an age without a guiding star, an age whose firmament has been shaken and is shaking, an unmoored epoch, seemingly without bearings, where the future of humanity, if not life itself, is in question, under the shadow of totalitarian rule and nuclear destruction. It has never been more difficult to think, but not just because the quantity of accumulated and available information has increased geometrically and geographically, as it has; nor only because, having tried and exhausted more than two millennia of self-interpretations, and having recently tried several brilliant and varied renewals, thought no longer knows what to think of itself, no longer has words for itself, can push its hyper-self-reflection no further; but, more profoundly, because thought can no longer think *in good conscience*. Good conscience is not good enough.

To live the *end* of metaphysics, its fulfillment and termination, requires,

---

19. Emmanuel Levinas, "Useless Suffering," translated by Richard A. Cohen, in *The Provocation of Levinas*, edited by Robert Bernasconi and David Wood (New York: Routledge, 1988), 156–67.

Levinas insists, that we take *bad conscience*[20] seriously, that we recognize the full extent and weight of our debts and obligations to the other and to others, that we value goodness and justice above being and order. It requires, in a word, that we live seriously under the constraints of time.

20. See Emmanuel Levinas, "Bad Conscience and the Inexorable," translated by Richard A. Cohen, in *Face to Face with Levinas*, edited by Richard A. Cohen (Albany: SUNY Press, 1986), 35–40.

SEVEN

Non-in-difference

The central inspiration guiding Levinas's thought is at the same time the central inspiration guiding Rosenzweig's.[1] The inspiration they share is the recognition that there is a mode of relation both *more concrete and more important* than the modes of relation that have hitherto constituted and concerned philosophical comprehension. This relation is the intersubjective relation.[2] The greater immediacy and significance of the intersubjective relation come from its terms and its orientation. As early as 1948, in *Time and the Other,* Levinas writes a sentence that in outline is a prospectus of his own thought and a summary of Rosenzweig's: "Set against the cosmos that is Plato's world, is the world of the spirit, where the implications of eros are not reduced to the logic of genus, and where the ego takes the place of the same and the *Other* [i.e., the personal Other, the other person][3] takes the place of the other" (*TO* 94).

The terms of the intersubjective relation, the I and the Other, form what Levinas calls a "new modality" (*CPP* 66, 67) and what Rosenzweig calls a "new thinking"—"new" because they are each independent, separate from one another, absolutely *out* of relation to one another, *and* at the same time absolutely *in* relation to one another. Furthermore, the relation joining the I and the Other is an asymmetrical orientation wherein the Other's relation to the I is not equivalent to the I's relation to the

1. There is much that separates the thought of Franz Rosenzweig from the thought of Emmanuel Levinas. To name only a few of the more obvious differences: there is the essential role in holy history that Rosenzweig grants specifically to Christianity; there are Rosenzweig's religious calendars; there is Schelling's influence and the lack of Heidegger's influence on Rosenzweig; and, like a vast black wall or plague, there is the Holocaust. There are many doctrines and insights that unite their thought, too. Far more important, however, than their particular differences and similarities, is the essential affinity, the brotherhood, the proximity, that brings these two major thinkers together.

2. In *Dieu qui vient a l'idée* (Paris: Vrin, 1982), Levinas writes: "Immediacy par excellence, the relation to the Other is the sole relation which has value only as immediate" (129); and in the preface: "We think that the idea-of-Infinity-in-me—or my relation to God—comes to me in the concreteness of my relation to the other man, in the sociality which is my responsibility for the neighbor" (11).

3. In French *autrui* is used for the personal other, the "other person," and *autre* for the "other" more broadly. In this chapter personal alterity will be designated by a capital "O" on Other, to follow through with what is at stake in this sentence from *TO*. In other chapters in this volume, however, *autrui* and *autre* are both translated as "other," with a small "o." Levinas himself often uses *autre* to mean *autrui*.

Other, where the Other takes priority over the I, where the I is reconditioned by its relation to the Other, and where one is in every instance and inescapably in relation starting from oneself, from myself, in the first person singular.

Straightaway, to propose such a relation will have two interrelated consequences: First, Rosenzweig and Levinas must and do express themselves negatively and positively. Negativity comes first, against the philosophical comprehension which cannot comprehend the concreteness and importance, the immediacy and significance, of intersubjectivity. Both Levinas and Rosenzweig commence thinking "against the cosmos which is Plato's world." Positivity comes second, when expressing what is closer and higher than traditional philosophy, when signifying directly from within the significance of what Levinas calls the "face-to-face" encounter and what Rosenzweig calls "love," a non-place (u-topia) which overflows all forms. Even a cursory reading of the works of Rosenzweig and Levinas reveals that they constantly go back and forth, on every page, within every paragraph, and even within sentences, from the negative to the positive. Both Rosenzweig and Levinas employ a *superlative* negativity and positivity, that is to say, a negativity more negative than philosophical negativity and a positivity more positive than philosophical positivity.

Second, because their "thought" is not a thought but an exceeding of thought, a teaching, not a nominative but a nomination, a moving toward what Rosenzweig calls "life" and what Levinas calls, among other names, "proximity," it has no (negative!) adequate conceptual expression, but must be enacted (positive!) across various but always concrete manifestations: as an erotic encounter, a family relation, a laboring, an ethical behavior, a prayer, a conversation, a ritual. Intersubjectivity never occurs as it is "in itself," in the purity and universality which for philosophy betoken essence. Intersubjectivity is always too close and too demanding for a thought that can and must capture the "in itself," the essence, that is to say, for philosophy.

I will attempt to illuminate both these points, and at the same time show that these two thinkers do indeed share a central inspiration, by explicating the sense of an expression Levinas uses to characterize the relation of the ego to the Other, namely, "non-in-difference." Here, to elucidate Levinas is to implicate Rosenzweig, and vice versa; I hope this proximity will be evident in what follows.

In the intersubjective relation, the I which by itself is in-different becomes non-in-different to the Other. Although Levinas is far more attached to the parallel expression *dis-inter-essement,* which refers to the status of the I stripped of its egocentric "inter-ests" in the intersubjective relation, invoking the *esse* and the "inter-esse" of the ontological difference, and hence calling to mind Levinas's great antagonist, Heidegger, I have chosen nonetheless to focus on the expression "non-in-difference." I have done this not only because the significance of "non-in-difference" parallels the more frequently used "dis-inter-estedness," but because it refers more directly to Hegelian thought, and by referring more directly to Hegelian thought it better serves the purpose of relating Levinas's thought to Rosenzweig's. Rosenzweig's great antagonist is, of course, Hegel. Both thinkers oppose Hegel, which is to say, philosophy "from Ionia to Jena,"[4] from Greek cosmos to German system, philosophy as total comprehension.

One straightforward meaning of the ego's non-in-difference to the Other is clear. Levinas writes that he wants "to account for the impossible indifference with regard to the human which does not succeed in dissimulating itself in the incessant discourse about the death of God, the end of man, and the disintegration of the world" (*OBBE* 59). The reference to G-d, man, and world recalls Rosenzweig, but the main point, the "impossible indifference with regard to the human," is central to both Levinas and Rosenzweig. To G-d, man, and world grasped by historical comprehension—a comprehension which today dissolves them in historical crisis, as it was wont to dissolve them, in the period of philosophy from Parmenides to Hegel, in concepts—Levinas opposes something which cannot dissimulate itself, something therefore irreducibly naked or sincere, namely, the impossibility of being indifferent. The meaning of "indifference" in this quotation is the ordinary one: unconcern, apathy, lack of interest, uninvolvement. There is a concern, an interest, an involvement "with regard to the human," that persists, despite and beyond all comprehension, and which is in truth "impossible" to comprehend. A fine sentiment, true, but what is the significance of the circumlocution? Why must Levinas say "*im*possible *in*difference" or "*non*indifference" rather than simply "concern" or "interest"?

Indifference comes first: the indifference of the self satisfied with itself, content with its enjoyments, wrapped up in its concerns and interests, and also more deeply the in-difference of the intellect caught up in the "life of the mind," in the reflection and consciousness which are always self-reflection and self-consciousness, whether transcendental, dialectical, egological, or ontological, but whose insistent claim to philosophical priority both Levinas and Rosenzweig recognize and attack. Auto-affectation, freedom, egology, self-reference, come first. Philosophy—

4. "Von Jonien bis Jena," in Franz Rosenzweig, *Der Stern der Erlösung* (Berlin: Schocken Verlag, 1930), 2:18; *SR* 12. Everywhere else in the *Star* Rosenzweig writes "from Parmenides to Hegel"; see *SR* 13, 15, 47, et passim.

which is at bottom always first philosophy—is always the elaboration, on the plane of language, of an original or Archimedean self-reference.

Because the self by itself naturally persists in its being, *conatus essendi,* Levinas understands that genuine concern for the Other, a concern going beyond all the ego's own initiatives, even its own acts of charity, is provoked *by* the Other, that the alterity of the Other is imposed on the self, disturbs and disrupts the freedom of the self, awakens another independence in the self, upsetting what Rosenzweig calls the self's solitary and pagan "character" for the sake of its "soul,"[5] or, as Levinas puts it, *electing* the for-itself to the irreplacability of the for-the-other. By itself the ego is not interested in the alterity of the Other—"No one is good voluntarily," Levinas has said (*OBBE* 11)—for the ego's interests are precisely the interests of the ego, its self-enclosure, its "tragic" pride, Rosenzweig would say. The I is concerned to integrate the other, to reduce the other to the same. The I's concern for the alterity of the Other comes in a *non*-indifference, rather than in a primary concern, because precisely a natural and original indifference to the alterity of the Other must be disrupted.

But does not the intellect already perform this function by grasping difference conceptually? Does not the mind, without the disruptive reconditioning effected by an irreducible alterity, already make contact with otherness, with difference? It does, but at a price. The difference that can be comprehended, the difference between the same and the other, is not the difference between the I and the Other. It is to indicate the explosion of the comprehension that comprehends the same and the other that Levinas uses the circumlocution "non-in-difference," using hyphens to break the expression up into its parts to reveal a fundamental non-Hegelian opposition to Hegel. Let us start with the root "difference"; we must distinguish differences.

In *Totality and Infinity* Levinas writes that the "difference between the Other and me does not depend on different 'properties' that would be inherent in the 'I,' on the one hand, and, on the other hand, in the Other" (*TI* 215). That is to say, the differences which make the I-Other relation extra-ordinarily concrete and immediate do not depend on any eccentricity of the I or the Other, on idiosyncracies or unique attributes, whether of genius or monstrosity. This sort of difference derives from what Hegel called "particularity." To scrutinize such differences is to open the door to a genuinely bad infinite, an endlessly microscopic empiricism that always escapes philosophy, but in a loss that is of insignificant consequence.

The difference between two terms that interests philosophy does not

5. See chapter 2 in this volume.

derive from particularity, but from the differentiation of a genus, "the logic of genus," where difference divides individuals that can nonetheless be united within the same species. Here difference is not only that which can be united in thought, in concepts, but is the very element of thought, difference brought to identity or synchrony, or a deferred identity or synchrony, through synthesis. Under the sign of the universal, ultimately of the first principle, the absolute origin, thought gathers different individuals together into identity. One of the most important advances in philosophy after Parmenides was the recognition that in gathering different individuals into an identity, into comprehension, difference itself could not be annihilated but would somehow have to be retained. The history of philosophy is the attempt to lose no difference while still achieving complete identity. The modern turn in philosophy is the account which unifies the difference between the mind that unifies differences and the differences unified.

Hegel is the last master of the thought that retains difference through identification. What he calls the "concrete universal" is the individual as locus of all possible universality, the individual as an integrated element within a systematic and total whole, which is itself, in its entirety, the absolute and comprehensive individual, the One, the equation of subject and substance. Hegel does not merely identify differences, as if consciousness, which is the very the power of identification, of synthesis, were outside the differences it identifies. To identify and retain all differences, all specifications of all genuses, without exception, Hegel understands that consciousness also identifies the difference between identity and difference. It does this through the "positive" power of negation, which is the mind's synthesizing power purified of all givenness, integrating subject and object through the ability to be both what is and what is not, to be what is by being what is not: the famous negation of negation.

This, then, is the deeper Hegelian signification of "in-difference": identity-in-difference. Here in-difference is more than a mundane lack of concern for the Other, more than a slip of the mind or a preoccupation; it is the negation of all radical alterity, or the integration of all alterity, whereby alterity is only retained qua negated, retained for the sake of a higher identity, which is ultimately nothing other than the activity of spirit. It is more than a curiosity that one of the longest citations quoted in *Totality and Infinity* (36–37) is taken from *The Phenomenology of Mind*, and is on the activity of differentiation that Hegel equates with the activity, the "freedom," of self-consciousness, and ultimately with the activity of being itself. In quoting Hegel at length, Levinas wants to show that despite the brilliantly managed retention of difference in the identity of identity and difference, the emphasis in the final account lies not with difference but with identity, with the totality formed through the identification of identity and difference. "The difference [in Hegel's phenomenology]," Levinas explicates, "is not a difference; the I, as other, is not an other. . . . The negation of the I by the self is precisely one of the modes of identification of the I" (*TI* 37). It is precisely in order to reject this sort of difference, a self-differentiation which is equivalent to self-identification, that Levinas uses the expression "*non*-in-difference." But we must be very careful at this juncture to properly grasp the non-Hegelian or non-negative sense of the "non."

To *really* reject Hegel and not merely to up the Hegelian stakes, to avoid a "beyond Hegel" which falsely attempts to free itself from the Hegelian totality by means of a negation of the identification which is itself the negation of negation, that is to say, to avoid a criticism of Hegel which Hegel has already comprehended, which in fact is already included within the concrete universal as its very power of identification, the *non* of Levinas's "non-in-difference" cannot be understood as a negativity, either in the straightforward formal sense or in the dialectical Hegelian sense. Indeed, the section of *Totality and Infinity* coming right after the long Hegel citation is entitled "Transcendence Is Not Negativity." Levinas constantly reminds his readers not to understand his claims within the bounds of the "negative and formal,"[6] within the "logic of genus."

Of course, Levinas's words seem to trip him up. But Levinas, like Rosenzweig, is not a mystic. He is not advocating the annihilation of difference. Rather he is indicating another sort of difference, a difference operating in another modality than philosophical difference, different, that is, than the differences available through possibility, probability, and necessity. Levinas's point does not lie in his formal theses alone, in the words said. It is "beyond the book," Rosenzweig would say. His point lies rather in a philosophical pointlessness, or, positively, in a pointedness, a piercing, an emphasis, a hyperbole, an excellence, an inspiration, which exceeds even the most determinate thought because its *orientation*, the I subject to the Other, the Other prior to the I, is the invisible condition of all thought. Levinas's words do not trip him up, he trips them up.

Both Levinas and Rosenzweig understand the necessity to start with philosophy, the requirement that they use words and prefixes such as "non," "not," "dis," "beyond," "meta," "other," and that these words constitute and are caught up in a logic of their own, the logic of signification. But this starting point, so evident in part 1 of Rosenzweig's *Star,* does not mean that Hegelian philosophy triumphs, or that philosophy

---

6. "The impossibility of killing does not have a simply negative and formal signification; the relation with infinity, the idea of infinity in us, conditions it positively" (*TI* 199).

definitively defeats the skepticism that dogs it, or that the subject is always only substance because even when it is *not* the individual of a genus it is the individual of a genus because not-being is still being through the dialectic of negation. Rather, it means that *philosophy cannot handle what transcends negativity, self-consciousness, substance, and freedom,* which are all equivalent expressions for Hegel; it cannot handle the *positivity* of the ego's non-in-difference to the Other, which, as was indicated in our first quotation from Levinas, is an "impossible indifference"—"beyond the possible" (*OBBE* 58)—but one which nonetheless cannot be "dissimulated." Non-in-difference in its nonphilosophical irreducibility is a *surplus* above and beyond the philosophical comprehension whose condition it is. "A relation might be possible," Levinas writes, "without common ground, that is to say, a relationship in difference; that the difference signifies a non-indifference."[7] This relationship, "without a common ground," exceeds philosophical comprehension, yet is the very bridge between the I and the Other that makes philosophy possible, or, positively, that makes philosophy alive or good, or, as Levinas would say, that gives philosophy "dignity."

At this juncture, or rupture, or break, or overflow, in the movement from in-difference to non-in-difference, or the movement from inter-est to dis-inter-est, Levinas, like Rosenzweig and Schelling, will speak of a "reversal" of thought, of its "inverse," where thought is "put into question." Grasping the I's non-in-difference to the Other in its positivity means grasping it beyond comprehension, *suffering* it in a first-person singularity that increases its singularity, its irreplacability, in the very measure that it is imposed upon not by itself, through auto-affectation or self-reflection, but by the immediacy and excellence of the Other's alterity. The positivity of Levinas's non-in-difference breaks out of quotation marks, out of the themes in which it is said, into what Rosenzweig calls "the bookless present" (*JL* 61). In ethical terms—and we can no longer put off the specific language of the always specific contexts in which non-in-difference occurs—subjectivity is pierced by something *better* than being or nonbeing, an excellence rather than a possibility or an impossibility.

Levinas characterizes the relation of the I to the Other in terms of a desire, a metaphysical desire which does not follow "the implications of eros," of philosophical eros. It is a relation "from the Good to me" where the ego's desire is "responsibility for the neighbor," where the ego's non-in-difference toward the Other "preserves *difference* in the non-indifference

---

7. Emmanuel Levinas, "Ideology and Idealism," translated by Arthur Lesley and Sanford Ames, in *Modern Jewish Ethics,* edited by Marvin Fox (Columbus: Ohio State University Press, 1975), 132.

of the Good, which chooses me before I welcome it . . . in the trauma suffered prior to any auto-identification, in an unrepresentable *before*" (*OBBE* 123). Prior to *because* better than philosophical priority are the priorities of intersubjectivity. Prior to the a priori of philosophical in-difference is the emphatic priority of non-in-difference.

At this point I would like to continue developing Levinas's thought by moving closer to the *Star*, to Rosenzweig's analysis of the ego's non-in-difference to the Other, which he calls, using only a slightly more religious terminology than Levinas, "revelation" *(Offenbarung)*. Because the rela-tion to the alterity of the Other that Rosenzweig calls revelation is central to his thought, it is not surprising that its analysis occurs at the heart and center of the *Star*, in book 2 of part 2. In describing revelation, Rosen-zweig does not use the expression "non-in-difference," but his own equiv-alent expression: "thus and not-otherwise" *(So und Nichtanders)*. In using this expression he is also deliberately rejecting the Hegelian comprehen-sion of individuals through internal and external negation, through the logic of genus. "We could not be satisfied," he writes, "with a *sic et non* based on the Scholastic model, we had to assert a Thus and not-otherwise, thus replacing the *non* with the double negative of a not-otherwise" (*SR* 173). Rosenzweig's double negative, like Levinas's "non" of non-in-difference, will be quite unlike and indeed will subvert Hegel's double negation.

The self is "thus and not-otherwise": *thus* because it is separate, inde-pendent, itself; *not-otherwise* because it is nonetheless in relation to all things, to G-d, man, and world. According to Rosenzweig: "It is already posited as otherwise than everything by the 'thus'—the 'not otherwise' coupled with the 'thus' means precisely that, though otherwise, it is never-theless not at the same time otherwise than everything, that is, capable of being related to everything" (*SR* 174). Here again, at the center of Rosenzweig's thought is an I that is both in relation and out of relation.

How does Rosenzweig understand the I's connection to and separation from alterity, its seemingly contradictory nature? "The 'I' always involves a contradiction," Rosenzweig writes, "it is always underlined, always em-phasized, always an 'I, however'" (*SR* 173). The I that is "thus and not-otherwise," which is equivalent to the I that is "emphatic and underlined," the "actual I," is contradictory not because it is turned against itself through self-negating in the Hegelian manner, divided against itself but on the same plane as itself, where difference is unified through a compre-hension of the identity of identity and difference, the *sic et non* of the Scholastic model. Rather the I is "thus and not otherwise" because it is ruptured or exceeded precisely by its relation to the other person, the interlocutor, the thou, from whence the self gains its emphatic or under-

lined status.[8] The I's separation, its independence, its *thus* (which philosophy turns into a totality by integrating, through negation, whatever is
"otherwise") maintains itself as itself and at the same time in relation to
alterity, by becoming a "thus and *not-otherwise*"—what Levinas speaks of
as an "otherwise than being and not a being otherwise"—precisely and
only in relation to the other person, precisely and only through an immediate and excellent relation to the Other, where the Other comes first and
takes priority over the I even while constituting, or re-constituting, the I.

I quote Rosenzweig at some length here to obviate the suggestion that
I am putting words, Levinasian words, into Rosenzweig's mouth, and,
more importantly, to underline this crucial point about the priority of the
Other in self-constitution:

> Only when the I acknowledges the Thou as something external to itself, that is,
> only when it makes the transition from monologue to authentic dialogue, only
> then does it become that I which we have just claimed. . . . The I of the monologue
> is not yet an "I, however." It is an unemphatic I, an I that is also self-understood
> precisely because it is only self-addressed. . . . Only in the discovery of a Thou is
> it possible to hear an actual I, an I that is not self-evident but emphatic and
> underlined. . . . "Where are Thou?" . . . The I discovers itself at the moment when
> it asserts the existence of the Thou by inquiring into its Where. (*SR* 174–75)

The I becomes an I in its non-in-difference to the Other, when it is put
into question by the Other, when its monologue is interrupted by the
questioning of the Other. Rosenzweig understands that the question
"Where art thou?" is not first the ego's guiding clue to discovering itself
or the Other, since for Rosenzweig, too, the ego's contact with the Other
depends not on the ego's initiative but on the Other's original contact
with the ego. This is to say that the Other is first encountered as a questioning of the ego, through a pre-original contact which though shining
through the *face* of the other, Rosenzweig understands as G-d's question
to man. It is, Rosenzweig writes, "the call that goes out to what cannot
flee, to the utterly particular, to the nonconceptual" (*SR* 175). Levinas
would call this inability to flee the ego's "passivity more passive than all
receptivity," its undeclinable "election" to itself. Rosenzweig will refer
to the ego's beginning after its creation, or to the necessary *sequence* of
creation-revelation-redemption (*SR* 189), a sequentiality or irreversibility
invisible to philosophy but its very condition.

With Rosenzweig's notion of sequence we can finally understand the
priority of intersubjectivity in relation to the priority of philosophy, the
firstness of philosophy in relation to the greater importance of intersubjec-

8. "Only in the discovery of a Thou is it possible to hear an actual I, an I that is not
self-evident but emphatic and underlined" (*SR* 175).

tivity where the I's secondness is its very firstness. The philosophical subject, he or it that comes first, becomes truly subject ("soul") subjected to the Other, second to the Other. Philosophy is always first philosophy in the sense that its eros always seeks the origin, the foundation, the absolute. In relation to this philosophical eros where difference becomes indifference, the desire for the Other comes second, non-in-difference. The soul, Rosenzweig would say, comes after the self; the self must be loved by the other to become the beloved soul that can love others in turn. The ego is disrupted *after* its own origins, it *begins after* its *origin,* just as Rosenzweig's *Star* starts with Hegel's system and Levinas starts with the "cosmos that is Plato's world," both in order to show what cosmos and system cannot contain though they are all inclusive. Levinas refers to the movement in Descartes' third Meditation, where Descartes is "dazzled" by the idea of G-d—by the *priority* which can only be G-d's—put into him *after* he has already found his absolute origin in the *cogito.* "In some way I have in me," Descartes' writes, "the notion of the infinite earlier than the finite—to wit, the notion of God before that of myself."[9] To return to Rosenzweig's terminology: the intersubjective *beginning,* the beloved self, comes after the *origin,* whether that origin be on the intelligible plane of the philosophical subject or on the existential plane of the tragic self. The true self begins after its origin, is struck by what does not originate in its origin. In the same disturbing movement the self discovers that it is given prior to its positings, discovers itself to have been *created* prior to its origin.

The self of the intersubjective relation, the soul, "the beloved self," according to Rosenzweig's formulae, the elected self, "the self despite-itself," according to Levinas, comes *after* and *before* the ego of the philosophical quest for origins, even (and especially) when that philosophical ego knows itself to be substance. The soul is pre-original and post-original. Levinas will speak of a "future that is always future," an illeity, and of an "immemorial past" or passivity that was never present. For the post-original future and the pre-original past Rosenzweig uses the terms redemption and creation. To redeem and to have been created are movements which disrupt the autonomy of the self-originating self, in a disruption Rosenzweig calls revelation: an immediacy and excellence which constitute the very presence of the present.

Undercutting the notion of autonomy, both Levinas and Rosenzweig defend the scandalous notion of the subject's finite freedom. In relation

---

9. Descartes, "Meditation Three: Of God: That He exists," in *The Philosophical Works of Descartes,* translated by Elizabeth S. Haldane and G. R. T. Ross (Cambridge: Cambridge University Press, 1968), 166.

to the face of the Other, the self in dialogue "answers, all unlocked, all spread apart, all ready, all-soul: 'Here I am'" (*SR* 176). Levinas, of course, also uses this expression, "Here I am," to characterize the very subjectivity of the subject, a subjectivity already subject to the Other, recalling along with Rosenzweig the biblical *hineni* spoken by Abraham and Isaiah in answer—however inadequate, and always inadequate—to G-d.

Of the combination of concreteness and excellence which orients the intersubjective relation, which gives it its absolute "above and below" (*SR* 422), and which Rosenzweig like Levinas "locates" in the face of the Other,[10] Rosenzweig writes (perhaps optimistically?) that prior to the crises of our day, "up to the threshold of the nineteenth century," before the rise of modern subjectivism, "one simply knew that the I and Thou of human discourse is without more ado also the I and Thou between God and man. One knew that the distinction between immanence and transcendence disappears in language. . . . Man loves because God loves and as God loves. His human soul is the soul awakened and loved by God" (*SR* 199). "Love simply cannot be 'purely human'" (*SR* 201). And like Levinas Rosenzweig admits that his own words betray him, that they must be resaid, because "all true statements about love must be words from its own mouth, borne by the I" (*SR* 202); "love is not to be a case of love" (*SR* 202).

The central inspiration of Rosenzweig and Levinas, call it proximity or love, emerges because both thinkers shift from a comprehension which sacrifices its terms to its relations, to the extra-ordinary relation between the I and the Other, whose "terms"—starting from the I but beginning with the Other—remain separate and related, through the inescapability of obligation rather than through the necessity of thought. Both thinkers grant philosophy the first word only in order to deny it the last.

10. See the remarkable concluding pages of the *Star* (422–23).

EIGHT

G-d in Levinas: The Justification of Justice and Philosophy

Reconciling Two G-ds

The topic of this chapter is Emmanuel Levinas's conception of G-d. All direct quotations from Levinas are taken, however, not from his many "Jewish writings"[1] but rather from his two major philosophical works, *Totality and Infinity* (1961) and *Otherwise than Being or Beyond Essence* (1974), and from an article entitled "God and Philosophy" (1975).[2] Although the reason for this formal stress upon philosophy can only become fully clear at the conclusion of the chapter, the coupling of this stress with the knowledge that Levinas's thought is committed to the Jewish tradition, to a properly Jewish conception of G-d, already provides a preliminary indication of the direction the task at hand will take. In unfolding Levinas's nuanced conception of G-d, I hope to show both that and how Levinas *resolves* the modern opposition between the universalist *ratio* which determines the "god of the philosophers," on the one side, and the demanding personal encounter so essential to the "G-d of Abraham, Isaac and Jacob," on the other, the opposition, that is, between Athens and Jerusalem, reason and revelation, being and the Bible.[3]

In a "Note" preceding the first page of *Otherwise than Being or Beyond Essence,* Levinas writes of its accomplishment:

The difficulties of the climb, as well as its failures and renewed attempts, are marked in the writing, which no doubt also shows the breathlessness of the author. But to hear a God not contaminated by Being is a human possibility no less

---

1. As to Levinas's Jewish writings, one thinks of his annual talmudic readings, nine of which have been collected together and translated into English in *NTR,* or the collection of "Essays on Judaism" in *DF.* This chapter will make clear that such a division, legitimate as far as it goes, between properly philosophical and properly Jewish writings, is not for Levinas a hard or absolute one.

2. Emmanuel Levinas, "God and Philosophy," translated by Richard A. Cohen, *Philosophy Today* 22, no. 2 (Summer 1978): 127–45; reprinted in *LR* 167–89, and in *CPP* 153–73; the latter will be used for references.

3. Given the long history and the great magnitude of this opposition, Levinas's resolution can hardly be expected to satisfy all interested or affected parties. Nonetheless, his contribution is not only unique and therefore original, but sufficiently subtle and persuasive to deserve universal hearing and consideration.

important and no less precarious than to bring Being out of the oblivion in which it is said to have fallen in metaphysics and in onto-theology. (*OBBE* xlii)

Levinas is obviously referring to Heidegger. But his claim is a much larger one than a critical response to a philosophical contemporary. His claim is that the discourse on or of G-d is, while "no less precarious" than ontology or traditional philosophy, also "no less important." It is perhaps both even more precarious and even more important. Perhaps it is precisely the greater precariousness of divine discourse that makes for its greater importance than philosophy. What is certain is that for Levinas, G-d and philosophy are neither incompatible nor can one encompass or substitute for the other.

There is a further suggestion in this note. In the conjunction of an apparently biographical aside, those "markings" in the text that testify to "the difficulties of the climb" and to "failures and renewed attempts," not to mention the author's "breathlessness," on the one hand, and the awesome philosophical claim regarding the importance and precariousness of the discourse on G-d in comparison to the importance and precariousness of ontological disclosure, that is to say, the balancing of G-d and philosophy, on the other, there is more, I think, than an incidental or accidental insertion of the "merely" biographical. This "apology" is essential to Levinas's thought. It is not accidental, obviously, from the side of Levinas's person, where it originates, but neither is it accidental, more importantly, from the side of philosophy. Perhaps, tentatively, we can formulate what is suggested by this conjunction as follows. Attentiveness to the manner in which the opposition between Athens and Jerusalem is resolved requires at the same time an attentiveness to the medium of this resolution, to that "something" whose own precariousness, slightness, and fragility threatens to be lost to meaning and is at the same time "present" to meaning by way of—or in the passage, trace, or inspiration of—a breath. Or to say this still more precisely, one must be attentive to the "breathlessness" by which even the essentially Greek, the "winged words" of truth—*especially* the winged words of truth—retain the mark of their true author and also, thereby, so Levinas intimates, gain the wings of their truth. This chapter will pursue precisely these suggestions.

From March 1973 to March 1974, just before and after the appearance of *Otherwise than Being or Beyond Essence*, Levinas went on a lecture tour. He gave six invited talks on the topic of G-d and philosophy at universities in almost as many different cities in Western Europe and Israel. The itinerary began in Lille, moved to Paris, Jerusalem, and Brussels, and ended in Geneva. The talks were sponsored by philosophy and theology departments, under the auspices of secular, Catholic, Protestant, and Jewish institutions. Levinas spoke in French except in Jerusalem, where he spoke in Hebrew.

This factual information can be found in another note, the "Preliminary Note" which precedes the article which was published after the lecture tour. The article, entitled "God and Philosophy," appeared in the spring of 1975 in the French literary and philosophical journal *Le Nouveau Commerce*.[4] The significance of this factual information is explained as follows by Levinas, in the concluding sentences of the preliminary note:

> The text we are publishing here is based on the core content of each of these lectures. This itinerary of lectures has given it an ecumenical character. We mention this especially in order to render homage to the life and work of Professor Hugo Bergman who, having very early settled in Jerusalem, was always faithful to Israel's universal vocation which the state of Zion ought to serve only, to make possible a discourse addressed to all men in their human dignity, so as then to be able to answer for all men, our neighbors. (*CPP* 154)

The homage to Hugo Bergman confirms once again the "ecumenical character" of Levinas's thought.[5] It is not just that Levinas's thought contains the prudent rhetorical cautions required of a sensitive discourse intended for Jewish and gentile audiences, but that it is intended to bring together, as its title indicates, "God and philosophy."

There is more, then, in this preliminary note than an homage to the person of Hugo Bergman, or, again more precisely, there is more in an homage to Hugo Bergman than a "merely" personal testimony. The proclamation of "Israel's universal vocation," as the making possible of "a discourse addressed to all men in their human dignity," locates Levinas's thought within the modern Western tradition of enlightened humanism. More specifically, the vocabulary and sense indicates that Levinas is locat-

---

4. Emmanuel Levinas, "Dieu et la philosophie," *Le Nouveau Commerce* 30-31 (Spring 1975): 97–128; this article, again prefaced by the same "Preliminary Note," also appears in Emmanuel Levinas, *De Dieu qui vient a l'idée*, 93–127.

5. Samuel Hugo Bergman (1883–1975), to whom Levinas renders homage, writes in *Faith and Reason:* "Pascal was right: he used to wear an amulet with the inscription, 'God of Abraham, Isaac and Jacob—not the god of the philosophers.' The god of the philosophers is at best a scientific hypothesis. You cannot pray to a scientific hypothesis. The Lord of Hosts wants not to be proved but to be called upon in perfect truth" (*Faith and Reason: Modern Jewish Thought,* translated by Alfred Jospe [New York: Schocken Books, 1963], 21). Levinas has hit the mark, of course, in rendering homage to Bergman, whose position, as one easily discovers by reading the whole text from which the above is taken, is to defend and articulate "a synthesis between faith and reason" (26).

ing his own thought close to the enlightened humanism of Immanuel Kant, a rational ethical universalism.

This rational ethical universalism, however, is meant to make possible the fulfillment of a further goal, a discourse "able to answer for all men," where Levinas specifies the expression "all men" as "our neighbors." *This* language, in contrast to the language of dignity, locates Levinas's thought within an equally modern, though differently based, universalist tradition, namely that of Jewish humanism. Here G-d's biblical command to the Jews to "love thy neighbor" is taken beyond the confines of the Jewish people proper, beyond the restrictions of tribal or exclusively inter-Jewish relations, and universalized to include "all men."

These two references—to the *dignity* of a rational humanist universalism and to the *love of the neighbor* of biblical humanist universalism (one might think here of Franz Rosenzweig and Hermann Cohen)—must be born in mind if we are not to misunderstand what is characteristic about Levinas's attempt to think G-d and philosophy together.

Levinas, as we know, is not alone is attempting to juggle two traditions, the biblical and the rational. Ever since the Enlightenment all Western religious thought, and especially Jewish religious thought, has found itself torn, in one way or another, "between two worlds." What is characteristic about Levinas's attempt to think G-d and philosophy together— and by philosophy we must understand what Levinas, and not he alone, understands by it, namely, that "philosophy is the bearer of the spirituality of the West" (*CPP* 155)—is that his thinking together of G-d and philosophy is done in a manner different from, indeed opposed to, those for whom these two terms are in irreconcilable conflict.

Levinas neither glorifies a conflict nor reduces one term to the other, whether G-d to philosophy or philosophy to G-d. Positively, then, his is an attempt to weigh and respect the proper value of both terms and to bring them into a resolution which both may recognize as genuine.

Levinas concludes the first subsection of "God and Philosophy" with an assertion of precisely this bold intention. It is bold because it calls into question what has arguably been the most fundamental distinction regarding G-d within modern Jewish and Christian thought, a distinction that makes this thought both modern and at the same time religious: the distinction between the god of the philosophers and the G-d of Abraham, Isaac, and Jacob. This distinction appears eminently already in Judah Halevi and Blaise Pascal, and then later also in Søren Kierkegaard, Martin Buber, Leo Strauss, and other modern religious thinkers. In contrast to that other group of moderns whose modernity hinges on foreswearing the institutions and realities of living religion entirely, these latter thinkers, like Halevi and Pascal before them, distance themselves from the rational but cold "god of the philosophers" by means of various intimate alliances with the G-d of Abraham, Isaac, and Jacob.

I will cite only Martin Buber and Leo Strauss, not only because they are important thinkers in their own right, but also, in this context, because they are Levinas's contemporaries and are quite clear on the significance of the distinction at hand.

In a 1943 article on Hermann Cohen's intellectual development, whose title, "The Love of God and the Idea of Deity," is itself but another formulation of this very distinction, Buber begins with the following dramatic invocation of Pascal:

In those scribbled lines affecting us as cries of the very soul, which Pascal wrote after two ecstatic hours, and which he carried about with him until his death, sewn into the lining of his doublet, we find under the heading *Fire* the note: "God of Abraham, God of Isaac, God of Jacob—not of the philosophers and scholars."[6]

Buber then spends the rest of his article attempting to show that, despite Cohen's predilection for idealist philosophy and hence despite his intellectual commitments to the merely ideational and therefore abstract deity of the philosophers ("the Idea of Deity" of Buber's title), his thought was nonetheless moving toward, or was perhaps even already within the orbit of the concrete and loving G-d of Abraham, Isaac, and Jacob ("The Love of God"). Buber, for his part, sides unambiguously with the latter, the personal G-d of the Bible, whom he understands as the mysterious presence animating and revealed in the interhuman "I-Thou" encounter.

Indeed, so deep and one-sided is Buber's commitment to the personal G-d of the Bible against the abstract god of the philosophers that the rhetorical force of his writing leads one to think that "I-It" experience, whose cognitive abstractness stands in stark opposition to the living mystery of the "I-Thou" relation that it eclipses, represents for Buber *evil* itself.[7]

Leo Strauss, too, is also very much taken by this distinction, which appears often and in various guises in his work. In the concluding section of an article whose themes were first formulated in the early 1950s, and

6. Martin Buber, "The Love of God and the Idea of Deity" (1943), translated by I. M. Lask, in *The Eclipse of God: Studies in the Relation Between Religion and Philosophy* (New York: Harper & Row, 1957), 49.

7. Professor Norbert Samuelson, among others, recently proposed such an interpretation at his presentation on December 17, 1990, at the 22d annual conference of the Association for Jewish Studies, in Boston, Massachusetts.

whose title, "Progress or Return? The Contemporary Crisis in Western Civilization,"[8] contains yet another even more succinct formulation of the same distinction, Strauss's argument drives him to accept the "often-made remark that the god of Aristotle is not the God of Abraham, Isaac, and Jacob."[9] Here as elsewhere Strauss takes this distinction to be fundamental, indeed decisive, for the very definition of the "West." In contrast to Buber, who, as we have seen, sides unambiguously with the G-d of the Bible *against* the god of reason, Strauss understands the value of the distinction to lie in the irreducible yet ineradicable *conflict* of its terms. He finds this conflict manifest in a variety of registers, in the opposition between progress and return, the new and the old, reason and revelation, Athens and Jerusalem, Greek philosophy and the Hebrew Bible, freedom and covenant, the primacy of speech and the primacy of deed, to name a few.

Unlike Buber, who, to say it again, rails from the side of the loving G-d of Abraham, Isaac, and Jacob against the abstract god of the philosophers, Strauss, who also, with extreme caution, takes the biblical side, recognizes the opposition itself as not only irreducible and irreconcilable, having its source, as he writes, in "a fundamental dualism in man,"[10] but also as the most inevitable and fruitful of all conflicts. "It seems to me," he goes so far as to say, "that this unresolved conflict is the secret of the vitality of Western civilization."[11]

My point, however, is not to explicate Buber or Strauss, but far more simply to illustrate how the distinction between the philosophical god and the biblical G-d is typically understood by contemporary and modern Jewish thought as an opposition, conflict, or crisis. It appears as nothing less than the great divide, a rift running through Western spirituality from beginning to end, making the famous "quarrel of the ancients and the moderns" a family affair. On the one side there is the god of the philosophers and scholars, an abstract, depersonalized, rationally absolutized G-d, to put this in modern terms, a god whose attributes of omniscience, omnipotence, omnipresence, and beneficence serve both as the products of ratiocination and as sacrifices to the same. Despite the "G-d talk," it is theology, the *logos,* reason, which rules on this side. And on the other side there is the G-d of Abraham, the G-d of Isaac, the G-d of Jacob, the G-d of the Bible, intervening at will in history, establishing personal rela-

8. Leo Strauss, "Progress or Return? The Contemporary Crisis in Western Civilization," *An Introduction to Political Philosophy: Ten Essays by Leo Strauss,* edited by Hilail Gildin (Detroit: Wayne State University Press, 1989), 248–310.

9. Ibid., 295.

10. Ibid., 294.

11. Ibid., 289.

tions with select individuals and nations, the ultimate support and witness to the drama of human morality and mortality. The thinkers named above—Halevi, Pascal, Kierkegaard, Buber, and Strauss—are religious thinkers precisely to the extent that each in his own way promotes the latter, submits to the latter, the G-d of Abraham, Isaac, and Jacob, against the former, the god of the philosophers.

It is *against* this entire oppositional tradition that Levinas takes his stand within religious thought. Elaborating an "alternative" to it is indeed the explicit aim of "God and Philosophy." It is this intention, as I have indicated, that Levinas expresses in the concluding sentences of the introductory section:

To ask, as we are trying to do here, if God can be expressed in a rational discourse which would be neither ontology nor faith is implicitly to doubt the formal opposition, established by Yehouda Halevy and taken up by Pascal, between the God of Abraham, Isaac, and Jacob, invoked in faith without philosophy *(sans philosophie),* and the god of the philosophers. It is to doubt that this opposition constitutes an alternative. *(CPP* 155)

The object of this chapter, then, is to show how Levinas thinks the personal G-d of Abraham, Isaac, and Jacob philosophically, to show how Levinas thinks the biblical G-d without reducing Him to philosophy, to the god of the philosophers, on the one hand, and without sidestepping or belittling philosophy, on the other.

One, Two, Three . . . G-d

I will present Levinas's position in seven statements, each followed by a commentary. The seven statements are taken verbatim from *Totality and Infinity* and *Otherwise than Being or Beyond Essence.* Their number could doubtlessly be increased or decreased; it is of no intrinsic significance. The order, on the other hand, is both significant and not significant. It is not significant because Levinas's position must be seen in its entirety, as a complex and unified vision. It is significant, on the other hand, for at least two reasons: first because it too reminds us that philosophical articulation, the development of thought, testifies not only to what is being said, the content of thought, but to the saying of it, by which I do not mean the formal qualities of style and composition alone, but the "trace," perhaps only a tempo or a resonance—less than the fluttering of wings—of the author; and second because the order is one of ascent, of increasing moral exigency and acuity, moving toward the good.

In all of Levinas's work the primacy of the good orders the priority of the true, and not the reverse. Thus the order of the seven statements below is not another updated version of Plato's *Symposium* or of the beautiful tale of the cave, that arduous climb from the shadows and dark of ignorance to the brilliance of a world illuminated by the sun above and the challenge of a difficult descent to enlighten all those who still remain below. Rather it is a movement rising from atheism to G-d and then back to philosophy, for it is not a daimon or a god but G-d who demands philosophy.

1. *"Atheism conditions a veritable relationship with a true God* kath auto *[self-caused]"* (TI 77).

By this Levinas means that in order to enter into that special relationship which is the relationship with G-d, the human being must be sufficiently separated from G-d not to be obliterated, annihilated, extinguished, or erased by that relationship. To express this in a "religious" terminology that Levinas sometimes calls "obsolete" (e.g., *CPP* 156), what Levinas is saying is that though man is G-d's creation, he is that element of creation which was created with the resources to remain independent of the Creator, that is to say, to willfully refuse G-d, to be atheist. Here, for humans, it is G-d who is made to suffer a precarious existence.[12] Here, too, in his freedom, it is man who is created in the "image of G-d." A being without the capacity to refuse G-d could not enter into relationship with G-d and remain in relationship with G-d.

Of course, from a purely logical point of view, this conception of man's freedom could be used to call into question G-d's omnipotence. This age-old paradox, with its many attempted resolutions and long history, does not concern us directly, but it does bring into focus what is important about Levinas's "method."[13] In *Totality and Infinity* as elsewhere, Levinas's claims are not the product of a deductive logic, an *ordine geometrico demonstrata;* rather, they are the result of phenomenological investigations. Such

---

12. Franz Rosenzweig finds a positive religious consequence in the possibility of atheism as follows: "A rabbinical legend spins a tale of a river in a distant land, a river so pious that it supposedly halted its flow on the Sabbath. If but this river flowed through Frankfort instead of the Main River—no doubt all Jewry there would strictly observe the Sabbath. But God does not deal in such signs. Apparently he dreads the inevitable consequences: that in this case precisely those least free, those most fearful and miserable, would become the most 'pious.' Evidently God wants for his own only those who are free" (*SR* 266; also cited in *FR* 284).

13. I put "method" in scare quotes because it is not entirely correct to say that Levinas has a *method* at all. See Charles William Reed, "Levinas' Question," *Face to Face with Levinas,* 73–82.

Though in this paragraph, for the sake of brevity and to respect Levinas's self-interpretation, I call Levinas's manner of philosophizing "phenomenology," to be more exact his philosophy is rather an "ethical overloading of phenomenology," or an "ethical overloading of philosophy." On this topic, see chapter 12 in this volume.

investigations require careful, detailed, "genetic" archaeological description. One entire section of *Totality and Infinity,* for example, making up
one quarter of its pages, is devoted to describing the structures of human
being qua "separated," the sphere of significations which constitute immanence and worldly being. These claims, like all the claims of phenomenology and philosophy more generally, can be challenged, to be sure. A more
rigorous, accurate, inclusive, well-ordered description would supplant one
that is less so. But this is not what concerns us here either. What should
be noted is, first of all, as mentioned, that Levinas's claims do not derive
from and hence are not subject solely to the stringencies of pure logic,
and second, and therefore, that for Levinas humanity's independence from
G-d hinges not on pure will or pure freedom abstractly conceived (as it
does within the *rational* systems of Kant and Sartre, to take two contrary
instances), but rather on a "finite freedom," where finitude refers to sensual and worldly being, what Levinas calls humanity's "created" being.

This said, the issue at hand is to understand what is at stake in the first
statement, namely, the claim that *atheism* is the condition for a relationship
with G-d. Putting the matter in the most general or abstract terms, what
Levinas realizes is that a "veritable relationship" must begin and end with
two terms or it is no longer a relationship. Neither term can be reduced
to the other or considered its dialectical equivalent.[14] The divine-human
relationship cannot collapse from either of its two sides, from the side of
man or the side of G-d. Levinas is neither an idealist nor a mystic.[15]

If man reduces G-d to the human level, then G-d is not G-d but a
human invention, projection, idea, or myth. To avoid this sort of reduction—whether cognitive, psychological, sociological, anthropological, or

14. Hermann Cohen has made a similar point. "In Judaism," he writes, "God and man
maintain their respective distinctiveness . . . though they are necessarily correlated. That
means, on the one hand, that man's individuality remains intact, and on the other that the
concept of 'spirit of holiness' effects a union between God and man" (*Reason and Hope:
Selections from the Jewish Writings of Hermann Cohen,* translated and edited by Eva Jospe
[New York: W. W. Norton, 1971], 150).

Gilles Deleuze, a contemporary French philosopher antipathetic to the transcendence of
G-d, nonetheless desperately seeks a relation such as the one Levinas and Hermann Cohen
affirm, a nondialectical relation respecting the singularity of terms. It is not so surprising,
then, that he finds its secular analog in the possibility allegedly opened up by Nietzsche's
overman. Unfortunately by rejecting true transcendence he, as Nietzsche before him, and
all those confirmed in a Spinozist monism, cannot avoid—and even ends by affirming—
monadicism, the solitary. See Gilles Deleuze, *Nietzsche and Philosophy,* translated by Hugh
Tomlinson (New York: Columbia University Press, 1983), chapter 5, "The Overman:
Against the Dialectic," 147–94.

15. For Levinas's relation to Jewish mysticism, see chapter 11 in this volume. Levinas
always rejects mysticism understood as union with G-d by means of the obliteration of self,
total absorption of self into G-d, indistinction of self and G-d.

historical—G-d's transcendence must be respected. For this reason Levinas refers to the G-d of a "veritable relationship" not simply as "G-d," but as the "true God *kath auto*," meaning the transcendent G-d. The true G-d cannot be reduced to the human level.[16]

But so too from the other side, which is perhaps of greater interest here, where, knowing *that* Levinas affirms the true G-d, one might be surprised by the status given to atheism, which signals not the end of religion but its condition. The only term sufficient to maintain a relationship with the true G-d, to not be reduced by G-d to G-dhood, to not become wholly absorbed into and indistinguishable from G-d, is a being capable of atheism, that is to say, more simply and more phenomenologically, a being *capable,* a being with its own capacities. Levinas clearly has Heidegger's "Dasein analytic" in mind, though unlike Heidegger he does not, as one might well anticipate, limit human being to possibilities, ownmost or otherwise.[17]

Atheism is the possibility of a being capable of putting up a determined, resolute, or willful resistance to G-d. Only an able being is a being able to refuse G-d. And, only a being able to refuse G-d is a being able to be moved by G-d.

Of course, having the *capacity* for independence does not mean that "veritable relationship" with G-d occurs *when* man is atheist. Not at all. It means only, as Levinas has written, that "atheism *conditions* [my italics] a veritable relationship with a true God." Though the "veritable relationship" will, as we shall see, transform both terms (though differently), both terms must at the same time retain their independence throughout, G-d His absoluteness and man his finitude.

2. *"The dimension of the divine opens forth from the human face"* (TI 78).

The only place where Levinas finds a relationship such as the one necessitated above, where one term of the relation is absolute and the other term

16. "The incapacity 'to interpret God as a Reality' "is, according to Leo Strauss in 1935, "the characteristic embarrassment for the modern 'philosophy of religion' inaugurated by Schleiermacher" ("The Conflict of Ancients and Moderns in the Philosophy of Judaism," *Philosophy and Law,* translated by Fred Baumann [Philadelphia: Jewish Publication Society, 1987], 28). Levinas is able to break with *this* incapacity by means of a phenomenological interpretation of being. It may well be that it is precisely because Strauss maintains a pre-Kantian conception of "reality," as in the above citation, that he always ends up caught in the same unresolved and unresolvable conflict between Athens and Jerusalem—a conflict based on what Kant called an antinomy.

17. Levinas's high regard for *BT* is long standing, well known, and a matter of record. His criticisms of Heidegger the man are perhaps less well known, but are also long standing and a matter of record. See, for example, Emmanuel Levinas, "Comme un consentement à l'horrible," *Le Nouvel Observateur,* no. 1211, January 22–28, 1988, 82–83.

nonetheless retains its independence, is the interhuman relationship, the one-on-one or face-to-face relationship between two humans. He names the relationality at work here "proximity." It is more, however, than a spatial nearness or contiguity. By the *human* face and the *dimension* of the divine it brings to bear, Levinas means that which is from the first moral, that whose primacy is ethical rather than cognitive or aesthetic.

This comment, however, requires the qualification, the further development, of the third statement, which must be expressed in the same breath, as it were—breathlessly!—as the second:

3. *"The Other is not the incarnation of God, but precisely by his face, in which he is disincarnate, is the manifestation of the height in which God is revealed"* (TI 79).

Here then is a further determination of the "dimension of the divine": not the other's face itself, its surface, the skin, but rather the height that opens up through this surface, this skin. The face, for Levinas, is a height.[18] It is not the incarnation of G-d, but rather and precisely the "disincarnation." G-d is revealed in a disincarnation, a dimension, a height: "the height in which G-d is revealed."

The second statement did not say that the divine is a being, or even the being of beings, but rather, and more precisely, a "dimension." The dimension of the divine is height. But this height is not that of the sky above, or it is that height only indirectly. It is rather the height found nowhere else or nowhere more than in the human face, in the face-to-face. This dimensionality, which is that of the divine, and which is at the same time, again attending to Levinas's words, that of the human, what is human about the human face, not to be mistaken for a spatial relation, is a *moral* dimension, the dimension of moral height, goodness.

This is perhaps *the* central claim of all Levinas's thought, about which his entire work revolves: the face of the other manifests and is manifest in a moral height which is the dimension of G-d, the revelation of G-d. Prophecy, revelation, occurs between interlocutors.

Only the moral relationship with the other relates two terms while

18. In a recent interview which appeared in *Autrement,* no. 102, November 1988, reprinted in Emmanuel Levinas, *Entre nous: Essais sur le penser-à-l'autre* (Paris: Editions Grasset et Fasquelle, 1991), Levinas has said: "It is necessary to also say that in my way of expressing myself the word 'face' must not be understood narrowly. The possibility for the human to signify in his unicity, in the humility of his nakedness and mortality, the lordship of his call—word of God—of my responsibility for him, and my unique election to this responsibility, can come from the nudity of an arm sculpted by Rodin" (*Entre nous* 262 [my translation]). Nonetheless, as is evident in even this "disclaimer," the primary or exemplary place, as it were, of the "face" is certainly that of the flesh and blood human person who faces another face-to-face.

respecting[19] their irreducible differences. This is why Levinas characterizes the relationship in terms of height. We might imagine this relationship

19. I have deliberately chosen the term "respect," with Kant foremost in mind, for the sake of a brief excursus to indicate important differences separating Levinas and Kant and, in a moment, Sartre, regarding the encounter with moral alterity.

Most broadly, Kant and Levinas differ regarding what counts as reason. Levinas's thought comes out of and overloads *phenomenology*. His "inquiry concerning human understanding" is thus from the start wider than Kant's, which is, as Kant formulates it, a "critique of pure reason." Even if practical reason takes precedence in Kant over pure reason, the two are made to conform to one another, hence the limitations of the latter limit the former.

For Kant the encounter with moral otherness is effected across what he calls respect *(Achtung)*. But what the Kantian moral ego respects in the other is not the alterity of the other but precisely the law, the same law that commands both self and other, universal law. Moral alterity for Kant means raising the anthropological to the rational, raising subjective maxims to objective maxims, raising rules to laws. Both the other person and the self as free moral agents must obey the same law. Their reason for doing so, however, is philosophy's oldest reason: fulfilling the demands of rationality, in Kant's case, a rational "faculty." This rational faculty, however, both its existence and telos, are simply given. Precisely at this point, then, Kant cannot say *why* man should be rational, except that man *has* a rational faculty. Of attempts to justify or provide the rationale for commitment to free respect for law, Kant writes: "This is circular because freedom and self-legislation of the will are both autonomy and thus are reciprocal concepts, and for that reason one of them cannot be used to explain the other and to furnish a ground for it" (*Foundations of the Metaphysics of Morals*, translated by Lewis White Beck [Indianapolis: Bobbs-Merrill, 1980], 69). This insuperable failure of reason to justify or even explain itself beyond its own pure self-relationship (principle of noncontradiction) is also grasped by Kant in the same text as follows: "How pure reason can be practical—to explain this, all human reason is wholly incompetent, and all the pains and work of seeking an explanation of it are wasted" (*Foundations* 81). Levinas, in contrast, as we shall see at the conclusion of this chapter, can justify philosophy. Kant's rationalism cannot see beyond consciousness, a limitation which is both the excellence and the limitation of Kant's entire philosophy.

Sartre, too, whose "existentialism" seems to have gone beyond the bounds of Kantian rationality, has in fact come no closer to Levinas's insights regarding alterity or the "ground" of rationality than Kant. Even when Sartre tries to establish an intersubjective morality, he can say nothing more, or support nothing more than his original claim, namely, that freedom aims for freedom. In his 1946 article "Existentialism is a Humanism," where more than anywhere else Sartre attempts to escape this trap, he writes that "freedom in every concrete circumstance can have no other end or aim but itself" ("Existentialism is a Humanism," translated by Philip Mairet, in *The Existentialist Tradition*, edited by Nino Langiulli [Garden City, N.J.: Doubleday, 1971], 412. It is this circularity or mirror that explains for us why Sartre is unconvincing when he tries to persuade his readers that his form of existentialism is a humanism. It is rather an egology. When Sartre gets to the central point of his article, when he writes that "when we say that man is responsible for himself, we do not mean that he is responsible only for his own individuality, but that he is responsible for all men" (396), his claim rings hollow and is unconvincing. It is unconvincing because by "responsibility for all men" Sartre means a responsibility unalterably trapped within the confines of its own freedom, hence incapable of any genuine *outside* responsibilities. Less than Kant, there is not even law. "Responsibility for all men" could just as well mean "responsibility for all toadstools" or "responsibility for all quarks." Subjectivity is, as Sartre himself put it, "conas a diagonal, with the other person above and the self below. The point is that the self and the other are related asymmetrically. Thus in the face-to-face there are not only two terms, but two relations. In one and the same relationship, and yet without recourse to the sociological notion of "roles," my relation to the other person is not at all the same as the other person's relation to me. Such a relationship can only be "understood"— really *undergone*—morally, as Levinas accounts for it in the following:

In proximity the other obsesses me according to the absolute asymmetry of signification, of the one-for-the-other: I substitute myself for him, whereas no one can replace me, and the substitution of the one for the other does not signify the substitution of the other for the one. (*OBBE* 158).

By "height" Levinas means the *moral* force encountered in the *other's* face *as* the *subject's* obligation to and responsibility for that other person. Formally, moral obligation and responsibility for the other mean the breaking down or the breaking open of the subject's natural self-oriented being. The I is no longer "for itself," as it is in all the varieties of its atheist being, but "for the other," what Levinas calls the "one-for-the-other." Historically or concretely, this moral disruption of the self means obligation and responsibility to feed the hungry, to protect and provide for the widow and orphan, to welcome the stranger, to heal the sick, and the like.

Responsibility and obligation to the other, solicitude, however, is infinite and "one-way," which is why, at this point, Levinas characterizes the "one-for-the-other" as "obsession" or "substitution" for the other. In the one-way responsiveness of the ethical subject, the self is obligated to the other all the way, is responsible for the other's death and responsible for the other's responsibility—one is one's brother's keeper. *But* the other is not, at least at this point in the exposition, or, more properly, from the point of view of the ethical subject, likewise responsible for the self, for me. Nowhere in the obligations and responsibilities of the self as moral I in relation to the other, as the one-for-the-other, is there a place[20] for, or

---

demned" to freedom, like it or not. Sartre's error, if I may say it so bluntly, is that he has equated the repetitive structure of consciousness, which he understands as pure activity or complete transparency, hence complete freedom, with subjectivity itself. Compounding this error Sartre then equates freedom with responsibility. Consciousness encounters nothing but itself, not humanity but "humanity," that is, its own free choices, its own meanings.

Because Levinas is a phenomenologist rather than a rationalist like Kant and Sartre, he is able to break the bounds of consciousness, uncovering a lapse or trace in consciousness itself whereby the very lucidity, the illuminating power of consciousness, is overcharged.

20. Regarding the notion of "place": one of the epigrams Levinas puts at the front of *OBBE* is the following taken from Pascal (*Pensées* 112): " 'That is my place in the sun.' That is how the usurpation of the whole world began."

a word about, the other's obligations and responsibilities for me. On this point Levinas is distinctive and seems to differ from most other ethical theorists. Where they argue for an ethics of intersubjective symmetry, he delineates an ethics of intersubjective asymmetry.

The responsiveness of the subject's obligation to and responsibility for the other is set off in the self neither as an animal reflex nor as a rational enactment or thematization. Morality is its own "level," which must be understood in its own terms, ethical terms, as moral exigency and not ontological necessity. Of course, this makes the philosophical task of thematizing morality, that is, ethics, all the more difficult, as we saw Levinas admitting from the start in a necessary admission. But this epistemological difficulty cannot be made to obscure the rupture effected by morality; the call of being cannot be allowed to usurp the primacy of responsibility and obligation. The only way to encounter the alterity of the other person is morally, where the other is put into the self, disrupting the intimacy of the self's relationship with its very self, or, for that matter, disrupting any iterative self-relationship. The self of such a relation is "an-archic" in the precise sense of this term: lacking principle. The self is cut to the quick prior to the adherence to a principle or ground of being or action. It is no longer manifestation, unveiling, disclosure but exposure, suffering, not being but beholden.

In "God and Philosophy" Levinas characterizes the extremity of what he elsewhere calls the "transubstantiation," "denucleation," or alter-ation of the self in its encounter with the other's alterity in the following dramatic terms:

This putting in without a corresponding recollecting devastates its site like a devouring fire, catastrophying its site, in the etymological sense of the word. It is a dazzling, where the eye takes more than it can hold, an igniting of the skin which touches and does not touch what is beyond the graspable, and burns. It is a passivity or a passion in which desire can be recognized, in which the "*more* in the *less*" awakens by its most ardent, noblest and most ancient flame a thought given over to thinking more than it thinks. (*CPP* 163)

The other's face calls the self higher than the faculties, capacities, or possibilities whose reflexive structure, whether ideational or existential, define selfhood in its autonomy, its "as for me." What is demanded is more, better, or greater than the otherwise deflective structure of selfhood, whether its characteristic iteration be named "being" or "consciousness." Moral exigencies at once overload and uplift, raising the self above itself, beyond itself, to greater responsibilities, than those which revolve around its own self, however extensive the self be conceived, whether reified as Hegel's *Geist* or verbalized as Heidegger's *Seinsfrage,* or however intensive the self be conceived, whether as Kant's transcendental ego, Locke's "I know not what," Hume's habituations, or Spinoza's *conatus essendi*. The self cannot escape but can only shirk the force of morality by its extensions—*divertissements* Pascal might say, or its intensifications, into projective structures, however amplified or playful. It is the taxing and inescapable excessiveness of this uplifting—moral introjection—that brings Levinas to characterize the face-to-face relation, proximity, in terms of the encounter of human and divine.

Levinas always links the moral dimension, the height of the other person, to religion, in a broad nondenominational sense. Indeed, it is precisely the ethical face-to-face relationship that Levinas calls "religion." As we have seen, in both statements two and three above, Levinas takes the asymmetrical moral implosion effected in the interhuman relationship to be "the dimension of the divine," "the height in which God is revealed." It is not, Levinas would have us think, that religion is reduced to intersubjectivity, in the manner of a Feuerbach, but rather that intersubjectivity is raised to religion, that is to say, raised above its own ontological possibilities.[21] By this I mean to say that for Levinas *G-d imposes Himself on humankind, commands humans, by way of and exclusively by way of interhuman relationships.*

The moral dimension, man's humanity to man, is G-d's detour. Furthermore, for Levinas G-d has and can have no other or no better route than this as far as humanity is concerned. It is for this reason, too, that in "God and Philosophy" Levinas rejects the path of *faith* as a route to G-d, or as an appropriate discourse for the truth of religion. There is no recourse to "religious experience," in other words, to an allegedly direct human encounter with G-d.[22] All experience, owing to its essentially intentional and synthetic character, as Edmund Husserl understood it, where the intended is always cut to the measure of the intention, where past and future, far and wide, are gathered together, is incapable of reaching G-d. It is the interhuman relation of morality, and only of morality, the face-to-face, that upsets the very intentional character of experience, overloading consciousness with more than it can think, putting the self up to an an-archy of infinite obligation and responsibility which have neither origin nor end in the self, where transcendence is encountered.

Levinas is adamant and clear that interhuman relations are the zero

---

21. This issue doubtlessly can not be resolved so simply in one sentence. What counts is making good on the intention expressed.

22. For Buber too the way to G-d is not direct but rather through the world. This is his reason for rejecting the direct and exclusive love of G-d of Kierkegaard's celibate Christianity. See Buber, "The Question to the Single One," *Between Man and Man* (New York: Macmillan, 1965), especially 50–58.

point of religion: "Everything that cannot be reduced to an interhuman relation," he writes, "represents not the superior form but the forever primitive form of religion" (*TI* 79).[23]

4. *"God rises to his supreme and ultimate presence as correlative to the justice rendered unto men"* (TI 78).

In a sense, this fourth statement regarding justice brings the other three to their full consequence. If the ethical dimension of the face-to-face relation is the authentic entry or dimension of the divine, if the demands expressed by the other's face are therefore G-d's revelation, then the wider impact of this dimension, meaning the spread of morality, up to its social and political institutionalization (in other words, the spread and establishment of justice), means at the same time the spread of G-d's presence on earth, or what is traditionally called redemption. The infinite ethical responsibilities and obligations of the face-to-face turn out to be insufficiently moral! There arises a further demand, for justice, justice for all. Ethics satisfying its own demand for justice would be G-d's "supreme and ultimate presence."

Once again I want to move directly—breathlessly, revealing the ineradicably human in all discourse—to the fifth and sixth statements to make sense of this fourth one, which is really no more than a declaration. Our aim is to discover what more precisely Levinas means by justice, and in what sense it goes beyond ethics. But before doing so I want to pause for a moment to sum up what has been said thus far in the first four statements above.

Morally hearkening to the height or good that beckons in the other person's face turns out to be Levinas's way of speaking about being drawn upward by and to the divine. Levinas later calls this movement, with a play on words, the *à-Dieu*. The diagonal dimension of morality, the call beckoning in the height of the other, the self's asymmetrical and one-way relation to the other, one-for-the-other, is the "to-God," the very dimension of divinity. Hearkening to the height which beckons in the other person's face does not mean theorizing, deliberating, or even willing, but rather, in a stunning upset of ontological, epistemological, and aesthetic reflexivity, it is a juncture of activity and passivity which is as much an undergoing as an effecting, at once response and responsibility. It is to be taken up with what is always already a prior summons, an an-archic summons, whose antecedence and precedence cannot be recuperated—

23. Here is not the place to enter into the perhaps ideological question of whether Levinas's restriction of religion to the interhuman retains or does not retain sufficient links to the Jewish religious tradition. Chapter 5 approaches this question; see also Chapter 11.

which is the very temporal and moral structure of the divine. Doing morally, aiding, comes before analyzing. Hearkening to the good means the moral agent is caught up in the infinity of an obligation whose primacy has priority over the "a priori" of consciousness itself, doing good before knowing the good, in the overwhelming or burning immediacy of an otherness "put" into the self.[24]

One could cite here, and perhaps Levinas's entire account of G-d is but a commentary upon, the famous biblical words of the Jewish people spoken to G-d at Mount Sinai: "We will do and we will hearken" *(naaseh v'nishma)*, and the prophetic words Micah (6:8) later speaks to the Jewish people: "What does the Lord require of thee but to do justice and to love mercy and to walk humbly with thy God."[25]

24. On the primacy of "doing good" over the priority of "knowing the good," especially in relation to Heidegger, see chapter 13 in this volume.

25. Franz Rosenzweig cites the same words from Micah on the concluding page of the *Star*.

Here is perhaps a good place to cite from Levinas's "Jewish" writings. In "The Temptation of Temptation," given in 1964 as a commentary on the Babylonian Talmud, tractate *Shabbat*, 88a–88b, Levinas makes the following preliminary remark: "Finally, in my commentary, the word 'God' will occur rarely. It expresses a notion religiously of utmost clarity but philosophically most obscure. This notion could become clearer for philosophers on the basis of the human ethical situations the Talmudic texts describe. The reverse procedure would no doubt be more edifying and more pious but it would no longer be philosophical at all. Theosophy is the very negation of philosophy. We have no right to start from a pretentious familiarity with the 'psychology' of God and with his 'behavior' in order to understand these texts, in which we see traces of the difficult paths which lead to the comprehension of the Divine coming to light only at the crossroads of human journeyings, if one can express it thus. It is these human journeyings which call to or announce the Divine" *(NTR* 32).

In his "Talmudic Reading" given the year before, on *Yoma* 85a–85b, entitled "Toward the Other," we find the following very similar preliminary remark: "My effort always consists in extricating from this theological language meanings addressing themselves to reason. The rationalism of the method does not, thank God, lie in replacing God by Supreme Being or Nature or, as some young men do in Israel, by the Jewish People or the Working Class. It consists, first of all, in a mistrust of everything in the texts studied that could pass for a piece of information about God's life, for a theosophy; it consists in being preoccupied, in the face of each of these apparent news items about the beyond, with what this information can mean in and for man's life.

"We know since Maimonides that all that is said of God in Judaism *signifies* through human *praxis*. Judging that the very name 'God,' the most familiar to men, also remains the most obscure and subject to every abuse, I am trying to shine a light on it that derives from the very place it has in the texts, from its context, which is understandable to us to the degree that it speaks of the moral experience of human beings. God—whatever his ultimate and, in some sense, naked meaning—appears to human consciousness (and especially in Jewish experience) 'clothed' in values; and this clothing is not foreign to his nature or to his supra-nature. The ideal, the rational, the universal, the eternal, the very high, the trans-subjective, etc., notions accessible to the intellect are his moral clothing. I therefore

But what more precisely does Levinas mean by *justice*, where beyond the infinity of ethics "God rises to his supreme and ultimate presence"?

5. *"In the proximity of the other, all the others than the other obsess me, and already this obsession cries out for justice, demands measure and knowing, is consciousness"* (OBBE 158).

Thus far, the other encountered in the moral dimension of the face-to-face has been described as an overwhelming force, a devastating, a "catastrophying," the irrecuperability of an antecedence and precedence which impinges on the self deeper than the self's otherwise autonomous self-relationships. The obligations and responsibilities generated by such an impingement are infinite, without end, not grounded or anchored in a principle but an-archic, always ever greater. The relationship is "one-way," asymmetrical, obligating the self but not the other. The demands of the other on the self are in nowise converted by the self into the mutuality or reciprocity of demands placed by the self on the other. Such would be an economics not an ethics.

It is worth noting, in passing, that it is because Buber does characterize the movements of the "I-Thou" relationship in terms of mutuality and reciprocity that Levinas has always criticized him.

"In proximity," we quoted Levinas above as saying, "the other obsesses me according to the absolute asymmetry of signification, of the one-for-the-other: I substitute myself for him, whereas no one can replace me, and the substitution of the one for the other does not signify the substitution of the other for the one." But now, in the fifth statement above, in sharp contrast, Levinas is putting forth another idea. In the obsession of the one-for-the-other, "in the proximity of the other, *all the others* [my italics] than the other obsess me." In the face of the other, in other words, the self is subjected not simply to the other who faces, but to all others: all the others who are other to this other and other to the self. One is no longer or not only in the Garden of Eden, in the society of two, of love and infinite obligation and responsibility. "The third party," Levinas

---

think that whatever the ultimate experience of the Divine and its ultimate religious and philosophical meaning might be, these cannot be separated from penultimate experiences and meanings. They cannot but include the values through which the divine shines forth. Religious experience, at least for the Talmud, can only be primarily a moral experience" (*NTR* 14–15).

In these instances we catch a glimmer of the fine discretion, so rare today, of an alert and subtle philosophical approach which is at the same time fully appreciative of G-d's transcendence, for instance, in admitting and opening up a distinction between "penultimate experiences and meanings" of G-d (which are the topic of this chapter) and "the ultimate experience of the Divine and its ultimate religious and philosophical meaning," which Levinas leaves deliberately undetermined ("whatever").

writes, "is other than the neighbor, but also another neighbor, and also a neighbor of the other, and not simply his fellow" (*OBBE* 157).[26] Alterization is then far more complex and far-reaching than its initial impact.

Just as the shift from one person to two is the transformative shift from atheism to ethics, the shift from two persons to three is the equally transformative shift from ethics to justice. It is not only the other to whom the self is beholden, but also to others, others whose relations bear upon the other, and hence indirectly, invisibly, upon the self, and also to others whose relations bear upon the self, but again invisibly, not as this very one who faces me. It is this indirection that introduces the concern for justice. "The other and the third party, my neighbors, contemporaries of one another," Levinas writes, "put distance between me and the other and the third party" (*OBBE* 157). The self is indeed morally beholden, infinitely beholden, to the one who faces, but justice is required of the self in relation to all others. And the demands of justice require a rectifying distancing from the infinity of one's infinite obligation to the other.

6. *"The relationship with the third party is an incessant correction of the asymmetry of proximity in which the face is looked at"* (OBBE 158).

I take the liberty of continuing the thought above by quoting the sentences which follow, because they flesh out the wide-ranging significance of the demand for justice and its relation to the divine that we are seeking.

There is weighing, thought, objectification, and thus a decree in which my anarchic relationship with illeity [i.e., *he* who faces] is betrayed, but in which it is conveyed before us. There is a betrayal of my anarchic relation with illeity, but also a new relationship with it: it is only thanks to God that, as a subject incomparable with the other, I am approached as an other by the others, that is, "for myself." "Thanks to God" I am another for the others. (*OBBE* 158)

Because in the face of the other there is a deeper obsession than the infinite ethical adventure, namely, obligations and responsibilities to "all the others"—the others who are other to the other and who are also, but not immediately, other to the self—the infinite ethical relation, the face-to-face, is not sufficient for the moral desire with which it burns. Even more is demanded than aiding the neighbor; one must aid all mankind. And aiding all mankind demands a different sort of aid than the infinite solicitude that one desires to give the other. It requires, in a word, *justice*, that is to say, *law*.

26. Levinas's thoughts on "the third," or the "third party," are complex and have developed over many years and writings. I will not enter into all the nuances and consequences of this notion, nor bring out possible shifts in Levinas's thought regarding its significance. Nonetheless, the rest of this chapter will focus on what I take to be its most important consequence, namely, the shift from ethics to justice and to the justification of philosophy.

But the I, as inexhaustible an-archic source of moral attention to the other, cannot provide what justice demands, since justice is the demand of all others, a demand that does not originate with the self but, and this is the important point, *includes* the self. Here, unlike the face-to-face, *but demanded by the unequal exigency of the face-to-face itself,* the self must be made *comparable* to others, put on the same plane as they, subject to law, not to mention the "laws" of exchange, the exchanges of money. Thus justice is both the "betrayal" of the self's incomparable and infinite obligation to *this* other, and nonetheless the *rectification* of that very obligation's neglect of *all* others. This necessary rectification, justice, demands that the self treat others as well as itself the same, that the self treat itself as other to itself. Such alienation of an original goodness, the "for itself" erected on the "for the other," is the very origin of consciousness. "The foundation of consciousness," Levinas writes, "is justice" (*OBBE* 160).

And where is G-d in this? Levinas calls the shift from the two to the three "the passing of God" or "grace," and terms it the "correction of the asymmetry of proximity" (*OBBE* 158). It is the shift *from* ethics, where the I is wholly "hostage" to the other, where the self is obsession unto infinity, *to* justice, to law, where the I is like the others, subject to objective judgment. Levinas invokes the everyday expression "Thank God" to characterize the saving relief the self experiences not only in being disburdened of its infinite obligation to this other for the sake of all others, but in being treated equally. " 'Thank God'," Levinas writes, "I am another for the others" (*OBBE* 158):[27] "The passing of God, of whom I can speak only by reference to this aid or this grace, is precisely the reverting of the incomparable subject into a member of society" (*OBBE* 158). It is literally incomprehensible to the moral self, whose obligations are unlimited, that it too is included as a member of society. The justice that comes out of this incomprehensibility is nothing other than "thanks to G-d," for it is in it that G-d comes to have a concrete significance in the world, that G-d works justice in the world.

Here, then, is Levinas's resolution to the problem of two G-ds. Though he does not in any way, for reasons given, directly invoke the biblical G-d of Abraham, Isaac, and Jacob as proof text, Levinas does bring together G-d's personal, immediate presence, and therefore this aspect of the religious sense of the divine, and the very requirement for impersonal, reflected, and universal consciousness, and therefore philosophical under-

27. Alphonso Lingis translates "grace à Dieu," as "thanks to God," thereby retaining the "to G-d" of the expression Levinas later favors, "à Dieu." In everyday English, however, the "grace à Dieu" would be rendered more naturally as "thank G-d." I have made this change, translating "grace à Dieu" as "thank G-d," for the sake of naturalness, though Lingis's translation is also precise.

standing (which would necessarily include, therefore, a philosophical understanding of G-d). It is not so much the philosophical G-d that Levinas brings into harmony—per impossible—with the personal G-d of the patriarchs, but rather the moral requirement for philosophy in the first place. The infinity of ethics is too much but nonetheless never enough: out of the binding intensity of an infinite desire for goodness emerges a wider rectifying demand for the inclusion of all others, the demand for justice, and hence for consciousness, judgment, objectification, fairness, science, in a word, philosophy in the broad sense.

This leads to the seventh and last statement, which addresses this issue directly:

7. *"Justice, society, the State and its institutions, exchanges and work are comprehensible out of proximity"* (OBBE 159).

Once again I will allow Levinas to continue his thought by citing the sentences which follow:

This means that nothing is outside of the control of the responsibility of the one for the other. It is important to recover all these forms beginning with proximity, in which being, totality, the State, politics, techniques, work are at every moment on the point of having their center of gravity in themselves, and weighing on their own account. (*OBBE* 159)

Justice itself, then, has an outside standard: proximity. Ordinary moral sentiment and moral dicta recognize this truth in such expressions as "justice must be tempered by mercy," or "justice without mercy is tyranny." For Levinas it is philosophy itself—and here we might well think of Levinas's own philosophy—that both establishes justice, in thematizing and objectifying it, and keeps what is just from becoming tyrannical. "Philosophy," Levinas writes, "is this measure brought to the infinity of the being-for-the-other of proximity" (*OBBE* 161).

Levinas resolves the conflict of G-d and philosophy by putting philosophy in the service of G-d. Not, however, in a way repugnant to philosophy, but in the context of giving the highest significance conceivable to the very interhuman relationality to which the love of wisdom is (though ofttimes unwillingly) committed. The love of wisdom is spurred by the "wisdom of love" *OBBE* 161.

The genuine task of philosophy, then, is to keep consciousness attuned not to its own immanent or independent tendencies, its own relative gravity, but to the higher and elliptical moral imperatives deriving from the absolute seriousness of the other's alterity encountered in proximity, and through that other, the imperative of all others, justice. Justice is both the rectification of ethical excess, "thank G-d," through which the I becomes an equal member of society, and inevitably at the same time the betrayal of the ethical. It is not only in the task of justification, but in taking a stand against the tendency of justification to turn into an allegedly fully autonomous self-justification that philosophy finds its worth. Several times Levinas repeats one formula to characterize the task of philosophy: "philosophy is called upon to reduce that betrayal" (*OBBE* 152, 156, 162).

In this way Levinas can dare to ask, because he is able to answer, a question so radical that philosophy itself—despite all its claims to get to the bottom of all things—too often shirks or ridicules, namely, "Why philosophy?" (*OBBE* 157). G-d demands philosophy because G-d demands justice. Indeed, G-d passes into the realm of human signification by means of precisely these demands, which themselves originate in a deeper dimension of the divine, namely, the disturbing anarchy of infinite responsibility one-for-the-other, in a proximity which is morality itself, and, again, "the dimension of the divine."

"The word God," Levinas writes, "is an overwhelming semantic event" (*OBBE* 151).

NINE

The Metaphysics of Gender

Whatever their ultimate link, one must distinguish metaphor from metaphysics. The first part of this chapter aims to display the role and explain the significance of the primary gender metaphors—the feminine and the masculine—operative in Levinas's writings. Such an exposition is worthwhile not only for its own sake, to clarify a stratum of meaning in Levinas's writings, but also to avoid likely and dangerous confusions when in its second part this chapter turns to a display and exposition of the significance of Levinas's metaphysics of eros and fecundity. While the center of Levinas's thought is elsewhere, in the metaphysical ethics of the face, eros and fecundity provide the "material" condition of ethics, produce beings who face and are faced, and hence are of considerable significance in the overall economy of Levinas's thought.[1]

1. Three articles appeared recently on the topic "Levinas and the Feminine," as part 3 of *Re-Reading Levinas*, edited by Robert Bernasconi and Simon Critchley (Bloomington: Indiana University Press, 1991), 109–46.

The first, "Questions to Emmanuel Levinas: On the Divinity of Love," by Luce Irigaray (translated by Margaret Whitford), evidences hardly any understanding of even the most basic features of Levinas's thought, let alone his thoughts regarding the feminine. Irigaray is more interested in what she has to say than what Levinas has to say. Fine, but the article is ostensively directed to Levinas's thought and is in fact part of a book devoted to Levinas's thought. For example, because Irigaray wants to defend, as her own, the idea that the erotic embrace must be understood in terms of shared pleasure, she attacks Levinas: "He [Levinas] knows nothing of communion in pleasure" (110). But however convenient such a bold statement is to make a contrast, it is nonetheless not true. Or, to take another example, later in her article she asks, rhetorically, "Is monotheism wisdom or a patriarchal and masculine passion?" And continues: "The obligation to believe or to give one's allegiance, the injunction not to touch, form an integral part of a monotheism which conceals its passional nature" (114) Irigaray is entitled to her opinions—who isn't?—but what on earth does this have to do with Levinas's nuanced conception of monotheism? Nothing. Irigaray is obviously serving her own feminist agenda, and is using Levinas as the usual sexist fall guy.

"Antigone's Dilemma" by Tina Chanter is, like Irigaray's article, another instance of a feminist agenda overpowering the difficult effort required to understand another thinker's thought or to assess its merits or demerits. The real interest seems to be in scoring points than in genuine study and education. For example, speaking of the continuity or discontinuity of Levinas's analyses of "the feminine and paternity" found in *Time and the Other* (1948), *Totality and Infinity* (1961), and *Otherwise than Being or Beyond Essence* (1974), Chanter charges that "contradictions emerge between the earlier and later texts. Not only between earlier and later texts but even within the same texts" (134). Certainly a very serious charge. But when she attempts to make good on it, we are given quotes taken out of context from here and there in Levinas's works, presented, furthermore, with no effort to understand them, such that anyone familiar with Levinas's thought—and without a feminist ax to grind—will feel shortchanged. It is a hatchet job. Levinas is once more made to play the tired role of male fall guy. What really interests and influences Chanter is Derrida's thought. Levinas is an occasion, as it were.

So why even bother with Levinas, one wonders, that sophisticated intellectual male chauvinist pig? But one must rather turn the table on ideologues, assuming that one genuinely does wants to understand Levinas (obviously a precarious assumption in part 3 of *Re-Reading Levinas*) rather than demonstrate loyalty to a party or school: why should one bother to be bothered by Chanter and Irigaray?

In stark contrast, the third article, "Ethics and the Feminine" by Catherine Chalier, is a nuanced and attentive reading of Levinas on the very important topic of the relation between what Levinas says about the "feminine" and the ethical core of his thought. One can see here, as elsewhere in her work, that Chalier is a knowledgeable and careful reader of the whole of Levinas's extensive work. I happen not to be in agreement with one of the central theses of this particular article, namely, that "maternity" is "the very pattern of substitution" (126) and hence of ethics, but this not because I believe she is entirely wrong everywhere. Here I think Chalier has mistaken a condition of ethics, "maternity," for the ethical relation itself; but the two intersubjective relations are close indeed, and perhaps not so easily disentangled. Chalier is right, on the other hand, to associate the "masculine" with *conatus*, perseverance in being; this is an important insight regarding Levinas. Chalier has had the wisdom and integrity to apply her deep understanding of Levinas to raise a central question, that of the precise relation between "Ethics and the Feminine," a topic which is not addressed directly in this book, but one which must be addressed.

For another attentive and thoughtful examination of Levinas's reflections on eros and fecundity, again by someone familiar with the whole of Levinas's thought, one should read a work by Levinas's main English translator, Alphonso Lingis, *Libido: The French Existential Theories* (Bloomington: Indiana University Press, 1985), chapter 3, "Phenomenology of the Face and Carnal Intimacy," 58–73. Again, as with Chalier, I do not agree with everything Lingis says—for instance, I do not know why he speaks of the "voluptuous care of the parents for the child" (70), since for Levinas the parental relationship is not a voluptuous one; or why he says that "to love someone carnally . . . is to be anxious for mortal flesh and blood" (63), since Levinas nowhere speaks of carnal love in terms of anxiety—but for the most part, and in its interests, the article provides useful insights into this complex and nuanced area of Levinas's thought.

A fifth article, published in 1991, "Thinking the Other Without Violence? An Analysis of the Relations Between the Philosophy of Emmanuel Levinas and Feminism," by Robert Manning (*The Journal of Speculative Philosophy* 5, no. 2: 132–43), entirely misses the difference and the relationship between a gendered metaphysics and gender metaphors. In the process Manning not only badly mangles Levinas's account of eros, fecundity, paternity, etc., and not only badly mangles feminism by facile invocation of the usual charge of sexism ("Levinas's philosophy is a male philosophy, written from a man's point of view. . . . " [137]), but, and far worse, Manning also stoops to making completely unsubstantiated, uncritical, gratuitous, yet allegedly progressive and feminist/Christian, attacks on the Jewishness of Levinas's thought ("Levinas's philosophy is always Jewish philosophy. . . . This means that Levinas writes out of a profoundly sexist and patriarchal tradition, out of a tradition that has perpetuated the evil of the oppression of women" [140]). Either such crude prejudices are the product of an immaturity still caught up in popular or herd thinking, which is still no excuse, or if deliberate and well considered . . . I shudder to think what else. The only redeeming value of Manning's article is that it correctly exposes the limitations of the passing criticism Simone de Beauvoir leveled against Levinas in *The Second Sex*.

The Metaphors of Masculine and Feminine

Levinas's use of feminine and masculine metaphors, his use of such terms as "feminine," "woman," "masculine," and "virile" metaphorically, is both extraordinary and unremarkable, and for the same reason. It is unremarkable because he uses these terms in their most conventional senses. For example, what he calls "woman" or "feminine" is a gentle, intimate, warm, and personal presence. What is called "virile" or "masculine," in contrast, is the impersonal and cold. But at the same time this completely conventional use of gender terms is extraordinary, and not simply because Levinas uses such terms at all in the emancipated temper of our times. What is extraordinary, rather, is the anthropology and its concreteness. We are compelled by its very strangeness, at the least, to ask why Levinas retains a deliberately gendered anthropological language to describe, as we shall see, regions of being that Husserlian phenomenologists or empirical scientists would take great pains to describe or explain in strictly sex neutral terms, in as impersonal or objective a language as possible. Let us see where, and then why, Levinas finds it appropriate to invoke the metaphors of gender.

The most outstanding use of the feminine or woman metaphor occurs in Levinas's magnum opus, *Totality and Infinity,* in the subsection entitled "Habitation and the Feminine" (which appears in part D, "The Dwelling," of section 2, "Interiority and Economy").[2] At this stage of his developmental phenomenology of the human and exteriority (*Totality and Infinity* is subtitled "An Essay on Exteriority"), Levinas is concerned to describe the initial emergence and primitive existence of the independent (in his terminology "separated") existent, nascent subjectivity. He is therefore still far from describing the fully constituted human being and world encountered across the ethics of face-to-face relations, an analysis which appears later, in section 3. Subjectivity—always embodied for Levinas—emerges sheltered by a gentleness. It is in the description of the warmth, shelter, and nestled protection which constitute the initial environment (or "intentionality") of a nascent independently existing existent, the first engagement of protosubjectivity in worldly existence, the environment which enables a break with what Levinas had already described as the murky indistinction of the "there is" *(il y a),* that the terms "feminine" and "woman" are first invoked. Their use is descriptive, metaphorical:

2. *TI* 154–58. No doubt gender metaphors occur importantly elsewhere in Levinas's work, especially after the publication of *TI*—for example, throughout *OBBE,* Levinas's second great work, and in several articles, of which I cite the most important in this chapter. Still, the subsection "Habitation and the Feminine," along with all of section 4 of *TI,* have elicited the greatest critical response in the secondary literature and crystallize the core of gendered language in Levinas.

Familiarity and intimacy are produced as a gentleness that spreads over the face of things . . . a gentleness coming from an affection for the I. The intimacy which familiarity already presupposes is an *intimacy with someone*. . . . The presence of the other must not only be revealed in the face which breaks through its own plastic image, but must be revealed, simultaneously with this presence, in its withdrawal and in its absence. This simultaneity is not an abstract construction of dialectics, but the very essence of discretion. And the other whose presence is discreetly an absence, with which is accomplished the primary hospitable welcome which describes the field of intimacy, is the woman. The woman is the condition for recollection, the interiority of the home, and inhabitation. . . . The discretion of this presence ["feminine alterity"] . . . its function of interiorization . . . is a new and irreducible possibility, a delightful lapse in being, and the source of gentleness in itself. (*TI* 155)

What is "feminine" or "woman" is a gentleness in being, the world *as* shelter, nestling place, the discreet gentle alterity of habitation. What justifies the use of anthropological terms is that such an initial sheltering environment of gentleness—the world as habitation—does not emerge from the world itself by itself, is not a *physus,* but depends on a type of personal alterity. Identifying or specifying the particular type of personal alterity constitutive of habitation—gentle, sheltering, familiar, intimate— with the term "feminine," used metaphorically, is a purely conventional gesture, like the expression "mother nature."

The same conjunction of meanings, the "feminine" gentleness of habitation, appears with even less restraint in another text written at the same time, "Judaism and the Feminine," published in 1960.[3] In this article Levinas offers "modest reflections" on "woman in Jewish thought," thought, that is, which is "inseparable from the rabbinic sources" (*DF* 31). At the same time, Levinas does not hesitate to relate his Jewish sources to certain conceptual alternatives articulated in the philosophical tradition proper. The following two passages illuminate and supplement what we have already discovered regarding the significance of the feminine in Levinas's thought:

"The house is woman," the Talmud tells us. Beyond the psychological and socio-logical obviousness of such an affirmation, the rabbinic tradition experiences this affirmation as a primordial truth. The last chapter of Proverbs, in which woman,

---

3. Because it is a short journal article, "Judaism and the Feminine" was published one year prior to *TI*, in *L'Age Nouveau,* no. 107–8. It was thereafter reprinted in both editions (1963, 1976) of *DF*.

"Judaism and the Feminine" happens also to be one of the first of Levinas's writings to appear in English, translated by Edith Wyschogrod, in *Judaism* 18, no. 1 (1969): 30–38, just prior to the English translation of *TI*, by Alphonso Lingis, in 1969. It has been translated a second time, by Sean Hand, for the English translation of the second edition of *DF*.

without regard for 'beauty and grace,' appears as the genius of the hearth, and precisely as such makes the public life of man possible, can, if necessary, be read as a moral paradigm. But in Judaism the moral always has the weight of an ontological base: the feminine figures among the categories of Being. (*DF* 31–32)

To return to the peace and ease of being at home, the strange flow of gentleness must enter into the geometry of infinite and cold space. Its name is woman. . . . The return of self, this gathering or appearance of *place* in space, does not result, as in Heidegger, from the gesture of building, from an architecture that shapes a countryside, but from the interiority of the House . . . but for the essential moderation of feminine existence living there, which is habitation itself. . . . The wife, the betrothed, is not the coming together in a human being of all the perfections of tenderness and goodness which subsist in themselves. Everything indicates that the feminine is the original manifestation of these perfections, of gentleness itself, the origin of all gentleness on earth. (*DF* 33)

Here, too, then, "woman" and "feminine" are associated with habitation. What receives more emphasis in the above citations, however, is the contrast between the private sphere of habitation, the sphere of feminine gentleness, and the colder, harsher sphere of public life, which Levinas characterizes as "masculine."

Let us then turn to the masculine, to the masculine as metaphor. Although one finds masculine metaphors—"masculine," "virile," "heroic"—employed in *Totality and Infinity,* their use there is diffuse, less focused, than metaphors of the feminine. If we continue to provisionally exclude the domain of the erotic (section 4 of *Totality and Infinity*), to which I will turn later, one sees that while feminine metaphors are reserved almost exclusively to characterize the gentleness of habitation, no such focus applies to metaphors of masculinity, which appear in the text posterior to habitation, both prior to the emergence of ethics proper, in phenomenologies of possession, labor, economy, consciousness, and representation (i.e., parts D and E of section 2), and in the midst of the analysis of ethics (section 3), especially in a subsection entitled "Commerce, the Historical Relation, and the Face" (*TI* 226–32). Levinas considers all the products of visible history as deriving from a "virile and heroic I," the I of "self-possession," and "self-positing" (*TI* 270).

In view of this diffusion in *Totality and Infinity,* I will turn once again to "Judaism and the Feminine." There Levinas has already referred to the feminine gentleness of the home as refuge from "the public life of man," from "the geometry of infinite and cold space." The appearance of masculine metaphors in an article devoted to the feminine is, of course, unsurprising, inasmuch as metaphors of masculinity obviously form a neat dyad with metaphors of femininity. In "Judaism and the Feminine," Levinas discusses the masculine, and its relation to the feminine, beginning with a talmudic text (no specific reference given) in which the prophet Elijah answers Rabbi Yossi's question regarding the meaning of the verse from Genesis on "woman lending aid to Adam." His answer, and Levinas's commentary, are as follows:

[Elijah:] "Man brings home corn—does he chew corn? He brings flax—can he clothe himself in flax? The woman is the light of his eyes. She puts him back on his feet." [Levinas:] Is it really just to grind the corn and spin the flax that woman exists? A slave would be good enough for such a task. One could certainly see in this text confirmation of the ancillary status of woman. Yet a more subtle interpretation is required. . . . This corn and flax are wrenched from nature by the work of man. They testify to the break with spontaneous life, to the ending of instinctive life buried in the immediacy of nature as given. They mark the beginning of what one can accurately call the life of spirit. But an insurmountable "rawness" remains in the products of our conquering civilization.

The world in which reason becomes more and more self-conscious is not habitable. It is hard and cold . . . it can neither clothe those who are naked nor feed those who are hungry; it is impersonal. . . . This is spirit in all its masculine essence. It *lives outdoors,* exposed . . . in a world that offers it no inner refuge, in which it is disoriented, solitary, and wandering, and even as such is already alienated by the products it had helped to create, which rise up untamed and hostile.

To add the work of servant to that of lord and master does not resolve the contradiction. To light eyes that are blind, to restore to equilibrium, and so overcome an alienation which ultimately results from the very virility of the universal and all-conquering *logos* that stalks the very shadows that could have sheltered it, should be the ontological function of the feminine. . . . She answers to . . . a solitude in the universal, to the inhuman which continues to well up even when the human has mastered nature and raised it to thought. For the inevitable uprooting of thought, which dominates the world, to return to the peace and ease of being at home, the strange flow of gentleness must enter into the geometry of infinite and cold space. Its name is woman. (*DF* 32–33)

The citation speaks for itself.

Derived from all the texts cited thus far, the following two somewhat imperfectly parallel lists summarize the clustered pairs of significations, all quite ordinary and conventional, upon which Levinas's gender metaphors are based:

Feminine	*Masculine*
private, sheltered, indoors	public, exposed, outdoors
instinct, nature	spirit, civilization
gentle, affection, peace, ease	raw, untamed, hostile, conquering
familiarity, intimacy	impersonal, solitary

| place, home, situated, warm | cold space, disoriented, alienated, uprooted, universal |
| absence, discretion, reserve | presence, logos, self-consciousness |

It should be obvious that Levinas is using gendered terms to characterize two distinct ontological regions: "feminine" for a private, gentle, warm, protected, personal sphere; "masculine" for a public, harsh, cold, impersonal sphere, which is subdivided into the realm of possession and economy, on the one hand, and representation and logos, on the other.

Levinas understands ontology phenomenologically; regions of being, such as "at homeness" or "economic exchange," are distinguished according to essence, that is, according to irreducible differences which unlike the differences which count in the natural or mathematical sciences are distinguished descriptively rather than statistically or quantitatively, and distinguished by an attentiveness to the correlation of noeses and noemas in the constitution of meaning. Unavoidably, then, barring a purely technical language, metaphors of some sort will be necessary at some level to describe and distinguish essential regions of being. It is precisely because Levinas's feminine and masculine metaphors are so ordinary and conventional that they can serve him as part of the common language necessary for phenomenological descriptions. Whether his descriptions and distinctions are accurate is one matter; how one evaluates the moral significance of regions of being is another. No doubt these two questions are not entirely unrelated.

Levinas is not, in any event, presenting, defending, or glorifying a biological thought, or, for that matter, a psychological or sociological one. His claim is not that a woman's place is in the home or a man's is at work, but rather that essentially different ontological regions such as "at homeness" or "economic exchange" exhibit characteristics whose contours follow the same contours as those expressed in the conventional language of gender discrimination. If Levinas is to be found at fault for being injudicious (rather than simply incorrect or inaccurate about his phenomenological discriminations), it cannot be for distinguishing regions of being which follow the same contours as do conventional gender stereotypes, but rather for perpetuating these stereotypes by utilizing a language to describe regions which in all likelihood could be described and distinguished without reference to gender whatsoever.[4] On the other hand, one

4. More radically, one might say that not merely the regions distinguished ("at homeness," "economy," "representation"), but all distinguishing of regions as such, is a function of gender determination (doubtlessly, in this case, "male"). Such a view, however, not only mobilizes a relativism which forecloses possible argumentation, whether toward agreement

could equally argue that Levinas is not so much perpetuating gender stereotypes as situating them in their appropriate ontological context. Addressing these questions in 1981, Levinas asks himself whether his use of gendered language is perhaps an "anachronism" (*EI* 66). But rather than answer the question directly, he sidesteps it by insisting on the greater importance which pertains to the ontological discriminations which this language is enlisted to reveal: "What importance the ultimate pertinence of these views and the important correctives they demand have! They permit grasping in what sense, irreducible to that of numerical difference or a difference in nature, one can think the alterity which commands the erotic relation" (*EI* 66). At this juncture, what is more important to Levinas than cultural variability and its moral consequences is the recognition that being must be grasped within a philosophical anthropology, that is, in terms of universals dependent on an always concrete human alterity, through which reality itself takes on feminine and masculine characteristics.

Being must be thought not according to the limits of thought, but rather according to the surplus significations of an always concrete human alterity. Indeed, the tendency to think being independently of the anthropological is precisely one of the characteristics of thought Levinas names "masculine." Two years after the publication of *Totality and Infinity,* in 1963, in his annual address to a colloquium of French Jewish intellectuals, Levinas refers to any proposition which "puts the universal order above the inter-individual order" as a "virile, overly virile, proposition" (*NTR* 20). (One might suppose, then, that Levinas's own thought must then be a "feminine" thought in contrast. Rather, it is an ethically based thought, "dis-inter-ested." But this question, which is no doubt more complicated than this, is not the issue directly at hand.) The point is that being and signification are inseparable, and that signification is inseparable from human existence. Levinas (like Heidegger before him) is translating Husserl's epistemological turn to the *noetic,* to overcome the realist prejudices of the "natural attitude" and of unreflective natural science, into an existential register. Thus being manifests a dimension of "at homeness" because at a certain constitutive level it emerges in relation to a gentle, affectionate, discreet alterity, which Levinas names "woman" and "feminine presence." So, too, being manifests dimensions of possession, both physical and intellectual, because it emerges in relation to an alienating, disorienting, willful, impersonal alterity, which Levinas names "masculine" or "virile."

---

or disagreement, but, more profoundly, it forecloses any possible communication, even its own enunciation to another.

In the above sense, ontology is philosophical anthropology is phenomenology. Levinas's constitutive phenomenology, in contrast to the phenomenological drama of Plato's *Symposium* or the conceptual phenomenology of Hegel's *Phenomenology of Spirit,* is guided not by progressively more comprehensive integrations of impersonal truth but rather by encounters with a progressively radicalized personal alterity. It is not that the phenomena or their sequence—being, sense-perception, consciousness, self-consciousness, civil society, government, art, religion, philosophy—or even their direction—from the indefinite to the definite—differ in these various thinkers. They are more or less the same. Plato in the *Symposium* and *Republic,* Hegel in the *Phenomenology* and *Logic,* and Levinas in *Existence and Existents, Time and the Other,* and *Totality and Infinity* (sections 2, 3, and 4), present parallel stages of an upward partially cumulative constitutive development. It is the endings, the ends, and hence each and every movement of development, that differ profoundly. Philosophy, the "love of wisdom," aims for comprehensive knowledge, seeks a fully discursive intellective satisfaction, whether the grand conclusion it seeks remains elusive, as in the metaphysics of Plato and Aristotle, or is attained in the active and circular dialectic of Hegelian logic. Levinas's thought, in contrast, is a "wisdom of love" (*OBBE* 153), not loving friendship above truth, to be sure, but loving the truth of friendship and of love. Its primary concern is to address the irreducible alterities constitutive of singular and social life. Hence, to speak negatively, it is driven by a desire to break out of cognitive circuits of self-sameness, out of thought thinking thought, or, to speak in a more modern idiom, out of questioning questioning questioning. Positively, owing to an attentiveness to the demands of alterity as alterity, Levinas's thought is driven by a desire for goodness and for justice, that is to say, by obligations and responsibilities.

Levinas does not, then, suggest restricting females to homes and gardens and males to work and civilization. To the contrary, following Husserl's famous "Prolegomena" to the *Logical Investigations,* his writings identify regions of signification, such as "home," "work," and "representation," and in the process detach them from the naivete of biological, psychological, sociological, or naturalist determinism. Levinas is quite able to distinguish description from prescription. Thus a house, as we are fond of saying in English, is not always a home. But for a house to be a home it must function as a zone of feminine presence, even if only males have ever inhabited it. The significance "home," in other words, depends on gentleness, warmth, welcome, intimacy, familiarity, ease, shelter, and not on the biological sex of its inhabitants. So, too, with the masculinity of the public spheres of work and representation.

Being, for Levinas, is inseparable from signification. Signification is inseparable from the irreducible alterity of a human transcendence, which is manifest concretely across such characteristics as gender, age, family, and pedagogic relationships. It should come as no surprise, then, that certain regions of being are hence describable in terms borrowed from the conventional language of gender discrimination, stripped, to be sure, of its natural but naive realism.

Turning to carnal eros, however, while yet avoiding the naivete of naive realism, the matter of gender nevertheless stands unlike that of the metaphorical femininity of the home or the masculinity of the workplace and scientific thought. Here the desires of carnal desire require the gender of engendering and of generations, that is to say, they express and are anchored in a metaphysics of desire which reaches beyond and breaks through any mere play of metaphors.

The Metaphysics of Love
Time and the Other *(1948)*

The definitive statement of Levinas's metaphysics of eros appears in 1961, in section 4 of *Totality and Infinity,* entitled "Beyond the Face." Levinas tells us in the Preface to *Existence and Existents* (15) that earlier reflections on this topic were pursued during his internment in Germany as a Jewish French prisoner of war from 1940 to 1945. These earlier reflections first appear in print in 1948, in one sentence, the last, of the penultimate chapter of *Existence and Existents.* The inaugural sentence is as follows:

Asymmetrical intersubjectivity is the locus of transcendence in which the subject, while preserving its subject structure, has the possibility of not inevitably returning to itself, the possibility of being fecund and (to anticipate what we shall examine later) having a son. (*EE* 96)

Levinas was able to announce his forthcoming examination of fecundity and paternity, even if somewhat cryptically in *Existence and Existents,* because it had already in fact been made in 1947 as part of the last of the four lectures he gave at Jean Wahl's Philosophical College in Paris. These lectures were published in 1948, just after *Existence and Existents,* under the title "Time and the Other," as Levinas's contribution to an anthology of several lectures given at the College. It was not until 1979 that these lectures were again published, now as a separate volume entitled *Time and the Other.* The last two sections of the fourth lecture are entitled "Eros" and "Fecundity" respectively. Before turning to section 4 of *Totality and Infinity,* then, we will be much rewarded by dwelling briefly on the last two sections of *Time and the Other,* not only because this earlier text is less complex and hence clearer (but also sparser) than the later one, but also because the theses regarding eros and fecundity which Levinas elaborates in *Time and the Other* in 1948 will remain essentially the same, and will have a fundamental importance, as they will have later in the ethical context of *Totality and Infinity* in 1961.

In sexual difference Levinas sees a difference radically different than the differences with which philosophy has hitherto concerned itself. Indeed, and no doubt expressing the same thought more sharply, in sexual difference Levinas sees a difference radically different than the differences which constitute philosophical thought itself. Levinas begins by sharply distinguishing sexual difference from genera and specification. He writes:

Sex is not some specific difference. It is situated beside the logical division into genera and species. . . . The difference between the sexes is a formal structure, but one that carves up reality in another sense and conditions the very possibility of reality as multiple, against the unity of being proclaimed by Parmenides. (*TO* 85)

Sexual difference presents a multiplicity irreducible to the unity of Parmenidean being, the touchstone of all philosophy. The significance of sexual difference (one cannot even say "specific to sexual difference") can thus hardly be overestimated.

It is not only the philosophical tools of genus and species, with which all definitions and classificatory systems are constructed, that prove inadequate to the difference constitutive of sexual difference. Even more fundamentally, sexual difference is maintained otherwise than by overcoming contradiction and by adherence to the principle of noncontradiction, and hence otherwise than the very rock bottom of philosophy. Sexual difference is not an instance of the identity and nonidentity of being and nothingness. "The contradiction of being and nothingness," Levinas writes, "leads from one to the other, leaving no room for [sexual] distance" (*EE* 85). That is to say, the parameters opened up by the thought of noncontradiction, which is to say, philosophy, leave no room to conceptualize the difference operative in sexual difference, in eros and fecundity. "Neither," Levinas continues, "is the difference between the sexes the duality of two complementary terms, for two complementary terms presuppose a preexisting whole. To say that sexual duality presupposes a whole is to posit love beforehand as fusion. The pathos of love, however"—and here we first glimpse Levinas's metaphysics—"consists in an insurmountable duality of beings. . . . The relationship does not *ipso facto* neutralize alterity but preserves it" (*EE* 86).

The difference of sexual difference, in sum, cannot be resolved, grasped, or comprehended by conceiving it as the particularity which separates species subsumable under a higher genus, or as the tension of contradictories in opposition, or of noncontradictories provisionally in tension but ultimately in harmony or harmonizable in principle, or as parts which complement one another to form a larger whole or gestalt. These options, however, are the very resources of thought, of philosophy.

In the sexual difference, then, Levinas has found a concrete instance of precisely what his entire philosophy seeks and supports, and which Parmenidean philosophy, in contrast, denies and denigrates, namely, a relation whose terms are both radically in relation and radically out of relation, terms linked and separate at the same time. Such are the "I" and the "you" of ethics, such are lover and beloved of eros. But one must tread carefully. So peculiar is the link and the separation between self and other that it is not correct to say, as I have just casually said, that they are "at the same time." A whole new structure of time, which Levinas names "diachrony," opens up across the fundamental relation of intersubjectivity, and hence also across sexual difference, which is the material condition of all intersubjectivity. It turns out, then, that the difference which emerges in and out of sexual difference is also the difference constitutive of time, that is, the manner in which a future and past are irreducibly dephased from the present and from all synthetic operations of self-presence.[5]

In *Time and the Other* Levinas distinguishes the *erotic embrace* of lovers from the relation of *paternity,* and both from the possibilities of Parmenidean philosophy. What makes the embrace of a carnal eros erotic, that is to say, what excites desire, what is the very desire of desire, is not a melding of lovers but rather the acuity of a duality on the cusp of unity, two lovers feeling one another and feeling one another's feelings without attaining complete identity. The "pathos of voluptuousness," Levinas writes, "lies in the fact of being two" (*TO* 86). In contrast to this pleasurable frustration, paternity exceeds voluptuous duality such that two are one while remaining two. In *Time and the Other,* Levinas already understands the paternal relation ontologically as "the relationship with a stranger who, entirely while being other, is myself, the relationship of the ego with a myself who is nonetheless a stranger to me. . . . I do not *have* my child, I *am* in some way my child" (*TO* 91). Later, as we shall see in a moment, in *Totality and Infinity,* Levinas names this peculiar non-Parmenidean but ontological relation of fecundity with a term borrowed from religion: "transubstantiation" (*TI* 271).

It is time to turn to section 4 of *Totality and Infinity.* Before doing so, however, the following three points summarize the relevant grounds already covered in *Time and the Other.* First and most general, what is

---

5. For more on time, especially in *Time and the Other,* see chapter 6 in this volume.

metaphysical is what exceeds the unity of being and thought, a transcendence or alterity that remains out of relation precisely when and while it is in relation. Genuine metaphysics, then, in contrast to philosophy conceived along Parmenidean lines, requires the articulation of a difference which differs otherwise than by specification, noncontradiction, or complementarity, which reduce alterity to sameness. Second, a concrete instance of metaphysical excess occurs in carnal erotic embrace, where two beings, lovers, make intimate contact without fusion, experiencing each other's alterity, drawn together while remaining separated by the "pathos of voluptuousness." Third, the farthest reach of erotic transcendence occurs in paternity, where one being, the father, both is and is not another being, the son. These three elements, the metaphysics of alterity versus the unity of Parmenidean ontology and philosophy, the unquenchable erotic pathos of lovers' contact and duality experienced across voluptuousness, and the metaphysical rupture of being effected by paternity, provide the frame for Levinas's future meditations on eros and fecundity in *Totality and Infinity*.

Totality and Infinity *(1961)*
CARNAL EROS AND EROTIC FEMININITY

As a student of phenomenology, Levinas begins with a primal phenomenon: erotic nudity. To faithfully describe this phenomenon he is forced to move his analyses "beyond the face," that is, beyond the ethical signification of intersubjectivity laid out earlier in section 3, the apex of *Totality and Infinity*. The sequence is important, but before seeking its explanation, let us first note that Levinas does not characterize the self and other of ethical intersubjectivity in gendered terms. Neither the other faced ethically nor the morally elected self are described as male or female or masculine or feminine, although it is obvious that Levinas envisions the ethical encounter taking place between gendered human beings. The point is that the ethics laid out in section 3 of *Totality and Infinity*, unlike the regions of meanings which are described earlier in section 2, where Levinas does not hesitate to invoke gendered metaphors, and unlike the regions of erotic meaning which will be described afterwards in section 4, which we are considering, is the domain of the *human*, described without reference to gender.[6]

Levinas's sequence: ethics first, eros second, reveals the "beyond the face" character of eros itself. It is not that eros is extraneous to ethics, or that ethics is extraneous to eros, for that matter, but rather that erotic

---

6. Regarding the other encountered ethically, Levinas says: "The best way of encountering the other is not even to notice the color of his eyes" (*EI* 85).

nudity involves a specific subversion of an intersubjectivity already constituted ethically. Erotic nudity cannot be subsumed under purely ethical terms. But neither can it be accounted for without the significations already established through ethical encounter. In erotic nudity the alterity of the other person not only presents itself as ethical command, and the correlated "agency" of the self is not only elicited as moral election. Rather, both terms, erotic other and erotic self, call for a compression, as it were, of other and self into materiality, sensibility, into a sensuousness wrapped up in the non-signifyingness of carnal passion. Levinas is forced by this subversion of signification, quite unlike the elevation effected by ethical transcendence, to describe a transcendence no longer coming from "above," but coming from "below" or "beyond" ethical responsibility. To be sure, this does not make the encounter with erotic nudity immoral or unethical. It rather places it outside, otherwise, differently than the straightforwardness of ethical encounter.[7]

The "intentionality"[8] proper to erotic nudity is the correlation caressing-carnal. Erotic nudity, the carnal, the "noematic" or "object" pole of erotic passion is what Levinas calls "woman" or "femininity." This is not, however, the "feminine" which in section 2 of *Totality and Infinity* Levinas describes in terms of the interiority of the home, the discreet, maternal feminine. But neither, in a simple opposition, is it a pure indiscretion or exhibitionism.[9] Indeed, the feminine remains, here too, a discretion and an interiority, but as the term of erotic love, i.e. sensual desire (not labor) and seeking (but not inquiry), it is "inwardness" as "frailty" *(faiblesse)*, "tenderness," "vulnerability" *(TI* 256). Erotic femininity is a tenderness touched, a body withdrawing as it is caressed. Unlike the discreet feminine of the home, an interiority which is not caressed but within which one rests, erotic femininity is touched and at once exposed and hidden. Whether one views the phenomenality or exposure of erotic nudity from

---

7. One can say, further, that the subversion effected by eros operates in a manner inverse from the equally extra-ethical (not unethical or immoral) subversion of ethics and language effected by prayer, which, according to Levinas, is a striving of the soul to free itself from the body. For Levinas, or rather for Rabbi Hayyim of Volozhyn as Levinas cites him from the *Nefesh HaHayyim* (1824), to pray is "to strip the soul of the clothes of the body," or "to pour out one's soul"; in Emmanuel Levinas, "Prayer Without Demand," translated by Sarah Richmond, in *The Levinas Reader,* edited by Sean Hand (Cambridge, Mass.: Basil Blackwell, 1989), 232. In eros, as we shall see, the soul is not stripped of the clothes of the body but is rather more fully "clothed." In eros, ethics and signification are subverted by the striving of a soul for greater embodiment, for "ultramateriality."

8. On the inadequacy of phenomenological description to characterize ethical alterity, see chapter 12 in this volume.

9. Such exhibitionism, the simple reverse of "feminine" discretion, would comprise the project of pornography, an artform not a lifeform.

the side of the caress's caressing or from the side of the nude body exposing itself, it is what remains hidden even without clothing or covering, dark even with bright lights on.

Before following Levinas's analysis further, let us note here, already, the appearance of one of the most remarkable features of his account of erotic nudity: eros appears under the sign of the "feminine." The passion of erotic love, for both men and women, is a "feminine" affair, at least initially. From the viewpoint of what Levinas metaphorically calls the "masculine" regions of being, such as work and logic, eros effects an "effemination" (*TI* 270). Let us note, too, that the shift from metaphor (section 2) to metaphysics (section 4) which we are anticipating does not occur in one fell swoop. The moment of the literal, the transcendent breaking through the phenomenal and through the metaphorical, does indeed occur in the region of eros, as we shall see, but it is not the whole and certainly not the initial stage of erotic passion. I return to Levinas's phenomenology of erotic nudity.

What is hidden in erotic nudity is not merely "the other side" or "the inside," as with objects, things. Rather, erotic nudity is the exhibition of sensibility under the dark light of passion, the exhibition of what Levinas calls "an exorbitant ultramateriality" (*TI* 256). When speaking of erotic nudity as "femininity," then, Levinas invokes a complex conjuncture of significations, indeed an ambiguous, ambivalent, essentially equivocal conjunction of signification and nonsignification. The key to this complex of meanings, however, lies not only in the specific meanings, but more especially in their equivocation. "The simultaneity or the equivocation of this fragility and this weight or non-signifyingness, heavier than the weight of the formless real," Levinas writes, "we shall call *femininity.*"

The proper "noetic" approach to, or contact with the essentially equivocal feminine, the frail, vulnerable, desired body, is the *caress*. Again, just as the erotic feminine is neither property nor representation, the caress is not a grasping, either of labor or of thought. The correlation of caress and erotic nudity constitutes a field of eros, of erotic sensibility, where voluptuousness and profanation meet. The links are as follows: the *eros* of erotic nudity is precisely the correlation of caress and femininity. The caress, for its part, *profanes,* because however loving, caring, sensitive, or attuned it is to erotic nudity, that is to say, however bold or shy its sensual indulgence, that which it caresses, qua feminine, slips away, remains hidden, escapes what would otherwise be betrayal. The erotic feminine is the essentially hidden. *Voluptuousness,* then, is the other side of profanation, the felt acuity which comes from the inability, the frustration of the caress to ever be done.

Precisely while accomplishing eros one never finally once and for all finishes caressing one's lover. Levinas reminds us here of Aristophanes's insight in the *Symposium* (192c), that when lifelong love partners are asked what they gain from one another, what they are aiming for in one another, they are at a loss for words. Voluptuosity is the pleasure which derives from the separation of lovers entwined in carnal embrace. Hence the invocation of an ambivalence named "feminine." "The feminine, essentially violable and inviolable . . . is an incessant recommencement of virginity, the untouchable in the very contact of voluptuosity, future in the present" (*TI* 258). Erotic sensibility is a skin that is both touched and still to be touched; given but not fully given; exhibited and at the same time hidden; present, contacted, touched, caressed, but nonetheless absent, futural, beyond the touch; exciting the caress while withdrawing, hence agitating; at once satisfying and frustrating, hence voluptuous.

> Voluptuosity begins . . . in erotic desire and remains desire at each instant. Voluptuosity does not come to gratify desire; it is this desire itself. This is why voluptuosity is not only impatient, but is impatience itself. . . .
>
> The equivocal does not play between two meanings of speech, but between speech and the renouncement of speech, between the signifyingness of language and the non-signifyingness of the lustful. Voluptuosity profanes; it does not see. *An intentionality without vision,* discovery does not shed light: what it discovers does not present itself as *signification* and illuminates no horizon. The feminine presents a face that goes beyond the face. The face of the beloved . . . ceases to express, or, if one prefers, it expresses only this refusal to express, this end of discourse and decency, this abrupt interruption of the order of presences. (*TI* 259–60)

Levinas insists that the nonsignifying aspect of the carnal opened up by eros does not refer to what philosophy knows as formless matter, *hyle,* which Levinas refers to as "the stupid indifference of matter" (*TI* 264). Rather, "beyond the face," it is an "inverted signification," the underbelly, as it were, of sense, a clouding of clarity, "laughter" in contrast to seriousness, innuendo and allusion rather than straight talk. It is not as if lovers retreated to a paradise prior to signification, as if significations never signified, had not yet occurred. Rather, established significations are short circuited, in the actuality or acuity of a logically impossible private language, the sweet nothings whispered not just to the beloved but breathed upon the beloved's ear.

Eros, then, stands to the fully human tasks of ethics and justice as an interlude, intermission, or vacation. It is play, the lighter side of life, "dual solitude, closed society, the supremely non-public" (*TI* 265). A sexual revolution, then, as envisioned by a Charles Fourier, Wilhelm Reich, or Gilles Deleuze, say, or by certain strains within feminism today (see note 1 to this chapter), which would make ethics and justice dependent on a new sexuality, would be beside the point, a distraction leaving the ongoing and unfinished business of ethics and social justice untouched.[10] Eros subverts society and civilization, yes, but it does so playfully and privately, as in the well-known scene where Tom Jones and his mistress turn dinner in a public restaurant into a lustful, though wanton, foreplay. Precisely one of the virtues, if one may so speak, of eros, is not only its pleasures but its privacy, its dual solitude, permitting a temporary refuge, as it were, from the serious and unending tasks of ethics and politics in an unredeemed world.[11]

Lovers are enclosed within a sphere of sensing and sensations, in an intimacy and privacy oblivious of others, and invisible to others. Within love's precincts, even the personality can prove to be a hinderance or a mask.[12] Indeed, in carnal eros one does not even aim at the other person, the other to whom one is obligated morally. Rather, one aims at the other's voluptuosity, the other's sensing of sensations. Of this, Levinas writes: "Voluptuosity . . . is voluptuosity of voluptuosity, love of the love of the other. Love accordingly does not represent a particular case of friendship. . . . I love fully only if the other loves me, not because I need the recognition of the other, but because my voluptuosity delights in his voluptuosity" (*TI* 266). Nor does this ultimate structure of erotic passion, loving the other's loving, exhaust the reach of erotic desire. For Levinas there is an even more extreme—excessive to the point of metaphysics— "intention" to erotic encounter than the voluptuosity which aims at the other's voluptuosity.

FECUNDITY, PATERNITY, AND FILIALITY

Erotic desire aims beyond the love of the other's love and, breaking with the logic of Parmenidean being, accomplishes its aim in fecundity.

Desire desires more than the piquant delight and intense sharing which

10. See *NTR* 170: "What is challenged here is the revolution which thinks it has achieved the ultimate by destroying the family so as to liberate imprisoned sexuality. What is challenged is the claim of accomplishing on the sexual plane the real liberation of man. Real evil would be elsewhere. . . . Libidinous relations in themselves would not contain the mystery of the human psyche."

11. One can see, then, in an unremittingly public commitment to ethics and justice, the justification for vows of celibacy and chastity. One must wonder, however, whether such vows, spoken for the sake of an unredeemed world, are, in the name of the same unredeemed world, angelic or inhuman?

12. See *TI* 264–65. Camille Paglia also argues for the disjunction between personality and sexuality, in the first chapter of her book *Sexual Personae* (New York: Vintage Books, 1991). Tracing different lines, Georges Bataille makes a similar point regarding the dissolution of personality in sexual relations in *Death and Sexuality* (1962; New York: Ballantine Books, 1969).

transpire across the equivocal transcendence of sensations. What is voluptuous about voluptuosity is its combination of satisfaction and frustration,
"simultaneously fusion and distinction" (*TI* 270),[13] the peculiar correlation of caress and femininity, the acuity of touching the untouchable. But
the caress's groping delineates an impossible desire. Ultimately, in the
love for the other's love, the lover wants, per impossible, to *be* the other,
to be lover and beloved at once, to be same and other. Erotic desire, then,
is ontological, but the logic of the sort of being it desires essentially
exceeds the unity of Parmenidean ontology: the desire of desire is metaphysical.

What this means is that voluptuosity, the crescendo of sense pleasure
thus far described, does not in itself go far enough. "If to love is to love
the love the Beloved bears me," Levinas writes, "to love is also to love
oneself in love, and thus to return to oneself. Love does not transcend
unequivocally—it is complacent, it is pleasure and dual egoism" (*TI* 266).
But rather than leaving love there, bracketed by the cigarette or shower,
as in a Hollywood take, in the discontinuity or metaphorical death of
which Bataille writes, Levinas sees in the impossible desire of carnal
love—its desire for unequivocal transcendence, departure from self without return, disencumberment—the *desire to engender a child,* fecundity.
Desire desires complete alterity, is metaphysical; only for a fecund being
can such a desire find fruition.[14] The child both *is* and *is not* the parent.
Fecundity—"paternity" from the side of the parent, "filiality" from the
side of the child—the most extreme extension of carnal eros, is not only
the ultimate desire of sensuous desire; it is the concrete condition of all
desire for transcendence, and hence, as we shall see, for ethical transcendence also.

Locating the desire for absolute transcendence in carnal eros means,
first of all, that the desire for fecundity, far from being imposed upon
eros externally—by the divine fiat or dogma of religious authority, or by
the inherited ties of a hypothetical and immemorial social contract, or
by force of a legislation inspired by demo-political calculation, or even by
the inescapable cunning of a subconscious biology—expresses rather the
innermost and most intense desire of carnal eros itself. The carnal begets
the carnal. Erotic bonds generate family bonds. Though he fully appreciates the disruptions that these relations present for thinking, Levinas does
not hypostatize a third term, as does Merleau-Ponty with his notion of

13. That in eros there is not only frustration but also *fusion* is the point Irigaray misses;
see note 1 above.

14. That the fecundity or sterility of eros is a central issue in the contest of encomia on
love in Plato's *Symposium* is brought out and emphasized in *Plato's Symposium* by Stanley
Rosen (New Haven: Yale University Press, 1968; 2d ed., 1987).

"the flesh of the world."[15] To describe the complex relationships of fecundity, paternity, and filiality, which also serve as the concrete conditioning of consciousness itself, thought is compelled to think a new relationship of being.[16] Levinas writes:

Already the relation with the child—the coveting of the child, both other and myself—takes form in voluptuosity, to be accomplished in the child himself (as a desire can be accomplished that is not extinguished in its end nor appeased in its satisfaction). We are here before a new category. (*TI* 266)

Fecundity is a new category precisely because it overflows categorical analysis, joining disparate terms, accomplishing in desire and birth what is impossible for thought, or, more precisely, impossible for the Parmenidean thought of being. Paternity and filiality are the concrete accomplishment of the metaphysics of gender, fecund desire.

The language Levinas uses to affirm the ontological but extra-Parmenidean link joining parent and child shifts back and forth between the impersonality of the third person singular and the personal testimony of the first person singular. The following are three illustrations regarding paternity: In the first person singular, he writes: "My child is a stranger (Isaiah 49), but a stranger who is not only mine, for he *is* me. He is me a stranger to myself" (*TI* 267). In the third person singular, Levinas sometimes writes in the specific language of paternity, the language of "father" and "son," as, for example, in the following: "the father discovers himself not only in the gestures of his son, but in his substance and his unicity" (*TI* 267), and other times in the more general language of "child" rather than "son," as we saw just above and, to give one final example, in the following: "the I is, in the child, an other" (*TI* 267). This shifting is not only natural (and occurs whenever the topic is intersubjectivity), insofar as Levinas is describing a relationship within which he is himself implicated, or, more precisely, regarding paternity and filiality, by which he is himself conditioned, but is also another sign, a "pointer," of the rupture of Parmenidean discourse, the inadequacy of the impersonality of the third person to fully absorb or contain the first person singular. The point is important, but having noted it I will pursue it no further here.

15. See Maurice Merleau-Ponty, *The Visible and the Invisible,* edited by Claude Lefort, translated by Alphonso Lingis (Evanston: Northwestern University Press, 1968), especially chapter 4, "The Intertwining—The Chiasm," 130–55.

16. Though Levinas often uses the words "fecundity" and "paternity" interchangeably, there are clearly two distinguishable significations at work in his analysis. One is the metaphysics of desire, or gender, from the perspective of the lovers, for which we could reserve the term "fecundity." The other is the metaphysics of desire from the perspective of its concrete accomplishment in parent-child relationships, called "paternity" from the side of the parent, and "filiality" from the side of the child.

Let us ask, however, why Levinas uses terms such as "paternity" and "son," rather than "maternity" and "daughter," say, or, more to the point, the more general and nongendered terms "parent" and "child" or "offspring"? I offer the following six reasons, in a vaguely ascending order of importance, to explain Levinas's choice of the gendered and masculine term "paternity." First, in French the term parent does not flow as naturally or readily as it does in English. One would sooner say "my father" or "my mother" than "my parent." Second, faithful to phenomenology and to contemporary philosophy more generally, Levinas always opts for a more concrete rather than a less concrete language, "paternity," in this instance, rather than "parental." Third, the term "paternity," precisely by retaining a sense of gender that the term "parent" does not, recalls the metaphysics of gender, the fecund desire, which is its source, and of which it too, more remotely, will be a source. Fourth, each of us remains a son or a daughter throughout the whole of life, even after the death of one's parents, while it is not true, or not true in the same sense, that one remains a child all one's life. Fifth, Levinas utilizes the term "maternity" for another aspect of the parent-child relationship, nurture, rather than, as we shall see in paternity, singularization. Sixth, then, and related to this last point (which is itself related to the previous points), it is because what is at issue in paternity is the unicity, the self-identity, the ipseity (from the latin *ipse*, meaning "self"), the singularization of the child. While "maternity" refers to the "soft," "sweet," or gentle nestlike aspect of childhood and of adult life too, to shelter, indeed, to what in section 2 Levinas calls "feminine presence," "paternity" refers to a "hard" or "harsh" side of social life, to character formation, indeed, more deeply, to the very ontological formation of the self, being on one's own, the finite freedom of creatureliness.

Through paternity the self is same and other at once: self-same, to be sure, but also same in the other, in the child who one is and one is not, but who for his part remains other. "By a total transcendence," Levinas writes, "the transcendence of trans-substantiation, the I is, in the child, an other. Paternity remains a self-identification, but also a distinction within identification—a structure unforeseeable in formal logic" (*TI* 267). In English we sometimes speak (in a disparaging tone) of parents "living through their children." Putting aside the disparagement, or perhaps simply accounting for its possibility, we can see in this expression the depth of the link, the ontological depth, established across generations in fecundity and paternity as Levinas understands these terms. One lives one's own life, but one also lives through one's children, meaning that the parent is vulnerable in the child. It is as if parents were not merely responsible for the birth of the child but extended amoebalike into the child.

Levinas will say that it is insufficient to think of this link as one of "sympathy or compassion" (*TI* 271), that is to say, as a psychological attribute, an emotion. Rather, it is shared being: "The I springs forth without returning, finds itself the self of an other: its pleasure, its pain, is pleasure over the pleasure of the other or over his pain—though not through sympathy or compassion" (*TI* 271).

Fecundity, then, yields the concrete production of multiple being and hence also yields the *diachrony* which for Levinas is the root constitutive meaning of time itself. Fecundity yields de-phased being, being out of phase with itself. It is not the case that being is first one and then made multiple by fecundity, or that time is first self-presence and then de-phased into past and future by fecundity, as if fecundity were added to an already constituted reality like yeast to dough. One should rather say that being is multiple and time diachronous, or that the time of being is not simultaneity but diachrony, because being and time are significations originally constituted across the interval of fecundity, which is to say, across generations.[17]

Because the significance of being is dependent upon intersubjectivity, it is conditioned by the significations which inhere in the production of intersubjectivity itself, one of whose fundamental movements is that of time as recommencement, time as the recurrence and displacement of youth and age. Levinas writes:

A being capable of another fate than its own is a fecund being. In paternity, where the I, across the definitiveness of an inevitable death, prolongs itself in the other, time triumphs over old age and fate by its discontinuity. . . . The discontinuous time of fecundity makes possible an absolute youth and recommencement. (*TI* 282)

In contrast to Bataille, for whom the rupture or discontinuity of eros is that of the self torn from itself, but always by itself, for Levinas the ultimate structure of rupture or discontinuity is intersubjective, occurring across the generations of humankind, that is to say, as paternity and filiality. Deliberately invoking a religious terminology, then, Levinas calls the extra-Parmenidean movement of this deep structure of time "resurrection." "Resurrection," he writes, "constitutes the principal event of time" (*TI* 284).

---

17. See the final section (prior to Levinas's "Conclusions") of part 4 of *TI* "The Infinity of Time," 281–85; and Levinas's two very important articles on time included in the English edition of *TO* 97–138: "Diachrony and Representation" (1982) and "The Old and the New" (1980). Also see chapter 6, "On Temporality and Time," in this volume. "From generation to generation" is, of course, a very common Hebrew expression especially in sacred texts.

With the notion of resurrection Levinas is not limiting himself to a reference or allusion to the Christian Gospel narrative. Nor, for that matter, is he limiting himself to its sense in an even more ancient Jewish usage. Rather, and more broadly, indeed universally, in addition to the ontological rupture which constitutes paternity from the side of the parent, he is referring to the "other side" of paternity, to filiality. Filiality, the relation of the child to the parent, son to father, is, it is true, the "converse of paternity" (*TI* 278), but the sense of renewal in filiality is different than that of the father's sense of renewal in the child. Both directions, however, parent to child and child to parent, paternity and filiality, are constituted by structures of "rupture and recourse" (*TI* 278). Let us turn, then, to the two poles of this double structure.

For the father, the son undoes the definitiveness of a life always already more or less lived, aged, and hence defined. Aging is the concrete sense of life's one-way direction, the definitiveness of the definitive. In this setting, the son marks a new beginning, an opening up of paths not taken, possibilities unchosen or possibilities previously unavailable. "The son," Levinas writes, "resumes the unicity of the father and yet remains exterior to the father: the son is a unique son. Not by number; each son of the father is the unique son, the chosen one" (*TI* 279). The son, then, for the father, represents the unknotting of the definitive, resurrection, the phoenix coming out of ashes, youth unwrinkling the experience of age, even as the father ages in an aging marked by the son's youth and aging.

Conversely, the son, for his part, represents originality in a resumption: "The originality of this resumption," Levinas writes, "distinct from continuity, is attested in the revolt or the permanent revolution that constitutes ipseity" (*TI* 278). The identity of the son, one's uniqueness, then, is not a function either of particular differences or of the difference of particularity, as if the distinctiveness of the son were that of a unique specification of a genus. Nor is its identity the pure freedom of a self-positing, as if unicity were sheer indetermination, *tabula rasa,* as Sartre strained to represent subjectivity. Rather the son's unicity, its self-identity, is a singularity, a partial freedom constituted by recourse and rupture with a paternal trust or deputation. Such is the unique status of a being both born and borne. Just as the father is and is not the son, the son is and is not the father. The new self of the son is sovereign, to be sure, but through an investiture by the father. Levinas writes:

The paternal *eros* first invests the unicity of the son, his I qua filial commences . . . in election. He is unique for himself because he is unique for his father. . . . And because the son owes his unicity to the paternal election he can be brought up, be commanded, and can obey, and the strange conjunction of the family is possible. (*TI* 279)

In recognizing the ontological weight of the metaphysics of gender as it manifests itself in paternity and filiality, Levinas is able to account for selfhood as that peculiar conjuncture of independence and dependence, sovereignty and vulnerability, that is the condition of ethical social life wherein the human is constituted as human. The family, in other words, is not some accident of biology, but the condition of the human, of the human as *created* being.

The consequences of this recognition are profound and far reaching. For one, Levinas is able to avoid the classic philosophical errors and aporias of a thought torn between freedom and determinism. By acknowledging the irreducible metaphysical and ontological originality of the family, Levinas can build an account of the human based upon the finite freedom of created beings whose status as sons, as daughters, is not some irrational natural or conventional accident but an irreducible condition of human being, one with repercussions felt throughout all human dimensions. Created being is quite a different kind of being, time, and significance than the kind of being (or becoming) to which modern philosophy (and in a different sense ancient and medieval philosophy) had hitherto and erroneously reduced the human, namely, causal being. By a single stroke one is no longer forced to decide whether humans are free or unfree, that is to say, caused or self-caused. Human freedom is indeed finite, but not because humans are somehow, impossibly, partially caused, but rather because causality is an inappropriate category with which to grasp a human or finite freedom. Neither, then, is an individual's freedom self-caused, *ex nihilo*, hence fully autonomous and atomic. Rather, freedom emerges in and out of familial relations, tempered by families which are themselves located within larger finite contexts such as nations and traditions, such that the finitude of human freedom is also tempered by the finitude of humanity as a whole. Levinas writes: "Creation contradicts the freedom of the creature only when creation is confused with causality. Whereas creation as a relation of transcendence, of union and fecundity, conditions the positing of a unique being, and his ipseity qua elected" (*TI* 279). Considerations such as these, starting in fecundity, paternity, and filiality, lead beyond the family proper, to the "family of man," fraternity.

FRATERNITY AND ETHICS

While each son is unique to each father, the son is at the same time not wholly or only a unique son. Unique sons live among one another, with other unique sons, each created, singular, elected, an ipseity. No one's self is originally distinguished merely as the specification of a genus, or the instance of a generality, or the term of a dialectic. The uniqueness of the son, singular, created, is what permits one, as one, to stand in relation to another, as another, to stand, that is, in relation and remain out of relation "at the same time." The uniqueness of the son is the condition of the nonreductiveness of intersubjectivity, the inexhaustible resilience of the I in the face of the other.

Philosophy overlooks the metaphysical and ontological significance of familial relations. The fundamentally ethical and familial significance of intersubjectivity escapes its epistemological focus, which knows only universals and individuals, where the latter are really only nexi of the former (the famous "concrete universal"). As for "particularity," it is only the indigestible and insignificant residue of universals and individuals. The uniqueness of the son, however, is a function of neither universalization, individuation, nor particularity, but of paternity, or the paternity and rebellion which constitute filiality. The son's singularity is relational and nonrelational. Once again, the significance of conceiving selfhood as filiality has profound and far-reaching consequences. First of all, because singularity—as the uniqueness of the son—is constituted as a relation to transcendence, it remains a susceptibility to transcendence. Such a relationship, to transcendence, to the alterity of the other, which always only occurs in the first person singular, unique relating to unique, is what Levinas understands as the ethical one-for-the-other, fraternity. The family, then, as the condition for fraternity, would be the condition for ethics, and beyond ethics, the condition for justice, the human.

"The I engendered," Levinas writes, "exists at the same time as unique in the world and as brother among brothers" (*TI* 279). If humans were only fellow citizens, or fellow *Homo sapiens,* the unicity of each would be lost in a genus or geist. The violation of the uniqueness of the self by assimilating it to its social relations is what Levinas calls the "tyranny of the state." If humans were only unique, on the other hand, each person a world unto himself, not only out of relation to radical alterity but incapable of such a relation, then each person would be (by a violation whose insufficiency always already shows up in and belies the very language used to express it) a monad without windows, solitary, insular monarch of the one and only realm, hence in a war of all against all.[18] But because paternal and filial love join father and son without absorbing son into father or father into son, fraternity joins singular beings without reducing one to another, or all of them to a greater whole.

Fraternity, then, conditioned by paternity and filiality, is nothing other than the condition for ethical relations—for, that is, the face-to-face en-

18. Beyond Hobbes, one thinks of Max Stirner and Nietzsche, but also of Sade and Leibniz.

counter between unique beings, the I susceptible to the other's command and, through that command, an I concerned for all others, for the others who are other to the other who faces; an I concerned, that is to say, for all humankind, for justice. This relation, the ethical relation, conditioned by human fraternity, stands at the center of Levinas's thought. Only between unique beings, beings who are born, members of families, can there be a responsibility for oneself which is from the first a responsibility for and an obligation to others. Only when conditioned by eros, then, by fecundity, paternity, and filiality, can there be fraternity, which is the condition for ethics, for the face-to-face relations which by their own (non-Parmenidean) logic extend to the struggle for justice for all, the struggle by and for the fraternity of humankind.

Of ethics and fraternity, Levinas writes:

> The I as I hence remains turned ethically to the face of the other: fraternity is the very relation with the face in which at the same time my election and equality, that is, the mastery exercised over me by the other, are accomplished. The election of the I, its very ipseity, is revealed to be a privilege and a subordination, because it does not place it among the other chosen ones, but rather in the face of them, to serve them, and because no one can be substituted for the I to measure the extent of its responsibilities. (*TI* 279)

Levinas elaborates a metaphysics of gender as the condition, rather than the equivalent, of ethics and the quest for justice, though the latter, ethics and justice, can in no manner be indifferent to the former, to eros, fecundity, and familiality. "What is challenged," Levinas writes in one of his talmudic studies, "is the claim of accomplishing on the sexual plane the real liberation of man. Real evil would be elsewhere" (*NTR* 170). To be human is not as easy as rejecting real conditions in the name of an abstract but clear conscience, or self-legislating rationality, or good citizenship. Moral responsibilities—for good, against evil, for justice, against injustice—are demanding not because responsibility or justice are male or female, or even masculine or feminine, which reduction would undermine justice, but because in these human tasks we rise, as members of families, and members of nations, to the full height of our humanity.

PART THREE

ROSENZWEIG, LEVINAS, AND OTHERS

TEN

Levinas, Rosenzweig, and the Phenomenologies of Husserl and Heidegger

There is a moment of exceptional humility in *Totality and Infinity*. In the preface, Emmanuel Levinas acknowledges a profound indebtedness to a book published forty years earlier, Franz Rosenzweig's *The Star of Redemption*. He writes: "We were impressed by the opposition to the idea of totality in Franz Rosenzweig's *The Star of Redemption,* a work too often present in this book to be cited" (*TI* 28). This is certainly high praise and the admission of a great debt.[1]

The magnitude of indebtedness is even more striking when viewed in the light of a letter unknown to Levinas, a letter by Franz to his mother, dated 5 October 1921. Rosenzweig writes:

I understand I was put in a [rabbi's] sermon yesterday and my book referred to as "the sublime book of a new thinker who lives in our midst." But it won't be really good until they use me in sermons without quoting me, and best of all, without even knowing that it is me that they are using. (*FR* 104)

Franz's words to his mother are partially fulfilled by Levinas's words to his readers.

We might therefore begin to understand the place of the *Star* in *Totality and Infinity* by interpreting these private words by Rosenzweig in a public, Levinasian way. "Really good" words, we would say, are not scholastic exercises, not recitations, but words freely used "without quoting"; they are the speech or *saying* of a thinker whose living presence is always "new," always beyond what happens to be *said,* subject matter, contents, or themes. The new would not just be the novelty resulting from an author's craft or artistry, but the freshness of he "who lives in our midst," he who faces us *face to face.* "Best," to continue this reading, would be words used "without even knowing," words used without the shadows cast by

---

1. In addition to the chapters in this volume which focus on the link between Rosenzweig and Levinas, let us here note that Levinas has written two long articles on Rosenzweig: "Franz Rosenzweig: Entre deux mondes," first published in 1959, which appears in an edited English translation by Richard A. Cohen in *Midstream* (November 1983): 33–40; and "Franz Rosenzweig: une pensée juive moderne," first published in 1965. Levinas has also written the preface to Stéphane Mosès's *System and Revelation: The Philosophy of Franz Rosenzweig* (1992; originally published in 1982 [Paris: Editions du Seuil]).

reflection, without the echoes of mental life, without the distances of its caution, reserve, and irony. Genuine words would be those disrupting knowledge from outside its grasp, words escaping the superior and synoptic gaze of comprehension, words making greater *demands* on knowing than knowing knows or demands of itself. Interpreted in this fashion, Rosenzweig's *Star* would be the "sublime" book, the overflow, which serves as both mount and "sermon" of *Totality and Infinity*. And it certainly is such a book.

Yet Levinas's thankful words force us to do more than discover the place, however cleverly detected, of the *Star* in the general economy of *Totality and Infinity*. Levinas forces us to do more because directly after acknowledging the incalculable debt *Totality and Infinity* owes to the *Star*, Levinas acknowledges an even greater debt to Edmund Husserl's phenomenological method. The next sentence reads: "But the presentation and the development of the notions employed owe everything *(doivent tout)* to the phenomenological method." Owe everything! It cannot be accidental that right after acknowledging an immeasurable—or unmeasurable— indebtedness to Rosenzweig's *Star*, Levinas acknowledges an even greater indebtedness to Husserl's phenomenological method.

What is at stake here? Why *these* acknowledgements? Why this "timidity and audacity" (to take up the title of a talk Levinas gave on Rosenzweig in 1959,[2] one year before the publication of *Totality and Infinity*)? What timidity it is, after all, to be in such debt, to owe so much to these giants of early twentieth-century thought. What audacity it is, nonetheless, to admit to such a debt, to proceed on one's own in the face of two such thinkers. Why, more to the point, this unmistakable link between the *Star* and phenomenology?

To have an even preliminary feel for the weight of these two sentences within *Totality and Infinity*, we must be reminded that Levinas's preface is in no way a polite litany of acknowledgements. Though it is tacked onto the front of an already completed book, neither is it a preliminary map or guide to the text which follows it. Nor, for that matter, is the preface a preemptive criticism, spoken from some laborious and superior vantage point achieved only by the book's conclusion, as if Levinas were surveying both text and reader like the adult whose condescending gaze looks down upon the innocent child at the start of an arduous education. In its last sentence Levinas reveals the purpose of the preface: "attempting to restate without ceremonies what has already been ill understood in the

2. Levinas's talk was given in September 1959, i.e., before the publication of *TI*. It was published in *La Conscience Juive*, edited by Amado Levy-Valensi and Jean Halperin (Paris: Presses Universitaires de France, 1963), 121–37, along with a record of the discussion which followed, 137–49. See note 1 above; also DF 181–201.

inevitable ceremonial in which the said delights." The *said* here is the body of *Totality and Infinity*. It is both inevitably and, so it seems, quickly ill understood. It is so quickly misunderstood that the very preface to *Totality and Infinity* is already a corrective for *Totality and Infinity*. Of course, the preface too, though it valiantly attempts to forestall the inevitable misunderstanding of the text, will with equal inevitability be itself misunderstood. To counter these inevitable misunderstandings without affirming some impossibly absolute word, some "magical" word which always rings true, Levinas links end and beginning. By joining beginning to end and end to beginning, he sets in motion a circular and therefore unending reading of the text, a reading resembling nothing so much as the annual reading of the Torah in the Jewish liturgical year. The reading is endless, but at no point is it done merely for the sake of the text alone. Each time the text is ill understood, inevitably, quickly, yet each time something more is understood, something deeper—something not in the text, life "beyond the book."

The preface both begins and carries on the philosophical claim, life, truth, spirit which animates *Totality and Infinity,* despite the inevitable and quick loss of whatever it is (Rosenzweig's *Star?*) that drives this text, that is in it but not of it. I use these particular verbs and nouns deliberately because on Levinasian "grounds" one must be wary of characterizing the achievement or accomplishment of *Totality and Infinity* in such traditional terms as "themes," "contents," "grounds," "essences," "theories," and the like. One must be wary, even and especially in view of the unavoidable peculiarity of speaking of contents, themes, and grounds which are neither contents, themes, or grounds nor the negation of contents, themes, or grounds. It is precisely *this* distance from traditional philosophical positions—and the word "wariness," like all words, is not quite right either, thank goodness—that is already on display in the structural relation of the preface to the rest of *Totality and Infinity*. If we take Levinas at his word, is it not strange, to say the least, for a preface to come before what it continues? How can what has not yet begun be continued? Does this not already hint at a beginning prior to the origin? If being has an origin, as philosophy has always maintained (regardless of whether philosophy can or cannot discover that origin), then what is the sense of "is" in this suggestion that there "is" a beginning prior to the origin? Such a beginning would already be a challenge to the firstness of first philosophy, would already be a challenge to the "is" that attempts to discover its origin, the original, of itself, by itself, courageously, invoking all of history and nature if that is what it takes to be free of outside help, to outgrow self-incurred tutelage. Perhaps this peculiar structure is the first signal or the first shot of the revolution which is the true *work*—the accomplishment, the achievement[3]—of Levinas's text: a pacific but fundamental inversion of philosophical discourse, an inversion of the order of justification and being. Is this not the sign or trace of the peculiar way that the "really good," to return to Rosenzweig's letter, enters philosophy? Is it not also and already a clue regarding the strange presence of Rosenzweig's *Star* in Levinas's *Totality and Infinity*? Surely if in the discipline of philosophy one were *to continue what has not yet originated,* "its" presence would be overwhelming at the same time that it could not be quoted.

Stepping back from the pursuit of these lines of inquiry, these intrigues, however fascinating or fruitful they may prove, let us for the moment just say that the glimpses they yield succeed in showing that Levinas's acknowledgements of indebtedness to both Rosenzweig and Husserl, far from being merely private or professional discharges of obligation, are in fact essential ingredients of Levinas's philosophy.

To lend further credence to Levinas's timidity and audacity, and to gain a further but still preliminary insight into the significance of his debts, that is to say, insight into the relation between Rosenzweig's *Star* and Husserl's phenomenological method, and both to Levinas's thought, we have to look closely at the specific context of these two sentences. We have to be reminded that the acknowledgement of indebtedness to Rosenzweig begins two paragraphs and follows one paragraph entirely devoted otherwise to phenomenology. The very first appearance in *Totality and Infinity* of the word "phenomenology" is in the paragraph directly preceding the appearance of Rosenzweig's name. Levinas's acknowledgement of indebtedness to Rosenzweig's *Star* is, in a word, sandwiched between two prolonged discussions of the phenomenological method. The two acknowledgements are not just linked by their contiguity and their hyperbole, but as if to answer doubts about their veracity they are both immediately played out: the *Star* vanishes and phenomenology looms large. The *Star* is but an island in a sea of phenomenology. Or, to change metaphors, the *Star's* place in *Totality and Infinity* recalls "those figures of Silenus in statuaries' shops" (Plato *Symp.* 214e), where a center of astonishing purity is hidden by an ungainly exterior—a burning star encased within philosophy's familiar scientific pose.

There is yet another enigma. Just before announcing that his text "owes everything" to the phenomenological method, that is to say, in the paragraph preceding Rosenzweig's name, Levinas lashes out against one of the most fundamental tenets of the whole of phenomenology, namely, the idea that consciousness is always intentional consciousness. The soon-to-be-praised method turns out to be already fundamentally flawed. Against the idea fundamental to phenomenology that consciousness is

---

3. See *TI* 28.

adequate to its objects, Levinas defends the existence and status of a more fundamental non-adequation, an extraordinary "relation" to the idea of infinity. All of *Totality and Infinity* is "about" this relation, which the text will later call an "unrelating relation" (*TI* 295). Thirteen years later, in *Otherwise than Being or Beyond Essence*—where, still true to the earlier work, Rosenzweig and the *Star* receive no mention—it is precisely this relation again that is "otherwise than being or beyond essence." It is already "at work" or "at play" or "in effect" or "operative" in a preface that comes both before and after a text.

Levinas's criticism of phenomenology occurs in the paragraph preceding the mention of Rosenzweig, and reads, with minor deletions, as follows:

> Consciousness then does not consist in equaling being with representation, in tending to the full light in which this adequation is to be sought, but rather in overflowing this play of lights—this phenomenology—and in accomplishing *events* whose ultimate signification (contrary to the Heideggerian conception) does not lie in *disclosing*. . . . The welcoming of the face and the work of justice—which condition the birth of truth itself—are not interpretable in terms of disclosure. Phenomenology is a method for philosophy, but phenomenology—the comprehension effected through a bringing to light—does not constitute the ultimate event of being itself. (*TI* 27–28)

Only after this harsh indictment of phenomenology does Levinas acknowledge his debt to Rosenzweig's *Star,* in the space opened by the indictment. The peculiarity or paradox thus increases: it is not only after having acknowledged an inordinate debt to Rosenzweig's *Star* but also after having attacked phenomenology at its roots that Levinas acknowledges his massive debt to the phenomenological method. Only in the light of these peculiar preparations does Levinas finally proceed to a prolonged and relatively positive discussion of phenomenology, though at this point the reader may not quite know whether this discussion is more or less paradoxical, given all that has preceded it.

Rather than say that Levinas's acknowledgement of Rosenzweig is sandwiched between two separate discussions of the phenomenological method, it is more accurate to say that Levinas's acknowledgement of Rosenzweig *interrupts* one extended discussion of phenomenology. I use the term "interruption" deliberately, not only to recall the dynamics of the living face-to-face conversation which is so important to both Rosenzweig and Levinas, and not only to recall the sense in which Levinas takes skepticism to be a refutable but irrepressible interruption of philosophy,[4]

---

4. See the section on "Skepticism and Reason" in *OBBE* 165–71. Also see the analysis of this section given by Jan de Greef in "Skepticism and Reason," in *Face to Face with Levinas,* edited by Richard A. Cohen (Albany: SUNY Press, 1986), 159–79.

in a conflict of epistemologies, but also and most importantly to invoke the manner in which knowledge itself is permanently ruptured not by *what* comes from another dimension, but by the *otherness* of another dimension, by the difference between that other dimension's slant onto knowledge, its *absolute* "opposition" to knowledge, if you will, and the slant of knowledge itself with its many but always relative oppositions. Again, here "is" the peculiar presence of the "really good," a good which is not real but is *really*, is neither ontic nor ontologic but emphatic.

Again let us take a step back from *these* heady developments to return to a simpler, more prosaic point, to the fact obvious by now that the Rosenzweig sentence interrupts many sentences having to do with phenomenology, and indeed, to perhaps only restate the same claim, that it interrupts all the sentences of *Totality and Infinity*. Rosenzweig's name and the name of his book appear in only this one sentence, one out of thousands. The contributions of Husserl and Heidegger, on the other hand, figure explicitly or implicitly on nearly every page of *Totality and Infinity*, as one would expect from an author whose worldwide scholarly reputation came initially from several excellent expositions of the phenomenologies of Husserl and Heidegger.

Can it be that we are on the wrong track and this scarcity betokens insignificance? One sentence—is it possible, contrary to everything thus far indicated, including Levinas's own testimony, that this means that Rosenzweig is *not* important? I raise this objection rhetorically, only in order to make a final preliminary point. A Jew—Levinas is certainly Jewish—or the Jewish people—the *Star* is certainly a book for (but not only for) the Jewish people—or a Christian, or anyone else for that matter who stands in solidarity with the fundamental humanism and monotheism of the West (however little these noble causes may be in evidence), cannot be so jaded as to be impressed only by large numbers, as if *one*—the one above and each and every one below—were not the most impressive of all "numbers," or as if *two* and *three* did not already set in motion innumerable infinities. Levinas is meticulously true to his few words about Rosenzweig's *Star*. We never hear of Rosenzweig or the *Star* again! They are "invisible to history," to use an expression dear to both Levinas and Rosenzweig; they are *almost* lost in the "inevitable ceremonial in which the said delights." It is *almost as if* nothing had been said.[5] It is in this *almost*

---

5. Levinas begins his 1957 article, "Phenomenon and Enigma," with the following quotation from Ionesco's *The Bald Soprano:* "In short, we still do not know if, when someone rings the doorbell, there is someone there or not . . ." *CPP* 61. In a note to the same article Levinas acknowledges another intellectual debt, this time to Vladimir Jankelevitch, especially to his *Philosophie première: Introduction à une philosophie du 'presque'* (Paris: Presses Universitaires de France, 1954). "Our own project," Levinas writes, "owes a great deal to his work" *CPP* 63.

and in this *as if*—lighter than winged words, heavier than the universe—
that a world of difference lies. Can one imagine a finer distinction, a more
refined discretion, a greater dignity and trust, to be thus mentioned once
and once only?

In view of these two peculiarities, (1) the eminent but brief appearance
of Rosenzweig (like a shooting star) within an extended discussion of
phenomenology, and (2) the allegation of the *Star's* exorbitant presence
in absentia in *Totality and Infinity*, we are prompted to ask two questions.
First, what connection is there for Levinas between Rosenzweig's *Star*
and the phenomenologies of Husserl and Heidegger? Second, what is the
deeper meaning of Rosenzweig's excessive presence and absence in *Totality and Infinity*? How can a thought be *too often* present? When quantity
becomes quality, when excess becomes invisibility, are we not already in
the presence of the idea of infinity? Though I will start with the question
of the relation between the *Star* and phenomenology, it will become apparent that the two questions and their answers are inseparable.

In the main, the discussion before the Rosenzweig sentence is, as we
have seen, critical of phenomenology, while the discussion afterwards, as
we have yet to see, is laudatory.

Returning to the discussion beforehand, to the criticism of phenomenology quoted above, where phenomenology's central methodological
and structural notion of intentionality—all consciousness is consciousness
of its object—is challenged in the name of the idea of infinity, one can
see the logic whereby Levinas concludes his discussion with glowing
praise for Rosenzweig's *Star*, more specifically for its "opposition to the
idea of totality." Levinas's logic would be as follows: the primordial
"*events* whose ultimate signification" exceed phenomenology are "the welcoming of the face and the work of justice." These two events, as events,[6]
are precisely the central message of Rosenzweig's *Star*, its revelatory love
of the neighbor and its redemptive call to save the world, a revelation and
a redemption whose imperative force enable the *Star* to oppose the idea
of totality.

Just as Rosenzweig strives to break up the classical philosophical equation of thinking and being, especially as found in the Hegelian dialectic,

6. See *SR* 108: "And theology itself conceives of its contents as event, not as 'content';
that is to say, as that which is lived, not as 'life'."

The invisibility of great events is a "theme," touched on in this chapter, that is crucial
in bringing Rosenzweig and Levinas together. Rosenzweig has written: "perhaps the great
events in a man's life always begin undetected by human eyes," in Franz Rosenzweig,
Kleinere Schriften (Berlin: Schocken, 1937), 325, quoted by Else-Rahel Freund in *Franz
Rosenzweig's Philosophy of Existence*, translated by Stephen L. Weinstein and Robert Israel
(The Hague: Martinus Nijhoff, 1979), 64. Levinas: "The great 'experiences' of our life have
properly speaking never been lived," in "Phenomenon and Enigma," *CPP* 68. I will return
to this theme and these two claims elsewhere.

that is to say, in the dynamic identity (whether open or closed) of identity and difference, Levinas opposes phenomenology's fundamental idea of intentionality, the idea of a thoroughgoing correlation of consciousness and its objects. By defining consciousness as intentional from top to bottom, from its most transcendent to its most immanent significations, as intentional even in its own self-constitution, phenomenology sees no exit from the circuit of noema and noesis. The mercy and justice which Rosenzweig's *Star* sets up against the conceptual totalizing of "philosophy from Parmenides to Hegel" also inspire Levinas in his opposition to the noetic-noematic totality of phenomenology.

The inspiration of the concluding words of the *Star* is intended not merely as another philosophical discourse, nor merely as another philosophical intuition, but rather as a *call* to and from above. Rosenzweig has chosen his words deliberately, borrowing from the Bible, in order to *stir* his readers, not merely to persuade but to exhort them "to do justice and to love mercy," and "to walk humbly with thy God" (*SR* 424). When concluding his text with these words, Rosenzweig explicitly warns his readers that love and justice are not to be taken as "goals," that is to say, as ideas in the Kantian sense.[7] "To love mercy" is to aid the nearest one, the neighbor, and this (more than the ten or the "six hundred and thirteen" commandments given on Mount Sinai, by the way) is the core "content" or overwhelming event of revelation. "To do justice," likewise, is to save the world, to complete it in and through history, to actively engage in hastening the Kingdom of G-d. "The Kingdom of God," Rosenzweig writes, "prevails in the world by being prevalent in the world" (*SR* 239); neither revelation nor redemption are "goals," for they are "wholly today, and thus wholly eternal as life and the way" (*SR* 424). They are the inwardly burning fire of Judaism, its life, and the outwardly spreading rays of Christianity, its way. Rosenzweig intends the imperatives of love and justice to be taken—here interpreting Levinas's criticism of phenomenology as a commentary on Rosenzweig—as precisely those "*events* whose ultimate signification (contrary to the Heideggerian conception) does not lie in *disclosing*." Loving mercy and doing justice, whether in their Jewish or Christian modalities, are the events—"beyond the book"—which exceed the phenomenology which is today's philosophical version of the German idealism criticized by Rosenzweig.

7. Characterizing the ends of Rosenzweig's redemptive ethics and justice in terms of asymptotes, Norbert Samuelson gets carried away with a mathematical analogy and makes imperfection of ethical behavior and social justice essential to Rosenzweig's notion of redemption. But there is no reason to believe that hopelessness, the foreknowledge of inevitable failure, or an eternal commitment to improvement, an eternal commitment to moral criticism and only moral criticism, are essential ingredients to even the tasks of ethics and social justice, let alone their fulfillment, as Rosenzweig conceives them.

This answer draws Rosenzweig into Levinas's criticism of phenomenology. By orienting their thought in ethics and social justice rather than grounding it in disclosure, by remaining true to the concrete persons and demands of social life rather than to the constitutive requirements of the "life of the mind," Levinas and Rosenzweig together oppose the idea of totality—whether the sophisticated and complex totalities found in the modern German idealisms of Fichte and Hegel or those found in the contemporary German idealisms of Husserl and Heidegger. Levinas and Rosenzweig oppose totality in fundamentally the same way.

Beyond this critical antitotalitarian dimension of the Rosenzweig-Husserl relation which *Totality and Infinity* sets up and maintains, we must also account for the seemingly paradoxical conjunction of the *Star* and Levinas's positive appraisal of phenomenology. Having insisted *prior* to the Rosenzweig sentence that "phenomenology—the comprehension effected through a bringing to light—does not constitute the ultimate event of being itself," and having insisted that "the welcoming of the face and the work of justice—which condition the birth of truth itself—are not interpretable in terms of disclosure," we must ask how it is that *after* mentioning Rosenzweig, Levinas can assert that "the presentation and development of the notions employed [in *Totality and Infinity*] owe everything to the phenomenological method"? If Husserl and Heidegger are wrong about the extension of intentional analysis, then why does Levinas use phenomenology as his method? Why, furthermore, does Levinas go out of his way to highlight his use of the phenomenological method in conjunction with his praise of Rosenzweig's *Star*? Certainly the textual contiguity, the shared excess, and the several speculations begun above, suggest an important link between Levinas's two positive appraisals.

At this juncture it is time to note Rosenzweig's own neglect of phenomenology. The *Star*, after all, was published more than two decades after the publication of Husserl's *Logical Investigations* (1899–1901), decades which saw this new phenomenology widely discussed in German philosophical circles. The *Star* was, in addition, written right after the publication of Husserl's *Ideas Pertaining to a Pure Phenomenology and to a Phenomenological Philosophy* (1913). During Rosenzweig's formative and creative years, then, Husserl was recognized in German-speaking circles as Germany's leading philosopher. Nonetheless, despite the chronological, geographical, and professional proximity, Rosenzweig neither uses nor criticizes the phenomenological method. He never even mentions it. While it is true that shortly after the publication of Heidegger's celebrated *Being and Time* (which totally ignores his *Star*) in 1927, Rosenzweig, though quite ill and only able to communicate with the greatest difficulty, does devote a few pages of reflection upon what he generously takes to be its proximity to the *Star*, he still neither discusses nor so much as mentions Husserl. Phenomenology is neither present nor present in absentia in Rosenzweig's work—it is totally absent. This silence, however, speaks (though with quite a different voice than Heidegger's several silences).

Despite Rosenzweig's silence, we have nonetheless seen how Levinas could bring the *Star* to bear on a criticism of phenomenology, by opposing ethics and justice to the residual philosophical idealism of phenomenology. Now, in contrast, we are asking how Levinas can praise the *Star* in nearly the same breath with which he praises the phenomenological method.

The answer lies in grasping exactly what Levinas praises in phenomenology. Putting aside his earlier role as faithful hermeneutic expositor, when Levinas creatively appropriates phenomenology for his own purposes, he is no longer interested in the chimera of a pure phenomenological method. Though Levinas always prefers phenomenology in its Husserlian form, his own philosophical task is not the defense of that form against other alternative versions of phenomenology. In a word, one must distinguish what Levinas finds wrong and what he finds right about phenomenology. Because like all of Husserl's great "students," Levinas has his own philosophy, one must discover his own phenomenology.

In the discussion that *concludes* with Rosenzweig, Levinas focused on the revelatory aspect of phenomenology, phenomenology as "the comprehension effected through a bringing to light," what he labels "the Heideggerian conception." This aspect, luminous phenomenology, intuitional, evidential phenomenology, is what Levinas criticized for not being able to reach, for covering up in the brilliance of its light, what is truly primordial, i.e., "the welcome of the face and the work of justice." Disclosure, though essential to phenomenology, as Heidegger saw even more deeply than Husserl, is inadequate to the "phenomena"—properly speaking, the "enigma"[8]—that interest Levinas: the events of ethics and justice. And these events, to repeat, are precisely what Levinas has so gratefully learned from Rosenzweig's *Star*.

In the discussion that *commences* with Rosenzweig, however, Levinas's focus is on two different aspects of phenomenology: its concreteness and its break-up of representation. Directly after saying that "the notions employed [in *Totality and Infinity*] owe everything to the phenomenological method," Levinas tells his readers what, in his eyes, this method is. He writes:

Intentional analysis is the search for the concrete. Notions held under the direct gaze of the thought that defines them are nevertheless, unbeknown to this naive

8. See Levinas, "Phenomenon and Enigma," *CPP* 61–73.

thought, revealed to be implanted in horizons unsuspected by this thought; these horizons endow them with a meaning—such is the essential teaching of Husserl. What does it matter if in the Husserlian phenomenology taken literally these unsuspected horizons are in their turn interpreted as thoughts aiming at objects! What counts is the idea of the overflowing of objectifying thought by a forgotten experience from which it lives. The break-up of the formal structure of thought (the noema of a noesis) into events which this structure dissimulates, but which sustain it and restore its concrete significance, constitutes a *deduction*—necessary and yet non-analytical. (*TI* 28)

The focus now is on the nonformal, "concrete" sources of the formal structures of thought, and on the way these "events," as Levinas (and Rosenzweig) calls them, break up and sustain the formal structures of thought.

To maintain this shift in focus and evaluation, Levinas makes an important distinction. He contrasts "Husserlian phenomenology taken literally," which he opposes in intellectual fellowship with Rosenzweig, and "the essential teaching of Husserl," to which he is indebted even more so than to Rosenzweig for the "presentation and development of the notions employed" in *Totality and Infinity.*

It is by means of a heightened attention to the concrete sources of formal thought—the "essential teaching of Husserl"—that Levinas finds the all-important double-edged *event,* the event both violent and nurturing which breaks up and sustains representation. First, starting with objective thought, there is a destructive side to the concrete: "the overflowing of objectifying thought," "the break-up of the formal structure of thought." This movement reinforces Levinas's alliance with Rosenzweig, reinforces their mutual "opposition to the idea of totality." Second, starting now with what *truly* comes first, there is a positive side to the concrete: the recognition that that which overflows and breaks up formal objectifying thought is at the same time that "from which it lives," what can "sustain and restore its concrete significance," what can "endow" it with meaning. For "Husserlian phenomenology taken literally," in contrast, the radicalness of its destructive work is undone by a reconstruction of the same formal objectifying thought at a deeper constitutive level. Like a Medusa's head, formal thought returns with a vengeance, reconstituting itself at deeper levels of consciousness, closer to and finally at the very heart of consciousness itself. Now even if one were to take exception to this line of thought, that is to say, even if one were to object and argue that "Husserlian phenomenology taken literally" is innocent, that it does not reestablish the primacy of formal objectifying thought, it would still be the case, by all accounts, that it reestablishes according to its unshakable tenet the primacy of intentional thought, the primacy of "thoughts aiming at objects." Levinas contests not only the formal objectifying character of absolute consciousness, but also its very intentionality. The coup de grace, however, as we shall see before concluding, is that to effect this contestation, to "prove" it, he enlists the evidence of phenomenology! Phenomenology, the latest and strongest form of philosophy as a science, destroys itself. Thus Levinas's contestation of phenomenology, and through phenomenology his contestation of philosophy, takes the form of critique rather than criticism. Phenomenology is permitted to show its glory, its science, and at the same time, through this same success, it is made to display its breakdown, its wounds. Precisely as such, in its success and in its failure, in the failure of its success and the success of its failure, it is invaluable.

It is instructive at this juncture to note that the manner in which Levinas distinguishes between the essential and the literal in Husserl, between what one can learn and what one must guard against, reproduces his earlier 1930 reading of Husserl in *The Theory of Intuition in Husserl's Phenomenology*.[9] Though the primary intent of this early work was to provide the French intellectual world with a faithful exposition of Husserl's theory of intuition, Levinas does manage here and there, already in 1930, to take an independent stand. The general criticism of phenomenology that permits him to take this stand is essentially the same as that found forty years later in *Totality and Infinity*. That is to say, Levinas's criticism of phenomenology in 1930 and in 1961 is that Husserl founds representational thought on representational thought, that for Husserl consciousness is always and ultimately representational consciousness, a predicative synthesis. But what is instructive for our current discussion is to see that in contrast to 1961, where, enlisting Rosenzweig, Levinas criticizes Husserl in the name of ethics and justice, in 1930, in *Theory of Intuition*, Levinas criticizes Husserl under the influence of Heidegger, that is to say, in the name of being. Beneath representation he sees not more representation but presence to being, i.e., an ontological thinking.

To be sure, Levinas was not a Heideggerian in 1930, or in 1961, nor is he one today. Though profoundly influenced then and now by the power of Heidegger's thought, influenced so far as to insist that all philosophy must "go though" (*EI* 42) Heideggerian thought, Levinas has never been a Heideggerian. One interesting result of our investigation into Levinas's joint appropriation of the *Star* and phenomenology, as we shall see in a moment, is to clarify the precise nature of Levinas's ambivalence

---

9. In *TI* Levinas refers to his 1959 article "The Ruin of Representation," to be published in English translation by Richard A. Cohen and Michael B. Smith in a collection of Levinas's writings on Husserl, *Discovering Existence with Husserl* (forthcoming).

toward Heidegger. It is on this ambivalence that the general significance of phenomenology for Levinas will hinge. In 1930, in any event, Levinas's work evidences an ambivalence toward both Husserl and Heidegger. In *Theory of Intuition,* Levinas attributes to Husserl a theory of consciousness grounded in representation *and* a theory of consciousness grounded in presence to being.[10] In so doing, Levinas keeps his distance from Heidegger (who nonetheless "inspired" Levinas, by his own admission)[11] by crediting Husserl with being Heidegger's teacher in ontology. For those who know better, it is clear that Levinas is praising and blaming both thinkers at the same time.

The 1930 distinction between a representational foundation for consciousness and an ontological foundation for consciousness does not, however, and not just because of its ambivalence, reproduce the 1961 distinction between a literal and an essential reading of Husserl's phenomenology. Or at best it half reproduces it. In both instances Husserl's phenomenological method is credited with breaking up the formal level of representation. Furthermore, in both instances Husserl is understood to have grounded representation on more representation, and to be found lacking for so doing. So much for sameness. The difference between the 1930 account and the 1961 account is far more striking, and with regard to the question of Rosenzweig's role, it is far more illuminating. It is clear on any reading that Levinas was from the first dissatisfied with the foundations of Husserlian phenomenology. To assuage this dissatisfaction in 1930 Levinas was tempted, albeit hesitantly, in a cautious or veiled manner, by the Heideggerian turn toward being, by Heidegger's reading of phenomenology as fundamental ontology. Levinas had just recently read Heidegger's brilliant ontological and hermeneutical appropriation of phenomenology in paragraph seven of *Being and Time.*[12] Levinas was

10. Levinas himself admits to having given a Heideggerian reading to Husserl in *The Theory of Intuition in Husserl's Phenomenology;* see *EI* 39.

11. *Theory of Intuition in Husserl's Phenomenology,* 155.

12. *BT* 49–63. Although for our purposes what I have said is sufficient, it should be noted that for Heidegger the relation between phenomenology and ontology is more complex than indicated. Towards the end of paragraph 7 Heidegger writes: "Ontology and phenomenology are not two distinct philosophical disciplines among others. These terms characterize philosophy itself with regard to its object and its way of treating that object. Philosophy is universal phenomenological ontology, and takes it departure from the hermeneutic of Dasein. . . ." In a complete treatment of this question, then, care would have to be taken to distinguish between philosophy, phenomenology, ontology, and hermeneutics.

It is also of interest to note, with regard to what has been said about Levinas's relation to Rosenzweig and phenomenology, that towards the end of section 7 of *BT* Heidegger acknowledges his indebtedness to Husserl, and at the same time takes a critical distance from his mentor. Heidegger's criticism relies on the same sort of discrimination later used by Levinas, i.e., between what is essential to phenomenology and what is not essen-

actually in Freiburg during the 1928/29 school year, attending private philosophical discussions led by Husserl (who had officially retired from the university the year earlier), but also attending the celebrated seminars of Husserl's successor, Professor Martin Heidegger, who if he had not yet eclipsed Husserl was surely the new and still rising star of German philosophy. What, then, convinces Levinas to turn away from Heidegger in his turn away from Husserl?

To answer this question, our account of Levinas's relation to Husserl and Heidegger requires one further nuance. In both *Totality and Infinity* and in *Theory of Intuition*, Levinas understands ontological thinking as an alternative and profounder *ground* for representational thinking. In both cases Levinas sees that not more representations but the truth of being, truth as the disclosure of being, as Heidegger understood it, underlies representational thought. But despite this genuine and continued appreciation for Heideggerian ontology, there is still a wide gap separating Levinas's assessment of Heidegger and phenomenology in 1930 and his assessment of Heidegger and phenomenology in 1961. In 1930 Levinas opposes Husserlian representation with Heideggerian ontology. In 1961 Levinas opposes both the Husserlian phenomenology, as representationally grounded, *and* the Heideggerian phenomenology, as ontologically grounded, in the name of "the welcoming of the face and the work of justice." Levinas now opposes Husserlian representation and Heideggerian disclosure for the sake of ethics, even though he takes Heidegger to be essentially correct, against Husserl, in asserting that ontological disclosure *is* the foundation of representation.

It is precisely the encounter with Rosenzweig's *Star* that enables Levinas to make his subtler and more fundamental critique of phenomenology. It turns out that Levinas's dissatisfaction with the foundations of Husserlian phenomenology stems from two sources, one more profound than the other. It is not until he encounters Rosenzweig's *Star*, because it is the more profound alternative, that Levinas can fully assuage this dissatisfaction. *Heidegger's ontology permits Levinas to see beneath the representational character of Husserl's phenomenology, true, but the ethics and justice of Rosenzweig's 'Star' permit him to see through the ontological character of Heidegger's regrounding of phenomenology.* Heidegger frees Levinas from Husserl and at the same time deepens his appreciation for phenomenology,

---

tial. "The following investigation," Heidegger writes, "would not have been possible if the ground had not been prepared by Edmund Husserl, with whose *Logische Untersuchungen* phenomenology first emerged. . . . What is essential in it does not lie in its *actuality* as a philosophical 'movement.' Higher than actuality stands *possibility*. We can understand phenomenology only by seizing upon it as a possibility."

but Rosenzweig frees Levinas from phenomenology by deepening his appreciation for ethics and justice.

Thus in the discussion of phenomenology in the preface to *Totality and Infinity*, which *commences* with praise for Rosenzweig's *Star*, the opposition between what is essential and therefore still acceptable in phenomenology and what is literal and therefore unacceptable in phenomenology will place both Husserl and Heidegger on the side of the literal. Now the literal means not just founding representation in more representation, *à la* Husserl, nor the founding of representation in ontological thinking, *à la* Heidegger, but the very idea or form of *Grund* (and its partner, *Abgrund*) as such, i.e., the standard of *adequation*, the thinking of thinking as sustained by adequation. It is this difference between Levinas's earlier and his later assessment of phenomenology that is the meaning of Levinas's acknowledgement of Rosenzweig's *Star* in close proximity to the phenomenological method. It is comforting to note, by way of biographical support for this thesis, that Levinas first read the *Star* in 1935.[13]

Under the influence of Rosenzweig's *Star*, Levinas will now oppose not just the formality and objectification of representation, an opposition also proposed by Heidegger, but the notion of adequation as such, whether of the intentional-consciousness sort proposed by Husserl, the correlation of noema to noeses, or of the existential-ontological sort proposed by Heidegger, the correlation of Dasein to Sein. What is also important to realize, in grasping this connection between Levinas's debt to Rosenzweig's *Star* and Levinas's positive evaluation of phenomenology, is that he finds within phenomenology itself the resources for its own undoing.

In his reading of phenomenology, against both Husserl and Heidegger, Levinas finds not only the recognition of a movement of thought which breaks up correlation as such, whether formal or existential, but the recognition that this break-up comes from an irrecuperably nonadequate relation—an ethical relation—whose significance is prior to the significations established through intentional correlation. Underneath the structure of founded and founding which dominates both Husserlian and Heideggerian phenomenology, Levinas, along with Rosenzweig, asserts the primacy of *metaphysics*, the unquenched and unquenchable thirst for alterity, the always inadequate desire for the inordinate.

We can see now, then, that when Levinas writes that the "notions

---

13. See Francois Poirié, *Emmanuel Levinas: Qui êtes-vous?* 121. Unaware of Poirié's book, in October 1987 I asked Levinas when he had first read Rosenzweig's *Star*. His answer was the same: 1935.

employed" in *Totality and Infinity* "owe everything to the phenomenological method," he means that the notions employed in the work are indebted to phenomenology for three interrelated movements or dimensions: (1) the turn to the concrete, (2) the break-up of the formal structures of representation, and (3) the recognition that the formal structures of representation "live from" and are "endowed" with significance by horizons unsuspected by intentional thought. It is the combined movement of all three of these components that Levinas calls "a *deduction*—necessary and yet non-analytical."

What phenomenological deduction reveals is the truth of metaphysics, metaphysical truth: the priority of goodness and justice. It is as if the phenomenological deduction forced philosophy, per impossible, one step beyond its maximum capacities, as in a quantum leap, or the abutment of one topological dimension by another of a different order. Ethics and justice would no longer provide "principles" or "grounds" for philosophy, nor, certainly, would they be subsumed by philosophy, nor, worse, would they be excluded from philosophy altogether. Rather, philosophy, thought through to the end, to the end of its end, troubled by Husserl's phenomenological deduction, would acknowledge itself as a *mode* of ethics and justice. "Husserlian phenomenology," Levinas writes in the concluding sentence of the two paragraph discussion of phenomenology which follows the acknowledgement of Rosenzweig's *Star*, "has made possible this passage from ethics to metaphysical exteriority" (*TI* 29).

Having achieved an insight into the metaphysical dimension which both undermines and nurtures philosophy qua phenomenology, we are now in a position (or "non-position," Levinas would say) to appreciate the extraordinary absence and presence of the *Star*, its presence in absentia, in *Totality and Infinity*, to appreciate both why this absence is necessary and how it relates specifically to phenomenology. There are two sides to the absence of the *Star* in *Totality and Infinity*, and both of them, of necessity, have their parallels in the *Star's* relation to itself and in *Totality and Infinity's* relation to itself.

First, to say that the *Star* is present in *Totality and Infinity* only by being absent, that the *Star* "is" extraordinarily absent, that it is "otherwise than being," is another way of saying that phenomenology—to which *Totality and Infinity* owes everything—is precisely what permits glimpsing the true sources of thought, sources which lie outside of phenomenology and outside of thought altogether. Rosenzweig shows Levinas the way free from phenomenology just as Schelling showed Rosenzweig the way free from idealism. It is not a simple curiosity that in the *Star* and elsewhere, Rosenzweig reveals his own hyperbolic modesty and audacity in relation to Friedrich von Schelling, giving credit to Schelling for having shown the way out of idealist philosophy. It is Rosenzweig's contention that had Schelling only completed his project of a positive philosophy, which was begun in *The Ages of the World* (1820), then the *Star* "would not have been worthy of anyone's attention except the Jews."[14] What he means is that the philosophical possibility of the *Star's* basic message comes from Schelling, from Schelling's argument against nineteenth-century German idealism, his positive argument that if thought through to the end idealism can itself be made to glimpse its own true sources outside of idealism—in existence.[15] Levinas is clearly making a similar claim with regard to phenomenology. Both idealism and phenomenology can be made to see—not, however, with the necessity that makes for their own sight, the sight that can be blinded by its own light—or made to *suffer*, one should perhaps say, the *weight* of metaphysics, the superlative of the divine, which "appears" in the face of the other person and "unfolds" in the struggle for justice. Phenomenology, so Levinas claims by invoking the "opposition to totality" found in Rosenzweig's *Star*, reveals its own shortcomings, its own inadequacy.

Second, just as idealism was for Rosenzweig not just any philosophy, randomly selected for criticism, but the essence of philosophy, philosophy itself, for Levinas it is phenomenology that is now philosophy's most rigorous form. If philosophy stayed put, if it never advanced, then Rosenzweig (or perhaps Schelling) could have done his critical work and we would all be done with philosophical pretensions once and for all. But philosophy does not stay put, even if it does not necessarily "advance" either. Just as idealism was yesterday's misunderstanding of metaphysics, corrected by phenomenology, phenomenology is today's misunderstanding of metaphysics (and increasingly phenomenology in our day has also become yesterday's understanding of metaphysics). We must understand that it is not just the text of *Totality and Infinity* that is inevitably ill understood and immediately calls for a preface. Neither, more broadly,

---

14. Quoted by Ernst Akiva Simon in "Reflections of a Disciple," in *The Philosophy of Franz Rosenzweig*, edited by Paul Mendes-Flohr (Hanover: Brandeis University Press, 1988), 205–6. For readers interested in Schelling's impact on Paul Tillich, Karl Barth, I. A. Dorner, and Heidegger, see Robert P. Scharlemann, "Schelling's Impact on Protestant Theology," in his *Inscriptions and Reflections: Essays in Philosophical Theology* (Charlottesville: University Press of Virginia, 1989), 92–105.

15. Rosenzweig's Schellingian argument occurs in part 1 of the *Star* and no doubt accounts for its difficulty. Cf. Paul Tillich, *The Construction of the History of Religion in Schelling's Positive Philosophy*, trans. Victor Nuovo (Lewisburg: Bucknell University Press, 1974), and Tillich, *Mysticism and Guilt-Consciousness in Schelling's Philosophical Development*, trans. Victor Nuovo (Lewisburg: Bucknell University Press, 1974). It is no accident that in 1841 Kierkegaard attended Schelling's lectures in Berlin criticizing Hegelian idealism, although he was disappointed in Schelling.

is it just phenomenology or idealism that are always inevitably ill understood. These are not the *only* but the *latest* philosophical "ceremonies" in which goodness delights in expressing and losing itself. Philosophy itself, or, even more broadly, the world itself, expresses and loses the metaphysical, the meta-physical. To reanimate the very same inspiration that animates the *Star,* then, Levinas must grapple with phenomenology rather than with nineteenth-century Germany idealism.

The necessary undoing of philosophy (which is itself, in another sense, *philosophy,* in a new key: the unsaying of the saying that has become said) is historical in the sense that philosophy, like the world of which it is a part, takes on different historical forms, forms which both complete and at the same time disfigure the metaphysical. But at the same time the undoing of philosophy so understood is ahistorical insofar as it is the very same metaphysical claim—always absent, always overwhelmingly present, better than being, otherwise than being—that undoes each and every philosophical form, each and every "ceremony," each and every provisional stopping place that takes itself too seriously, that is to say, that takes the genuine ethical and social claims of humanity too lightly. The undoing of philosophy is as eternal and as temporal as philosophy itself. "Thinking," Levinas has written, "has never been more difficult." Thinking, we could add, has at each time always been most difficult. But perhaps, let us add in a final suggestion which returns to *philosophy* in another sense, the ideal of a life not just of knowledge but of *wisdom*—the "wisdom of love" (see *OBBE* 153–62), Levinas writes—is how philosophy itself acknowledges the difficulty of thinking that which transcends thought itself.

ELEVEN

The Face of Truth and Jewish Mysticism

In all faces is seen the Face of faces, veiled, and in a riddle.

Nicolas of Cusa

The Vision of G-d

For both Franz Rosenzweig and Emmanuel Levinas the human face is the site of truth. The face is where truth *happens* in its *absoluteness,* that is to say, in its divinity. "Truth is from God," writes Rosenzweig in his great work, *The Star of Redemption* (*SR* 388). Truth is "to God" *(à-Dieu),* writes Levinas in many of his later texts. Clearly, neither Rosenzweig nor Levinas thinks of truth simply as the coherence of a set of propositions or their correspondence to a state of affairs. Neither, of course, do they simply exclude or ignore these forms truth takes, as if they did not exist. For both thinkers, however, the truths of coherence and correspondence are based on the transcendence of *revelatory truth*—truth as expression, sincerity, and moral force. It is truth in this social and ethical sense that is ultimate. It is truth in this sense that opens up *in and as the face,* in the face-to-face where one person faces the alterity of the other person. Truth thus emerges in an excessive proximity, a proximity to the otherness of the other closer than being, yet one wherein the other's alterity remains absolute. Truth is produced in an excessive nearness and distance whose claim is nothing other than the call of a moral force. Thus an always utterly unique relation—the face-to-face relation—becomes the source of universality.

To articulate and legitimate this peculiar combination of ethics, religion, and epistemology, Rosenzweig and Levinas have much to say about the face. They have much to say, and there is much for expositors to explain about what these two thinkers say about the interpersonal orientation of truth. The aim of this chapter, however, is limited to illuminating the faces in Rosenzweig and Levinas in the light cast by the many faces found in the Jewish mystical tradition. Such a line of inquiry would be of interest under any number of circumstances, especially given the general neglect of Jewish studies in mainstream philosophical discussions. That it is specifically called for to illuminate the philosophies of Rosenzweig and Levinas, however, is triply justified regarding the former by the unexpected epiphany of the extraordinary "face of man" *(Das Menschen-Gesicht)* which appears on the penultimate page of the *Star,* in its gateway *(Tor)* to life, and for the latter by the profound influence that Rosenzweig's prodigious masterwork has exerted on the whole of Levinas's thought. Rosenzweig's description of the face at the end of the *Star* manifestly resonates with the Jewish mystical tradition. My objective here is to trace that resonance.[1]

Related to the question of truth, but over and beyond our more partic- ular interest in the faces in Rosenzweig and Levinas, their link, and their link to the Jewish mystical tradition, the human face has always been surrounded by a host of wider significations and resonances. The image of the human face has for millennia served the entire West—indeed, the entire world—not merely as the place of this or that truth, but as a primary and primordial opening between the human and the divine, as the place and test of truth, as the very "truth" of truth.

Before entering into the faces of Rosenzweig, Levinas, and Jewish mysticism, then, I am going to begin with a brief look at the face in the broader spiritual heritage of the West. I am going to begin, that is to say, by giving three general reasons why the human face plays a middle role between the divine and the human. In attending to these reasons one must not forget that the Western tradition, even when it is most reasonable, has at least two beginnings, or rather, the Western tradition has an origin and a beginning: an origin in Greece and a beginning in the Holy Land.

The Preeminence of the Face

Perhaps the most obvious reason for the preeminence of the face, for its quasi-divine stature, is its natural verticality, the "above and below" it orients in conjunction with the natural verticality of the standing human body. Erwin Straus's famous study of the body's upright posture has made us familiar with the phenomenological significance of this aspect of human physiology.[2] The human body and the human face are both upright, or should be. Physical and ethical significations parallel and shade into one another: in facing another person one's attention is oriented toward and by the uppermost part of the other's body; in like manner one is oriented upward to G-d. The face looks out from atop the body; G-d looks out from above creation. A spirituality articulated in terms of the dimensions of height, of the above and the below, *axis mundi,* joins the experience

1. Stéphane Mosès, in *System and Revelation,* has also emphasized certain connections between the *Star,* mysticism, Jewish mysticism, and the face; see especially 127–28, 279–86.

2. See Erwin Straus, "The Upright Posture," in *Phenomenological Psychology* (New York: Basic Books, 1966), ch. 7; reprinted in *Phenomenology and Existentialism,* edited by Richard Zaner and Don Ihde (New York, G. P. Putnam's Sons, 1973), 232–59.

of verticality encountered in the human face and body. This verticality is at play in the *Star* in an important passage, where just before introducing the "face of man," Rosenzweig writes:

There is an Above and a Below, inexchangeable and irreversible. . . . And just because there is an Above and a Below in the truth, therefore we may, nay we must call it God's countenance. . . . Man has an above and a below in his own corporeality. . . . It is not human illusion if Scripture speaks of God's countenance and even of his separate bodily parts. There is no other way to express the Truth. Only when we see the Star as countenance do we transcend every possibility and simply see. (*SR* 422)

A second reason for situating the juncture of man and G-d in the image of the face is that the human face not only is vertical or upright physically and morally, but also is the locus of more kinds of openings than any other place on the surface of the human body. The body is nowhere more open. All senses are at play there: seeing, hearing, smelling, tasting, touching. Here too one thinks, wrinkles one's brow. Of all human faculties, activities, and desires, perhaps only feelings, full body gymnastics and athletics, and certain urgent dimensions of eros, are more powerfully focused elsewhere than the face. The face is alive with expressions and impressions. Thus again physiological and ethical-spiritual significations shade off into one another: as the place of so many openings and sensitivities, it is *the place*;[3] as the center of such a multitude of exchanges and passages, it is *the center*. No other comparably compact area of the body or world is open to a greater range of give and take. The face is by nature intense, a zone of intensities and exchanges. The true *omphalos* is the face.

A third reason lies in the very life of the face. That the face is alive means, of course, that it is active, fluid, moving and moved, physically and emotionally, that it is expressive. But also and more importantly it means that the face is irreversible, that it is indelibly oriented and marked by a past, present, and future. When he joins truth to the verticality of human and divine countenance, in the passage cited just above, Rosenzweig also notes the link between truth and the irreversibility of life: "We speak in images [i.e., of the countenance]. But the images are not arbitrary. There are essential images and coincidental ones. The irreversibility of the truth can only be enunciated in the image of a living being" (*SR* 422). Living beings grow, their life travels one way from birth to death, passing through infancy, youth, maturity, and old age, never returning the same or to the same like reflection. The face of the other, Levinas has taught since 1946, is precisely the excessive dimensionality of time,

3. In religious Hebrew, "the place," *ha-makom,* is often used synonymously for G-d, or for where His presence never departs, His holy temple in Jerusalem.

"diachrony," irreversibility, the transcendence of an immemorial irrecoverable past and an always surprising future.[4] At the same time, without contradiction, the face crystallizes a whole life; it gives evidence of accumulated and accumulating vulnerabilities and powers, of experiences etched as character in lines and wrinkles on its skin. Thus it is at once whole and part, presence and passage, living now and through all its times—a fitting image of the divine-human juncture, where time and eternity meet.

These three reasons alone would suffice to "explain" the biblical *panim 'el panim*,[5] the excessive rectitude, openness, and directness of the *face to face* between G-d and the human. Because both Rosenzweig and Levinas are cognizant of all these reasons, it is obvious that additional factors must account for the differences in the faces found in their writings, to which we now turn.

The Difference between the Face in Rosenzweig and the Face in Levinas

One of the most striking moments at the end of Rosenzweig's *Star*, even more so than the transcending intention dramatized by the triangular arrangement of the book's final sentences,[6] is the appearance of the human face *(Gesicht, Antlitz)* described on its penultimate page. In an altogether brilliant and astonishing book, this epiphany stands out as one of the

4. See *TO* and chapter 6 in this volume.

5. The expression *panim 'el panim,* literally "face-to-face," is found in Exodus 33:11, where God speaks to Moses who is within the "tent of the meeting" at the foot of Mount Sinai: "And God spoke to Moses face to face"; and in Deuteronomy 5:4, where Moses reminds the people Israel of their covenant with G-d which was made in Horeb: "The Lord spoke with you face to face."

Of these two instances, Moses Maimonides, in *The Guide of the Perplexed,* part 1, chapter 37, says that "face to face" means "the presence and station of an individual." Maimonides writes: " 'And the Lord spoke unto Moses face to face'—which means, as a presence to another presence without an intermediary, as it is said: 'Come, let us look one another in the face' (2 Kings 14:8). Thus Scripture says: 'The Lord spoke with you face to face' (Deuteronomy 5:4). In another passage it explains: 'Ye heard the voice of words, but ye saw no figure, only a voice' (Deuteronomy 4:12). Hence this kind of speaking and hearing are described as being 'face to face'." Moses Maimonides, *The Guide of the Perplexed,* vol. 1, translated by Shlomo Pines (Chicago: University of Chicago Press, 1963), 85–86.

6. See p. 297 below. As we have seen, the *Star* moves from death to life, literally beginning with the word "death" and ending with the word "life." The book passes from critique through a variety of positive stages in self-development and authentic encounter with reality, from erotic love to the loves which drive ethics and religious community, concluding in life in the everyday world with others *(Der Alltag des Lebens),* life "beyond the book."

It is interesting to note that Rabbi Simeon ben Yochai (of the *Zohar*) is said to have died with the word "life" on his lips.

most astonishing moments. What makes for the amazement it inspires is both a surprise at its appearance, to be sure, but also the details of its description. With regard to its surprise, upon reflection we realize that it is no accident that Rosenzweig describes the human face just before making the final and ultimate gesture of the *Star:* launching out from text into life, from conceptual or imaginary truth into *eternal* truth, truth lived as love for the neighbor within a revealed religious community. Eternal truth, as Rosenzweig understands it, is found in a return from concepts and images to face-to-face relations, to faces encountered in love, ethics, and spirituality, faces at once human and divine.

The details of Rosenzweig's graphic description of the face, on the other hand, stand out precisely in their detail, their particularity. This detail stands out even more for readers familiar with the face in Levinas's thought. The face is more essential, if this is possible to say, to Levinas than to Rosenzweig. Even apart from Rosenzweig's influence, the entirety of Levinas's thought can be correctly characterized as a long and profound meditation on the significance of the face. When the influence of Rosenzweig on Levinas is taken into account, what becomes conspicuous is the contrast between Rosenzweig's "face of man" and the ethical face of the other person in Levinas. Rosenzweig's description of the face on barely one page of the *Star* presents a face far more *graphic* and *symbolic* than anything found anywhere in the entire oeuvre of Levinas. There are, indeed, no comparable descriptions of the face in Levinas, not even in *Totality and Infinity,* to take the prime example, where fully one quarter of the text is explicitly devoted to the face *(la visage).*[7] The difference is one of quality. In contrast to the face in Levinas, Rosenzweig's face is both *graphic,* meaning that it details concrete features: eyes, ears, cheeks, mouth, etc.; and *symbolic,* meaning that these features are distributed according to the geometry of the Mogen David, the six pointed star of the *Star,* thus also according to the fundamental elements and structures developed in the *Star.*

The differences between the faces in Rosenzweig and Levinas are at first glance all the more difficult to explain inasmuch as it is Levinas who is trained in the *descriptive* phenomenology of Husserl, and Rosenzweig who is trained in the *conceptual* phenomenology of Hegel. That is to say, one might quite naturally have expected concepts from Rosenzweig and descriptions from Levinas. But this expectation is not met. It is not met for the obvious reason that Rosenzweig rejects the Hegelian mode of

---

7. *TI* represents the prime example of salient differences separating Levinas from Rosenzweig not only because of its lengthy treatment of the face, but because overall it is a book closer to Rosenzweig's *Star* than *any* other book of its stature.

philosophizing and Levinas rejects the Husserlian mode. But here lies a great hint as to why one finds such graphic detail and symbolism in Rosenzweig but not in Levinas. Rosenzweig, unlike Levinas, rejects Hegelian conceptualization without the aid of Husserlian phenomenology. His is the bolder, less mediated leap. Levinas, in contrast, appropriates Rosenzweig's criticism of Hegelian totalization, but utilizes it not to get beyond Hegel, a critical task already well argued for by Rosenzweig and effected by the work of Heidegger and Husserl; rather, Levinas uses it to get beyond the limits of fundamental ontology and descriptive phenomenology themselves. Thus Levinas feels no compulsion to *describe* a face— graphic, symbolic—a face that surpasses the logic of Hegelian ontology, as does Rosenzweig. Rather, in contrast to Rosenzweig, he is compelled to articulate a face that not only surpasses the resources of Hegelian logic, but *also* surpasses the resources of Heideggerian ontology and Husserlian descriptive phenomenology.

But our current attention is not focused on these relations and developments.[8] Our question has to do with the truths expressed by these faces and their relation to Jewish mysticism: What truths do the faces in Rosenzweig and Levinas manifest? How do these faces, and the differences which clearly distinguish them, relate to the Jewish mystical tradition?

Rosenzweig's Face

I will begin by quoting the paragraph of the *Star* where the "face of man" appears. This paragraph occurs in the final section of the *Star, after* the third book of part 3, in the section entitled "Gate," a gate which leads into real life "beyond the book." Rather than apologize for the length of the following citation, I rather insist on the importance of reading it in full, attentively. Everything in this chapter assumes a familiarity with Rosenzweig's "face of man":

Just as the Star mirrors its elements and the combination of the elements into one route in its two superimposed triangles, so too the organs of the countenance divide into two levels. For the life-points of the countenance are, after all, the points where the countenance comes into contact with the world above, be it in passive or active contact. The basic level is ordered according to the receptive organs; they are the building blocks, as it were, which together compose the face, the mask, namely forehead and cheeks, to which belong respectively nose and ears. Nose and ears are the organs of pure receptivity. The nose belongs to the forehead; in the sacred [Hebrew] tongue it veritably stands for the face as a whole. The scent of offerings turns to it as the motion of the lips to the ears. This first

8. See chapters 10 and 12 in this volume.

triangle is thus formed by the midpoint of the forehead, as the dominant point of the entire face, and the midpoints of the cheeks. Over it is now imposed a second triangle, composed of the organs whose activity quickens the rigid mask of the first: eyes and mouth. Not that the eyes are mutually equivalent in a mimic sense, for while the left one views more receptively and evenly, the right one "flashes"—a division of labor which frequently leaves its mark deep in the soft neighborhood of the eye-sockets of a hoary head; this asymmetric facial formation, which otherwise is generally conspicuous only in the familiar difference between the two profiles, then becomes perceptible also en face. Just as the structure of the face is dominated by the forehead, so its life, all that surrounds the eyes and shines forth from the eyes, is gathered in the mouth. The mouth is consummator and fulfiller of all expression of which the countenance is capable, both in speech, as, at last, in the silence beyond which speech retreats: in the kiss. It is in the eyes that the eternal countenance shines for man; it is the mouth by whose words man lives. But for our teacher Moses, who in his lifetime was privileged only to see the land of his desire, not to enter it, God sealed this completed life with a kiss of his mouth. Thus does God seal and so too does man. (*SR* 422–33)

The following illustrations are provided in the hope that they will be helpful aids to visualizing what Rosenzweig has articulated.[9]

The correlations are artful, indeed artificial. Thankfully, Rosenzweig

---

9. These illustrations would be even better if they were each printed on a clear medium so that they could be laminated one on top of the other.

For a brief history of the Star of David symbol in Judaism, see Gershom Scholem, "The Star of David: History of a Symbol," *The Messianic Idea in Judaism,* translated by Michael A. Meyer (New York: Schocken Books, 1971), 257–81; and Gershom Scholem, "Magen David," *Kabbalah* (Jerusalem: Keter Publishing Company, 1974), 362-368. Especially interesting and somewhat ironic, regarding Rosenzweig's fascination with the star, is that, as Scholem notes in the conclusion to both articles, the Star of David, or more literally the Shield of David, did not become a symbol of Judaism in the way that the cross was a symbol of Christianity until the nineteenth century. In the latter article, "Magan David," he writes: "The prime motive behind the wide diffusion of the sign in the 19th century was the desire to imitate Christianity. The Jews looked for a striking and simple sign which would 'symbolize' Judaism in the same way as the cross symbolizes Christianity" (367–68). The traditional "symbol" of Judaism for Jews is, of course, the Menorah, the candelabra which stood in the Temple in Jerusalem; it is today the "official" symbol of the State of Israel (which, by the way, has also lent legitimacy to the Star of David by putting it on the state flag). Prior to the nineteenth century, Scholem points out, the Star of David was most often either an ornament or a magical sign, and not just a Jewish one at that.

With regard to these drawings, which are my own and not Rosenzweig's, it is instructive to contrast the sense Rosenzweig makes of his two triangles (Creation, Revelation, Redemption, and God, Man, World) with that of the two triangles making up the "vortexes" which, at precisely the same time Rosenzweig was conceiving and writing the *Star,* William Butler Yeats and his wife were (automatically) depicting in their work, *A Vision* (1925). The Yeatses

THE FACE OF MAN

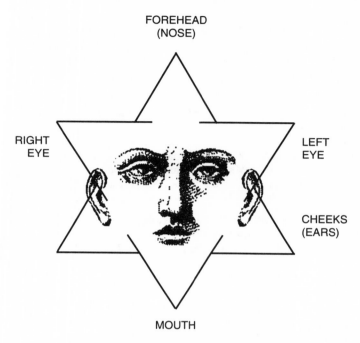

FOREHEAD
(NOSE)

RIGHT
EYE

LEFT
EYE

CHEEKS
(EARS)

MOUTH

Rosenzweig's face in relation to the Mogen David.

does not belabor their geometrical aspect. The reader is not expected to henceforth imagine something like a Mogen David tatoo on the human face, superimposing the primary elements, structures, and religions elaborated in the *Star* onto human faces encountered socially. The primary intent is, I think, simply to accentuate and accelerate a deliberate movement "beyond the book." To go beyond the book is not at all to forget or to ignore the rigorous and demanding itinerary of the *Star,* lest one

articulated a complicated "system" of symbolic thought based on two intersecting triangles and a circle. Their visions, in contrast to Rosenzweig's use of the Star of David, remained personal, within the "legislation" of the artist, attached neither to a revealed tradition nor to a philosophical justification. Rosenzweig detects a similar but far more consequential detachment from tradition in Masonic "religion"; see *SR* 285.

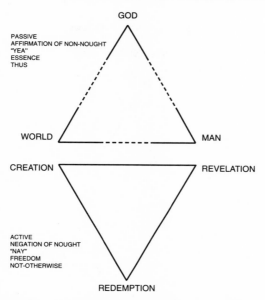

Some of the significations correlated to the two triangles of the Mogen David as elaborated in part 1 of the *Star*.

THE STAR OF REDEMPTION

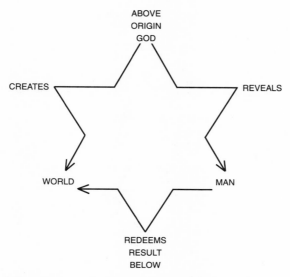

The Mogen David as the symbol of the primary elements and structures organizing and elaborated in the *Star*. This star is *the* star.

CHRISTIANITY: THE RAYS

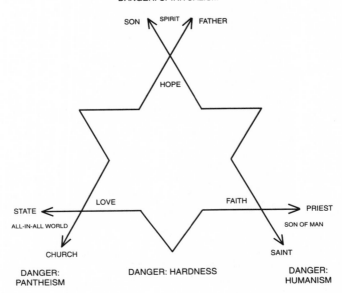

JUDAISM: THE FIRE

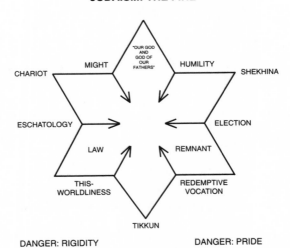

The Mogen David as symbol of the eternal fire of Judaism and the historical rays of Christianity as elaborated in part 3 of the *Star*.

either fall back into patterns of thought and behavior criticized or not be instructed by the positive contents of Rosenzweig's "new thinking." The point of those positive contents, however, is to turn readers from the hypotheses, theses, and doctrines of the *Star* to the place where these contents lead, one might even say are "tested"—to ethical and religious life with others. The "face of man" is Rosenzweig's final gesture, in other words, in his effort to turn his readers to real human faces "beyond the book." Thus one must not get bogged down, speculatively, contemplatively (beyond the healthy rational skepticism always demanded of astute readers, and certainly always demanded of Rosenzweig's readers) in the "face of man," which remains in the final account a literary description, however graphic, symbol laden, and linked to the contents of the *Star*. The enigmatic description of the "face of man" opens up and upon a new register of meaning for the entire *Star*. To accomplish this exceeding, this transcending, this surpassing, this "beyond the book," Rosenzweig's graphic and symbolic image of the "face of man" calls to mind sources and resources other than those found within the Greek philosophical tradition; indeed, it draws upon currents running deep within the Jewish religious tradition.

When Rosenzweig writes that "the Star must once more mirror itself in that which, within the corporeality, is again the Upper: the countenance. Thus it is not human illusion if Scripture speaks of God's countenance and even of his separate bodily parts" (*SR* 422), or when he writes that "the life-points of the [human] countenance are, after all, those points where the countenance comes into contact with the world above" (*SR* 422), emphasizing the absoluteness and unity of the divine above and the human below, a unity found precisely in the human face as a mirror of G-d's face, these words echo with meanings coming out of the long mystical tradition of Judaism. Such statements, coupled with their attachment to the graphic and symbolic correspondences illustrated in the figures of the "face of man," indicate the importance in Rosenzweig of this tradition. It is to the Jewish mystical tradition that we must then turn to flesh out what is at stake in the face in Rosenzweig, and then in the face in Levinas.

The Jewish Mystical Tradition

In attending to the Jewish mystical tradition, I must begin with several disclaimers, the first quite general and the others less so. First, my survey is driven by a limited purpose, which one might call intellectual analysis rather than historical or historiological research. This survey will not, therefore, decide issues best left to qualified historians of Jewish mysticism, issues having to do with the precise dating of manuscripts, for example, or, in some controversial areas, determining historical influences upon certain texts.[10] Historical questions are particularly tricky in the Jewish mystical tradition, owing to the undeniable impact of oral tradition. Because my primary purpose is intellectual analysis, however, if the scholarly historical assessments of certain texts upon which I rely are later refined or revised, the points I aim to establish will nonetheless remain firm, even if their historical anchorage may have to be shifted more or less.

Second, I do not claim to read the minds of Rosenzweig or Levinas, or to reveal their hidden intentions. Third, I make no claims about how much or in some instances even whether Rosenzweig or Levinas knew about particular mystical texts. Fourth, my object is not to label Rosenzweig or Levinas "mystics."[11] Fifth, my aim is not to show that Rosenzweig or Levinas tapped Jewish mystical sources to prove their philosophies. Though their written words show beyond a shadow of doubt that both Rosenzweig and Levinas are not merely aware in some vague way of a Jewish mystical tradition but directly refer and allude to Jewish mystical sources, their philosophies nevertheless do not in any essential way rely on these references and allusions for their truth. The purpose of my examination of Jewish mystical sources is not, therefore, to reveal the hitherto concealed bases of the thought of Rosenzweig and Levinas, but rather, more appropriately and modestly, to show as precisely as possible how an attunement to the subtle resonances of the Jewish mystical tradition can cast light on the faces which appear in Rosenzweig and Levinas.

Before proceeding to these resonances, however, I must briefly take up a more general question of method in mysticism. The term "resonance" is deliberately vague. I have used it because to the philosophically trained mind, that is to say, to the mind trained in reason, in giving reasons, all of the connections, correlations, correspondences whose meanings are legitimized by Jewish mysticism seem highly unregulated. Within certain boundaries almost "anything goes," almost any association of meaning is tolerated and exploited.

The restriction of meaning, or the meaning of restriction, in Jewish mysticism is primarily of two sorts: first, mystical claims are bounded by Torah and Talmud insofar as mystical claims cannot ultimately contradict the higher authority accorded to halakah (Jewish law) and aggadah (Jew-

---

10. The reader will see that in what follows I rely on the pioneering interpretations of Jewish mysticism developed by Gershom Scholem and extended by his successor at Hebrew University in Jerusalem, Joseph Dan. In recent years, however, Moshe Idel, also at Hebrew University in Jerusalem, in *Kabbalah: New Perspectives* (New Haven: Yale University Press, 1988), without revolutionizing the field, has argued for some interesting and sometimes far-reaching revisions of Scholem's theses.

11. Both thinkers explicitly deny the label "mystic." But in these matters, affirmative or negative avowals are of little account. Such is the freedom or mystery of mystical thought.

ish mores). A mystical claim will certainly deepen the meaning of a halakic regulation, but it will never contradict or overturn it. The same holds for the incidents and ethical truths of aggadah, where mystical interpretations will deepen but not nullify other nonmystical readings. Second, the connections made by mystical interpretation are bounded by the connections that have already been made within the Jewish mystical tradition. That is to say, mystical claims are bounded by the authority of transmitted tradition. Indeed, the authority of mystical claims, at whatever historical time they are formulated, depends precisely on the authority of transmitted tradition, since the antiquity of a claim strengthens its credibility because it signifies closeness to the revelation at Mount Sinai, and going beyond Sinai it signifies closeness to G-d in His undiminished unity prior to creation. It is only within these strictures, and woven into them—halakah, aggadah, and tradition—that "anything is possible" in Jewish mysticism.

Given these restrictions, one may question the aptness of the expression "anything is possible," but the latitude left to mystical interpretation, from highly imaginative glosses on prophetic visions (especially of G-d's chariot, throne, and palace; see *SR* 408), to exotic correlations of meaning established through gematria, to clever manipulations of Hebrew letters and parts of Hebrew letters which border on the stunning, all seem adequate to justify this characterization. However irregular these "methods" may appear when compared to the rigorous standards of philosophy, to Greek standards, the meanings established are not, from the perspective of the Jewish mystical tradition itself, in any way arbitrary or subjective, and, as we shall see, the connections established by their means, and possible through no other means, are often quite suggestive and illuminating.

Jewish mysticism is not poetry. The Jewish prophet or sage is never confused with the Greek oracle or poet. Jewish mysticism is the sense one makes of the divinity of the created universe over and beyond the authority of halakic and haggadic significations.

The wide-ranging freedom of the mystical reading is one of its prime virtues, and with equal certainty one of its prime dangers. That it is a danger Jewish tradition has underlined by setting restrictions onto who and how one can enter into mystical studies. That it is a danger is further emphasized by the famous and oft repeated story of the four rabbis who entered the garden of mystical knowledge, from out which only Rabbi Akiba emerged sane and with his faith intact.[12] At the same time, interpre-

---

12. This story appears in the Babylonian Talmud, *Hagigah* 14b, and in the Jerusalem Talmud, *Hagigah* 2:3–4. The four rabbis are: Rabbi ben Zoma, who went mad (or died young); Rabbi ben Azzai, who died; Rabbi Acher (Elisha ben Abuyah), who became an apostate; and Rabbi Akiva. For one version of this story with commentaries, see Louis Jacobs, *Jewish Mystical Testimonies* (New York: Schocken, 1977), 21–25.

tive freedom is the virtue of mysticism because it enables its devotees to mine a wealth of significations otherwise inaccessible to the Greek logic of affirmation and negation, or to the limitations of human poetical production. This mining is based on the genuinely religious insight, expressed in its fullest force within the Jewish tradition by Rabbi Moses ben Jacob Cordovero, that in a world absolutely sacred, created and sustained by G-d, each and every entity contains and is therefore related to all other entities in all ways. Thus the mystical interpretative tradition—*sod*, secret—is within certain strictures the least determinate and most unregulated of the traditional interpretative approaches which make sense of the sacred universe.[13] The symbol is not equivalent to thought; it "gives rise to thought."[14]

A final disclaimer is required: my aim in the following is not to enter as a privileged initiate into the infinite terrain of infinite possible interpretations. My aim is not to "do" mysticism in this sense. Rather, I intend to invoke only those corporeal and facial symbols and interpretations that have already been made in the Jewish mystical tradition. My overall purpose, to repeat, is to better understand the significance of the faces which orient the thought of Rosenzweig and Levinas.

The proximate motivation for this voyage into Jewish mysticism is the manifest link between this tradition and the face which appears at the conclusion of Rosenzweig's *Star*. The face in Levinas is at first sight far less evidently connected to the Jewish mystical tradition, but excluding other fairly compelling reasons which I have not mentioned,[15] its close association with the face in Rosenzweig is reason enough to pursue its link to this tradition.

The entire Jewish mystical tradition is an attempt on the symbolic plane to solve a central religious-metaphysical problem, namely, the problem of making sense in a finite world of G-d's absolute transcendence. The key here is the term "G-d." What is at stake in the Jewish tradition is determining the singular relationship between a perfect and good G-d (who as one is the totality), and the imperfection, remoteness, or evil of His creation. Metaphysics for the Jew is not the abstract science of the Greeks but

13. The other interpretative approaches, according the schema known by the acronym *pardes*, are *peshat*, the "plain" meaning, *remez*, the "allusive" meaning, and *derash*, the "solicited" meaning. To a certain limited extent, one can consider *peshat* the level of philosophical interpretation, *remez* the level of haggadic interpretation, and *derash* the level of halakic interpretation. *Sod* takes care of everything else after the other three approaches have produced their results, including the reinterpretation of the results of these other approaches.

14. See Paul Ricoeur, *The Symbolism of Evil*, translated by Emerson Buchanan (Boston: Beacon Press, 1969), especially the conclusion, 347–57.

15. For instance, Levinas's oft acknowledged indebtedness to Rabbi Hayim of Volozhin, whose work is thoroughly imbued with mystical knowledge, as we shall see below.

an always specific ontology regulated by G-d's goodness. It is not only knowledge but worship.

Within Jewish mysticism there are many sets of symbols designed to show or manifest the link between the infinite and the finite, the perfect and the imperfect, between G-d and His creation. All of these symbolisms by necessity can only utilize elements taken from the finite world. Elements of the finite world are, when given mystical significance, taken to be signs, metaphors, ciphers, or mirrors, which when appropriately manipulated, through praxis or intellect or both, manifest the infinite or bring it near. It is no accident that the precise term or movement of this juncture cannot be fully articulated. One must have recourse to symbols. In the course of its long history,[16] Jewish tradition has already articulated many sets of symbols, of which the most outstanding are: names of God, the letters of the aleph-bet, parts of letters, letters of particular words, personal pronouns, the human body, biblical personages, celestial spheres, family trees, lovers, nations, colors, days of the week, attributes of G-d, and numbers. In this tradition one finds the human face within the set of symbols that utilizes the figure of the finite human body. Within this set of symbols there are innumerable faces and interfaces of faces.

I will now turn to examine four types of corporeal symbolism: one from the ancient period, two from the medieval period, and one from the modern period. The first comes from a very early Jewish mystical text devoted entirely to the body of G-d, the *Shi'ur Qomah*,[17] a title which can be translated either as *Measurement of Body* or *Measurement of Height*. The two sets of medieval symbolisms come, first, from three relatively early portions of the *Zohar*, which are attributed to Moses de Leon (b. 1240), of Catalonia, and second from kabbalah texts written by Moses ben Jacob

---

16. It can be quite a sobering thought to realize that for the Jews the classical period of Greek antiquity, indeed the entire epoch of Greek antiquity, appears late in sacred history. Another reason for the eternal youth of the Greeks.

In contrast to the traditional Jewish interpretation of its own sources, according to modern academic scholarship Jewish mystical sources all appear long after the fall of Greece to Rome.

In such debates even the most objective historian must pause for some length of time to wonder, and doubt, whether definitive dates can ever be attached to the historical origins of mystical claims which claim, after all, to have been part of a strictly oral tradition for centuries if not millennia. What, after all, is the compelling reason for thinking that the history of documents is conterminous with the history of thought, that earlier insights and teachings have not been reworked again and again in the language of later times, especially in a mystical tradition?

17. Martin Samuel Cohen, *The Shi'ur Qomah: Liturgy and Theurgy in Pre-Kabbalistic Jewish Mysticism* (Lanham, Maryland: University Press of America, 1963). One text of the *Shi'ur Qomah*, translated and annotated in detail by Martin Samuel Cohen, is found on 187–266.

Cordovero (1522–70) and Elijah de Vida (d. ca. 1593), of Safed in the upper Galilee. In the modern period, finally, we will examine the corporeal symbolism found in a book dear to Emmanuel Levinas, *The Soul of Life (Nefesh Hahayim)*,[18] by Rabbi Hayim of Volozhim, Lithuania (1759–1821).

It goes without saying that throughout any examination of Jewish mystical sources one must keep in mind what the authors of these sources certainly had in mind, namely, the Jewish prohibition against idolatry. The symbols used in the Jewish mystical tradition are not meant as independently divine agents or intermediaries between G-d and humankind. Rather, they are meant as openings, openings from G-d to the human and from the human to G-d.[19] "World and man," writes Rosenzweig, "are deified without being idolized" (*SR* 421).

The Ancient Period: The *Shi'ur Qomah*

The content of the *Shi'ur Qomah* is basically quite simple. It provides exact numerical dimensions of a gigantic humanlike body—millions and millions of miles high and wide—which is meant to be G-d's body. Of course, G-d has no body. The size of the divine figure whose measurements are given in the *Shi'ur Qomah* is so large, so vast, as to defy the capacities of human visualization and imagination. It thus "solves" the religious-metaphysical problem of uniting divine and human by means of giganticism, that is to say, by an excessive amplification of finite spatiality, overloading, overwhelming, and thus transcending the finite powers of human visualization and imagination. In a word, it explodes visions and images.[20]

Whatever other awe-inspiring and inspired insights motivated the authors of the *Shi'ur Qomah,* the text presents a bodily image that opens up

18. The first and relevant part of this book, "On the Soul and Repentance," can be found in English translation in *An Anthology of Jewish Mysticism,* edited and translated by Raphael ben Zion (New York: Yesod Publishers, n.d.), 129–204, 225–33. Raphael ben Zion's anthology also contains an English translation of Rabbi Cordovero's text, *The Palm Tree of Devorah* (9–85, 211–19).

Levinas has written the preface to the French translation of Rabbi Hayim's work, *L'Ame de la vie,* vii–x (cf. chapter 6, note 17); he has also written an article on Rabbi Hayim's thought, "A l'image de Dieu: d'apres Rabbi Haim Voloziner," which appears in *L'au-delà du verset* (Paris: Editions de Minuit, 1982), 182–200.

19. See Moses Maimonides, *Mishneh Torah,* I, ch. 1; and *The Guide of the Perplexed,* part 1, chap. 36.

20. One might think here of what Kant says in the third *Critique* of the sublime, particularly the mathematical sublime.

a passage between G-d and man precisely because it destroys images. It short-circuits perceptual intentionality, breaks the correlation of perceiving and perceived, by means of the apparently simple mechanism of hyperbolic enlargement.[21] The dimensions of space are abused, as it were, to create an appreciation for our inability to reduce the divine to them. The body delineated is not contradictory, to be sure, like a round square or a four-sided triangle, but is rather excessive in a manner that strains finite human capacities, overloading them to demonstrate their finitude in relation to G-d's infinitude. Thus in an almost ironic rejoinder to Maimonides' reservations about mysticism, the divine body of the *Shi'ur Qomah* precisely prevents the idolization of space.

Both Rosenzweig and Levinas, though they do not themselves utilize giganticism as a technique, are, along with everyone else in the Jewish tradition, in agreement with the *Shi'ur Qomah* that the alterity of G-d is not a spatial exteriority. But something more specific is at stake. Like the effect of the *Shi'ur Qomah*, as I have interpreted it, both thinkers recognize an exteriority in the other's face which, despite the finite sense in which the term "exteriority" refers to space, i.e., to the opposition of interior and exterior, nevertheless precisely explodes the very spatiality or form of exteriority. In encountering the face of the other, like the divine body of the *Shi'ur Qomah*, one enters into a non-place, an u-topia.

The Medieval Period and Rosenzweig

The method of deliberate exaggeration utilized in the *Shi'ur Qomah* is a technique so simple and so focused on visual perception and imagination that it could hardly be long satisfactory as a conduit between man and G-d. It does little more with the finite organs, shape, and posture of the human body than give them huge dimensions. Moving beyond gigan-

---

21. It has been suggested that this mechanism, giganticism, is childish. In his carefully researched study of the *Shi'ur Qomah*, Martin Samuel Cohen is doubtlessly correct to join Gershom Scholem in criticizing those scholars—Philipp Bloch (1844–1923) is named—who believed the *Shi'ur Qomah* was actually intended only for grade school children (see Cohen, *Shi'ur Qomah*, 18; Gershom Scholem, *Major Trends in Jewish Mysticism*, 2d ed. [New York: Shocken, 1961], 66–67). Nonetheless, given the central or most immediately striking idea of the *Shi'ur Qomah*, i.e., the hyperbolic bigness of G-d (M. S. Cohen writes: "The bigness of the godhead is, of course, the key idea in the *Shi'ur Qomah*," (93)), the sense of Bloch's thesis can still be affirmed, regardless of its literal truth, without slighting the text. Whether the *Shi'ur Qomah* was actually used in grade school or in advanced study, its "key idea" undoubtedly has its childish side: that G-d is too big to see or imagine.

None of the above is intended to suggest that there are not other significations at stake in the *Shi'ur Qomah*.

ticism, two developments occur in the medieval period which are of successively increasing significance in the interpretation of the human body as a mystical symbol.

The earlier of the two developments is the supplementation of the *Shi'ur Qomah*'s exclusively quantitative gloss with a plurality of qualitative glosses. The symbolism of G-d's body is overlaid with many other sets of symbols, symbols which are loosely attached to the facial organs and to their functions and relative positions within the facial and corporeal schema. Beyond biblical citations, this loose attachment can be "legitimized" (to the mind looking for reasons, for justifications) by an appeal to resemblance, but as often as not the connections are merely a matter of *juxtaposition*.

The second development occurs three centuries later. It radically alters the significance of the entire mystical enterprise. All the quantitative and qualitative correspondences of the earlier mystical texts, which operate within the assumptions of a contemplative approach to G-d, and hence are subject to the seductions of aestheticism and ultimately to idolatry, are now shifted to an active and ethical model of *imitation*.

The magnitude of this latter shift, where Jewish mysticism moves from contemplative absorption in symbolic correspondences to an ethical imitation of G-d, appears forcefully when one compares the thirteenth-century Catalonian texts of the early Zohar to the sixteenth-century Safed texts of the Kabbalah.[22] The thirteenth-century texts that have most to say about the divine body and face are three: *The Book of Concealment (Sifra di-Tseni uta), The Great Holy Assembly (Idra raba),* and *The Lesser Holy Assembly (Idra zutra),* all by Moses de Leon.[23] The sixteenth-century text that has most to say—and is most original—about the divine body and face is without question the famous *The Palm Tree of Devorah (Tomer Devorah)* by Moses ben Jacob Cordovero. Acknowledging their faithfulness to Cordovero and their widespread popularity, two additional sixteenth-century texts must also be mentioned, and will be cited later: the *Beginning of Wisdom (Reshit Hokhmah)* by Cordovero's disciple Elijah de Vida, and its abbreviated version *The Abbreviated Beginning of Wisdom (Reshit Hokhmah ha-Qasar)* by Jacob Poyetto. The faces which appear in these two texts

22. It is perhaps noteworthy, given the shift from contemplation to ethics marked by the sixteenth-century texts, that they appear less than three generations after the disruptive mass migrations (and conversions) which resulted from the forced expulsion of all Jews from Spain, in 1492, after the Jews had sojourned a long and productive fourteen hundred years there.

23. These three texts are collected together in English translation in *The Anatomy of God,* edited and translated by Roy A. Rosenberg (New York: KTAV, 1973).

are nearly exact duplicates of the face which appears originally in *The Palm Tree of Devorah*.

The Earlier Medieval Period of the Zohar

Rosenzweig describes the "face of man" graphically, in terms of its forehead, eyes (right and left distinguished), ears, nose, cheeks, mouth, and the placement and coordination of these facial elements on the symbolic grid of the two overlapping triangles of the Mogen David.

Moses de Leon's works also provide detailed accounts of two faces: the face of the "ancient one" and the "small countenance." Both are divine faces. In *The Great Holy Assembly* and *The Lesser Holy Assembly* the faces of the ancient one and the small countenance are described and compared in terms of skull, hair, forehead, eyes, nose, nostrils, and beard. In both of de Leon's texts the ears are mentioned only in the accounts of the small countenance, and not as part of the head of the ancient one. The small countenance listens to the ancient one; what the small countenance hears are tales of evil and suffering. Only in *The Lesser Holy Assembly* do the mouth and lips of the small countenance appear. The third text attributed to Moses de Leon, *The Book of Concealment*, is but a few pages long. Though brief, it includes all the facial features found in the other two texts, but in addition speaks of the cheeks of the ancient one. These differences are doubtlessly important for reasons internal to the hermeneutics of the Zohar. For our purposes I mention them to indicate the similarity in detail with Rosenzweig's face of man.

Like the *Shi'ur Qomah*, there is giganticism in de Leon's works. One reads, for example: "it is taught that the length of his [small countenance] nose fills 375 worlds."[24] Yet unlike the *Shi'ur Qomah*, large and precise measurements (and hence the attendant explosion of humanly conceivable spatiality) are no longer the primary features of these divine heads. Along with a shift to greater detail regarding the face's features, not measurements but descriptive qualities, moral characteristics, and other attributes now take center stage.

The features of the faces of the ancient one and the small countenance—skull, forehead, hair, eyes, ears, nose, mouth, and especially the beard—are associated with divine attributes (such as will, judgment, and mercy), with biblical words and passages, with names of G-d, with colors, with natural phenomena (such as dew, snow, and smoke), with numbers, and to a lesser degree with other sets of symbols. To the uninitiated and to the philosopher seeking reasons, the associations that are made seem

24. Rosenberg, *Anatomy of God*, 62.

haphazard. Patterns of the same associative characterizations recur throughout the three texts, yet except for their consistency they seem no more "logical" or "legitimate" than the correspondences that do not recur. No legitimization is given, either for the correspondences, *tout simple,* or for the differences between the ones that recur and the ones that differ from one text to another. In some cases there is a modicum of logic. For example, in all three texts the nose of the ancient one and the nose of the small countenance are associated with life. The "logic" is that G-d originally animated man with the "breath of life." But even such "logic" or "reason" as there is is never too rigorous, and often it is barely if at all visible. In all three the ears are spoken of in terms of hearing good and evil; in all three the eyes are spoken of in terms of seeing good and evil; and in all three the forehead is associated with will. The correspondences, whether appearing once or repeated in two or three texts, are no more and no less than associative connections whose sense is established intuitively rather than argued discursively or deductively. This is the same impression one gets when reading Rosenzweig's "face of man"—or so its correspondences are presented.

The correspondences of the Zohar are correspondences of juxtaposition; reasons or explanations, in a strict scientific sense, are not given.[25] We never find out, for example, why the ears hear only good and evil, rather than tales of brave Ulysses, or names of insects, or jokes. Nor is it the case that the characteristics associated with the features of the divine head are limited to what at that historical time was thought to be "empirically" known about human heads. Rather, almost anything that can be said about the human head and its features—or about almost any entity, for that matter—is here also said about the divine head. Ultimately the "logic" or "reason" for these attributions is inscrutable. The correspondences linking attributes to the divine body, like the correspondences linking the human body to the divine body altogether, are as if established by their very assertion, by the authority of fiat, by the greater or lesser intuitive impressiveness of their display. To accept these correspondences as valid, based on the "proofs" given in the texts alone, would be a form of reverence rather than rationality. That reverence is involved is borne out by the fact that none of the correspondences asserted in the three texts are presented by Moses de Leon as his own creative inventions.

The connections, then, are not only curious and suggestive; standing outside a Jewish interpretive tradition, or any interpretive tradition, they

---

25. See Joseph Dan, *Jewish Mysticism and Jewish Ethics* (Seattle: University of Washington Press, 1986), 90–91. "The mystic . . . does not know the 'true' reasons, only the vague hints suggested by the symbols" (91).

are arbitrary. But precisely because they are arbitrary (or fully rooted in an extra-rational interpretive tradition), they disturb the objective universality and necessity which together constitute the logic of a scientific perspective. By the end of the thirteenth century, then, we find a Jewish mysticism conceiving itself in terms of a dual negative task: clearing a channel between G-d and humankind *otherwise than by images and otherwise than by logic*. In their mystical usage, images and concepts are made to violate the natural limits of imagination and the logic of discursive reason. Human consciousness and its contents are undermined, subverted, and shattered by their contact with the divine. In another context, but regarding the same disruptive distance between the above and the below, Levinas writes: "The relationship with alterity is neither spatial nor conceptual" (*TO* 84). The same holds for Rosenzweig. Despite the agreement of these two modern thinkers with this medieval outlook, it is obvious nonetheless that the face does not serve Rosenzweig and Levinas as it serves Moses de Leon, as a magnet attracting symbols arbitrarily (or by tradition) brought close to it.

There is, of course, one major exception to the abyss separating the modern thought of Rosenzweig and Levinas from the medieval mysticism of Moses de Leon. One bridge clearly does link Rosenzweig's *Star* to the Zohar, namely, Rosenzweig's organization of the features of the "face of man" in terms of the geometry of the Mogen David. Such an association is precisely the sort sanctioned by the Zohar.

Having duly noted this, however, and also duly noting that Rosenzweig nowhere makes explicit this connection with early medieval Jewish hermeneutics, and, more importantly, duly noting that Rosenzweig also nowhere makes explicit the significance of his own overlapping of the Mogen David with the "face of man," it is time to turn to the second development in medieval Jewish mysticism, to the Kabbalah of Moses ben Jacob Cordovero, to uncover a far more profound affinity which joins the Jewish mystical tradition to the face in Rosenzweig.

The Later Medieval Period of the Kabbalah

The change in the meaning of Jewish mystical symbolism which occurs in the sixteenth-century Kabbalah texts of Safed has with good reason been characterized by Lawrence Fine, a contemporary scholar of this period, as "one of the most significant and remarkable chapters in the history of Judaism."[26] The change is radical and its consequences far-reaching. What occurs is *the unification of what was until then an exclusively contempla-*

---

26. *Safed Spirituality: "Rules of Mystical Piety," "The Beginning of Wisdom,"* trans. Lawrence Fine (New York: Paulist Press, 1984), xiii.

tive and personal mysticism with the positivity and sociality of Jewish ethics. In this new union the entire sense of the mystical body and face changes.

In the mysticism of the man whom Gershom Scholem has called "the greatest theoretician of Jewish mysticism,"[27] Moses ben Jacob Cordovero, this new union is both inaugurated and established. Indeed, the call to shift from contemplation to ethics is made in the very first paragraph of Cordovero's great work, *The Palm Tree of Devorah,* as follows:

> It is proper for man to imitate his Creator, resembling Him in both likeness and image according to the secret of the Supernal Form. Because the chief Supernal image and likeness is in deeds, a human resemblance merely in bodily appearance and not in deeds, abases that Form. Of the man who resembles the Form in body alone it is said: "A handsome form whose deeds are ugly." For what value can there be in man's resemblance to the Supernal Form in bodily limbs if his deeds have not resemblance to those of his Creator? Consequently, it is proper for man to imitate the acts of the Supernal Crown, which are the thirteen highest attributes of mercy.[28]

Jewish mysticism henceforth turns from solitary spiritual exercise, from contemplation and meditation, to the refined and regulated behavior of social ethics and moral piety.

As a result, too, for the first time mystical texts are widely read in the Jewish community and take their place in the mainstream of Jewish life. Elijah de Vida's ethical-mystical treatise, *Beginning of Wisdom,* which, as has been said, follows directly from Cordovero's *The Palm Tree of Devorah,* becomes (along with Bahya ibn Paquda's twelfth-century *Duties of the Heart*) one of "the several most influential Jewish ethical works ever written."[29] Elijah de Vida's treatise and Jacob Poyetto's abbreviated version of it together will go through fifty-five editions, from 1579 to 1937, published all over Western and Eastern Europe.

In place of the contemplative epistemology of association through resemblance and juxtaposition, the mystical tradition now presents an ethical model of behavioral imitation. The divine face (and body) is no longer either an exaggerated spatial image or the relatively arbitrary site of various

---

27. Scholem, *Major Trends,* 252.

28. Fine, *Safed Spirituality,* 31. See also Cordovero, *The Palm Tree of Devorah,* in ben Zion, *Anthology of Jewish Mysticism,* 15. Louis Jacobs, in his preface to Fine's collection, quotes the words of Dean Inge: "Religion is a way of walking, not a way of talking" (ix), to sum up the momentous change effected by Cordovero in the basic character of Jewish mysticism. If this change occurred earlier and developed gradually, its significance would nonetheless remain the same.

29. Lawrence Fine says this in *Safed Spirituality,* 84; he also puts the later eighteenth-century work of the Ramchal, Moses Hayyim Luzzatto, *The Path of the Righteous (Mesilat Yesharim),* in this category of the most influential Jewish ethical works.

qualities, but also and more importantly the moral exemplar par excellence, the divine paradigm, the absolute model from which human expressions and behaviors take on their fundamentally ethical-religious significance. It is precisely this development, we can now say, that attracts Rosenzweig. With Cordovero and de Vida not only are perceptual images and abstract conceptualizations of the divine broken, they are broken through and positively exceeded by ethics.

The ethical-mystical account of the divine head and face in Cordovero's *The Palm Tree of Devorah* and in de Vida's *Beginning of Wisdom* (and in Poyetto's *The Abbreviated Beginning of Wisdom*) are almost identical. Both texts devote about four pages to the divine head and face, treating them under the category or *sepharah* of divine humility *(keter)*.[30] In order, Cordovero writes of the mind, forehead, eyes, ears, nose, face, and mouth.[31] De Vida follows the same order, the sole difference being that (like Rosenzweig) he treats of the ears before the eyes.[32] Both texts bridge the gap between divine and human by moving from a perfect pattern above to the human below, aligning the above and below across terms such as "resemble," "imitate," and "just as." They teach that human expressions and deeds should *resemble* or *imitate* or be *just as* the divine head and face in order for the human to be ethical. A sample from Poyetto will make this movement and its divine standard clear:

It is good for an individual to regard himself as nought in comparison to the exaltednesss of God. . . . Just as the supernal Forehead is known as "gracious," . . . so too a person should not engage in strife and contention. . . . When it

---

30. The anthropomorphic symbolism that appears most often in Kabbalah is not the face alone but the figure of the whole human body, the *Adam Kadman,* which is at once divine cosmos above and human microcosmos below. Owing to the influence of Isaac Luria, ten *sepharot* or divine emanations are at this time especially emphasized and made to correspond to parts of the human body. The uppermost three *sepharot* correspond to the head and shoulders: (1) *keter,* "crown," corresponding to the head; (3) *binah,* "understanding," and (2) *hokhmah,* "wisdom," corresponding to the left and right shoulders respectively. The next six *sepharot* correspond to the arms, trunk, genitals, and legs: (5) *gevurah,* "power" (or *din,* "judgment"), and (4) *chesed,* "mercy," corresponding to left and right arms respectively; (6) *tif'eret,* "beauty" (or *rahamin,* "compassion"), which harmonizes *gevurah* and *hesed,* corresponding to the trunk; (8) *hod,* "majesty," and (7) *nesah,* "endurance" (or "victory"), corresponding to the left and right legs respectively; (9) *yesod,* "foundation," corresponding to the phallus. The tenth and lowest *sepharah,* (10) *malkos,* "kingdom" (or *shekhinah,* "God's presence"), corresponds to the feet.

The face, then, would have "only" to do with the uppermost *sepharah, keter,* the crown or head. This location gives it, in addition, the special significance of being both top and bottom at once, for the ten *sepharot* are repeated in each of four worlds which are serially and progressively distant from G-d. The terrestrial world is farthest from G-d.

31. Cordovero, *Palm Tree of Devorah,* in ben Zion, *Anthology,* 38–41.

32. See Fine, *Safed Spirituality,* 119–21.

comes to the eyes, one should be certain that his eyes are ever vigilant to show compassion to the poor and to care for them, just as the supernal Eye does. One's eyes ought to be downcast as is the supernal Eye for the purpose of nourishing the lower world. . . . With regard to one's ears, they must be alert in order to hearken to the sound of Torah and prayer, as well as to the voice of the poor so as to show them compassion. But the ears should pay no attention to the sounds of evil gossip and other such things which blemish an individual . . . for even the Holy One, blessed be He, pays no attention to the [moral] debts which men incur. . . . As for his nose, a person should imitate the quality of patience as it manifests itself in the supernal Nose. . . . With respect to the face, one should imitate those supernal qualities which are called Countenance. . . . As for his mouth, a person ought to resemble the supernal Mouth, uttering neither a curse nor words of ostracism, condemnation, impudence, or harshness. . . . An individual who avoids speaking much about worldly matters prolongs his days, inasmuch as his mouth thereby resembles the Supernal Mouth.[33]

With an eye to the influence of these Kabbalah texts on Rosenzweig, I deliberately highlight two points. First, there is the general shift from contemplation to ethics. Shifting from contemplation to ethics means, negatively, that both images and concepts are inadequate to bridge the gap between the finite and the infinite. Positively, it means that moral behavior is demanded. Torah means Torah-life, life lived according to Torah. Second, then, the ethical aspect of behavior—the true life—comes from a movement which begins with the infinite, as perfect model, and comes to the finite. Ethics is now a movement from top down, from above to below, the perfection of the divine head and face coming first and serving as the stable model, pattern, or paradigm to be imitated through the imperfect strivings of human ethical behavior. What ought to be is what already truly is in G-d.

It is this movement of imitation—*imitatio dei*[34]—that constitutes the *mystical* element in Cordovero's ethics. It must be noted that nothing about the ethical behavior recommended in the texts by Cordovero or de Vida is new, qua behavior, within the Jewish ethical tradition. The moral behavior and piety these kabbalists propose were normative to the Jewish community well before and continued to remain normative well after the sixteenth century. Indeed, they are still normative for Rosenzweig, Levinas, and the contemporary Jewish community. It is the significance of ethics, its meaning, its contextualization, that Cordovero and de Vida

33. Ibid. The text is from Poyetto's abbreviated version of Elijah de Vida's *Beginning of Wisdom;* it could just as well be from Cordovero's *The Palm Tree of Devorah* itself.

34. On the importance of the imitation of G-d—*hitdamut la'El*—in the ethics of halakah, see Joseph B. Soloveitchik, "Imitating God: The Basis of Jewish Morality," in *Reflections of the Rav,* adapted from the lectures of Joseph B. Soloveitchik by Abraham R. Besdin (Jerusalem: Publishing Department of the Jewish Agency at Alpha Press, 1979), 23–30.

alter. By joining the Jewish ethical tradition to the Jewish mystical tradition, they elevate the status of ethics. It is precisely this elevation of status that attracts Rosenzweig to Cordovero's Kabbalah. Henceforth the cosmic, or, if the term "cosmic" is too Greek, the divine status of ethics becomes the issue in Jewish mysticism, up to and including the reflections of Rabbi Hayyim of Volozhin. Once Cordovero elevates ethics by uniting it with mysticism, the essential role of mysticism within the normative Jewish tradition is never again seriously challenged—despite occasional recidivism—and the level of ethics is never again lowered.

Professor Joseph Dan—one of Gershom Scholem's preeminent students and the successor to Scholem's chair at the Hebrew University in Jerusalem—in his book on *Jewish Mysticism and Jewish Ethics* sums up the great significance of Cordovero's *The Palm Tree of Devorah* for Jewish ethics and mysticism:

Jewish ethics in the Middle Ages and modern times is not concerned so much with the problem of what should be done in a certain set of circumstances, as with the question of why should one follow the ethical demands. To this question Cordovero presents the first clear and unambiguous mystical answer: ethical behavior should be adopted and followed not only because God says so, but because God is so; one should conform not only to the divine laws, but to the divine nature. The righteous, thus, is not only an obedient servant of God, but an imitator of His essence, and therefore a part of the divine system as a whole. Mystical ascent and everyday ethics are fused into one, and the highest achievement of communion with God is attained by following the most mundane and elementary demands of social ethics. This is a revolution not in the behavior of the righteous, but in the meaning of this behavior. . . . The distinction between an ethical work and a mystical one was erased, and a whole literature came into being, the literature of mystical ethics, which dominated Jewish thought during the next three centuries.[35]

With Cordovero, in other words, there begins a tradition within which *ethics takes on a mystical dimension and mysticism takes on an ethical dimension.* It is this tradition which continues right up to the *Star* and beyond. Thus, in the tradition of Jewish mysticism Rosenzweig's face must be located alongside the face of Cordovero. Of course, there is one aspect of Rosenzweig's face, as we have remarked, its geometry, that harks back to an earlier mysticism. But with this one exception, the central point of Rosenzweig's face—its truth or life—is drawn from the deep well of Cordovero's mysticism.

Without invoking proper names, Rosenzweig labels the Cordoverian

35. Joseph Dan, *Jewish Mysticism and Jewish Ethics* (Seattle: University of Washington Press, 1986), 86–87.

structure of his thought "theomorphism." While this term does not appear in the *Star*, it is the central topic of a course entitled "The Science of God" which Rosenzweig gave at the Free House of Jewish Studies in the autumn of 1921, just after the publication of the *Star*.[36] The problem the term "theomorphism" is introduced to solve is a problem central to contemporary thought and central to the whole of the *Star*. It is the problem of how to criticize idealist philosophy and yet remain a philosopher; or, to express this in another register, it is the problem of how to criticize the orthodoxy of traditional revealed religion and remain genuinely religious. After having criticized the old philosophical "all" and the old theological G-d, Rosenzweig does not want to fall into the subjectivisms of Kierkegaard, Schopenhauer, and Nietzsche, on the side of the philosophers, or into the anthropomorphism of Schleiermacher and the theological historicists, on the side of the theologians. Rosenzweig realizes that after criticizing the old thinking for neglecting the mortal individual, religion and philosophy can henceforth neither be whole nor healthy if they too eliminate, gloss over, or minimize the subjectivity of the individual. But, on the other hand, contrary to the thinkers named just above, he also realizes that neither will the individual be in the truth if the objectivity and necessity of philosophy and religion are entirely abandoned.[37] It is precisely to escape this latter danger, while maintaining his radical criticism of the old thinking, that Rosenzweig takes up what he calls a "theomorphic" orientation, an orientation which is at the same time precisely the orientation of Moses Cordovero's ethical mysticism.

What is theomorphism and how does it embrace the finitude of the individual without succumbing to a subjectivist relativism? Instead of attempting to grasp this notion abstractly, let us see it at work in Rosenzweig's thought, where it is central, and where it appears most clearly in the pivotal notion of the *Star:* revelation. "The bridge from maximum subjectivity to maximum objectivity," Rosenzweig writes, "is formed by theology's concept of revelation" (*SR* 106). What Rosenzweig means by "theology's concept of revelation"—which is found quite literally at the center of the *Star,* in book 2 of part 2—are not the dicta of the ten commandments given to Moses on Mount Sinai, but the command that each man must love his neighbor *because* G-d loves man. To avoid subjectivism, to avoid anthropomorphism, to avoid historicism, while also

36. See Rivka Horwitz, "Franz Rosenzweig's Unpublished Writings," *The Journal of Jewish Studies* 20 (1969): 74.

37. See chapter 3 in this volume for a close look at how in the *Star* Rosenzweig appropriates Nietzsche for Nietzsche's critical turn against "old thinking" for the sake of the temporal and mortal individual, and at the same time rejects Nietzsche for the literary efforts Nietzsche makes in the name of an active and affirmative rejection of truth.

avoiding the old conceptualized thinking and the old orthodox theology, Rosenzweig appropriates the Cordoverian model: man must love his neighbor *just as* G-d loves man. To be good humankind must *imitate* or *resemble* G-d. By means of this theomorphic move Rosenzweig overcomes the sterility of the *old* thinking while insisting on the thoughtfulness, the truth, of the new. According to Rivka Horwitz's summary of Rosenzweig's 1921 lecture course:

Rosenzweig asserts that the only reason that man is capable of love at all is because God loves. All human action, speech, and thought are in the image of God. A God who is a reality has, according to Rosenzweig, of necessity to be integrally involved in corporeality. Man can speak because God speaks. . . . The Kabbalist, in saying that God's "hand" stands for a higher form of reality, is evincing a similar tendency. As in Platonism at its extreme, God is the archetype of all existence.[38]

The face of Rosenzweig is the face of Cordovero: the imitation of G-d.

The Modern Period and Levinas

Levinas, in contrast, is not a "theomorph" in Rosenzweig's sense. The face in Rosenzweig—bringing G-d's law down to earth, embodying G-d's commandments in the command to love the neighbor just as G-d loves man—is less like the face in Levinas than like the mezuzah on the doorway of the traditional Jewish household, containing G-d's word while welcoming the neighbor. To understand the face in Levinas we must move beyond the medieval mysticism of sixteenth-century Safed to the celebrated Yeshiva Judaism of eighteenth- and nineteenth-century Lithuania.

Rabbi Hayim ben Isaac of Volozhin's *The Soul of Life (Nefesh Hahayim)* was published in 1824, posthumously. As Scholem has noted, it is a text which reveals "a manifest indebtedness to kabbalistic sources on every page."[39] Like his famous teacher, Rabbi Elijah ben Solomon Zalman (1720–97), Gaon of Vilna, Rabbi Hayim's knowledge of the Jewish mystical tradition was thorough and profound. But *The Soul of Life* is not another version of Cordovero's Kabbalah. Two important and intimately connected developments make this text an original contribution to Jewish mysticism—and a decisive influence on Levinas's thought.

The Reversal: From Human to Divine

The first development is a reversal, a reversal so fundamental as to be more than a simple inversion. While *The Soul of Life* takes up and continues

38. Horwitz, "Franz Rosenzweig's Unpublished Writings," 74.
39. Gershom Scholem, *Kabbalah* (New York: Quadrangle, 1974), 196.

the central contribution initiated by Moses Cordovero, the union of ethics and mysticism, its originality lies in reversing the direction of that union. For Cordovero and de Vida—and, as we have seen, for Rosenzweig—human ethical behavior is modeled on divine ethical behavior: what is done above, because it is done above, should be done below. For Rabbi Hayim of Volozhin, in contrast, *the divine realm itself depends on human ethical behavior*. What is done below establishes the above, for better or worse. Instead of man imitating G-d, the divinely created realm is determined *by* the actions of man. Thus immoral behavior on the part of humans produces immorality or disorder in creation; moral behavior on the part of humans produces a "healing" or "repairing" *(Tikkun)* of the created realm.

These astonishing claims are made in the first chapter of *The Soul of Life*, in Rabbi Hayim's commentary on the three celebrated passages in Genesis having to do with the creation of man in G-d's image *(tselem)* and likeness *(d'muth)*, namely, Gen. 1:27: "And Elokim created man in His own image; in the image of Elokim created He him"; Gen. 9:6: "For in the image of Elokim made He man"; and Gen. 1:26: "Let us make man in our image, after our likeness." To be sure, the words "image" and "likeness" do not refer to a geometrical or spatial congruence. No one has lost sight of the fact that G-d has no body in an anthropomorphic or creaturely sense of body. To understand the meaning of man's likeness to G-d, Rabbi Hayim instead focuses on the Bible's use, in the above verses, of the name "Elokim" for G-d in His capacity as creator of man in the image and likeness of G-d. This name, Hayim reminds us, in contrast to the many other possible names used in the Bible to designate G-d, signifies "master of all powers." It is as master of all powers that Elokim "created man and gave *him* dominion over myriads of powers and over numberless worlds."[40] In other words, when the Bible teaches that man was created in the image and likeness of *Elokim,* it means that man has been given the absolute mastery that is the specific significance of this particular name of G-d; to be created in the image and likeness of Elokim is to be given the mastery which is Elokim's: the power over all worlds.

By transferring divine power to man, *the perfection of the divine realm now depends on the perfection of human behavior*. This is the key to Rabbi Hayim's reorientation of Cordovero's Kabbalah. Human behavior, bodily movements directed by the soul, now have cosmic repercussions. And this is precisely what Rabbi Hayim writes:

Just as each of his individual bodily acts is directed by the force of the soul within

40. *Nefesh Hahayim,* ch. 1, sect. 3.

him, so is man himself the force and living soul of unlimited numbers of upper and lower worlds which are dominated by his actions.[41]

From the point of view of the position of his body man is at the latter end of creation [the tenth *sephirah* (*malkhut*, "kingdom") of the fourth and bottom realm (*olam ha-asiyyah*, "the material world")], but with respect to the upper root of his living soul he rates before the works of the Chariot—even before the world of the Throne.[42]

To elaborate and justify this doctrine of man's ethical-cosmic centrality, Rabbi Hayim invokes the entire Jewish mystical tradition: the texts of the Zohar, the *Idra Zutra*, the Kabbalah of Cordovero and Isaac Luria, the Divine Palaces *(Hekhalot)*, Ezekiel's Throne of Glory and Holy Chariot *(Merkabah)*, and so forth. He invokes these texts to reorient them.

The point is not simply that the *Nefesh Hahayim* is strewn with mystical references, but, to repeat, that it takes up these references in order to reverse their orientation. *The Soul of Life* moves not from G-d's power and goodness to man's power and goodness, as do prior sources, but from G-d's power and goodness to man's power and goodness *back to* G-d's power and goodness. Human ethical behavior determines the orderliness of the cosmic order, its goodness. G-d's face reflects the human face:

In the measure that we present to Him a smiling and happy face, in that measure there appears to us below His smiling and happy Face.[43]

Thus God says to Israel . . . My connection with the worlds is entirely dependent, as it were, on the direction to which your deeds point. . . . The Sages had this in mind when they said that "human worship is a necessity for the One Above."[44]

The real truth is . . . that the World to Come is actually identical with Man's own deeds; it is that portion which he expanded, added and prepared by his own efforts.[45]

41. Ibid., ch. 1, sect. 5.

42. Ibid., ch. 1, sect. 6. What Norman Lamm, in *Torah Lishmah: Torah for Torah's Sake: In the Works of Rabbi Hayyim of Volozhin and his Contemporaries* (Hoboken: KTAV, 1989), finds groudbreaking in *The Soul of Life* is also the height to which Rabbi Hayim bring's the Torah . . . all the way to G-d, G-d in His pure unadulterated absoluteness ("before the works of the Chariot—even before the world of the Throne," as cited). See Lamm, *Torah Lishmah*, 102-37. Levinas focuses on this elevation, taking it to signify the all-encompassing importance and consequences of ethical responsibility. For Rabbi Hayim, too, ethics no doubt also has the highest significance and importance, but his emphasis lies on Torah study above all other *mitzvot*; see Lamm, *Torah Lishmah*, chapter 4, 138-189. It is possible that Levinas read and was influenced by Norman Lamm's book, *Torah Lishmah*, in its original 1972 Hebrew edition.

43. *Nefesh Hahayim*, ch. 1, sect. 9.

44. Ibid., ch. 1, sect. 9.

45. Ibid., ch. 1, sect. 12.

This orientation from man to G-d, we know, is precisely the orientation of Levinas's "face-to-face," where the movement of the one toward the other, of the subject subjected to the other who commands, an upright movement because an upward orientation, is nothing other than the movement "to-God."

The Correction: Reversal of the Reversal

It is clear, however, that an unchecked or simple reversal of the medieval orientation would tread dangerously close to a Feuerbachian (socialist) or Freudian (individualist) secular humanism, and to the subjectivisms and anthropomorphisms which so troubled Rosenzweig. This danger brings us to the second development of *The Soul of Life*.

An anthropological or subjectivist reading is obviated—in Rabbi Hayim of Volozhin and later also in Levinas—by a subtle, even paradoxical, but all-important nuance. For all that has been said thus far, Elokim still does *not* give up His mastery of all worlds when He creates man as master of all worlds. We must be very careful here. Elokim neither does nor does not give up His mastery. Either alternative, either affirmation or denial, either "yea" or "nay," would by itself paralyze reason. Rabbi Hayim is reminding us of what reason cannot remember, but what the flesh and blood individual somehow can remember: Elokim does not *posit* man, He *created* man. Humankind begins, is created, but to say that it *begins*, that it is created, is at the same to say that humankind does not have its *origin* in itself. Thus Elokim *created* man, according to Rabbi Hayim, "*as though* he were actually master of the energy of those worlds." This *as though* or *as if* makes for all the difference.

Against—or "otherwise than"—the exclusions of traditional logic's "either/or," its excluded middle, G-d *both* retains for Himself *and* gives to man *all* of His powers. Faithful to this overcharged "logic," to this ethical-religious dimension, Rabbi Hayim distinguishes—on quite a different plane than Kant—"God as He is for-Himself" and "God as He is for-man." The excess of one over the other is another reason, beyond the "borrowing" that Levinas so often acknowledges in relation to Descartes, for calling G-d the "Infinite." And here, finally, lies the explanation for the paradox of G-d giving away and yet retaining all power, the "otherwise" than rational logic: only an infinitely powerful being can give away an infinity of power without in the least diminishing His own original infinity.[46]

---

46. For Levinas the term "being" itself is inadequate to express the exceptional relation of infinity to infinity.

Perhaps all the paradoxes of "infinity," from Zeno to Russell, must find their ultimate "explanation" in religious-ethical terms.

The Levinasian Appropriation of the Subjunctive

What is crucial in Rabbi Hayim's distinction, as in all mysticism, and, we can now add, as in all ethics, is not simply the logical distinction between G-d-for-Himself and G-d-for-man, but the way the unity *(echod)* of G-d so distinguished is maintained. And this unity is maintained precisely through the ethical force of the "as though," or the "as though" understood as ethical force, which is precisely how Levinas understands ethical force and the movement he names "to-God." Man is created by G-d and at the same time man is an autonomous ethical agent insofar as he acts *as though* he himself, by his acts, were the irreplaceable—nonsubstitutable—center of the universe which his own acts create. It is precisely the subjunctive case that Levinas learns from Rabbi Hayim. The subject is he who supports everything, including the insupportable. Here we can recall the words of Dostoyevsky which Levinas is so fond of quoting: "We are all guilty of all and for all men before all, and I more than the others." Thus to be human is to strive to be divine, not as the Greek philosophical tradition understands such striving, i.e., in gnostic terms, as a thinking of G-d's thoughts, but as the Jewish religious tradition understands it, in ethical terms, in the "ought" which goes beyond being.

Levinas and Rosenzweig can both agree with Rabbi Hayim when he writes: "At the time of Creation God fixed all the rules by which the worlds are regulated, in such a manner that they should depend upon the good or evil deed of man."[47] But for Rosenzweig this means that to be good man should *imitate* G-d, while for Levinas it means that *in being good* man is *making* sacred history, making history sacred.

The Levinasian sense in which the face is language,[48] then, is precisely its subjunctive sense. Face-to-face with the other person, the command of the other person comes "as though" the I were commanded by G-d. Through the face-to-face relation the I is *ordained* as a responsible I, just as through another face-to-face relation, in love, the Rosenzweigian individual breaks out of the solitude of its character to enter into the higher challenges of the sociality of its soul.[49] The ethical I, which for Levinas is obligated to the other person infinitely, is "as though" it were obligated to G-d. It is precisely the *as though* structure, joined to the

47. *Nefesh Hahayim*, ch. 1, sect. 12.

48. There are some Levinas commentators, for example Robert Bernasconi and Simon Critchley, who claim that between *TI* and *OBBE* there is a fundamental shift in the concerns of Levinas's thought, a shift from being to language. But already in *TI* Levinas writes: "The calling in question of the I, coextensive with the manifestation of the Other in the face, we call language" (171); and, "The face opens the primordial discourse whose first word is obligation" (201).

49. See *SR* 68–71, 213–214, 392; and see chapter 2 in this volume.

orientation or movement from man to G-d, as in Rabbi Hayim of Volo-zhin, that is the face in Levinas. Though no attention is drawn to it, the "as though" *(comme si)* appears on almost every page of *Totality and Infinity*. It is perhaps the fundamental gesture of this demanding text, the "essence" of the ethics it proposes, the "saying of the said."

Many years later, in a collection entitled *Of God Who Comes to the Idea (De Dieu qui vient à l'idée)*, Levinas does take up this topic explicitly. He writes: "We understand in the 'as though' the equivocation or the enigma of the non-phenomenal, the non-representable: the testimony prior to thematization, testifying to a *'more' awakening-a-'less'-which-it-disturbs-or-inspires,* the 'idea of the infinite,' 'God in me'."[50] Such an "as though" derives, Levinas continues, not from the "uncertainty or simple resemblance of the philosophies of the *'als ob,'* "[51] nor, for that matter, we can add, does it derive from any logic or metaphorics of Greco-Christian hermeneutics.[52]

The structure of the "as though" is also found, as Rabbi Hayim and Levinas are both well aware, in the peculiar hermeneutics of the rabbis of the Talmud. Without sacrificing difference to identity or identity to difference, without submitting to the constraints of affirmation and denial, the "as though" *(kee lu)* maintains difference in identity. In a recent work Susan Handelman has quite perceptively pointed out that the "as though" effects a "perception of resemblance despite difference (not a collapse of difference)," and "leads not to statements of predication . . . but to inclusion without identity. . . . Here resemblance never effaces difference, *as if* never becomes *is*."[53] This last claim, that the *"as if* never becomes *is,"* is precisely Levinas's point. The "as though" never becomes an "is" because it is an "ought"; and it is an "ought" which never becomes an "is" because of its orientation: "to-God."

Just as man neither is nor is not G-d, but is created in the image and likeness of G-d, and just as man neither is nor is not the Creator of the universe, but acts *as though* he had divine creative power, the face of the other person neither is nor is not G-d's face—for G-d has no real face, no spatial or conceptual face. *Still*—a rejoinder than can only be effaced by

---

50. Levinas, *De Dieu qui vient à l'idée*, 51, n. 24.

51. Ibid. The reference is to Hans Vaihinger's *Die Philosphie des Als-Ob* (Berlin, 1911); *The Philosophy of 'As If'*, translated by C. K. Ogden (New York, 1924), where the "as though" is a form of pretending, a noble lie.

52. For a penetrating discussion of the important contrast between the rabbinic technique of *kal ve-chomer* and the related interpretive techniques in Greco-Christian thought, see Susan Handelman, *The Slayers of Moses* (Albany: State University of New York Press, 1982), 52–57.

53. Handelman, *The Slayers of Moses*, 54–55.

will power, by the will to power—the face of the other person *nonetheless, enigmatically, paradoxically, disturbingly* "appears" *as though* it were G-d's face. It obligates infinitely, making the subject responsible, Levinas will say, for the very responsibility of the other person, even beyond the death of the subject, whether that death be my own mortality or the death of the other to whom I am bound.

Conclusion

What Rosenzweig means by "eternal *truth*" is the face in its relation to the divine, the human face that imitates the divine face. "To do justice and to love mercy," he writes on the last page of the *Star* (invoking a sentence from Micah 6:8), one must come "to walk humbly with thy God" (*SR* 424). Justice and mercy follow from G-d. Rosenzweig's orientation is quite close to that of Levinas, but it is an all-important nuance away. For Levinas "to do justice and to love mercy" is also "to walk humbly with thy God," for walking humbly with G-d arises in the doing of justice and the loving of mercy. G-d is where there is justice and mercy. Or, to express this in a formula dear to Levinas and close to Rabbi Hayim of Volozhin, and close also to the transcending intention which bursts through the conclusion of the *Star,* to be face-to-face with the alterity of the other person, to be for-the-other-before-oneself, is to be for G-d, *à-Dieu.*

TWELVE

Absolute Positivity and Ultrapositivity: Beyond Husserl

The Radical Positivity of Phenomena

In book 1 of *Ideas Pertaining to a Pure Phenomenology and to a Phenomenological Philosophy,* Edmund Husserl speaks of phenomenology as a positivism based on direct intuition, and thus a positivism even more positive, so to speak, than the natural sciences which base themselves on and limit themselves to sense experience: "If *'positivism'* is tantamount to an absolutely unprejudiced grounding of all sciences on the 'positive,' that is to say, on what can be seized upon originaliter, then *we* are the genuine positivists."[1] The natural scientists of course think that they are "the genuine positivists," that they, like the practitioners of no other approach, ground themselves "on what can be seized upon originaliter," grasping what truly is inasmuch as reality and truth are within human grasp. But for Husserl the truth is otherwise. The natural sciences are encumbered by the prejudices of theory. Not so the phenomenologists: "We take our start from what lies *prior to* all standpoints: from the total realm of whatever is itself given intuitionally and prior to all theorizing, from everything that one can immediately see and seize upon."[2]

The famous "principle of all principles" of Husserl's phenomenology combines the broadest possible definition of phenomena with the most radical care to cast off all extraphenomenal presuppositions. It says that to count as truth a truth claim must be supported by nothing but the evidence of a direct intuition into the phenomenon proper to the truth claim. Truths about perception must be backed by perceptions; truths about imagination must be backed by imaginings; truths about memory must be backed by memories. Intuition of "the thing itself" is the ultimate justification of all knowledge.

Extra-intuitive notions of what counts as real, notions which because they are not rooted in intuition are laden with unexamined theoretical baggage—for example, the famous "thesis of the natural attitude," but so too all natural scientific theorizing—must be rigorously put aside, brack-

---

1. Edmund Husserl, *Ideas Pertaining to a Pure Phenomenology and to a Phenomenological Philosophy,* translated by F. Kersten (The Hague: Martinus Nijhoff, 1982), 1:39.
2. Ibid., 1:38.

eted out of consideration, excluded, reduced, if one is to gain access to the things themselves. Deductions, inferences, analogies, indeed any accesses to "reality" that are not finally grounded in direct intuitions, are of no ultimate evidential value:

> Deductive theorizings are excluded from phenomenology. *Mediate inferences* are not exactly denied to it; but, since all its cognitions ought to be descriptive, purely befitting the immanental sphere, inferences, non-intuitive modes of procedure of any kind, only have the methodic function of leading us to the matters in question upon which a subsequent direct seeing of essences must make given. Analogies which emerge may suggest presumed likelihoods about concatenations of essences prior to actual intuition, and conclusions may be drawn from them; but ultimately an actual seeing of the concatenations of essences must redeem the presumed likelihoods. As long as that has not occurred, we have no phenomenological result. . . . It is now completely clear to us that nothing of value for the establishing of phenomenology can be gained by proceeding according to analogy.[3]

In contrast to all metatheories of reality built on the evidences of deductions, inferences, analogies, and any other indirect verification procedure, phenomenology not only contains its own final grounding within itself; that final grounding is indeed *the* final grounding: the things themselves. "Phenomenology . . . like any other descriptive, non-substructing and non-idealizing discipline, has its inherent legitimacy."[4]

"The great manifesto *Ideas I,*" Alphonso Lingis has written of the above texts and of Husserl's positivism, "declares heroically that what will be built is a philosophical discourse which from one end to the other will be grounded in immediate insight, the direct observation of what is given in evidence, and will consist nowhere of argumentation, nowhere of deduction, nowhere of induction, will not advance one sole statement that is not guaranteed by direct intuition ever available, ever repeatable."[5]

If Parmenides's theogony is the inaugural and founding statement of the Western thought that is scientific, which it is—excluding opinion, equating being with thinking, conceiving thought beyond the portals of "day and night" as the universally true—then surely Husserl's phenomenology is its concluding statement. Parmenides's dual insight is, first, that "thinking and the object of thought are the same" (the most celebrated modern version of which has been Hegel's "The real is rational and the rational real"), and second, that "never shall it be proven that non-being is" (hence *all* differences occur "within" being, nothing transcends being,

3. Ibid., 1:169.
4. Ibid., 1:167.
5. Alphonso Lingis, *Phenomenological Explanations* (Dordrecht: Martinus Nijhoff, 1986), 1–2.

and not even "nothing"). Parmenides sums up and justifies this dual insight in statements whose modal terms are those of *necessity* and *possibility:* "It is necessary both to say and to think that being is. For to be is possible and not-to-be is impossible."[6] Here lies the constitutional prescription for scientific positivity. In the historical contest between idealist and realist interpretations of this prescription, whether, basically, being conforms to thought, or thought to being, it has been the latter, what is now called the "realist" interpretation, which as natural or empirical science (whatever its exact nature or procedures are), that has won the laurels, to the exclusion of all other contenders, of the designation "science" and "true knowledge." By extending the positivity of evidence beyond the confines of experience as defined by empirical science, where experience is in some (difficult to define) manner limited to sense experience, by extending these confines to include all the evidences available to the full range of intuition, even and especially the evidences of an intellectual intuition into *essence,* Husserl in Freiburg concludes the long journey from myth to science that began with Parmenides in Elea.

With enough dedication and care, one can confirm the positivity of Husserl's principle of principles in such complex areas as perception, imagination, and memory, where judgments about perceiving and the perceived, or imagining and the imagined, or remembering and the remembered, are confirmed or denied on the evidence of actual perceptions, imaginations, and memories, evoked and carried through by the practicing phenomenologist and described as accurately as possible for repeatable intersubjective verification. Perceptual claims about the Statue of Liberty, for example, as Aaron Gurwitch was fond of saying, are ultimately validated not by literary descriptions, paintings, photographs, or souvenir miniatures, but by perceptions of the Statue of Liberty in New York harbor.

A hitch, however, in phenomenological investigation comes from the necessity to use language to describe or report on perception, imagination, memory, or, more broadly, on any and all regions of meaning. As a phenomenological propaedeutic to every other possible phenomenology, one would first have to ask if there is a phenomenological theory of judgment whose own positivity supports the positivity of all of phenomenology's other descriptive claims. Or, to express the matter more simply, one must first ask if the necessary use of language in phenomenological descriptions introduces a negativity of the sort that would undermine the full positivity of phenomenology and hence would undermine its claim to scientific status.

---

6. English translations from *The Presocratics,* edited and translated by Philip Wheelwright (Indianapolis: Bobbs-Merrill, 1960), 96–98.

A look at Husserl's *Formal and Transcendental Logic*,[7] where these sorts of questions are explicitly addressed, confirms the view that for Husserl phenomenology can succeed at the semiotic level in its efforts to ground its researches in absolutely positive evidence. Let us take a brief look at the results of Husserl's direct investigations of the phenomenon "judgment." First, at the least determinate, most formal level of judgment ("theory of forms"), what makes any judgment a judgment in the widest sense, and hence a judgment ultimately though not immediately capable of conveying truth scientifically, is its *distinctness*. And this distinctness, at the morphological base of any and all judgments, is or can be known through direct intuition. For example, one intuits that a cluster of words joined together, such as "the is cat brown" is confused in meaning, and that the cluster of words "the cat is brown" is distinct in meaning. When a judgment does have a morphologically correct form, and hence is a distinct judgment, a second positive intuition must still be possible before the judgment's candidacy as a knowledge claim can be registered. For Husserl, one must intuit, in an anticipatory intuition, that the distinct judgment does not and will not contradict other distinct judgments ("logic of noncontradiction"). In keeping with the commitment to a fully positive phenomenology, the criterion of noncontradiction or coherency is not given a priori or imposed a posteriori in the Husserlian analysis. It must be intuited, in an intuition Husserl calls an intuition of "clarity." Finally, before entering the body of established scientific knowledge, a distinct and clear judgment must be subject to fulfillment or lack of fulfillment in a further intuition to determine its truth claim ("logic of truth"). At no point is the language of judgment imported naively into phenomenology.

Thus, even when one turns to the area most likely to be nonintuitive, to the area most likely to introduce negativity into phenomenological positivity, one must at every point return to the positivity of intuition, to evidence which is, or is capable of being, brought into immediate presence to consciousness. We can understand, then, what one contemporary Husserl scholar means when he writes that "the distinctions between the different levels of logic are grounded on or founded in, at least in the final analysis, the distinctions between the different manners of intention and fulfillment."[8] All propositions of scientific knowledge, as well as all propositions which are to be considered as candidates for scientific knowledge,

7. Edmund Husserl, *Formal and Transcendental Logic,* translated by Dorion Cairns (The Hague: Martinus Nijhoff, 1969).
8. George Heffernan, "Old Wine in New Skins: Hermeneutical Remarks towards a Solution to the Problem of the Three-fold Structural Stratification of Formal Logic as Apophantical Analytics in the *Formal and Transcendental Logic* of Edmund Husserl," in *Proceedings of the Husserl Circle* (19th Meeting, Washington University, Saint Louis, Missouri, May 5–7, 1987), 114.

are accepted and confirmed through the positivity of intuitions whose fulfillment or lack of fulfillment weeds out falsehood as well as vagueness and confusion.

The Superlative Positivity of the Other Person

It seems incredible, therefore, that in response to the most radical positivity conceivable, the positivity of the Husserlian phenomenology, Emmanuel Levinas launches an attack on phenomenology not in the name of an irreducible negativity, as do Sartre and Adorno, nor in the name of a irrecuperable deferral of sense, as do Heidegger and Derrida, but precisely in the name of an immediacy and a concreteness, a positivity, *greater* than phenomenological positivity, an immediacy and a concreteness not only hidden to phenomenological positivity, despite its all-embracing egology and the infinity of its regions of investigation, but precisely hidden *by* phenomenological positivity itself. We are forced to ask, already with some degree of astonishment at the very question, how does Levinas make good on his extravagant claim?

Rather than simply quoting texts from Levinas's many writings to show that he makes this claim, that he indeed takes phenomenology to task for not being positive enough, and to show how he justifies this claim, re-presenting his arguments, let us be guided by Husserl's call to return to the things themselves, in conjunction with the special attention Levinas pays to the face of the other person, and *do* a phenomenology of the face. Let us do this in order to see for ourselves the outbreak of a positivity more positive than phenomenological positivity can admit, or failing that, to see the breakdown of Levinas's claim and the triumph of phenomenology.

Presumably a phenomenology of the face is a subset of a phenomenology of perception. Before proceeding any further, let me pause to note that when I say "our," "we," or "us," I mean that I as a phenomenological scientist am acting as a scout and a guide, for all other actual and potential phenomenological scientists, blazing or charting a univocal route into the workings of the constitution of a single self-same phenomenon, the thing itself, in this instance, the face. Every phenomenologist is entitled to object to "my" guidance at any step of the way, on the basis, though, of better (more accurate, closer, sharper) intuitions into the thing itself. But any sense of "my" and "yours" is inappropriate; the inquiry must be a disinterested one, impersonal, carried on by what is probably better called, as Husserl does call it, a "transcendental ego" of one sort and at one level or another. As a scientific inquiry, truth, impersonal truth, takes precedence over friendship, even my own "friendship" with myself, as Aristotle expressed it in the *Nicomachean Ethics*. So, to continue: in this investigation the face is to serve as our guiding clue and not just as an instance of a perceived object, or an instance of a perceptual phenomenon, but as an object or phenomenon in its own right. The phenomenologist might begin with a painting of a face, a photograph of a face, a marble bust, a death mask, or, even better, the phenomenologist's own face as seen in a mirror. But because we are guided in this investigation both by Husserl's call to the things themselves and by Levinas's directive that we attend to the face of the other person, the best (the most positive, direct, immediate) phenomenological evidence for a phenomenology of the face of the other person is nothing other than the flesh-and-blood face of another person.

So the phenomenologist, in search of the intuitionally most positive evidence, faces a face which faces the phenomenologist. The first step in doing any phenomenology is to get into contact with the phenomena. In order to get into contact with the *phenomenon* of the face of the other person the phenomenologist must first bracket his or her own "doxic thesis" of the "natural attitude," to employ Husserl's terminology. That is to say, the phenomenologist must put out of play or disconnect any naive beliefs regarding the *reality* of the face of the other person, in order to gain access to the presence of the phenomenon of another's face. This initial reduction is meant to put out of play historically determined presuppositions about such things as appropriate behaviors or good manners, but even more importantly, presuppositions about the reality or ontological status of the other's face must be put out of play.

Here already, however, with the very first step in the phenomenological procedure, a dilemma emerges that makes the investigation not merely difficult or impossible; rather, depending on how the phenomenologist responds, a dilemma emerges that puts the entire phenomenological investigation into ethical jeopardy. I think it is fair to say that the dilemma the phenomenologist encounters when investigating the face of the other person is analogous to the one summed up in the famous characterization of biological research where one must "kill to dissect." To disconnect the thesis of the natural attitude when facing the face of the other person is to treat the other person as in some sense nonreal, as a presentation to the consciousness of the investigator, as a perceptual phenomenon constitutionally correlated to perceiving. There is no doubt that the face is a perceptual phenomenon and that it can be treated as such. But is it not also *more* than a phenomenon? Why does the phenomenologist have a gnawing sense that something is awry, that something more than an unreflected doxic thesis is disconnected when the face of the other person is reduced to its phenomenality? Why does it seem that the face of the other person is not merely the ultimate positive basis for fulfilling judgments about portraits, busts, masks, and the like, but is somehow, in addition, or *otherwise,* something else altogether different, something more important?

Let us look more closely at this dilemma the "phenomenon" of the face seems to present for phenomenology. Perhaps the "gnawing sense that something is awry" is appropriate to all phenomenological investigations, or is merely personal, a beginner's uneasiness, say. Anything in the natural attitude—a stone, a dish, or an elephant's trunk—becomes "something else" when reduced to the phenomenological domain. This transformation is expected and deliberate. In a profound sense, it is the very point of phenomenological science. When treated as a phenomenon rather than as a real being, when treated as the *noema* of a *noesis* rather than as an object actually or potentially valued and used in everyday practice, the phenomenologist, unlike the ordinary person, can uncover his subject matter's essence, its *truth,* can articulate its proper intentional sense and the origin of its sense in the constitutional syntheses of consciousness. Again, this is the point of phenomenological science.

What then, if anything, makes the face any different? The difference is that in facing the face of the other person in the natural attitude there is already more at play than a doxic thesis and unreflected intentional correlations of sense. This *more,* to say it straightaway, refers to a qualitative difference rather than to a quantitative difference. The other person is not merely one real entity among others in the world of real things, a real entity with specific defining attributes, whether objective or subjective; nor is the other person fully explicable as a concatenation of sense, of meanings, even when constituted across associative syntheses as "another myself," according to the very suggestive analyses of Husserl's fifth Cartesian Meditation;[9] rather, beyond these characteristics, *the other person is someone who always already has a claim on me.*

9. See Edmund Husserl, *Cartesian Meditations,* translated by Dorion Cairns (The Hague: Martinus Nijhoff, 1970), 81–157. One should take careful note of the title of this meditation (which by itself is almost as long as all the four prior meditations combined): "Uncovering the Sphere of Transcendental Being as Monadological Intersubjectivity."

Husserl's fifth meditation, like Descartes's sixth, is notoriously filled with ambiguities. Especially with regard to the constitution of the sense "other person," Husserl sometimes verges on admitting to the limitations of phenomenological inquiry, though he never quite does so. The following is a representative sample of this ambiguity, specifically in response to the charge of "solipsism," taken from the third to the last section of this longest of meditations:

"Our actual explications have dissipated the objection as groundless. The following is to be noted above all. At no point was the transcendental attitude, the attitude of transcendental epoché, abandoned; and our 'theory' of experiencing someone else, our 'theory' of experiencing others, did not aim at being and was not at liberty to be anything but explication of the sense, 'others,' as it arises from the constitutive productivity of that experiencing: the

This all seems so simple and obvious that one wonders why it leads to an attack on phenomenology. The reason the other's alterity poses a problem for phenomenology is that the other person, which is what Levinas means by "the face," cannot be brought to full intuitive presence, and this precisely because the "presence" of the other person is an excess. The face of the other, the very alterity of the other, overwhelms subjectivity, overloads the subject, burdens the ego with more than its own abilities, more than its own active and passive syntheses can handle. The other, in sum, is too much for phenomenology. This is so because the face is not simply present but is *already present* (has already passed) *and* is *yet to come* (has not yet arrived into the present), such that the other cannot, in principle—and especially in principle—be brought to presence.

The face facing, before and after the phenomenological reduction, defies the constituting ego's synthesizing abilities, defies the ego's self-definition, defies the ownness of the ego's sphere of ownness. No matter how present the phenomenon of the face becomes to the consciousness of the phenomenologist, the face "itself" is out of phase, has always already been present, is always coming into presence. And yet, as we shall see in a moment, the disjointedness of the face is not simply the function of negation and nonbeing, which is how the ancient Greek scientists understood "passing away" and "coming to be." The language of science, even the broad descriptive language of phenomenological science, is simply and *essentially* inadequate to "account for" the overload of the face facing. That is to say, the other person, from the first and *prior to the constitution of meaning,* puts the self into a posture of debt that can best be character-

---

sense, 'truly existing others,' as it arises from the corresponding harmonious syntheses. What I demonstrate to myself harmoniously as 'someone else' and therefore have given to me, by necessity and not by choice, as an actuality to be acknowledged, is *eo ipso* the existing Other for me in the transcendental attitude: the alter ego demonstrated precisely within the experiencing intentionality of my ego. Within the bounds of positivity we say and find it obvious that, in my own experience, I experience not only myself but others—in the particular form: experiencing someone else." (148)

Ambiguities glimmer in the use and disuse of quotations marks: within the transcendental epoché quotation marks are not necessary, since what appears is understood as that which is limited to an appearance before the "constitutive productivity" of consciousness; prior to, or outside of, the transcendental epoché quotation marks are necessary, since what is referred to is not yet understood as that which is limited to an appearance before the constitutive productivity of consciousness.

For our purposes, the most revealing expression in this citation occurs when Husserl speaks of being "within the bounds of positivity." Positivity, for phenomenology, is always limited, as I have noted, to that which is correlated to consciousness. Of course, this is meant to be unlimited, to include all significations, all meaning, all sense. But is the objection that Husserl's account is a "solipsism" really only naive? Or always only naive? That is our question. It is Levinas's challenge.

ized in *ethical* rather than epistemological terms, as a responsibility and obligation to the other, rather than in terms of phenomenological depth and horizons of sense. To face the face of the other is to be made to assume the posture of being for-the-other prior to being for-oneself. It is to already be held "hostage" by the other. This structure of already-being-beholden to the other person, this being put into debt, is neither necessary, possible, nor meaningful, in the phenomenological senses of these terms, yet, as Levinas understood, it is the very heart, the very subjectivity, of the subject.

To be obligated by the other person is not necessary, as can be seen very simply by the fact that the phenomenologist *can* treat the face of the other person as a phenomenon, *can* simply apprehend a perceiving of the other as a perceived entity, even as an entity with a certain value and randomness. One does not *have* to face up to the prior claims of the other person; one *can refuse* the alterity of the other person, shake off, ignore, or repress whatever "gnawing sense" bothers the self. To some degree a version of this refusal is necessary for phenomenological inquiry, and is the price of its disinterested, dispassionate quest for truth. But this always means, however much it is forgotten in practice, that phenomenological reduction is far from being a purely neutral instrument for a purely neutral positive science: it is an act, like all acts, which is unalterably set within an ethical context. Like all human actions, phenomenological reduction is the always more or less justified act of someone who, for the purposes of science in this instance, more or less refuses the prior claims of the other person. Given the disinterest required of the phenomenologist in order to do scientific work scientifically, and given that the world which the phenomenologist investigates is an as yet unredeemed world, that is to say, a morally imperfect world, the alleged moral neutrality of phenomenological disinterest is local, temporary, and artificial, and as such stands in greater or lesser conflict with an always broader context of ethical demands, which may require, on a moral plane, the suspension of the phenomenological reductions themselves. That these conflicting exigencies, epistemological and moral, must be balanced is doubtlessly not specific to the phenomenological enterprise. Ethical necessity always claims priority, even if its claims, in the course of things, are not always met, and *should* not always be met.[10] It is this ethical priority that is *established*

___

10. I have deliberately formulated the restriction of moral priority in moral terms because purely moral relations (for example, the self giving all its food to the other facing) may at the same time produce injustice: in this instance, the self denying food to others who are also hungry but not currently present facing the self. I have written elsewhere about the relation of ethics to justice; see especially chapter 8 in this volume. As I point out there, the ethical responsibility and obligation of the face-to-face nonetheless always retain their

or *produced* (terms Levinas prefers to the term "constituted"; see *TI* 26) in the encounter with the face facing the "phenomenologist" (the moral agent really, the subject morally subject to the other), beyond the face apprehended phenomenologically. It occurs in an elicitation rather than an elucidation.

To be beholden to the other person is not a possibility, either, because unlike all possibilities, it is neither structured by sense conferral nor is it a condition of phenomenality. The other is not constituted by the self as one of the self's possibilities, but reconditions the self, transforms its natural or historical possibilities into moral choices, raises the self to moral agency, to self-as-response. Heidegger articulates a similarly peculiar conditionality when he distinguishes existential analysis from categorical analysis, where the former involves a hermeneutic circularity and depth of being hidden to the latter. The face, however, does not overload the abstract possibilities of mundane or transcendental reflection with the concrete possibilities of hermeneutic reflexivity, as in Heidegger; it overloads phenomenological reflexivity with an impossible but obligating ethical straightforwardness, a devotion and not a condition. The face of the other presents what is not necessary and what is im-possible, from the phenomenological point of view, by overloading manifestation with what is greater than the presence of either abstract or concrete essences.

But let us persist in questioning this extraordinary claim. Why insist on the term "more" rather than the term "less"? Why not simply revert to negatives, to the face *not* being a phenomenon, rather than the face being *more* than a phenomenon? In a sense this question has already been answered by the absolute positivity claimed by Husserlian phenomenology. If Husserlian phenomenology is absolute, then whatever overloads its grasp—not at all, therefore, unfulfilled, indistinct, vague, or empty intuitions, which are indeed *less* than its possibilities—must be more than a positivity. This is an overloading that Levinas, following Franz Rosenzweig, thinks of in terms of *emphasis* or hyperbole. The excess of the other's face is not itself a phenomenon. It is a non-phenomenal bursting of phenomenality. Its breakthrough is accomplished not as the entry of another world, but as an emphatic positivity, an excessive positivity, an ultrapositivity. The priority of the other person is a priority of greater concreteness and significance than the priority of scientific a prioris— because it is a moral priority. As moral, it is more glorious and has a higher exigency.

The constituting ego can constitute the signification "other person" by

_____

priority, for it is in the name of ethics that justice too is called for, and only in relation to ethics that justice can remain just. I call this "justice with a human face."

placing the other person within quotation marks, reducing alterity to "the sphere of transcendental being as monadological intersubjectivity."[11] These marks—so dear to Husserl—remind or rather warn us that a phenomenological reduction is in effect. To flesh out this signification is what we meant earlier by "doing" a phenomenology of the face. But the disturbance of the ego effected by the alterity of the other person is not itself constituted by the constituting ego. The alterity of the other person is not merely a signification in the sense of a sign signifying within a system of signs and referents, verifiable in an intuition now or later. The other person is not only the possible object of signifying acts; rather, the person signifies signification. This is not to say, simply, that we must not forget that the other person, too, is an origin or source-point of meaning *in the same way* "as I myself" but from elsewhere, grasped through analogy, where the "I" is Husserl's transcendental ego at the origin and source of all meaning, whether here (directly) or there (analogously, by associate pairing). It is not a question of relocating the constituting ego, giving it a new address, as if by placing the origin of constitution in the other person rather than in me or in a transpersonal transcendental ego to which I too have equal access, the alterity of the other person could be brought into phenomenology. In such a perspective, one would still have to account for the constituting ego's location in this particular other rather than in another particular other; one would have to account for the significance of "here" and "there," which would introduce precisely the same rupture that the associate pairing was intended to cover over. No, Levinas is not suggesting a simple relocation of the transcendental ego; he is contesting the originariness and also the comprehensiveness of the transcendental ego altogether.

In the face of the other person one finds that meaning is not simply constituted from a zero source point, mine or the other's; it requires the reception of meaning. Actually, one does not find this out, like the findings of an inquiry, one suffers it, one undergoes it. To be sure, to thematize something true, words must be morphologically organized in a distinct and clear way and open to intuitional confirmation. To be sure, too, meaning involves active and passive synthesis, is part of a differential field of meaning which is more or less held together at present and across history. But prior to the "originary" constitution of propositional meaning, words are meaningful because they are addressed to someone. This sense of *meaningful* is the ethical sense, one person responsible and obligated to another person, where what is at play has all the seriousness of *significance* and not just *signification*, where meaning is not reducible to

---

11. From the title of Husserl's fifth Cartesian Meditation; see note 9 above.

semantic or semiotic assemblages of signs, concatenations of sense and nodes of displacement within historically developing systems of signs (languages) grounded at some point, according to Husserl in any event, by intuitional confirmation. Prior to *what* is said, the alterity of the other person already has a claim on meaning, in the ethical encounter which brings together saying and responding.

The dative overloads the pure positivity of the nominative with a greater positivity, with higher exigencies, requiring more. Subjectivity, even transcendental subjectivity, even when it constitutes all meaning, does not at all constitute the alterity of the other person *to whom* all meaning is given. Rather, the ego presupposes the alterity of the other person in a presupposition, devotion, or moral stricture that can never be loosened without some degree of ethical lapse, even if that lapse is justified in the name of a phenomenological science dedicated to pure truth, and even if that truth is dedicated to the noblest purposes of social justice. In our historical time—perhaps this is the deepest sense of "history" itself— interpersonal ethics and social justice do not coincide, not yet. Thus the realm of truth, and the phenomenological science dedicated to that truth, still compromises the ethical presuppositions which make it possible and which provide its ultimate standard. All meanings are already subject to the other person, are already for-the-other, and thus are subjected to a meaningfulness greater, of greater significance, of more importance—in the ethical sense—than any and all meanings constituted or fulfilled within the parameters of science, phenomenological or otherwise.

In seeking for the *essence* "this face here and now facing" (in quotes, i.e., as a phenomenon), the face is necessarily reduced to being an instance of "faceness" or reduced to being the intuitional evidence for an essence. Yet the face is more concrete, *is otherwise,* than the species of a genus, or the instance of an essence, or the case of a generality, or anything else whereby the phenomenologist qua phenomenologist "grasps" the face. It is deeper than the originary "this *as* that" (see *OBBE* 35) constitutive of meaning because the alterity of the other is incomparable, *unique,* and the responsibility it elicits in subjectivity is irreplaceable, *elected.* The concreteness of the face is not a uniqueness derived from an exceptional singularity or an exceptional combination of attributes, for example, the length of this particular nose, the shape of this particular cheek, the curve of these lips, although every face, like everything else spatial and temporal, is particular, unique in this sense. Such particularity, based on the logic of contiguous space and irreversible time, always eludes thought, always opens out onto a so-called "bad infinite," an infinitely microscopic or macroscopic empiricism. Every perceptual thing is particular in this way, yet not every perceptual thing is a face. The uniqueness which breaks the "this *as* that" of constitutive meaning arises in the encounter with the face of the other person differently. The alterity of the other is unique in its very infinity, its very bursting of the bounds of manifestation, with a blacker black, to speak metaphorically, than the pupils of the other's eyes. On the side of the subject, it is a forcing of the self into a responsibility and obligation that cannot be shirked without moral fault, a self irreplaceable in its moral agency. The other person rivets the self to its place as irreplaceably beholden to the other, at the other's service, me—not "as for me" but for the other, for you. The face cannot be grasped, either intellectually or otherwise, without doing violence to the nonmediated claim it makes, the putting into question it effects, on the self of the investigating ego, the me that is responsible first before all else.

The ethical self underlies the investigating ego, not as one world lying beneath another or as one constitutive layer lying beneath and founding another, but as the rupture of the egoism of the ego. The alterity of the other person is already closer to the self, to the me, paradoxically, than is the transcendental ego which is the origin of all meaning. It is the always new beginning beneath such an origin. This is what Levinas means when he speaks of the subjection of subjectivity subject to the alterity of the other, subjectivity as a "passivity more passive than any receptivity."

The mushroom in the grass, the grass, the sky above, the stars beyond do not make claims on me, or question me, or hold me to my place, vigilant, obligated, in the disturbing way that the face of the other does. They are near and far, but the other is nearer and farther, too near and too far, too close and too distant. The concreteness and immediacy of the face—the alterity of the other person—plunges an exceptional hold or vigilance so deep into the self, endlessly, that the self is better than the ego, more alert, more ready for the other, before thinking of or for itself. Such a "hold" is not the grasp of consciousness, whether empirical or transcendental; its grip is ethical, the very orientation of myself toward the other person, myself beholden to, obligated to, in debt to, the other person, prior to any contracts or agreements about who owes what to whom.

The self finds its inexhaustible resources when and only when it is placed wholly and without reserve in the service of the other. Only in this way, by default as it were, can the phenomenologist "account for" the greater positivity, the ultrapositivity, that is the extraordinary irruption of the other's face.

THIRTEEN

On the Suffering of Meaning: Levinas "Outside" Heidegger's "Threshold" through Rosenzweig's "Gate"

For the stone cries out from the wall,
And the beam from the woodwork responds.
Woe to him who builds a town with blood,
And founds a city on iniquity!

Habakkuk 2:11–12

"Threshold," "Outside," and "Gate"—these are three names for passages in a time beyond the "end of philosophy," movements across the boundary between philosophy and nonphilosophy, but delineated and beckoning from the other side, at once destabilizing old spiritual adventures and establishing new ones.

Three very short texts explicitly concerned with barriers, boundaries, and breakthroughs will guide us. "Language,"[1] by Martin Heidegger, examines the birth of meaning out of language in the light of a poem entitled "A Winter Evening" by Georg Trakl. For Heidegger, the key to this poem lies in the second verse of the third stanza: "Pain has turned the threshold to stone." The second text is the solitary concluding chapter of Levinas's *Otherwise than Being or Beyond Essence,* entitled simply "Outside." It is the only chapter of the third and final general heading, "In Other Words," of this book, a point which I note because in this it resembles, both in structure and sense, the short final section of Rosenzweig's *The Star of Redemption,* also simply entitled "Gate," the third and final text to be considered here.

1. Heidegger's Threshold: For Poet-Thinkers Only

Heidegger's early concern for being led naturally, in his later writings, to a concern for language. Language must not be thought, however, as one

---

1. Martin Heidegger, "Language," in Martin Heidegger, *Poetry, Language, Thought,* translated by Albert Hofstadter (New York: Harper and Row, 1971), 187–210. Originally a lecture, "Die Sprache" first appeared in Martin Heidegger, *Unterwegs zur Sprache* (Pfullingen: Neske, 1959). Heidegger writes of it: "The lecture was given on October 7, 1950, at Bühlerhöhe in memory of Max Kommerell and was repeated on February 14, 1951, at the Württembergische Bibliotheksgesellschaft in Stuttgart." (Henceforth "Language.")

among several interesting topics. Rather it would be the very element of thought, the "home" of authentic thinking, the "field," "site," "dwelling" of a thoughtfulness deeper, more responsive to being, than the abstract representational forms of thinking which hitherto constituted philosophy. Precisely inasmuch as thinking thinks beyond philosophy, beyond representational, calculative, instrumental *ratio*, it lives in language, the dwelling house of being. Beneath and more original than the rigorously narrow correspondence of proposition and reality sanctioned by classical philosophy, language is the place where that ultimate eventfulness *(Ereignis)* occurs which is the origin of all meaning, of all history, and hence also of classical philosophy itself.

Because Heidegger takes the final truth of the philosophy he seeks to surpass to be a pure willfulness, unmasked in and by Nietzsche, he offers instead "to take up our stay with language, i.e., within *its* speaking, not within our own" ("Language" 190). Heidegger understands that to break with the willfulness of philosophy one cannot construct a more comprehensive barrier against it. One cannot construct anything. Opposing philosophy in such a manner would be as futile as putting out a fire with kerosine, or with "dynamite," as Nietzsche said of himself. Instead— precisely "instead"—the entire willful orientation of philosophy, whether willing for the will (Nietzsche) or willing against the will (Schopenhauer), must be disarmed, disengaged, side-stepped. Henceforth the true thinker is the one who attends to the way language breaks in upon humans rather than the way humans force themselves upon language. "We do not wish to assault language in order to force it into the grip of ideas already fixed beforehand. We do not wish to reduce the nature of language to a concept" ("Language" 190). What humans impose on language remains always only human, a mirror and not being. It is language, not man, that gives to thought what is thoughtful to think. Thinking is receptiveness to the thought which language gives. Heidegger's famous "turn," then, is not from being to language, but away from subjectivism, willfulness, imposition.

The barrier which bars the way to a proper relationship with language is precisely whatever barriers humans erect, constructions of any sort, precisely because they are constructed.[2] Heidegger specifies the essential failure of construction as "theory," "method," "mathesis":[3] the approach

---

2. For a careful conceptual-historical analysis of modernity defined by the idea of "construction," see David Lachterman, *The Ethics of Geometry: A Genealogy of Modernity* (New York: Routledge: 1990).

3. See Martin Heidegger, *What is a Thing?* translated by W. B. Barton, Jr., and Vera Deutsch (Chicago: Henry Regnery, 1967), especially part B, section 5, "The modern mathematical science of nature and the origin of a critique of pure reason," 65–108.

to reality which always *already* determines whatever is approached *prior* to any receptivity to what is given. Genuine thinking, in contrast, lets go, side-steps the preconceptions of philosophy, releases itself to what is. The thinker must be especially careful to avoid precisely those highways which philosophy itself meticulously constructs as privileged passages to truth. Method and thinking are incompatible.

Heidegger thus rejects a threefold interpretation of language as (1) "expression," the utterance which externalizes and communicates an otherwise merely internal message; (2) "an activity of man," the willful setting in motion of a historically determined set of signs, such as German, French, or English; and (3) "presentation and representation of the real and the unreal" ("Language" 193). Such interpretations of language are "correct," Heidegger writes, but only so far as they go, meaning only as far as the standard of "correctness" goes. But correctness, the carefully controlled correlation of proposition and reality, is itself but another instance of theory, method, mathesis, in a word, imposition. It is no wonder, therefore, that Heidegger turns to poets. Their art has always been a receptivity to muses. No wonder too, then, that Heidegger favors poets who poeticize about the poetic art itself, because in their self-consciousness Heidegger senses a hint of the self-reflection proper to thinking.

It is by listening in on poets, such a Trakl, who have listened to language's self-revelation, that Heidegger teaches. Language, Heidegger reports, gathers together a cosmos made up of four essential and elemental dimensions: mortals, divinity, earth, and sky. The specific style, manner, or way in which language gathers together the fourfold nexus at any particular time determines everything about a historical epoch or world. The world of today, for example, is a global technological world, a totalizing gathering of mortals, divinity, earth, and sky, under the sign of an infinitely resourceful and voracious know-how. The ancient Greek world and the medieval European world, in contrast, were gathered together quite otherwise. In any and all worlds, however, it is language and not humankind that "brings the presence of what was previously uncalled into a nearness" ("Language" 198). All of Heidegger's later writings, on various poems and pre-Socratic fragments, are so seemingly elusive, then, because they attempt not to define terms, as if what were important were terms already given, but rather to track down the very giving, sniffing out the glue, as it were, which first lays out and joins terms within a meaningful whole. "The intimacy of world and thing," Heidegger writes, "is present in the separation of the between; it is present in the dif-ference" ("Language" 202).

The last thing Heidegger wants to do, then, is to *interpret* Trakl's poem, if by "interpretation" one means exchanging an original set of obscure terms for another set of clearer ones. He aims, rather, to tease out, to attend to, to wait upon—"in the genuineness of hearkening"—the world-productive gift-giving of language. Heidegger's concern is the elemental gathering to which Trakl has given voice, or which finds a voice in Trakl's poem. The first stanza invokes *things;* the second stanza invokes *world;* the third and final stanza, whose second verse is "Pain has turned the threshold to stone," invokes the *between,* the intimacy, the "separateness and towardness" ("Language" 203), the "dif-ference," which joins things and world. The between which first gives rise to things and world, which holds them together while holding them apart, is for Heidegger a threshold. It is the always hidden horizon of a giving of the given, the very revelation of what is revealed, language as organizing host to and of entities.

What, then, is the meaning of "pain" in this context, where, according to Trakl, "Pain has turned the threshold to stone"? That the threshold is "stone," Heidegger informs us, indicates the hardiness of its drawing together, that "the settling of the between needs something that can endure" ("Language" 204). But why is that which makes for this enduring "pain"? Is the poet thinking of the hurt mortals suffer through wounds and diseases to flesh, blood, and bones, the aching and agony which cry out for relief? Heidegger rules out such an interpretation, with its anthropological, psychological, and moral overtones, as mere sentimentality: "We should not," he writes, "imagine pain anthropologically, as a sensation that makes us feel afflicted. We should not think of the intimacy psychologically as the sort in which sentimentality makes a nest for itself" ("Language" 205). Rather, Heidegger would have us think of a non-human *rending* which lies at the source of meaning, the "pain" of holding together what at the same time is held apart: precisely the threshold that language effects between things and world, the "pain" of an ontological horizon giving and maintaining beings qua beings. Trakl's "pain," then, is the "pain" of difference in identity, the "pain" of a world-productive differentiation opened up and held open by language, by what Heidegger in his earlier writings called "ontological difference," neither beings nor being but the difference between ("separateness and towardness") beings and their being.

Heidegger is obviously reading Trakl's "pain" metaphorically if not mythically, since language assuredly has no skin, nerves, or heart, and thus cannot suffer as sentient creatures suffer. To leave behind abstract conceptual language such as Hegel's "identity in difference," or Spinoza's "substance," "mode," and "attribute," Heidegger opts for the language of architecture, geology, and fecundity (and elsewhere agriculture). Language, the house of being, suffers labor pains to hold apart and together the meaningful: "Pain indeed tears asunder, it separates, yet so that at the same time it draws everything to itself, gathers it to itself." Further: "Pain is the joining agent in the rending that divides and gathers. Pain is the joining of the rift. The joining is the threshold. It settles the between, the middle of the two that are separated in it. Pain joins the rift of the difference. Pain is the dif-ference itself" ("Language" 204).

One is reminded of Empedocles' world-productive love and strife. Pain is the dif-ference, the rending between being and beings, which releases beings to be the beings they are, a releasing which is at once the very movement of language, its gift-giving.

Unlike any human all too human pain, in which sufferers cry out, moan, whimper, beg, scream, and plead, the "pain" of language is somehow always a silent gift-giving, "the peal of stillness" *(Geläut der Stille)*. Such is the strange "speaking" of language to which humans must harken: "Mortals speak insofar as they listen" ("Language" 209). Humans speak truly when they listen as gently as possible, quiet enough to hear the murmuring of stillness. But listening, by itself, is not enough. True listening, for Heidegger, must at the same time be an *accepting*. Only listening that accepts—without, let us note, any imposition of standards, values, or moral scruples—responds to language: "This speaking that listens and accepts is responding" ("Language" 209).

2. Levinas's Outside: For the Good Only

While Heidegger is at home quietly echoing a listening, responding to the world-historical generativity and generosity of language, Levinas finds the inauguration of the meaningful elsewhere, outside, subject to harsher and more piercing conditions, in response to moral demands, suffering for the suffering of others.

The epigram Levinas places before "Outside," the last short chapter of *Otherwise than Being or Beyond Essence,* is taken from Goethe's *Faust,* part 2, act 1 (*OBBE* 175).[4] It consists of a dialogue between Mephistopheles and Faust:

4. The only other German-language epigram of the eight epigrams found throughout *Otherwise than Being or Beyond Essence* is taken from the poet Paul Celan, a fellow Holocaust sufferer, and a poet whom Heidegger, for all his care for poets, never mentions, as far as I know, anywhere throughout his voluminous writings.

Mephistopheles: Would you only hear what you already heard?
Shy at no further sound, weird as it be,
Long since no more at odds with oddity.
Faust: Yet not in torpor would I comfort find;
Awe is the finest portion of mankind; . . . [5]

One can read this selection as highlighting Levinas's differences with Heidegger. Mephistopheles enunciates Heidegger's critique of mathesis ("only hear what you already heard") and his path into the strangeness of thinking ("weird as it be"), while Faust responds with Levinas's ethical-religious alternative ("awe"), from which perspective Heideggerian thinking is criticized for its complacency ("torpor").

Levinas hoists Heidegger on his own petard, discovering a fatal prolepsis, a mathesis, in the very thought whose highest aim is to escape mathesis. Thinking as listening, Levinas will claim, is a hearing limited to certain preconceived and very restricted wavelengths. It is a hearing seeking and satisfied only with the comforts of home, the closure of a cosmos, the quietude wherein language can be overheard whispering to itself. Levinas has Faust call this whispering and the stillness that makes it possible a "torpor" *(Erstarren)*. It is a torpor compared to the ethico-religious "awe" *(Schaudern)* which is "the finest portion of mankind."

Like Heidegger's later writings, *Otherwise than Being or Beyond Essence* is a sustained examination of the role of language in the origin of meaning. Like Heidegger, Levinas rejects any account of language restricted to predicative judgement, whether elaborated in terms of a coherence or a correspondence theory of truth, or some combination of both.[6] Levinas

---

5. The English translation is taken from Goethe, *Faust,* translated by Walter Arndt, edited by Cyrus Hamlin (New York: Norton, 1978), 158. Lingis, in his translation of *OBBE,* leaves Levinas's two German language epigrams in their original German. The other appears under the title of chapter 4 (99) and is from Paul Celan: "Ich bin du, wenn / ich ich bin" ("I am you when / I I am"). Of the other six epigrams (which Levinas cites in French), five appear after the title page: two are from the prophet Ezekiel, one is from Rashi's commentary on Ezekiel, and two are from Pascal's *Pensées;* while the sixth, which appears under the title of chapter 1, is from Jean Wahl's *Traité de métaphysique* (1953).

6. In rejecting the fundamental status of representation in the production of meaning, Levinas is of course rejecting the Husserl of his youth. As we saw in chapter 10, he was already influenced by Heidegger's critique of representation as early as 1930, as is clear from Levinas's reading of Husserl in *The Theory of Intuition in Husserl's Phenomenology.*

But in addition to a critique of Husserl, in following Heidegger Levinas is also rejecting the dominant French philosopher of the 1920s and 1930s: Leon Brunschvicg (1868–1951). In the glory of Henri Bergson's domination of French philosophy beforehand, and Jean-Paul Sartre's afterwards, and the continued interest in and impact of the thought of both, Brunschvicg's philosophical stature in France in the between-time is usually overlooked or entirely forgotten. Brunschvicg was an idealist. His main work, published in 1897, entitled *La*

also appreciates that the meaningfulness of language cannot be fully grasped if language is reduced to the representational functions either of expressing internal states or thematizing external reality. He appreciates, too, that language and history are conjoined. Still, Levinas does not pay obeisance to the Heideggerian coronation of language as the ontological-historical-hermeneutical fount of meaning. He sees in the ontological difference not only the bounteous generosity of world-giving but the sharper edge of a mocking *irony,* thinly veiling an abyss without bottom. Heidegger and Levinas agree that ontology is without foundation. For Levinas, however, ontology is not fundamental. From its depths come horrors as well as gifts. Levinas rejects a vision of humanity reduced to playing the role of "mortals" in a drama produced and directed by language. For Levinas, meaning originates in another sort of pain, a pain which pierces through all the generosity and irony of the play of language, ripping through its curtains in the superlative sobriety of moral responsiveness to the alterity of the other person, to the sufferings of others. Meaning, for Levinas, originates in the ethical structure of one-for-the-other.

More compelling than being's "pain" is the other's suffering. What is truly meaningful arises in the infinitesimal gap separating and joining the I and the other in ethical proximity, in the I morally subjected to the other's suffering. Here being and language do not call but are called into question by the urgency of moral demands. Meaning emerges from out of an urgency where material and spiritual needs meet, in "the pain lightly called physical" (*TO* 69). Meaning arises most primordially not in what languages gives to mortals, but in the acuity of the irreplacability—the over-exposure—of the I's responsibility to respond to the hurt and destitution of others. The other's pain pains the self, turns the self inside-out. This is the meaning of Levinas's *outside.* Meaning emerges in a burning care—like a burning bush, or a hot coal on one's tongue—to alleviate the suffering of others, to care not for one's self (or for language, or for being) but more immediately, in a "passivity greater than all receptivity,"

Modalité du jugement, begins by asserting: "Knowledge gives birth to a world which for us is the only world. Beyond that there is nothing; if there were anything beyond knowledge, its definition would be in terms of the inaccessible and the indeterminable, which would amount to nothing for us." (This passage is cited in I. M. Bochenski, *Contemporary European Philosophy* [Berkeley: University of California Press, 1969], 84). Interestingly enough, this did not prevent Brunschvicg from developing a religious philosophy, or a religious interpretation of philosophy, or, perhaps it is best to call his view a "gnosticism," because he claims that G-d is nothing other than the *copula* of predicative judgments. In any event, Levinas's criticism of the ultimacy of re-representation, i.e., the synthetic activity of predicative judgment, in the production of meaning, is an obvious and direct attack on the foundation and linchpin of Brunschvicg's idealism (or gnosticism).

for others, to aid them. Meaning arises in the pain of a excessive unwonted exposure to the alterity of the other, an exposure open not merely to the always veiled horizons of meaning, but open to—because opened by—the "height and destitution" through which the very alterity of the other person is constituted as other.

The other's suffering is meaningless, absurd, useless, until I respond to it, taking up that suffering as if it were my own, as pressing as would be my own, providing for the other before myself. Suffering for the other's suffering, expiation, describes the heart of the inordinate relationship of one-for-the-other that Levinas calls *ethics* rather than *epistemology, ontology,* or *aesthetics,* and which, in the final chapter of *Otherwise than Being or Beyond Essence,* he understands in the radical terms of a skin turned inside out, the self completely "outside" itself for-the-other. Classical thought is broken not because it was not quiet enough, not thankful enough, not sufficiently attuned to the gift-giving of language, but because it suffered too little, preferred to remain within, ensconced inside, dwelling upon its own threshold, not risking its skin. "Yet not in torpor would I comfort find," says Faust, "Awe is the finest portion of mankind."

Levinas insists that the over-exposure of the self—excessive and un-willed subjection to the other person whose needs get "under my skin"—cannot be understood in terms of disclosure, even when disclosure is understood beyond re-representation. The other's suffering does not take on meaning because it, or my associative pairing with it, or my sympathy for it, discloses, clarifies, manifests, or reveals something *about* the other's suffering, or my own. The intimacy of disclosure is still too distant, remote, even when gracious like a host. Rather, the I's suffering for the other is at one and the same moment the I's suffering and the suffering of another's suffering. The other is closer to the self than the ego—this is the deepest experience and condition of moral responsibility, and hence of meaning. The other breathes through the self, "inspires" the self—such is the true meaning of awe. In "Outside," Levinas writes:

The approach of the neighbor is a fission of the subject beyond lungs, in the resistant nucleus of the ego, in the undividedness of its individuality. It is a fission of the self, of the self as fissibility, a passivity more passive still than the passivity of matter. To open oneself as space, to free oneself by breathing from closure in oneself already presupposes this beyond: my responsibility for the other and my aspiration by the other, the crushing charge, the beyond, of alterity. (*OBBE* 180–81)

What is meaningful in the ultimate sense (and the meaningfulness of ultimacy itself) emerges neither from representation, will, nor disclosure, but from moral obligation, obligation put upon an I *elected* by the other, hence through the pain of an inescapably heteronomous autonomy.

Meaning originates in an I stripped to its rawest nerve by what has no *real* force, an I morally obligated to the other, torn inside out, exposed: "outside where nothing covers anything, non-protection, the reverse of a retreat, homelessness, non-world, non-inhabitation, layout without security" (*OBBE* 179). In this non-historical, non-ontological compression of I and other, Levinas discovers "the very signifyingness of signification" (*OBBE* 178), the meaningfulness of meaning. Meaning is not merely heard, it hurts.[7] But from this hurt not weakness but moral response and moral judgment arise.

Levinas is obviously opposing the immorality, implied or actual, of Heidegger's subservience to language. To not take seriously the self morally elected in the pain of an excessive exposure to the other's suffering, the other's suffering, if recognized at all, becomes a mere cog or sign in a calculus whose ultimate meaning lies hidden in the forever inscrutable and superior resources of language. Levinas writes:

In all the compunction of Heidegger's magical language, and the impressionism of his play of lights and shadows, and the mystery of light that comes from behind the curtains, in all this tip-toe or wolf stepping movement of discourse, where the extreme prudence to not frighten the game perhaps dissimulates the impossibility of flushing it out, where each contact is only tangency, does poetry succeed in lessening the rhetoric? Is not essence the very impossibility of anything else, of any revolution that would not be a revolving upon oneself? (*OBBE* 182)

In other words, Heideggerian attunement, wrapped up in itself, echoing language, is *inferior* to moral responsibility for others. Heidegger's *Gelassenheit* is philosophy in a new key, to be sure, but its silence is also the accomplice, willy-nilly, to suffering unaided, to evil and injustice unhindered, about which its beautiful rhetoric is ineffective from the outset. To hearken to the distant language of a being's horizon, one must first silence the distressful and all too immediate cries of other persons, cries which are meaningful only when they are too close for comfort, too close to be willed away, so close as to be overwhelming, forcing the self to suffer for what is not of its own doing, not its business, nor it *own* concern—the other.

What is most meaningful is not receiving the gift of language's quiet words of world-giving, but the always insufficient giving of food, clothing, shelter, to the needy, opening a door, sharing an umbrella, lending a hand, bolstering a shattered confidence. Other's are hungry—I must

7. And against Nietzsche, we can add that meaning is *harder,* sharper, than the ego.

feed them. Here lies the first and last word. Philosophy has yet to account for the priority of this demand, which is neither true nor beautiful. In this "must" before the other, overriding the quest for truth, the quest for truth finds its *worth*, rises to its worth.

"The threshold turns to stone"—the Heideggerian pain cannot shatter the threshold, for it is precisely the Heideggerian "pain," pain muffled within quotation marks, that hardens the threshold, turning it into stone in the first place, in a giving that feeds no hungry mouth. To rise to a fully human height it is not sufficient to respond to the gifts of being— which are not, after all, Levinas reminds us, always *gifts* for which one is *thankful:* who is thankful for Auschwitz? The willfulness of Nietzsche's will to power and Schopenhauer's will to nothingness is not rectified by Heidegger's rarified hearkening. Willfulness is also one of being's dispensations. Being and essential language do not and cannot give rightly because they are wrapped up in themselves, however great and worthy they proclaim their gifts. Neither more nor less is required, but better. The human rises to its full stature neither willfully positing being nor gently yielding to its dis-posal, but when one is de-posed by and for the other.

The contracts of re-presentational philosophy, objective thought, are grounded ultimately not in the horizon of being, even thought as language, but in the denucleation of the self. "To nullify the civic pact," Charles Peguy wrote in 1902, "it would be sufficient that a single man be wittingly held—or what comes to the same—be wittingly left in destitution. As long as one man remains outside, the door slammed in his face closes a city of injustice and hate."[8] The moral exigency Levinas describes in terms of the outside, the self turned inside-out, besides itself for another, is a response precisely to the exteriority of the outsider par excellence, the other.

3. Rosenzweig's Gate: For Jews and Christians Only

"Gate" is the heading of the final short section of Rosenzweig's *Star of Redemption*. The term appears three times in the concluding exhortatory (and triangulated) sentences of this book (*SR* 424). In these sentences, reproduced below, Rosenzweig urges his readers to trust G-d by following the prophetic words of Micah: "To do justice and to love mercy and to walk humbly with thy God," a path taken by exiting the book and entering "INTO LIFE," which are the final two words of the *Star*.

8. From, "Destitution and Poverty," in Charles Peguy, *Basic Verities: Prose and Poetry* (Chicago: Henry Regnery, 1965), 50.

To walk humbly with thy God—nothing more is demanded
there than a wholly present trust. But trust is a big word.
It is the seed whence grow faith, hope, and love, and the
fruit which ripens out of them. It is the very simplest
and just for that the most difficult. It dares at
every moment to say Truly to the truth. To
walk humbly with thy God—the words are
written over the gate, the gate which
leads   out   of   the   mysterious-
miraculous   light   of   the   divine
sanctuary   in   which   no   man
can   remain   alive.   Whither,
then,   do   the   wings   of
the   gate   open?   Thou
knowest   it   not?
INTO   LIFE.

Rosenzweig urges his readers to leave his book behind, not, to be sure,
to escape its meaning, but to escape entrapment in the immanent play of
its signifiers. One should escape the book for the sake of the far more
serious obligations of real life, constituted not only by familial, social,
economic, and political obligations, but also, and most deeply, by the
material and spiritual obligations of religious community. True life is
"beyond the book" in moral and religious life. Moral and religious life is
found in a contact closer than that conceivable by philosophy, with specific people at specific times in specific places, each person, place, and
time, unique.

But Rosenzweig's demand is even greater. It is not abstract "persons"
whom Rosenzweig urges through the gate of divine trust, nor does he
urge his readers into abstract or generic "religious communities." Rather,
Rosenzweig's urgent message is for *Jews* and *Christians*, for members of
the Jewish people and the Christian communion. Like Hegel's *Phenomenology* or Plato's *Symposium*, which are also spiritual ladders, propaedeutics
designed to produce, justify, and sustain the type of the *philosopher, The
Star of Redemption* demands spiritual *askesis*, ascension; but against the
current of what Rosenzweig understands to be the necessarily abstract
possibilities (the "perhaps") of philosophy, whether ruled by Platonic ideas
or Hegelian concepts, it moves toward and into the supra-ideational,
supra-conceptual concretude and actuality of Jewish and Christian life.
Morality and holiness, Jewish and Christian morality and holiness, revealed religion, exceed the resources of philosophy, exceed the book. Others, who are neither Jews nor Christians, Rosenzweig names "pagans,"
because that is who they are for Judaism and Christianity. Pagans are all

those who do not rise to authentic LIFE, to life in Jewish or Christian community, as described in books 1 (on Judaism) and 2 (on Christianity) of part 3 of the *Star*.

No doubt Rosenzweig was quite aware of the shocking non-liberal exclusiveness of his privileging of Judaism and Christianity. But it was not, or not merely, as some commentators have suggested, a residual and chauvinist Hegelianism tainting the universalism of his thought. His thought remains universal, but with a universality tempered by the concretude of *love*. His logic can be reconstructed as follows: humans are fully constituted only within religious community (without which one is alone, whether in the solipsism of philosophy or the tyranny of politics); religious communities can only be genuine founded upon love (which for Rosenzweig is the core sense of revelation); love has two and only two fundamental and complementary forms or aspects: being loved and loving; Judaism is the living community of being-loved, beloved of G-d (part 3, book 1), and Christianity is the living community of loving, loving one's neighbor (part 3, book 2).[9] One day these two communities will unite, when loving-the-neighbor and being-loved-by-G-d are united, after the Jewish and Christian work of sacred history, redemption, is completed, a work which for Jews means setting an eternal example and for Christians means historical missionizing, at which point everyone will live in "Truth" (part 3, book 3). Pagans, in contrast to Jews and Christians, neither grasp nor grapple with the centrality of love in all things human and divine.

At the center of Heidegger's thought lies the question of be-ing, care *(Sorge)* to be released *(Gelassenheit)* into the rift of language. At the center of Levinas's thought lies goodness, moral responsiveness to the suffering of the other. At the center of Rosenzweig's thought, and literally at the center of the *Star* (part 2, book 2), is love, love for the neighbor inspired by G-d's love. Unlike Heideggerian attunement to language, which calls for and calls forth the philosopher-poet, and unlike Levinasian obligation to the other, which elicits the morally elected self, Rosenzweigian love for the neighbor requires Jews and Christians, members of the two and only two communities capable of maintaining, continuing, and spreading love to all humankind. All the rest is pagan.

The issue at stake in situating Levinas and Heidegger along paths leading into and out of Rosenzweig's gate is not, to be sure, a matter of one man's private convictions or of a comforting topology. The issue is one

---

9. To the extent that other traditional religious communities embody and impart love, one could say that they too are acceptable within Rosenzweig's schema. Perhaps it is here in not allowing for this possibility that Rosenzweig perpetuates the sorry exclusiveness of Hegelian philosophy.

of evaluating fundamental and conflicting orientations in post-rationalist thought. Both Levinas and Heidegger reject the basic epistemological orientation of classical philosophy. But one, Levinas, does so by directing the human vertically, or diagonally, upward, toward what is above classical rationality, to that which is at once good and holy. The other, Heidegger, aims at that which is farther and nearer than the rational, directing humans to a participatory receptivity to language as the giver of the meaningful.

Levinas as Jew and Christian

To say that Levinas's thought is Jewish would mean, for Rosenzweig, that it is the thought of being-loved, a thought which follows after the priority of G-d's love. This would be the religious sense of the "passivity" or "subjection" of the ethically elected self which Levinas describes as "more passive than all receptivity." Levinas's Jewishness would be found, secondly, in his defense of the independence of moral judgment from history, which independence also allows, indeed obligates, the moral agent to render judgment upon history. Against the grain of much contemporary thought, for Levinas morality judges history and not the other way around. In Rosenzweig's vocabulary this would be the *eternality* of the Jewish people, their position outside history, as the community toward which history is driving, and at the same time as the community living in a humble righteousness sufficient to guarantee the rectitude of the moral judgments which currently drive history.[10] The exteriority of ethics, of the alterity constitutive of ethics, is for Levinas precisely the capacity, exceeding all the capacities of the autonomous subject, to judge history.

But Levinas's thought is also, from Rosenzweig's perspective, Christian, centrifugal as well as centripetal, a loving of others inspired by being loved, a global mission as well as an eternal example. Indeed, for Levinas, who nowhere expresses Rosenzweig's exclusionary commitments, these two moments are inseparable. Irreplaceable election of the self and responsiveness to the incomparable alterity of the other person are two aspects of the same ethics. To be good one must respond to the other, which also means responding to those who are other to the other. Hence to be good to the immediate other, the one who faces, ultimately requires justice for all, for all humankind. For Levinas, who reserves the language of "love" for the specifically erotic encounter, both of these dimensions, goodness to the other who faces and justice for all humankind, are structured by a dual transcendence: a breaking into the self by the other, and

---

10. On the Jews as the goal and driving force of history, it is likely that Rosenzweig was influenced by Nachman Krochmal's Jewish reworking of Hegel. See chapter 1, note 11.

a breaking out of the self toward the other.[11] Rosenzweig finds this dual excess in historically established traditions of love: being loved and loving in turn enacted in the Jewish and Christian communities respectively.

Looked at through Rosenzweig's lens we can grasp how and why Levinas avoids conceiving ethics in a way that is merely Jewish, for Jews only, or merely Christian, while at the same time we can see how his ethics may justifiably be situated within the "exclusiveness" of Rosenzweig's Jewish *and* Christian framework. For Rosenzweig, Jews have a universal message, but one which can only be grasped by seeing the Jewish community as an exemplary ethical and religious community, the end lived by Jews today in the meantime toward which all history drives, and is driven by Christians. In this context we can say that Levinas's thought is Jewish and Christian at once, exemplary and missionary, the former called "ethics," the immediacy of the face-to-face, and the latter called "justice," the ultimacy of spreading goodness to all humankind. To think along with Levinas, then, even when his vocabulary is Jewish and Christian (as it so often is), is to join in the genuine tasks—ethics, justice, holiness—of all humanity. Levinas notes, citing the rabbis, that wherever in the sacred writings one finds the term "Israel," one can always substitute "humanity."

Levinas does not thereby reduce Judaism to what is universal in an abstract sense, according to the standards of classical philosophy, as did so many nineteenth and twentieth-century liberal reformers of Judaism. Rather, he shows that what is most Jewish about Judaism, precisely and only when it is grasped within an irreducibly moral and religious context, is *at the same time* capable of teaching universal lessons for all humanity, capable of accomplishing that which is "the finest portion of man." Levinas's ethical thought demands both "fire" and "rays," to use Rosenzweig's terms, both example and mission, judging history and creating it at the same time.

Heidegger as Pagan

It is Hans Jonas who has, to my mind, shown "the profoundly pagan character of Heidegger's thought."[12]

11. In "Toward the Other," one of his annual "talmudic readings" (1963), Levinas distinguishes two dimensions within Jewish ethical life: "social morality" and "ritual practices" (*NTR* 16), but insists that both are necessary each for the other, the former emphasizing loving and the latter being-loved, to use Rosenzweig's terms.

12. "Heidegger and Theology," in Hans Jonas, *The Phenomenon of Life: Toward a Philosophical Biology* (New York, Dell, 1966), 235–61, at 248. This essay is the written version of Jonas's talk given at a colloquium on hermeneutics held at Drew University on April 9–11, 1964. Heidegger was meant to attend in person, but in fact was unable to do so. He sent his paper in a letter of March 11, 1964. It has been published under the title "The

Christians, he argues, should not embrace Heidegger, as does Richardson, but should rather be on their greatest guard against him, precisely because Heidegger's thinking represents yet another, indeed a most subtle form of the very paganism that Christianity is forever enjoined to struggle against. Rosenzweig is nowhere mentioned in this debate, but given Jonas's educational background and interests there is little reason to doubt that he was more or less familiar with the *Star*. Regardless, however, of whether Jonas knew Rosenzweig's work or not, his argument regarding Heidegger's paganism serves to support a Rosenzweigian reading of Heidegger as pagan.

Jonas's argument hinges on showing the insurmountable immanence, the rejection of genuine transcendence, which follows from Heidegger's questioning of be-ing, despite its deliberate and deliberative attempt to reorient thinking—the famous "turn"—away from philosophical construction. Moving from the calculus of beings within-the-world to thinking the very being of the world, thinking being-in-the-world as such, is nonetheless to remain within the confines of an inescapably worldly thinking. Jonas writes: "The being whose fate Heidegger ponders, is the quintessence of this world, it is *saeculum*. Against this, theology should guard the radical transcendence of its God, whose voice comes not out of being

---

Theological Discussion of 'The Problem of a Non-Objectifying Thinking and Speaking in Today's Theology'—Some Pointers to its Major Aspects," in Martin Heidegger, *The Piety of Thinking: Essays by Martin Heidegger,* edited and translated by James G. Hart and John C. Maraldo (Bloomington: Indiana University Press, 1976), 22–31. Jonas's paper, the opening address of the colloquium, was a direct response to Heidegger's letter, which was first publicly read. William J. Richardson's response to Jonas's paper, and his defense of a Christian reading of Heidegger, was given as a talk that same April, on the 27th, as the annual Suarez Lecture at Fordham University in New York. It was published under the title, "Heidegger and God—and Professor Jonas," in *Thought: Fordham University Quarterly* 40 (Spring 1965): 13–40. At the conclusion of his rebuttal (39), Richardson invokes a "gentleman"—there is no doubt that it is Emmanuel Levinas, though his name is not mentioned—who at a reception in 1962 reminded Richardson that Heidegger's "prolific year" of 1943, as Richardson had called it in his Heidegger book, was also the year that that person had been in a Jewish prisoner-of-war camp. Someone else "with the same experience," Richardson tells us, later asked him: "What can you hope for as a Christian from the thought of that God-less man?" (39). The following is Richardson's reply: "Because there is truth in Heidegger and wherever there is truth there is God" (40). He explains, in the concluding paragraphs of his article, that whether Heidegger recognizes it or not, in the opening or clearing where Heidegger awaits language "the voice of a radically transcendent God can at least make itself heard." But it is precisely this that Jonas, and Levinas, dispute about the Heideggerian topos. Precisely in the Heideggerian clearing, they argue, one will not and cannot, in principle, hear "the voice of a radically transcendent God." For that, one must rise to the higher call of the other person, beyond being.

I cannot recommend too highly that one read first Heidegger's paper, then Jonas's, then Richardson's. It is one of the more remarkable dialogues of our time.

but breaks into the kingdom of being from without."[13] The transcendence of the world, thought to its most extreme horizons in language, falls short of the transcendence of G-d.[14]

In criticizing Heidegger, Jonas grasps quite well what it is that tempts his Christian readers. Beyond Heidegger's early and almost Christian fascination with being-toward-death, conscience, and resolution in *Being and Time*, there lies the even greater seductiveness of the later Heidegger's "turn" away from subjectivism, willfulness, construction. The call to turn away from willfulness to a listening, hearkening, attunement to what is given to humans to think by language, seems very much like the Christian critique of pride and the concomitant Christian notion of divine grace, albeit couched in poetic language. But Jonas breaks the spell of this illusion by insisting upon a greater specificity: one must ask not only for a turning from the will to a receptivity, a giving, but for a *receptivity to G-d* and a *giving by G-d*. Heideggerian attentiveness listens, to be sure, but it listens to the silent voice of epochal being. Greek pagans read entrails and listened attentively to their oracles. The alleged generosity of being, however, is in no way equivalent to G-d's grace. To conflate the two, reducing G-d's grace to being's giving, is precisely the error into which Jonas sees Richardson falling. It is precisely the error Jonas attacks as a serious short-changing of a genuinely Christian conception of G-d, of G-d's relation to Christians, of Christians' relation to G-d, and hence of Christianity altogether.

What is "so seductive to Christian theologians," Jonas understands, is what he calls "the seeming, false humility of Heidegger's shifting the initiative to Being." Despite this turn, which is indeed the most characteristic move in Heidegger's later thought, Jonas sees that beyond an alleged humility before being lies "the most enormous hubris in the whole history of thought." Heideggerian humility is not that of the soul beloved by G-d, the soul called to serve G-d through service to his fellow creatures, as demanded by Christianity and Judaism, but rather an intoxication or self-obliteration before the oracle, an effacement careful to catch the most distant signals not of what *should* be but of what *is*, hence of what must be. Jonas fearlessly scourges Heidegger for a dangerous immoralism, an immoralism which, its tremendous danger notwithstanding, most twentieth-century continental philosophers influenced by Heidegger refused to even acknowledge until Victor Farias published his book, *Hei-*

13. Jonas, *Phenomenon of Life*, 248. Jean-Luc Marion, in France, has pursued this path.

14. Merleau-Ponty would thus reveal the Heideggerian influence on his thought when he writes that Christian ontology "arrives by an unavoidable dialectic at an anthropology and not a theology." Maurice Merleau-Ponty, *Sense and Non-Sense*, trans. Hubert Dreyfus and Patricia Dreyfus (Evanston: Northwestern University Press, 1964), 76.

degger and Nazism,[15] more than two decades after Jonas's talk at Drew University and the publication of his article, not to mention more than half a century after Heidegger first joined the Nazi party. Of Heidegger's promulgation of "the most enormous hubris in the whole history of thought," Jonas has the following to say:

For it is nothing less than the thinker's claiming that through him speaks the essence of things itself, and thus the claim to an authority which no thinker should ever claim. And moreover it is the claim that in principle the basic human condition, that of being at a distance to things . . . can be remitted, avoided, overcome. The claim, that is, to a possible immediacy that perhaps has a place in the person-to-person relation, but not in the relation to impersonal being and things and the world. . . .

Man: the shepherd of being—not, mind you, of beings! Apart from the blasphemous ring which this use of the hallowed title must have to Jewish and Christian ears: it is hard to hear man hailed as the shepherd of being when he has just so dismally failed to be his brother's keeper. The latter he is meant to be in the Bible. But the terrible anonymity of Heidegger's "being," illicitly decked out with personal characters, blocks out the personal call. Not by the being of another person am I grasped, but just by "being"! And my responsive thought is being's own event. But called as person by person—fellow beings or God—my response will not primarily be thinking but action (though this involves thinking), and the action may be one of love, responsibility, pity; also of wrath, indignation, hate, even fight to the death. . . . Such calls are drowned in the voice of being to which one cannot say No.[16]

These remarkable sentences pronounced in 1964 bring to mind the fundamental arguments and orientations of both Rosenzweig and Levinas, in critical opposition to what the former calls "pagan" and the latter calls "ontology" and "Heidegger." We should note that in contrast to Rosenzweig and Levinas, Jonas argues against Heidegger for the sake of the objectivity of science. Nevertheless, his incisive criticisms succeed, I think, in showing what it means to say, as Rosenzweig would say, that Heidegger's language-thinking is pagan.

The pagan hubris, what Levinas criticizes as the reductiveness of Heideggerian language-thinking, is its magisterial insistence that being or language counts more than beings, even when those "beings" are human beings. Jonas's challenge to Heidegger's resolute insistence that the *Seinsfrage* is the *only* question worthy of thought, that mortal perseverance in the rift (the metaphorical "pain") of language's disclosure is more mean-

---

15. Victor Farias, *Heidegger and Nazism.* See chapter 2, note 2; and chapter 14, note 22.

16. Jonas, *Phenomenon of Life,* 257–58.

ingful and takes priority over the moral demands of others, is a criticism which could be taken from the pages of either Rosenzweig or Levinas.

The enormous individual and social effort that Levinas names "sacred history" and Rosenzweig "redemption" is precisely the long and hard—and glorious—struggle against the persistent medusian hubris of paganism, a struggle against the totalitarianism of both its crude and its subtle forms, both in its social-political and individual manifestations. About the difficulty of this struggle, Rosenzweig and Levinas harbor no illusions or wishful optimism. The force of ontology, the *conatus* of being, is the natural and perennial opponent of the force of morality. This explains the *valuative force,* the opprobrium, in Rosenzweig's term "pagan." Here lies the power of his religious-philosophical "gate." Rosenzweig's concluding "INTO LIFE" is a beginning. It is at once a teaching, a warning, a challenge, and a watchword. Paganism, he well understands "will live on to the eternal end in its eternal gods, the state and art, the former the idol of the realists, the latter that of the individualists; but these gods are there put in chains by the true God" (*SR* 421).

The gateway out of the *Star* consists, then, of the obligations and responsibilities of a "religious" ethics. What is religious about this ethics is not only its basis in love, but its concrete existence in communal life, the specificity of social obligations and responsibilities, developed across living traditions, appearing not in ideas but in what we have seen both Rosenzweig and Levinas call the "face." Only through this gate, in social life, loving mercy, doing justice, can Jew and Christian "walk humbly with" God—one-for-the-other, G-d and humans for each other and for all others, torn inside-out, besides oneself, outside of one's own skin, in a suffering exposed to and for the other: higher than being. And, let us add, not only Jew and Christian.

FOURTEEN

Derrida's (Mal)reading of Levinas

This chapter focuses on Jacques Derrida's 1964 essay on Emmanuel Levinas, entitled "Violence and Metaphysics: An Essay on the Thought of Emmanuel Levinas." Derrida's essay is divided into three parts: a nine page introduction on Levinas and the question of philosophy and nonphilosophy; a ninety-nine page body presenting detailed "deconstructive" analyses of Levinas's writings up to 1964; and a five page conclusion which returns to the topic of the introduction, Levinas and the question of philosophy and nonphilosophy.[1] In this chapter I will take up Derrida's introduction and conclusion, that is to say, I will pass over the details of Derrida's ninety-nine page deconstruction[2] and attend to his contextual-

---

1. The page lengths refer to the original French version of 1964.

2. What Derrida does in the main body of his essay is twofold. He explicates Levinas, pointing out precisely how his thought intends to exceed ontology by means of the alterity of an intersubjective ethics. Second, he subverts, undermines, "deconstructs," the univocal signification and hence the univocal significance of Levinas's ethics.

Derrida's exposition and subversion of Levinas's writings are at one with his usual misreadings. The "criticisms" are various and do not add up to a systematic or even a coherent philosophical alternative. For Derrida this is not a failing, however, and not only because no one can question the right or legitimacy of criticisms which do not offer alternatives. When Derrida accuses Levinas of falling into negative theology, for example, it is by no means because Derrida intends to propose an alternative positive theology, or a systematic rejection of all theology, for that matter. Rather it is only to show that Levinas is not accomplishing what he thinks he is accomplishing. The same is true of Derrida's accusation that Levinas has misread Husserl. Rhetoric notwithstanding, Derrida does not propose a true reading of Husserl, as J. Claude Evans, in *Strategies of Deconstruction: Derrida and the Myth of the Voice*, has so patiently and brilliantly shown with Derrida's earlier (mis)readings of Husserl in *Speech and Phenomena* and *Of Grammatology* (cf. chapter 6, note 15). Again, it is only to show that Levinas is not accomplishing what he thinks he is accomplishing, and to show this by undermining the univocity of Levinas's significations.

By showing that Levinas's allegedly univocal exceeding of ontology in ethics in each and every instance must be interpreted equally as a linguistic rather than an ethical excess, a linguistic excess based on an anonymous and differential rather than a personal and referential interpretation of the interrelation between sign, signifying, and signified, Derrida undermines the significance or *force* that makes Levinas's interpretation an ethical one.

For Derrida univocity is always a mask, because "equivocality is original and irreducible" (*VM* 113). It is not the case, then, that against Levinas Derrida has an argument or a refutation in the traditional sense. Rather, what Derrida does is what he does, with all the keen sensitivity of his cultivated and incisive intelligence, against all his adversaries: uncover and release alternative meanings which lie hidden in an author's words and sentences, meanings whose open-endedness would otherwise be covered over by the coherence of the au-

ization of Levinas's thought within the question of the difference between philosophy and nonphilosophy.

I will begin by briefly reviewing Derrida's conception of philosophy, with an eye to both its incompatibility with Levinas's thought and its bond to Heideggerian thinking. It is difficult to doubt that Derrida has these two relations in mind as well. Derrida begins by reminding us that

---

thor's intentions or by a text's ostensive integrity. Derrida's reading is always a pluralizing one. One never makes sense of nonsense, for Derrida, because "nonsense" is already a sense, a "text," already and essentially in touch with sense as part of the sense of sense—"there is no immaculate perception." While both Levinas and Derrida are "postmodern" in the sense that their thought does not ultimately rest or rely on a rational foundation, or on the foundational demands of rationality, the salient difference separating them can be summed up as follows: whereas Levinas's words are intended to invoke and increase *responsibility,* Derrida's are intended to elicit and increase the *play* of meaning, or, more precisely, the *undecideability* between responsible and playful meaning, which in effect, in the effect it has on responsibility, amounts to the same thing as play.

Levinas and Derrida thus seem caught up in an endless dialogue or an endless game of leap frog, again depending on from whose side one sees and names their altercation. Three years after the publication of Levinas's first major book in 1961, his call to ethics in *TI,* in 1964 Derrida published the essay we are now considering, where for ninety-nine pages he makes play of Levinas's words. Nine years later, in 1973, in a short article on Derrida entitled "Wholly Otherwise" (translated by Simon Critchley, in *Re-Reading Levinas,* 3–10), then a year later, in 1974, in his second major book, *OBBE,* Levinas takes Derrida's words and enterprise seriously, responsibly. Six years later, in 1980, it is Derrida's turn. In an article entitled "At This Very Moment in This Work Here I Am" (translated by Ruben Berezdivin, in *Re-Reading Levinas,* 11–48), Derrida again makes play of Levinas, of precisely his most serious formulations. These exchanges are only the highlights. There are many intervening conversations on a smaller scale.

The entire conversation between Derrida and Levinas is, furthermore, and importantly, an extension of the earlier debate between Levinas and Heidegger, with Derrida taking up Heidegger's part. This link is important because Derrida's characterization of philosophy as a questioning (a determination central to the introduction and conclusion of his Levinas essay, see especially 80–82, and hence a determination central to the issues addressed by this chapter), is profoundly and unmistakably Heideggerian, as Derrida explicitly and repeatedly acknowledges. Jürgen Habermas says the following of their relationship, calling Derrida an "orthodox Heideggerian": "Derrida does not want to think theologically; as an orthodox Heideggerian, he is forbidden any thought about a supreme entity. Instead, similarly to Heidegger, Derrida sees the modern condition as constituted by phenomena of deprival that are not comprehensible within the horizon of the history of reason and of divine revelation. As he assures us at the start of his essay on 'differance,' he does not want to do any theology, not even negative theology" ("Beyond a Temporalized Philosophy of Origins: Jacques Derrida's Critique of Phonocentrism," in *The Philosophical Discourse of Modernity: Twelve Lectures,* translated by Frederick G. Lawrence [Cambridge, Mass.: MIT Press, 1987], 165).

Because this link is so clear (though one can certainly debate its precise character), I will spend little time developing it, except to occasionally introduce Heidegger's name along with Derrida's. It is a link that must be kept in mind, nonetheless, to gather the fuller import of my exposition and contextualization of the Levinas-Derrida conflict.

philosophy is said to have died, but also that the death of philosophy is today the topic that gives it life. That philosophy is now in question, and more, that philosophy proceeds as a self-questioning, a questioning without answer, a radical questioning, is for Derrida not merely another sign of the contemporary crisis of philosophy, but rather, and more deeply, the perennial form of philosophy itself, its purest possibility.

On the basis of this conception of philosophy Derrida is able to distinguish philosophy's various historical manifestations, or answers, from its pure form as questioning. He is able to distinguish, in other words, all the philosophies proposed in the history of philosophy from the pure form of philosophy itself. It is a matter of distinguishing, though not separating, the pure form and possibility of philosophy, i.e., open-ended questioning, from various historical and finite manifestations of that form, i.e., answers, closures.

Derrida's distinction between philosophy and nonphilosophy clearly mimics Heidegger's distinction between thinking being and calculating beings, the distinction between authentic being-in and inauthentic being-within. What can be called Derrida's "philosophical difference" is a variation on, and extension of, Heidegger's "ontological difference." The difference is only that Derrida begins and holds unremittingly to the register of language, a hold and a resolution which came to Heidegger at the end rather than from the start of his intellectual career. For Derrida the key to understanding the true nature of philosophy is to grasp "the difference between the question in general and 'philosophy' as a determined—finite and mortal—moment or mode of the question itself" (*VM* 81), "the difference between philosophy as a power and adventure *of* the question itself and philosophy as a determined event or turning point *within* this adventure" (*VM* 81).

By the opening that is philosophy, then, Derrida means the *nondetermination* of questioning, precisely the "freedom" Heidegger discovered in the essence of truth.[3] What is obvious from the start of Derrida's essay is that Levinas's ethical thought, oriented as it is by the extraordinary alterity of the other person, is already too determined, too "finite and mortal," to be counted as genuine philosophy. It seems that for Derrida too, following Heidegger, Levinas is not properly or sufficiently attuned to the gentle rustling of language. Making his differences from Levinas as stark as possible, Derrida lays out three specifications, or as he prefers to call them, "three motifs" (*VM* 82), that constitute philosophy as question-

---

3. See Martin Heidegger, "On the Essence of Truth," translated by R. F. C. Hull and Alan Crick, in Martin Heidegger, *Existence and Being* (Chicago: Henry Regnery Company, 1970), 292–323; especially section 4, "The Essential Nature of Freedom," 305–10.

ing. The link to Heidegger is too obvious to belabor. They are as follows: (1) "the founding concepts of philosophy are primarily Greek and it would not be possible to philosophize, or to speak philosophically, outside this medium" (*VM* 81); (2) philosophy "entails . . . a subordination or transgression, in any event a *reduction of metaphysics*" (*VM* 81); and (3) "the category of the *ethical* is not only dissociated from metaphysics but coordinated with something other than itself, a previous and more radical function" (*VM* 81).[4] So, to paraphrase Derrida's three point specification of philosophy: it is questioning, in the Greek manner, which entails a reduction of metaphysics, and the displacement and recontextualization of ethics.

Of course, the contrast between philosophy and nonphilosophy turns out to be nothing less than the contrast between Derrida's (and Heidegger's) thought and Levinas's. Following his three specifications of genuine philosophy, Derrida presents Levinas's thought in point by point contrast (see *VM* 82–83). To paraphrase, for Derrida, Levinas's thought is an ethical metaphysics[5] within but deeper than Greek philosophy. Though here Derrida introduces the expression "prophetic speech" (which may still be a Greek term), and speaks of the "messianic eschatology from which Levinas draws inspiration" (*VM* 83), and has, furthermore, placed at the head of his essay an epigram by Matthew Arnold distinguishing "Hebraism and Hellenism," at this stage of his inquiry he assures his readers that "in the last analysis [Levinas's thought] never bases its authority on Hebraic theses or texts" (*VM* 83).[6]

4. In *BT* it is clear that for Heidegger all morality is ontic, not ontological. The following passage is representative:

"Not only can entities whose Being is care load themselves with factical guilt, but they *are* guilty in the very basis of their Being; and this Being-guilty is what provides, above all, the ontological condition for Dasein's ability to come to owe anything in factically existing. This essential Being-guilty is, equiprimordially, the existential condition for the possibility of the 'morally' good and for that of the 'morally' evil—that is, for morality in general and for the possible forms which this may take factically. The primordial 'Being-guilty' cannot be defined by morality, since morality already presupposes it for itself" (332).

This is the reason Heidegger insists that his distinction between "authentic" (*eigentlich*) and "inauthentic" (*uneigentlich*) *Dasein* must *not* in any way be understood as a moral discrimination or evaluation. This, too, is why Dasein's "fall" (*Verfallen*) is not a moral category. It is an ontological characteristic of *Dasein* to fall.

5. Levinas studies are indebted to Edith Wyschogrod for this expression.

6. Derrida writes: "If the messianic eschatology from which Levinas draws inspiration seeks neither to assimilate itself into what is called a philosophical truism, nor even to 'complete' (*TI* 22) philosophical truisms, nevertheless, it is developed in its discourse neither as a theology, nor as a Jewish mysticism (it can even be understood as the trial of theology and mysticism); neither as a dogmatics, nor as *a* religion, nor as *a* morality. In the last analysis it never bases its authority on Hebraic theses or texts."

The "authority" for Levinas's thought comes not from "Hebraic theses or texts," but rather, as Derrida writes in the very next sentence, from an appeal to experience: "It seeks to be understood from within a *recourse to experience itself*" (*VM* 83). Of course, the term "experience" has had a long history in Western thought. Because of its all too many uses, its meaning "eludes definition," according to Nietzsche.[7] In the phenomenological movement alone, of which Levinas is a student, "experience" *(Urfahrung)* is precisely a central term over whose meaning and significance the major phenomenologists (certainly Husserl, Heidegger, Sartre, Merleau-Ponty, and Levinas) disagree and part company. Thus Derrida has told us precious little in revealing that the authority for Levinas's thought is "recourse to experience itself." Despite its indeterminacy, however, anchoring Levinas's thought in experience functions for Derrida as follows: it gives Levinas's thought sufficient *philosophical* legitimacy, however provisional, to justify Derrida's extensive and close inquiry.

Levinas's thought cannot be ruled out of philosophy a priori, despite what one senses to be the inevitability of this result given Derrida's three Heideggerian characterizations of philosophy, because its authority is not based on such obviously philosophically illegitimate grounds as divine revelation, sacred texts, or the transmissions of religious tradition. Because a thought based on experience has, at least provisionally and in contrast to alternative obviously illegitimate bases, some credibility, if only as a candidate petitioning for philosophical status, then it must be questioned, as Derrida will question it. Derrida's strategy for reading Levinas now becomes clear: showing that a thought based on experience, even when experience is taken in the strong sense in which Derrida knows Levinas takes it, namely, as "the passage and departure toward the other" person (*VM* 83), falls into the morass typical of all *empiricism:* the attempt to conceive exteriority. As such it is unfree, bogged down by the problems its own limitations, acknowledged and unacknowledged, generate; it is nonphilosophy.

For all the multiple readings, the "questions" (*VM* 84) and "perplexity" (*VM* 84), that Derrida manages in the ninety-nine page body of his essay to tease out of Levinas's writings, one result is certain by the essay's conclusion. Derrida's ultimate response to Levinas is ostracism, exile, exclusion, excision from what Derrida calls "the community, within the world, of those who are still called philosophers" (*VM* 79), the rarified community of those who still engage in philosophy as the most questionable question of all, "the dialogue of the question about itself and with

7. Friedrich Nietzsche, *On the Genealogy of Morals,* Essay II, section 13 (Kaufmann translation).

itself" (*VM* 80). Levinas, in contrast, has been caught dreaming the impossible dream of walking the forever blocked path Parmenides warned about, the path beyond the questionableness of philosophy into what can neither be nor be thought, even if Levinas gives it the name "otherwise than being or beyond essence."

But Derrida does not side with philosophy against Levinas. He merely uses it. On the concluding pages of his long essay, Derrida reiterates what is by now the most famous and characteristically Derridaian gesture, a gesture with which the introduction had earlier ended—undecidability. Having set philosophy against Levinas's thought, which the reader now understands is but an "empiricism" which must forever be excluded, as nonphilosophy, from "the community of the question about the possibility of the question" (*VM* 80), Derrida puts both philosophy and nonphilosophy, therefore Levinas's thought and genuine philosophy, into a new and now essentially unresolvable tension, a tension which, according to Derrida's own words, "is perhaps the unity of what is called history" (*VM* 153).

At the end of his introduction, Derrida left off embracing the somewhat startling and stark consequences of what he takes to be the correct posture, undecidability, toward the conflicting claims of philosophy and nonphilosophy. He refused to choose, thereby, between the opening or questioning which is philosophy and the totality or closure which is nonphilosophy or "empiricism." He wrote: "We will not choose between the opening and the totality. Therefore we will be incoherent, but without systematically resigning ourselves to incoherence. The possibility of the impossible system will be on the horizon to protect us from empiricism" (*VM* 84). Now, at the end of the penultimate paragraph of the conclusion, Derrida explicitly utilizes the language of the Athens-Jerusalem question, and strikes a very Straussian note with regard to it, and a Levinasian note too, to invoke the same undecidability. He writes:

Are we Jews? Are we Greeks? We live in the difference between the Jew and the Greek, which is perhaps the unity of what is called history. We live in and of difference, that is, in *hypocrisy,* about which Levinas so profoundly says that it is "not only a base contingent defect of man, but the underlying rending of a world attached to both the philosophers and the prophets." (*VM* 153)

Notice the shift. For strategic reasons, it seems, Derrida had to begin his essay with the question of the philosophical status of Levinas's thought, where its nonphilosophical character was called "empiricism," a term, apparently, with just enough philosophical dignity to make Derrida's question a fair one by lending its object a sufficient if provisional legitimacy. By the end of the essay, however, Levinas has been run over the racks of deconstruction, exposed as a marrano, first by having his alleged philosophy reduced to an "empiricism," shot through with all the unacceptable faults and failings of empiricism, and then, his philosophical mask torn, exposed as a Jew cloaked in a Greek tunic, but an ill-fitting one as Derrida has shown. No longer is the issue one of philosophy and empiricism, or philosophy and the pretense to philosophy, but rather it has become one of "philosophers" and "prophets." Here, too, Derrida will take a stance of undecidability.

But in this concluding (unscientific) undecidability Derrida now seems to be saying that the separation of philosophy from its other was all along *Levinas's* insight, encapsulated in the word "hypocrisy," a term and an opposition which Derrida is here taking from the Preface to *Totality and Infinity*. The confession has been extracted and now it is signed. Earlier, however, in the introduction, Derrida had already protected himself, had already protected the questionableness of questioning, even from Levinas's notion of "hypocrisy." Derrida wrote of the questionableness of questioning: "A community of the question, therefore, within that fragile moment when the question is not yet determined enough for the hypocrisy of an answer to have already initiated itself beneath the mask of the question, and not yet determined enough for its voice to have been already and fraudulently articulated within the very syntax of the question" (*VM* 80). Derrida's stance of undecidability, therefore, even when it invokes Levinas's notion of hypocrisy, distances itself from Levinas, maintains itself in "that fragile moment" of indetermination, which is, as we shall see, still a Greek moment, in contrast to Levinas's thought, which though admittedly a "hypocrisy" and hence ostensively in some manner both Greek and Jew, is not *fragile* enough for Derrida. It is Levinas's fault, according to Derrida, to have "already" given an "answer," to have overdetermined and thus ended genuine questioning "fraudulently," even if the failing has been perpetrated by something as slight as the "syntax of the question."

But Derrida grants a productive relation between philosophy and propheticism, between Levinas's thought and the questioning that is philosophy. The relevant passage from the conclusion has been cited just above. For Derrida, it is prophetic thought, beyond the bounds of philosophy, but precisely because it is beyond the bounds of philosophy, as nonphilosophy, that is the very provocation *of philosophy,* in a provocation which is at the same time "the unity of what is called history." Let me suggest, in a preliminary fashion, that when Derrida says that "we live in the difference between the Jew and the Greek, which is perhaps the unity of what is called history," this conjunction of unity and difference, history, is for Derrida neither philosophy nor propheticism.

Despite his grand concluding gesture of all-embracing recognition, about which Derrida invokes Levinas's term "hypocrisy," we must be careful to remember that Derrida is not concluding with a synthesis. His is not a "both/and" but an "either/or"; or, one would be closer to Derrida to say that it is neither a "both/and" nor an "either/or." As Derrida has structured this large issue, one stands either on the side of philosophy or on the side of philosophy's other, in this case what Derrida is calling "prophecy," of which Levinas's thought is the outstanding instance. However Derrida locates himself in relation to it, and however one adjudicates it, the dichotomy between philosophy and religion is an old one. Levinas clearly does stand on the side of prophecy; he makes philosophy the handmaiden of religion, albeit in his "postmodern" sense of religion.[8] As we saw in chapter 8, the objectivity and universalism of philosophy are necessary for justice, which is itself required by the moral exigencies released by an ethics exceeding ontology. Consequently, in this way ontology is subordinate to religion. Derrida, on the other hand, despite or rather *because* of his (un)principled decision not to choose, has made religion the handmaiden if not of philosophy then of a second fundamental dimension of Greece, the *aesthetic,* by which I mean not merely what this term has come to mean in modernity, essentially judgments of taste, but rather the entire realm of sensibility and imagination, inclusive of pagan mythos and athletics,[9] but perhaps best summed up in the word *poesis.*

To make sense of Derrida's avowed "incoherence" (*VM* 84), and of the manner in which it stands outside of and against both the closure of philosophy (Hegel) and the transcendence of prophecy (Levinas), yet within Greece, it is time to turn to Derrida's relation to Hegel, to turn, that is, to the final paragraph of Derrida's long essay on Levinas.

Derrida's concluding paragraph has been much cited in the secondary literature. Derrida writes:

8. In *TI,* in the second subsection of part A of section 1, entitled "The Breach of Totality," Levinas defines religion as follows: "We propose to call 'religion' the bond that is established between the same and the other without constituting a totality" (40).

Although Derrida mentions Levinas's indebtedness to Rosenzweig, citing the famous sentence from the Preface to *TI* (28), there is no indication in any of his writings, as far as I know, that Derrida takes into account Rosenzweig's critique of the Hegelian conception of religion comprehended by philosophy. On the first pages of the *Star* Rosenzweig succinctly traces the conflict between knowledge and belief and the Hegelian conceptual resolution that Rosenzweig's entire work positively contests. See *SR* 6–7.

9. It is too often forgotten that the ancient Greek Olympics were one of the most enduring of all human institutions, lasting approximately one thousand years and involving the entire Greek world.

Are we Greeks? Are we Jews? But who, we? Are we . . . *first* Jews or *first* Greeks? And does the strange dialogue between the Jew and the Greek, peace itself, have the form of the absolute, speculative logic of Hegel, the living logic which *reconciles* formal tautology and empirical heterology after having *thought* prophetic discourse in the preface to the *Phenomenology of Mind*? Or, on the contrary, does this peace have the form of infinite separation and of the unthinkable, unsayable transcendence of the other? To what horizon of peace does the language which asks this question belong? From whence does it draw the energy of its question? Can it account for the historical *coupling* of Judaism and Hellenism? And what is the legitimacy, what is the meaning of the *copula* in this proposition from perhaps the most Hegelian of modern novelists: "Jewgreek is greekjew. Extremes meet"? (*VM* 153)

These unanswered questions are certainly prime examples of Derrida's conception of philosophy as questioning.

In the fundamental and irreconcilable opposition between totality and opening, by "totality" Derrida means "the absolute, speculate logic of Hegel, the living logic which *reconciles* formal tautology and empirical heterology," which Derrida sees as the ultimate *philosophical* way of understanding the form of the Jew-Greek relation, in contrast to "opening," which means the prophetic way of grasping it, in "the form of infinite separation and of the unthinkable, unsayable transcendence of the other." To buttress his contention that transcendence must be thought *within* totality, Derrida appends a footnote containing a long quotation, taken from Hegel's *Science of Logic,* about "Absolute Difference," that is, difference as internal difference rather than a difference from something somehow (impossibly) irreducibly other. I will only cite a part of it: "difference in itself is difference in relation to itself; thus it is its own negativity, difference not in relation to an *other,* but in relation to itself" (*VM* 320).

Thus absolute difference, difference-in-itself, simple difference, what I will henceforth call "internal difference," is different from, superior to, more comprehensive than, what Hegel calls "pure difference," where the other remains other, which I will call "external difference." For the former, internal difference, the exteriority of different terms is an inner difference, a family quarrel as it were. For the latter, external difference, the exteriority of different terms reflects an unresolvable hiatus or disturbance. Of this distinction between "simple" or internal difference and "pure" or external difference, and Hegel's defense of the former over the latter, Derrida makes the following very interesting comment: "Hegel's critique of the concept of pure difference is for us here [in the Levinas essay], doubtless, the most uncircumventable theme" (*VM* 320). In other words, to undermine Levinas Derrida *adheres to* Hegel's conceptual lead, "Hegel's critique of the concept of pure difference," by showing how Levinas's notion of absolute alterity, despite the philosophical pretension it shares with all empiricist reflection, is actually caught up within the inescapable network of internal difference. "Pure difference," Derrida says in his own voice, "is not absolutely different" (*VM* 320).

But does not Derrida, at the same time, also maintain that Levinas's infinite, *as* external difference, does manage to somehow stand in fundamental opposition to Hegel's absolute, Jew against Greek? That is to say, has he not posed Levinas's infinite ethical difference as a genuine way to characterize the hiatus between Greek and Jew and Jew and Greek, in contrast to Hegel's absolute conceptual difference (= identification), as the other way to characterize and maintain difference? Whether the contrast be straightforward, Jew versus Greek and Greek versus Jew, or put onto a metalevel, the contrast nonetheless remains for Derrida unreconciled and irreconcilable, and like an antinomy, inevitable.

The point is that Derrida's "We will not choose between the opening and the totality" is, if not exactly on the side of totality, Hegel, and the closure of philosophy, because it denies the finality of synthesis, neither is it on the side of infinity. Not only is it not on the side of totality or infinity, it is *against* totality and infinity. That Derrida is against the closure of philosophy is perfectly clear. That he is against Levinas, however, is not as clear. To see why he is against Levinas is to see the reasons why Derrida's essay has been read, and rightfully, I think, as a polemic against Levinas rather than as a neutral or harmless "deconstruction" of him.[10]

For Levinas, ethics is a responsibility, a being held "hostage" by and for the other. While such is not an ethics based on choice, since "no one is good voluntarily," and the other's alterity disrupts the self prior to the self's intentions and abilities, it nonetheless hollows out a moral agency, a being for-the-other, a compression or fission of the self by and for the other's alterity, pressing the self into a "passivity more passive than all receptivity," into a service to the other, a responsibility for the other. Such a subjectivity does not merely or even *first* interpret the various possible significations of the other's cry for help—an endless task, as Derrida well shows—but rather, and rather immediately, *helps* the other.

Derrida's undecidability, his not choosing, his hovering between, his

10. Robert Bernasconi, among others, confirms this appraisal when he writes: "This is not the place to rehearse the argument as to whether 'Violence and Metaphysics' is a critique of Levinas or already a double reading. Whatever Derrida intended and however Levinas himself understood 'Violence and Metaphysics,' it was generally construed as a forceful critique . . ." ("Skepticism in the Face of Philosophy," in *Re-Reading Levinas*, 153). My intent is to explain why and with what good reason Derrida's essay has been construed as an attack on Levinas.

resolute indetermination, his agile logic of neither this or that nor not this and not that,[11] or various further permutations of what he calls "the liberty *of the question,*" his own *appreciation* of the equivocations of signification, is at the same time what Levinas would call *irresponsibility.* Derrida's neutrality on the Athens-Jerusalem question, which permits him in his own way to escape ontology, is nonetheless (and contrary to what non-Derridaians insist on calling Derrida's "intentions") not the absolute neutrality that it wants to appear to be on first, second, third, fourth . . . reading of it. It is not *morally* neutral. On this ultimate question, Athens or Jerusalem, philosophy or prophecy, reason or revelation, the true or the good, one must take sides, if not for one and against the other, then still for or against the latter, revelation, prophecy, the good. Derrida, by not taking sides, and thus avoiding the Greek *logos,* has precisely taken sides regarding morality. From the point of view of morality, the relation to the other has no other on a par with itself, which is to say, as Levinas has said, the good is not part of a dyad, it has no equal—which is precisely its goodness.

Though Derrida refers to the Hegel of the *Science of Logic,* there is an earlier work by Hegel that is in fact closer to the terms of Derrida's challenge to Levinas. This is Hegel's famous *Faith and Knowledge* essay, subtitled "The Kant-Jacobi-Fichte Philosophy," published in July 1802.[12] Here, in his polemic against the philosophical pretensions of Kant, Jacobi, and Fichte, we already find the basic thought of the Hegelian absolute (that true infinity is the identity of identity and difference) used to distinguish and critically contrast genuine philosophy, which at that time meant Hegel's and Shelling's absolute idealism, from what Hegel, like Derrida, calls "empiricism," which in this essay refers to the subjective idealisms of

11. One is tempted to compare Derrida's "logic" with that of the great second century C.E. Indian Buddhist thinker, Nagarjuna, or that of the Chinese Buddhist master, Chi-tsang (549–623), for whom the highest level of truth is to neither affirm nor deny both being *(yu)* and non-being *(wu).* For a fuller account of the latter's theory of truth, see Fung Yu-lan, *A History of Chinese Philosophy,* translated by Derk Bodde (Princeton: Princeton University Press, 1983), 2:293-99; and Garma C. C. Chang, *The Buddhist Teaching of Totality: The Philosophy of Hwa Yen Buddhism* (University Park: Pennsylvania State University Press, 1974), 107–10.

An important difference separating these thinkers from Derrida, however, is that for both Nagarjuna and Chi-tsang, unlike Derrida, the ultimate aim of such thought is a final and complete obliteration *(sunyata sunyata)* of every "affirmation," even the most fragile. Derrida, on the other hand, aims to multiply significations, not to transcend them.

12. G. W. F. Hegel, *Faith and Knowledge,* translated by Walter Cerf and H. S. Harris (Albany: State University of New York Press, 1977). For Friedrich Heinrich Jacobi's rejoinder, see his August 1802 letters to Friedrich Koppen, published as "On Faith and Knowledge," translated by Diana I. Behler, in *Philosophy of German Idealism,* edited by Ernst Behler (New York: Continuum, 1987), 142–57.

Kant, Jacobi, and Fichte. One already senses that the term "empiricism" in Hegel's hands, as in Derrida's, cuts a large swathe indeed.

What disturbs Hegel about Kant, Jacobi, and Fichte, and why he rules them out of genuine or absolute philosophy, is, as we can by now well imagine, that they attempt to maintain in their thinking a pure or external difference rather than a simple or internal difference. Hegel writes: "The fundamental principle common to the philosophies of Kant, Jacobi, and Fichte is, then, the absoluteness of finitude and, resulting from it, the absolute antithesis of finitude and infinity, reality and ideality, the sensuous and the supersensuous, and *the beyondness* [my italics] of what is truly real and absolute."[13] "Thus," Hegel continues in the next paragraph, "although these philosophies do battle with the empirical, they have remained directly within its sphere."[14] Kant, Jacobi and Fichte, in other words, do not reach the Hegelian idea, the idea in which "finite and infinite are one."[15] I think something important is revealed here about the alleged openness of philosophy, namely the narrowness of its openness, the narrowness of "essence," "being," the "thought of being," etc., such that Kant, Jacobi, and Fichte (philosophers one hardly thinks of as empiricists) can be ruled out of philosophy—as Derrida later rules out Levinas—in the name of their "empiricism" because they, like Levinas, have the audacity to recognize philosophy's limits, to recognize, that is, that philosophy, including the philosophical absolute, must stand in relation to an other irreducibly other.

For Hegel, true to form and in contrast to such ostensively "nonphilosophical" thinkers, the antithesis between finite and infinite understood as an external difference can and must be superseded by means of the higher *synthesis* of the absolute difference (or the absolute identity) of the idea, structured by internal difference, "which is philosophy's sole knowledge."[16] For Hegel, "the sole idea that has reality and true objectivity for philosophy, is the absolute suspendedness of the antithesis."[17] For Derrida, the antithesis between totality (internal difference) and opening (external difference) is understood as an external difference, but an external difference not to be superseded *à la* Hegel, or ethically interpreted *à la* Levinas, but one which must remain forever in *suspense,* even to the extent that its continued suspension is held in suspense, "without systematically resigning ourselves to incoherence."

The Hegelian *supersession by synthesis* and the Derridaian *suspense by*

13. Hegel, *Faith and Knowledge*, 62.
14. Ibid., 63.
15. Ibid., 66.
16. Ibid., 68.
17. Ibid., 68.

deferral are both opposed to *external difference,* but differently. This difference makes all the difference. The former, the Hegelian synthesis, the totality, the idea, absolute difference which is at once absolute identity, explicitly forecloses the transcendence of external difference as prephilosophical, as a partial moment serving philosophy's logical-historical striving for comprehensive truth. External differences, then, would be *provisional* philosophy, empiricism. The latter, the Derridaian suspense, play, multiple signification without unifying or ultimate coherence, undecidability, deferral, deference, and defense without end, differ*a*nce, questioning without answer, explicitly perverts the "pretended" univocity of the transcendence of external difference, without deciding for or against either side of that difference.

These two different ways of obviating the unmediated transcendence of external difference have two very different consequences with regard to their approach to Levinas's ethical interpretation of the exceeding of ontology. For Hegel, it is clear that the difference constitutive of Levinasian ethics—the transcendence of the good, the alterity of the other—can only be understood as a partial conceptualization, and as such a merely relative difference, subsumable by the higher level conceptualizations which manifest and constitute civil society in its relation to the state, and ultimately subsumable by the purely logical totality of philosophical conceptualization, as found in the *Science of Logic.* These latter, a fully rational politics and a fully rational philosophy, represent the cognitive totality against which Levinas inveighs, following Rosenzweig and more generally contemporary thought from Kierkegaard onwards.

For Derrida, in contrast, refusing the Hegelian synthesis in the name of its suspense, the problem with Levinas is not that his ethics effects a breach against the conceptual totality. That is his virtue. Derrida and Levinas are on the same side on this question, in their opposition, that is, to the Hegelian idea. What irks Derrida about Levinas, nonetheless, is his univocal and hierarchical interpretation of the alterity that does breach the totality. While for Levinas external difference takes *precedence* over internal difference, and as its *condition* is precisely the dimension of the ethical, for Derrida, in contrast, the price of escaping Hegel is that neither internal nor external difference can be made superior one to the other. All hierarchy is for Derrida onto-theo-logical, the unjustifiable privileging of a sign or a manner of signifying. Freedom is precisely *not* deciding between internal and external difference, and *not* determining this "not" in the manner of philosophical negation from Parmenides to Hegel, even if this refusal is "incoherent" *from Hegel's point of view.*

Any decision between them, whether Hegel's for internal difference, or Levinas's for external difference, must fall back, for Derrida, into . . .

Hegel. But while Derrida admits to the "incoherence" of his own thought, he has a blind spot regarding what, from the point of view of his rejection of Levinas, would have to be the *immorality* of his thought. He does not see this because here, in criticizing external difference, he is still aligned *with* Hegel, a filiation that he freely acknowledges even if not its full significance. Regarding this allegiance to Hegel, we must remember what Derrida said in his footnote to his final Hegel citation: "Hegel's critique of the concept of pure [external] difference is for us here, doubtless, the most uncircumventable theme." Derrida admits his incoherence but simply ignores what would be his immorality, although *both* follow from his rejection of external difference. Perhaps, too, Derrida does not see the immorality of his way because he is still following the path Heidegger, already in *Being and Time,* determined as the "condition for the possibility of the 'morally' good and for that of the 'morally' evil—that is, for morality in general and for the possible forms which this may take factically" (*BT* 332).[18] But for all his protean brilliance, for Derrida to stand outside of Athens and Jerusalem means to stand against them both.[19]

To summarize: because Derrida agrees with Hegel that external difference cannot escape the Hegelian *supersession,* i.e., the synthesis of internal difference, his own way out of Hegel is not to hold to external difference (in what could only be an empty and false gesture of useless desperation), but rather to remain in the no-man's-land of undecidability between external and internal difference, to hold them both in *suspense,* even if the price of this suspense is incoherence (though not a systematic incoherence, which is also suspended, that is to say, deferred). But in Derrida's view Levinas *has* attempted to escape Hegel by external difference, so Derrida must *reject* Levinas, which he does on Hegelian grounds. But since these are not Derrida's true grounds, he must at one and the same time also reject Levinas on post-Hegelian grounds, nowhere deciding between these two grounds, which yields the suspense, the undecidability, of what has come to be known today as deconstruction.

Being true to his own way of thinking, Derrida certainly has no grounds to insist that there is only one way out of Hegel. Levinas's ethical imperative may well be, indeed certainly is, another way out of Hegel,

---

18. For Heidegger all moralities, whether immanent or transcendent, are ontic affairs. More important as far as Heidegger is concerned, is as far, that is, as he thinks all "thinkers" should be concerned, is their condition: the ontological.

19. Derrida plays the role Machiavelli identified as the "doubtful friend": he who wanting safety above all takes neither side of a dispute, but thereby alienates both sides. See Niccolo Machiavelli, *The Prince,* chapter 21, "How a Prince Must Act to Win Honor." Whatever the political consequences, on moral questions one is always on one side or the other, even in abstention.

another signification. Derrida, in principle, cannot decide against Levinas, and as we know, his double reading always means for him, though not for Levinas certainly, that he has not decided against Levinas. For example, this enabled Derrida to give a talk entitled "The Politics of Friendship," in which the overall approach as well as the details of vocabulary and syntax are Levinasian, except that Derrida's talk, unlike Levinas's, remains within quotation marks.[20] This exception, and the exemption that is implied, makes all the difference from an ethical point of view. In the introduction to his Levinas essay, Derrida cleverly (disingenuously?) interprets his own questions to Levinas as "questions put to *us* by Levinas," notes "that by simply articulating it we have already come close to Levinas's own problematic" (*VM* 84), and in his conclusion agrees, as we have seen, that "we live in and of difference, that is, in *hypocrisy*" (*VM* 153) as *Levinas* has defined the term. But, from Levinas's point of view, not to decide the question of the primacy of ethics or ontology is most certainly to decide *against* ethics. Ethics is constituted as the primacy of the other, whereby ontology finds its condition outside of and prior to its own origins. So while Derrida can live with both Hegel *and* Levinas, which means that he can live *beyond* both Hegel and Levinas, Levinas cannot live with either Hegel or Derrida, that is to say, he cannot live with their self-interpretations, with the primacy each respectively accords to his own way of thinking, whether totality or undecidability. Levinas can abide neither by the cognitive totality of Hegelian philosophy, because it subsumes and thereby relativizes the good, nor by the *aesthetic* relativity of Derridaian deconstruction, because it undermines the imperative and elective exigency of the good.

In terms of the Greek *logos*, what is primary for Levinas is the Athens-Jerusalem question, the question of the opposition, as Derrida puts it,

---

20. Derrida's talk was given on December 30, 1988, at the Eastern Division meeting of the American Philosophical Association. His discourse was Levinasian more than anything else. Using the language of *Totality and Infinity*, Derrida attacked the "Greek model" of relationality in the name of friendship, which he conceived in terms of "heterology, asymmetry, and infinity," where "one *answers* first *to* the Other." For the published version, see Jacques Derrida, "The Politics of Friendship," *Journal of Philosophy* 85, no. 11 (November 1988): 632–44. One should also read the published version of the fine commentary given by Thomas A. McCarthy, entitled "On the Margin of Politics," which is found in the same issue of the *Journal of Philosophy*, 645–48. Without being "taken in" (into quotation marks, that is), and hence defending a more genuine politics against Derrida's deconstructive "politics," McCarthy right away in his very first sentence hits the nail on the head in characterizing Derrida's thoughts as "subtle variations on Levinasian and Heideggerian themes" (645).

For another instance of Derrida *seemingly* engaged in the positivity of ethics, explicitly in opposition to Hegelian thought, see the debates and discussions collected into the volume entitled *Altérités: Jacques Derrida et Pierre-Jean Labarriere* (Paris: Editions Osiris, 1986).

between totality and opening, between totality and infinity, between the true and the good. Levinas sides with the resources of Jerusalem, without thereby foregoing the achievements of Athens. For Levinas infinity and the good rectify and justify totality and truth.

In terms of the same Greek *logos,* what is primary for Derrida (and for Heidegger before him), in contrast to Levinas, is the *logos-poesis* question, the opposition between the philosophers and the poets, the struggle between Socrates and Agathon and Aristophanes, between *episteme* and *mythos.* For Derrida the latter condition the former.

In terms of Hegel's system, their attachment to different questions means that Levinas is pitting religion against the autonomy of philosophy and art, while Derrida (and Heidegger, and Nietzsche even earlier) is pitting art against an autonomous philosophy or religion.

Thus, the Levinas-Derrida debate turns out to be of the utmost importance and interest in a post-Hegelian frame, because unlike the Athens-Jerusalem question and the *logos-poesis* question, it represents the Jerusalem-*poesis* question. "Against epistemology," said Adorno (among others), but that still leaves unanswered the question of *from whence,* from whence is one against epistemology?[21] It is because Derrida is against epistemology differently, from the side of *poesis,* than Levinas, who stands on the side of ethics, that we can now understand why Derrida ends his essay neither with a philosopher of closure, Hegel, nor with a "prophetic" thinker, Levinas, but rather with a poet, James Joyce. But following poets freed from moral constraints, like following heros, can be a very dangerous enterprise, as the example of Heidegger—his delicate enthusiasm for the quiet voice of being was unable to keep him from an enthusiasm for the much louder mythology and murderous order of National Socialism[22]—

21. Because he not only had no answer to this question but thought no positive answer was possible in principle, or desirable either, Adorno insisted on the suitability of a completely "negative dialectics," which would nonetheless, he thought, retain its determinacy. See Theodor W. Adorno, *Against Epistemology,* translated by Willis Domingo (Cambridge, Mass.: MIT Press, 1983); and *Negative Dialectics,* translated by E. B. Ashton (New York: Seabury Press, 1973).

22. The important discussion of Heidegger's Nazism (not to mention the integrity of Paul de Man) is not irrelevant to a discussion of Derrida. Where is philosophy's moral strength if it can rely on no more than the good or bad fortune of a thinker's personality, itself something of a cult, rather than insisting upon the unity of life and thought, for goodness?

Recommended readings: Victor Farias, *Heidegger and Nazism* (cf. chapter 2, note 2); *Martin Heidegger and National Socialism,* edited by Gunther Neske and Emil Kettering, translated by Lisa Harries and Joachim Neugroschel (New York: Paragon House, 1990); Jacques Derrida, *Of Spirit: Heidegger and the Question,* translated by Geoffrey Bennington and Rachel Bowlby (Chicago: University of Chicago Press, 1989); Edith Wyschogrod, *Spirit in Ashes: Hegel, Heidegger, and Man-Made Mass Death* (New Haven: Yale University

shows. It is the Jerusalem-*poesis* question, and not the Athens-Jerusalem question, contrary to what most commentators have thought, that is ultimately at stake—and much is at stake—in the final and famous citation of Derrida's essay on Levinas: "Jewgreek is greekjew. Extremes meet" (*VM* 153).

Levinas would reply that this so-called meeting of extremes in the freedom and equivocations of *poesis* is but the aesthetic pretension to religion and philosophy, to turn Derrida's phrase around, a pretension acceptable to neither philosophy nor ethics nor religion.

Nazism as no more than the error of "his politics from May, 1933, through February, 1934." Karsten Harris, in an article entitled "Heidegger as a Political Thinker," which first appeared in *The Review of Metaphysics* 24 (June 1976), and was later reprinted in *Heidegger and Modern Philosophy*, edited by Michael Murray (New Haven: Yale University Press, 1978), finds that Heidegger uses nazi vocabulary. Harris finds this usage "embarrassing," nothing worse. For more on these points, and more generally and profoundly for a sustained philosophical and moral criticism of Heidegger (along with other philosophers and theologians) prior to Farias's book and in the dark light of the holocaust, a criticism which in addition is explicitly informed by Rosenzweig's thought, see Emil L. Fackenheim's important work, *To Mend the World: Foundations of Future Jewish Thought* (New York: Schocken Books, 1982).

Bibliography

Selected Rosenzweig Bibliography

Briefe. Edited by Edith Rosenzweig and Ernst Simon. Berlin: Schocken Verlag, 1935.

Franz Rosenzweig: His Life and Thought. Presented by Nahum N. Glatzer. New York: Schocken Books, 1953; 2d rev. ed., 1961.

Franz Rosenzweig: Der Mensch und sein Werk. Gesammelte Schriften. 4 vols. Edited by Rachel Rosenzweig and Edith Rosenzweig-Scheidmann, with Bernhard Casper. The Hague: Martinus Nijhoff, 1976–84.

Hegel und der Staat. 2 vols. Munich und Berlin: R. Oldenbourg, 1920; one vol. ed., Aalen: Scienta Verlag, 1962.

Judaism Despite Christianity: The "Letters on Christianity and Judaism" between Eugen Rosenstock-Huessy and Franz Rosenzweig. Edited by Eugen Rosenstock-Huessy. Translated by Dorothy Emmett. Tuscaloosa: University of Alabama Press, 1969; New York: Schocken Books, 1971.

Kleinere Schriften. Berlin: Schocken Verlag, 1937.

On Jewish Learning. Edited by Nahum N. Glatzer. Translated by Nahum N. Glatzer and William Wolf. New York: Schocken Books, 1955, 1989.

The Star of Redemption. Translated by William W. Hallo. New York: Holt, Rinehart and Winston, 1971; Boston: Beacon Press, 1972; Notre Dame, Ind.: University of Notre Dame Press, 1985.

> *Der Stern der Erlösung.* Frankfort, 1921; 2d ed., Frankfort, 1930; Heidelberg, 1954; The Hague, 1976.

Understanding the Sick and the Healthy: A View of World, Man, and God. Translated by Nahum N. Glatzer and T. Luckman. Edited by Nahum N. Glatzer. New York: Noonday Press, 1954.

> *Von gesunden und kranken Menschenverstand.* Written 1921, unpublished. Düsseldorf: Joseph Melzer Verlag, 1963.

Ninety-five Hymns and Poems of Judah Halevi. Edited by Richard A. Cohen. Translated by Eva Jospe, Tom Kovach, and Gilya Gerda Schmidt. Tuscaloosa: University of Alabama Press, forthcoming.

Judah Halevi: Zweiundneunzig Hymnen and Gedichte. Translation and commentary by Franz Rosenzweig. Berlin, 1927.

Sechzig Hymnen und Gedichte des Jehuda Halevi, deutsch. Translation and commentary by Franz Rosenzweig. Konstanz, 1924.

And Martin Buber. *Scripture and Translation.* Translated by Lawrence Rosenwald and Everett Fox. Bloomington: Indiana University Press, 1994.

Selected Secondary Works on Rosenzweig in English

Freund, Else-Rahel. *Franz Rosenzweig's Philosophy of Existence: An Analysis of 'The Star of Redemption'*. Translated by Stephen L. Weinstein and Robert Israel; edited by Paul Mendes-Flohr. The Hague: Martinus Nijhoff, 1979.

Gibbs, Robert. *Correlations in Rosenzweig and Levinas*. Princeton: Princeton University Press, 1992.

Mendes-Flohr, Paul, ed. *The Philosophy of Franz Rosenzweig*. Hanover: University Press of New England, 1988.

Miller, Ronald H. *The Challenge of Dialogue: The Contribution of Franz Rosenzweig to Jewish-Christian Understanding*. Washington, D.C.: University Press of America, 1992.

Mosès, Stéphane. *System and Revelation: The Philosophy of Franz Rosenzweig*. Translated by Catherine Tihanyi. Detroit: Wayne State University Press, 1992.

Schwarzchild, Steven S. *Franz Rosenzweig (1886-1929): Guide of Reversioners*. London: Education Committee of the Hillel Foundation, 1960.

Selected Levinas Bibliography

L'au-delà du verset. Paris: Editions de Minuit, 1982.

Collected Philosophical Papers. Edited and translated by Alphonso Lingis. Dordrecht: Martinus Nijhoff, 1987.

De l'évasion. 1935. Montpellier: Fata Morgana, 1982.

Dieu, la mort, et le temps. 1975–76. Edited by Jacques Rolland. Paris: Edition Grasset et Fasquelle, 1993. Previously published as: *La mort et le temps*. 1975–76. Edited by Jacques Rolland. Paris: Edition de l'Herne, 1991.

De Dieu qui vient a l'idée. Paris: J. Vrin, 1982.

Difficult Freedom: Essays on Judaism. Translated by Sean Hand. Baltimore, Johns Hopkins University Press, 1990.
    Difficile liberté: Essais sur le judaisme. Paris: Albin Michel, 1963; 2d ed., 1976.

Discovering Existence with Husserl. Edited by Richard A. Cohen. Translated by Richard A. Cohen and Michael B. Smith. Forthcoming.

En découvrant l'existence avec Husserl et Heidegger. Paris: Vrin, 1949; 2d ed., 1967.

Entre nous: Essais sur le penser-à-l'autre. Paris: Bernard Grasset, 1991.

Ethics and Infinity. Translated by Richard A. Cohen. Pittsburgh: Duquesne University Press, 1985.
    Éthique et infini. Paris: Fayard, 1982.

Existence and Existents. Translated by Alphonso Lingis. The Hague: Martinus Nijhoff, 1978.
    De l'existent à l'existence. Paris: Fontaine, 1947; Paris: Vrin, 1973, 1978.

Humanisme de l'autre homme. Montpellier: Fata Morgana, 1972.

Les imprévus de l'histoire. Montpellier: Fata Morgana, 1994.

In the Time of the Nations. Translated by Michael B. Smith. London: Athlone, forthcoming.

A l'heure des nations. Paris: Editions de Minuit, 1988.

The Levinas Reader. Edited by Sean Hand. Cambridge, Basil Blackwell, 1989.

Liberté et commandment. Montpellier: Fata Morgana, 1994.

Nine Talmudic Readings. Edited and translated by Annette Aronowicz. Bloomington: Indiana University Press, 1990.

Quatre lectures talmudiques. Paris: Editions de Minuit, 1968.

Du sacré au saint: cinq nouvelles lectures talmudiques. Paris: Editions de Minuit, 1977.

Noms propres. Montpellier: Fata Morgana, 1975.

Otherwise than Being or Beyond Essence. Translated by Alphonso Lingis. The Hague: Martinus Nijhoff, 1981.

    Autrement qu'être ou au-delà de l'essence. The Hague, Martinus Nijhoff, 1974.

Outside the Subject. Translated by Michael B. Smith. Stanford: Stanford University Press, 1993.

    Hors sujet. Montpellier: Fata Morgana, 1987.

Sur Maurice Blanchot. Montpellier: Fata Morgana, 1975.

The Theory of Intuition in Husserl's Phenomenology. Translated by André Orianne. Evanston: Northwestern University Press, 1973.

    La théorie de l'intuition dans la phénoménologie de Husserl. Paris: Alcan, 1930; Paris: J. Vrin, 1962, 1970, 1984.

Time and the Other, and Other Essays. Translated by Richard A. Cohen. Pittsburgh: Duquesne University Press, 1987.

    Le temps et l'autre. In J. Wahl, *Le Choix, Le Monde, L'Existence.* Grenoble and Paris: Arthaud, 1948, 125–96. With new preface, Montpellier: Fata Morgana, 1979.

Totality and Infinity: An Essay on Exteriority. Translated by Alphonso Lingis. The Hague: Martinus Nijhoff, 1969; Pittsburgh: Duquesne University Press, 1969, 1979.

    Totalité et infini: Essai sur l'extériorité. The Hague: Martinus Nijhoff, 1961.

Transcendence et intelligibilité. Geneve: Labor et Fides, 1984.

For the most complete Levinas bibliography, see Roger Burggraeve, *Emmanuel Levinas: Une bibliographie primaire et secondaire (1929–1989).* Leuven: Peeters, 1990.

Selected Secondary Works on Levinas in English

Bernasconi, Robert, and Simon Critchley, eds. *Re-Reading Levinas.* Bloomington: Indiana University Press, 1991.

Bernasconi, Robert, and David Wood, eds. *The Provocation of Levinas: Rethinking the Other.* London: Routledge, 1988.

Cohen, Richard A., ed. *Face to Face with Emmanuel Levinas.* Albany: State University of New York Press, 1986.

Critchley, Simon. *The Ethics of Deconstruction: Derrida and Levinas.* Oxford: Blackwell, 1992.

Manning, Robert J. S. *Interpreting Otherwise than Heidegger: Emmanuel Levinas's Ethics as First Philosophy.* Pittsburgh: Duquesne University Press, 1993.

Peperzak, Adriaan. *To the Other: An Introduction to the Philosophy of Emmanuel Levinas*. West Lafayette: Purdue University Press, 1993.

Smith, Steven G. *The Argument to the Other: Reason beyond Reason in the Thought of Karl Barth and E. Levinas*. Chico, California: Scholars Press, 1983.

Wyschogrod, Edith. *Emmanuel Levinas: The Problem of Ethical Metaphysics*. The Hague: Martinus Nijhoff, 1974.

Index

The Philosophical Discourse of Modernity (Habermas), 55n.13, 306n.2
Philosophie première: Introduction à une philosophie du 'presque' (Jankelevitch), 229n.5
Philosophy, Derrida on, 305–312; not empiricist, 309–311, 315–317; ethics, justice, and, 190–194, 196; essence, 163; overlooks family, 218; firstness, 163, 165, 169–171, 225; and God, 172–179, 190–194; Greek, 127; Hegel on, 315–317; justification for, 193–194; Kantian, 184n.19; life versus, 72–74; seeks origins, 72, 150–151, 166, 171, 225; misunderstands, 239–240; morality of, 320n.22; negation, 170; Parmenidean, 98–100, 205–207; as phenomenology, 235n.12; scientific, 78–79, 299; telos, 203; and time, 133, 146, 148; totality, 164, 167, 170; willful, 288
Philosophy and Law (Strauss), 182n.16
The Philosophy of "As If" (Vaihinger), 272n.51
The Philosophy of Franz Rosenzweig (Mendes-Flohr), 51n.9, 96n.14, 239n.14
Philosophy of German Idealism (Behler), 315n.12
The Philosophy of Martin Buber (Friedman, Schilpp), 93n.8
The Piety of Thinking (Heidegger), 301n.12
Pines, Shlomo, 244n.5
Place, center, 243; face, 243; God, 243n.3; usurpation, 185n.20
Plato, cosmos, 162–164, 171; drama, 203; *episteme, mythos,* 320; erotic fusion, 144, 210; fecundity, 212n.14; good beyond being, xii, 149; ideas, 297; platonism, 267; propaedeutic, 297; Silenus, 226; dying Socrates, 74; telos, 180, 203
Plato's Symposium (Rosen), 212n.14
Poet, meaning of being, 45; Celan, 291n.4; Derrida on, 312, 320–321; Goethe, 291–292; Heidegger on, 287–291, 298, 302; versus Jerusalem, 320–321; not Jewish prophet, 253; Joyce, 320–321; life of, 73; versus philosopher, 320; Trakl, 287, 289–291; fount of truth, 50
Poesis. See also Poet
Poetry, Language, Thought (Heidegger), 287n.1

Poirié, François, 116n.1, 237n.13
Politics, activism, 14n.10; Dasein, 56; and Derrida, 319n.20; eros, 210–211, 219; fecundity, 212; Heidegger's nazism, 321n.22; and love, 63–64, 77; Nazis, 128; totalitarian, 160, 304; World War II, 119
Possibility, and actuality, 236n.12; against 123; and death, 142
Postmodern, xii, 306n.2, 312
Poyetto, Jacob, 258, 262–264
Pradines, Maurice, 116
Prayer, and body, 208n.7; day and night, 99n.16; versus knowledge, xvii; for Messiah, 17, 19–20; mystic, 254; Sabbath, 11, 12, 13; and science, 157n.5; sinful, 82–83
The Presocratics (Wheelwright), 276n.6
The Prince (Machiavelli), 318n.19
Proceedings of the Husserl Circle, 277n.8
Proper Names (Levinas), 15n.11, 120
Prophecy. *See* Prophet
Prophet, Derrida on, 308, 310–312, 320; Elijah on woman, 200; and nations, 16; and philosopher, xvi, 308, 310–312, 320; not poet, 253, 320–321; speech, 130
Proust, Marcel, 119
The Provocation of Levinas (Bernasconi, Wood), 160n.19
Psychology, and gender, 201; of God, 189n.25; naive, 203; and Nietzsche, 88n.30; reductive, 181, 290; superficial, 36
The Pursuit of the Millennium (Cohn), 26n.14
Pushkin, Alexander, 115

Quatre lectures talmudiques (Levinas), 120

Rashi (Rabbi Shlomo Yitzaki), 128n.5, 292n.5
Reason, ethics exceeds, 125, 159; and faith, 175n.5; god of, 178; good beyond, 124; Kantian, 184–185n.19; versus mysticism, 252–253; versus revelation, 173, 176–179, 315, 320–321; unlimited, xiii; upset, 122
Reason and Hope (Cohen), 181n.14
Redemption, Christian contribution, 16–22, 64, 109–111; and eros,